PowerBuilder 4.0
for Windows
Power Toolkit

**Cutting-Edge
Tools & Techniques
for Programmers**

PowerBuilder 4.0 for Windows Power Toolkit

Cutting-Edge Tools & Techniques for Programmers

Ted Coombs, Jason Coombs & Ed Ashley

VENTANA

PowerBuilder 4.0 for Windows Power Toolkit: Cutting Edge Tools & Techniques for Programmers
Copyright ©1995 by Ted Coombs & Jason Coombs

Library of Congress Cataloging-in-Publication Data

Coombs, Ted.
    PowerBuilder 4.0 for Windows power toolkit: cutting-edge tools & techniques for programmers /
Ted Coombs & Jason Coombs. -- 1st ed.
        p. cm.
    Includes index.
    ISBN 1-56604-224-0
    1. Application software. 2. PowerBuilder. I. Title.
QA76.76.A65N48 1995
005.2--dc20   95-1921
                          CIP

Book design: Marcia Webb
Cover illustration: Lynn Brofsky, Jeff McCord

Acquisitions Editor: Cheri Robinson
Art Director: Marcia Webb
Companion CD-ROM: Kerry Foster, Cheryl Friedman, Cheri Robinson
Design staff: Bradley King, Charles Overbeck, Jennifer Rowe, Dawne Sherman
Developmental Editor: Tim C. Mattson
Editorial staff: J.J. Hohn, Kristin Miller, Amy Moyers, Beth Snowberger, Melanie Stepp
Managing Editor: Pam Richardson
Print Department: Dan Koeller
Production Manager: John Cotterman
Production staff: Patrick Berry, Scott Hosa, Jaimie Livingston
Technical Director: Cheryl Friedman

Copy Editors: Nancy Crumpton, Eric Edstam
Index service: Dianne Bertsch, Answers Plus
Proofreaders: Angela Anderson, Beth Snowberger, Sue Versenyi
Technical review: Ed Ashley, Jaqueline Wood Busby, Lance Tillman, Enrique Villalobos

First Edition 9 8 7 6 5 4 3 2 1
Printed in the United States of America

For information about our audio products, write us at Newbridge Book Clubs, 3000 Cindel Drive, Delran, NJ 08375.

Ventana Communications Group, Inc.
P.O. Box 13964
Research Triangle Park, NC 27709-3964
919/544-9404
FAX 919/544-9472

Limits of Liability and Disclaimer of Warranty
The authors and publisher of this book have used their best efforts in preparing the book and the programs contained in it. These efforts include the development, research and testing of the theories and programs to determine their effectiveness. The authors and publisher make no warranty of any kind, expressed or implied, with regard to these programs or the documentation contained in this book.
    The authors and publisher shall not be liable in the event of incidental or consequential damages in connection with, or arising out of, the furnishing, performance or use of the programs, associated instructions and/or claims of productivity gains.

Trademarks

Trademarked names appear throughout this book, and on the accompanying CD-ROM. Rather than list the names and entities that own the trademarks or insert a trademark symbol with each mention of the trademarked name, the publisher states that it is using the names only for editorial purposes and to the benefit of the trademark owner with no intention of infringing upon that trademark.

About the Authors

Ed Ashley is a Systems Engineer for Sun Microsystems. He has been in the IS industry for over 12 years and has spent the last six years developing transactional and informational client-server systems. In addition to software development, Ed teaches computer science courses at the University of California, San Diego extension.

Jason Coombs, scientist, engineer, entrepreneur and author, is vice president of Pacific Knowledge. He is coauthor of several books on such technologies as the Internet and software engineering tools, and his published works include *Setting Up Shop on the Internet for Dummies* and *PowerBuilder 4 Programming for Dummies* (both by IDG Books).

Since 1972, **Ted Coombs** has worked with various technologies—including electronics, lasers, robotics, computer networking, telecommunications, database and software development. A research scientist, he is president of the science and engineering think tank Pacific Knowledge of Santa Cruz, CA, as well as director of Pacific Knowledge Foundation and a researcher for the Center for Multidisciplinary Research (both in San Diego, CA).

Acknowledgments

Whew! What a project. When I first saw the outline for this book, I thought it would be a pretty tough undertaking. In retrospect, I suppose I was right. Although there are a handful of names on the cover, this book would not exist without the work of many others. I want to thank the people who jump through hoops daily as a part of their job description in order to produce quality books.

I would first like to thank Ted and Jason for starting this project and having the ambition to tackle all of the topics covered. I would also like to thank Jerry Singer at UCSD for not having me killed along the way. Kerri DeRosier batted "clean-up" and did so perfectly. Thanks also to Tim Beck at NexGen SI for the input on performance.

Without Matt Wagner, Margot Maley and all the folks at Waterside, we would not be able to function. They have an unbelievable tolerance for whining.

As this project came to fruition, a considerable number of people at Ventana rallied to make everything work. Many thanks to each of you. As you know, this book would not exist if not for all of your efforts. Particularly, thanks to "the eternal optimist," Cheri Robinson. Her shoulder has been a permanent crutch for me throughout this project. Special thanks also go to Eric Edstam, Tim Mattson, Enrique Villalobos, Pam Richardson, Walt Bruce, Nancy Crumpton, Lynn Jaluvka, Scott Hosa and John Cotterman.

Each of us would like to thank our wives and significant others for putting up with workaholic zombies for the last few months. I would especially like to thank my lifelong editor and best friend, my wife, Diana.

— *Ed Ashley*

Contents

Introduction

As you know, there is now a plethora of PowerBuilder books available on the shelves of your local bookstore. We wanted to develop this book to add value to the existing offerings, and we believe we've achieved that goal. Altogether, the authors of the *PowerBuilder 4.0 for Windows Power Toolkit* have over 10 years' experience developing PowerBuilder applications. We wanted to bring the benefit of our real-world experiences to you. This book focuses on advanced topics surrounding PowerBuilder development.

WHO SHOULD READ THIS BOOK

My experience in teaching PowerBuilder has been that it takes about six months to become comfortable with the PowerBuilder toolset. This book is intended to be a more advanced coverage of PowerBuilder topics. As a result, the targeted audience is those PowerBuilder developers with at least six months' PowerBuilder experience.

Developers who are ready to expand their toolset and experience level should read this book. We touch on topics that are not covered in the PowerBuilder manuals and that, in some cases, we've discovered by trial and error ourselves. You should be familiar with software development in general and have a willingness to explore development areas that are new to you.

WHAT'S IN THIS BOOK

In Chapter 1, "Programming With Objects," and Chapter 2, "Building a Class Library," we discuss object-oriented topics, particularly issues surrounding reusable software classes. Then we demonstrate how you can build your own reusable classes. We also offer some of our own for you to use.

Chapter 3, "DataWindows," and Chapter 4, "Advanced Reporting," address DataWindows, then extend the subject further by discussing the advanced reporting features. We feel this topic has not been well covered by other offerings.

Chapter 5, "OLE & DDE," brings you procedures for developing OLE applications and demonstrates with code how to build your own OLE-compliant apps.

In each of our PowerBuilder experiences, we have faced security issues of one kind or another. We dedicated Chapter 6, "Security," to addressing security concerns from within PowerBuilder. In addition, we discuss other areas of security that will certainly affect your PowerBuilder applications—database and network security.

In Chapter 7, "Advanced Database Techniques," and Chapter 8, "Advanced SQL," we demonstrate some advanced methods for working with databases and SQL. Two of the authors have worked as Database Administrators, and hopefully, we've brought some resulting insights to these chapters.

Chapter 9, "Advanced Programming Topics," is a discussion of advanced programming topics in general.

With Chapter 10, "Developing Cross-Platform Applications," we begin branching out from the core of PowerBuilder development and discussing topics ancillary to PowerBuilder. This chapter examines the differences in operating systems and helps you prepare now for the inevitable future of cross-platform development.

Chapter 11, "Handling Group Development," explains the issues and techniques of keeping all the members of a development team in sync.

In Chapter 12, "Tips for Creating a Windows 3.1 DLL," we discuss extending your PowerBuilder environment by building your own Windows Dynamic Link Libraries (DLLs). With DLLs, you can build better-performing code and call it from within PowerBuilder.

Seldom do we find that developers use only PowerBuilder when creating client-server applications. In Chapter 13, "Related Software Tools," we discuss the external utilities that come with PowerBuilder, such as the DataWindow Syntax utility and some third-party tools, such as RoboHELP.

Chapters 14, "Winsock TCP/IP Programming With PowerBuilder," and Chapter 15, "Programming With Internet Resources," deal with Internet resources and interacting with the Internet from within PowerBuilder. These chapters will help you start growing your toolset for PowerBuilder/Internet development.

To demonstrate some of the techniques we cover in this book, we've developed a sample application called the Student Registration System. In Chapter 16, we explain the sample application so that you can use it as a starting point for your own applications. The application is also included on the Companion CD-ROM.

Finally, we talk about a topic that is near to every developer's heart—performance. Like security issues, we face performance issues on every PowerBuilder project. In Chapter 17, "A Discussion of Performance," we share the tips and tricks we've discovered along the way.

Following Chapter 17 are several appendices:

❒ Appendix A, "About the Online Companion," tells how the online resources of the *PowerBuilder Online Companion*, located on the Ventana Online site on the World Wide Web, can be used to complement the information in this book.

❒ Appendix B, "About the Companion CD-ROM," describes the contents of this book's Companion CD-ROM. The CD-ROM includes third-party products that enhance the performance or usability of PowerBuilder. You'll also find examples that provide instructions for building applications described in this book.

❒ Appendix C, "PowerBuilder & Windows 95," is a reprint of a paper presented to the 1995 Mid-Atlantic PowerBuilder Users Conference by Dave Rensin, Gregory McIntyre, and Timothy Jarrett of American Management Systems, Inc. It attempts to address some of the major structural changes to the operating system and how they are likely to affect PowerBuilder programmers.

❒ Appendix D, "PBORCA Reference," contains a reprint of Powersoft's available documentation on its Open Repository CASE API (ORCA), which provides advanced developers and CASE vendors with a simple way to access PowerBuilder's library functions. The authors of this book extend their thanks to Powersoft for allowing the use of this documentation.

A Final Word

We certainly do not know everything about PowerBuilder. Frankly, I doubt anyone does. The more experience we gain when working on PowerBuilder development projects, the more techniques we have to add to our arsenal. And, of course, more techniques crop up every day. This book should serve as a reference, and we hope that you learn some techniques you can add to your toolset. We want to make your next PowerBuilder project that much better!

—Ed Ashley, Jason Coombs & Ted Coombs

Chapter 1

Programming With Objects

Dr. Kristin Nygaard of Norway invented object orientation (OO) in 1969 to handle the complex modeling problem of ships moving in and out of a Norwegian fjord. The challenge of creating a computer program that could handle all the variables of ships moving through a fjord was too great for traditional procedural programming. Your programming needs may not have the detail and the complexity of a Norwegian fjord, but they can benefit from the ideas and principles of using objects to model real-world things and events. In this chapter we'll talk about what objects are and why you would want to program with them, and we'll introduce some of the basics of object-oriented programming in PowerBuilder. (Some object-oriented topics will be covered in greater detail in the next chapter.)

PRINCIPLES OF OBJECT-ORIENTED PROGRAMMING

What are objects? A cliché often heard about object-oriented programming is that "everything is an object." Well, not exactly. A more accurate way of looking at it might be that, in a program, anything can be *represented* by an object. An object is a program entity that combines the properties and behavior of the real-world item it represents into a single unit of program code. This single unit of program code contains data elements that describe the real-world item and functions to manipulate those data elements. The data elements represent the properties of the object, and the functions represent the behaviors of the object. An object can model people, like employees; things you can see, like boats or machines; or things you can't see, like a process to manage data communications or a process to print a report. Some of the more common objects you might be familiar with are windows and controls, such as checkboxes or radio buttons.

The property data elements in an object are known as the object's *attributes*. An attribute is information that describes something about an object. For example, an employee object might contain attributes such as the employee's name, ID number, date of birth and date of hire.

Attributes are manipulated with the functions in an object. For example, the employee object could have functions to assign a new ID number, return the value of the ID number to other objects and terminate itself as an employee. These functions are known as an object's *methods*. (Throughout this book, we'll use the terms *method* and *function* interchangeably.)

Each object is built from a definition called an *object type* or a *class*. You can think of an object type as a template for logically related objects. This definition contains the functions, internal functions and variables to store attributes. It truly is a template in the sense that you don't manipulate the class itself; rather, you manipulate what is created or *instantiated* from the class. (To be technically precise, an object is an *instance* of a class.)

Object orientation can make a complex program simpler to model, often representing people and processes that actually exist in the world around you. For example, you can develop postman objects to deliver electronic mail, student objects that enroll in courses and accountant objects that will perform tax calculations. When the attributes and functions are contained with the object and the object represents a real-world entity, such as a student object, then the developer can identify with the architecture of the application more easily than when all of the code was in one large, sequential program. With the code all in one program, the different data elements and procedures for a given entity are scattered throughout the program, making the pertinent code difficult to find and to maintain. Let's take a closer look at the major OO principles and why you might want to use object orientation in developing applications.

Encapsulation

The object-oriented principle of storing attributes and functions together as a self-contained unit of code is called *encapsulation.* In traditional procedural languages, such as COBOL and C, procedures and data elements could be scattered throughout the source code. Having the functions and attributes stored together, encapsulated within the object, enables the object to easily be moved or reused. The attributes and functions are moved with the object because they are contained in it. In the procedural languages, the code for a single entity would have to be cut and pasted from several places in order to be copied or moved to other programs. Encapsulating functions (or methods) and attributes (or properties) into a single object provides for considerably easier maintenance. Because the code for manipulating a given entity is stored within the entity itself, the maintenance programmer knows exactly where to go to find an error or to make a change. For example, suppose an application contained a window, w_search, that prompted a user for search criteria and collected the search argument for use in an SQL query. If there was an error in the way the search argument was constructed, the developer would know the problem code was somewhere in the w_search window, and not in the code for other objects.

The rules of encapsulation require that functions in an object may manipulate only the attributes in the same object and may not manipulate the attributes of another object. Conversely, the attributes within an object may be manipulated only by the functions within that object and not by functions in another object. Thus, in an object-oriented application, ObjectA would not operate on ObjectB. In order to achieve the same result, ObjectA would send a *message* to ObjectB, telling it to operate on itself (to invoke an ObjectB function). In PowerBuilder, a message is the invoking of another object's function or triggering of another object's event.

Objects send messages to other objects using functions.

Rather than a linear series of commands sent to the computer, your program is a system of objects that communicate with one another by sending messages. Object messages are sent and received using functions or events. One object requests information from another object by calling a function designed to provide that information.

Objects become like building blocks, and developing an application becomes a matter of putting together the right objects in an environment that lets them communicate with one another via messages. In a well-designed object-oriented application, objects can be modified or replaced to add new functionality without changing any other parts of the application. New objects can simply be "dropped in."

There are many benefits to this design. If, for instance, there were a requirement to change the code for a given function in ObjectB, then only the code in ObjectB would need to be changed. ObjectA was coded to simply send a message to ObjectB, invoking some action. That has not changed. ObjectA still wants ObjectB to perform the action. It is the action itself that is changed. If there were code in ObjectA manipulating ObjectB, then changing a behavior of ObjectB would require the developer to make changes to both ObjectA and ObjectB. If only ObjectB requires a behavior change, why should a developer make code changes to ObjectA and risk causing new bugs there?

In an object-oriented application, one object does not operate on another.

Inheritance

The most valuable premise of object orientation is software reusability. The idea is that a program or part of a program can be written once and used in more than one place within an overall application. The benefit is that time is saved by designing the same or similar functionality only once, while using the functionality more than one time. And fewer bugs are introduced when code is written and debugged in only one place, regardless of how often it is used. Once object types are created, you can share them in the same application or in other applications that require them. Both the attributes and functions for an object may be reused. When one object type reuses the functions and attributes of another object type, it is called *inheritance*. Reuse is not the same thing as copying code; when code is reused, the original code is actually called when invoked from reused classes. *Ancestors* are the classes from which other classes are inherited. *Descendants* are the classes inherited from ancestors. Any number of new object types can be created from a single ancestor. Some object types can be both ancestor and descendant.

Inheritance is the object-oriented ability to create new object types from existing object types.

Multiple inheritance is when a descendant can inherit attributes and functions from more than one immediate ancestor—as a child inherits attributes from both its parents. (This is not the same as a descendant that inherits from an ancestor that is also a descendant—like a child-to-parent-to-grandparent relationship.) *Single inheritance* is when a descendant may inherit from only one immediate ancestor. PowerBuilder supports only single inheritance.

Inheriting from an ancestor gives the developer the ability to *extend* the attributes and functions of the descendant object types without affecting the ancestor. To extend the attributes and functions of an ancestor means to add to the capabilities of whatever was inherited. A newly created object type has all the same attributes and functions as its ancestor. A developer handles the inheritance of the ancestor's code by choosing to do one of the following:

The ability to add the to capabilities of an ancestor object is known as *extensibility*.

❐ Accept the ancestor's code as is.

❐ Extend the code of the ancestor.

❐ Completely override the code of the ancestor.

If the developer chooses to neither extend nor override the ancestor code, then the descendant object will behave exactly like the ancestor object.

Choosing to extend the ancestor's code makes the best use of inheritance. In this manner, the descendant uses the ancestor's code and requires additional code for only the differences between the ancestor and the descendant. For example, an ancestor window used for maintaining a "person" could be inherited and extended for maintaining a "student." Since a student is a person and has a name, address, etc., the student window would extend the code of the ancestor, adding code for manipulating the attributes specific to a student—student ID, declared major, etc. The ancestor's code for maintaining a person would be used in full by the student window, since it uses all the attributes of the person window. The developer would only add code specific to the new attributes.

Our Sample Application

The sample application we've developed for use in examples throughout this book is called the Student Registration System. It's included on the Companion CD-ROM and explained in detail in Chapter 16. This application illustrates the concepts of PowerBuilder development described in each chapter, and you can use it as a template for your own development.

If the developer chooses to override the ancestor code, then the descendant is effectively replacing the ancestor's code for that particular event. Should the developer override the majority of an ancestor's code, then he or she must decide whether another object is needed. There is little benefit to inheriting 50 functions from an ancestor, then overriding 48 of them. If this situation occurs, it is a clue that the ancestor should be redesigned or that a new ancestor object type is needed.

Polymorphism

Another feature of object orientation is polymorphism. The word *polymorphism* means "of many forms." This is the ability to add functionality to an object without having to create entirely new functions. Polymorphism enables us to add capabilities specific to each level of descendant objects. This ability is called *specificity*. Modifying the functions of objects inherited from a more general object type allows you to meet the needs of more specialized objects. In a technical sense, polymorphism is the ability to send messages of the same name to different objects and receive different behavior from these objects.

For example, you might have a general employee object type with a function called payment(). From this general object type, you create the more specialized types of SalariedEmployee and HourlyEmployee. The ancestor object, employee, has a very general function that ensures that employees get paid. The inherited HourlyEmployee object would have a modification to the payment() function to allow for things like the payment of overtime, or timecard tracking. The SalariedEmployee object has modifications to payment() that allow a fixed annual salary to be paid in equal installments. The essence of polymorphism is that both objects have a payment() function that makes sure the employee gets paid. Both the HourlyEmployee and SalariedEmployee object functions were built on the ancestor's payment() function using inheritance. Polymorphism can be thought of as the ability to send the same message to different objects, with each object responding in its own way.

OBJECT-ORIENTED VS. OBJECT-BASED

By a somewhat loose definition, the term *object-oriented* means any development language or environment that supports polymorphism, inheritance and encapsulation. A term used to describe a development language or development environment that is not purely object-oriented is *object-based*. PowerBuilder is an object-based development environment. One of a number of reasons for this is that PowerBuilder does not support multiple inheritance; it supports only single inheritance.

PowerBuilder is an *object-based* development environment.

PowerBuilder doesn't force you to develop in an object-oriented style. In fact, using PowerBuilder, you can break every single one of the OO rules. For example, you'll see that one of the very first things that happens when you try to write an object-oriented program that uses a relational database is that encapsulation can be violated. Information stored in a database is accessible to all the objects, and if an object needs a student's name, for instance, why ask a student object if it can get the name direct from the database?

It's easy to get caught up in the temptation to write traditional top-down applications using PowerBuilder. (Generally, top-down applications start with a menu and work from there.) There are many benefits to OO programming, however, as this and other books demonstrate. Even though PowerBuilder doesn't enforce complete object orientation, there is no reason that developers cannot follow the principles (within reason) by designing the program as if PowerBuilder *did* enforce those rules. The benefits of object orientation are still realized. Throughout this book, we describe various approaches, pros and cons, for handling inheritance, encapsulation and polymorphism in PowerBuilder. At this point, be aware that to varying degrees, each OO requisite can be accomplished in PowerBuilder.

WORKING WITH OBJECTS IN POWERBUILDER

PowerBuilder has a standard set of object types that you use to build your application. These object types have built-in behaviors and properties that you can use and manipulate. These are definitions of objects, and *not* actual objects. You can think of them as cookie cutters from which you'll eventually make cookies. The most commonly used object types are windows, user objects and menus. However, these object types are only a few of the descendants of higher-level classes that PowerBuilder provides.

Because object-oriented programs are designed to have objects that model people and processes in the real world, you're likely to need more than the standard PowerBuilder object types. PowerBuilder lets you create your own object types (using the User Object painter) rather than forcing you to use only the object types provided. These are known as *user objects*. Powersoft contends that DataWindows are the most powerful objects in PowerBuilder. User objects are a close second in terms of power and utility. You can also create user objects that enhance the built-in PowerBuilder object types. For example, you could build a command button that has added value, such as additional user-defined events.

In PowerBuilder, the distinction between creating an object type and creating an object is somewhat ambiguous. The PowerBuilder painters create definitions of objects. (You can use the library export function to output a definition created by a painter to an ASCII file. You can then look at the definition using the PowerBuilder editor. Press Shift+F6 from within the PowerBuilder development environment to use the editor.) When you create a window using the Window painter, you are creating an object type. You may *think* that you're creating an object. The documentation may even *tell* you that you're creating an object. But you're not. You are creating the definition for a window. Your window doesn't actually become an object that the user sees until the PowerScript Open() function is issued at run-time. At this point, PowerBuilder uses the new object type you have created and creates an object from it.

This ambiguity is not necessarily a bad thing. If we were coding in C++, we would have to create a class and then write the code to instantiate an object from the class. But in PowerBuilder, when a class is created, we have to do very little to create an instance of that class. For example, when we create a window with some controls on it in the Window painter, we are creating several classes. However, when we open the window, we don't have to write code to instantiate each of the controls on the window. PowerBuilder handles the instantiation of the controls for us. Since PowerBuilder does some of the work for us, it's not always clear that the object types and objects are actually different things.

The PowerBuilder painters create definitions of objects.

Objects are created from object types in several ways. We've shown you how it happens using the Open() function for windows. In the case of certain other standard and user objects, it's up to the developer to create the object. (Although it is only necessary to create the pointer variable for non-visual/class user objects, they can be used with most of the objects if the developer desires to gain tighter control over the memory allocation of the objects.) This involves two steps. Step one is to create a pointer variable. Unlike in C or C++, the fact that this variable is a pointer is just something to know and not really something to care much about beyond that. Create a pointer variable as you would any variable in PowerBuilder. The one exception is that instead of using String, Integer, Long or one of the other standard datatypes, the datatype of this variable will be any valid object type.

PowerBuilder automatically creates a global variable to point to a window object created with the Open() function.

Here's an example in which a programmer has created a menu using the Menu painter and saved it with the name m_menu1. There is now a new object type, m_menu1, derived from the PowerBuilder menu object type. Here we'll create a pointer variable to hold an m_menu1 object:

```
m_menu1 m_mymenu
```

We still don't have an object. But we have a place in memory to put one and a variable to point to it once it's there. You use the CREATE statement to actually create the object. CREATE manufactures the object in memory. It then returns the memory address of the new object, which is stored in the pointer variable. Here is an example of the syntax:

```
m_mymenu = CREATE m_menu1
```

From this point on, m_mymenu is a pointer to the new m_menu1 object. For simplicity, m_mymenu can now be thought of as a menu object. You can use this same syntax for any object you want to create.

The DESTROY statement obliterates any object in memory that was created using the CREATE statement. This obliteration returns the available memory to the operating system. It's a good idea to use DESTROY to do your housekeeping as soon as the object is no longer needed in the code. This is especially important in memory-intensive applications. Here's how we destroy our menu object:

```
DESTROY m_mymenu
```

The Close() function automatically destroys window objects.

Be aware that once you've destroyed an object, you cannot access it, because it no longer exists. You can no longer call its functions or reference its attributes because they are all part of the object.

Encapsulation in PowerBuilder

PowerBuilder provides a Function Painter button on the PowerBar. However, this button invokes what is effectively a "global" function painter. That is, the functions are forced to have scope global to the entire application. *Scope* is the term to indicate how long a function or variable exists and what accessibility it has in the application. These global functions are not encapsulated within another object. They are stand-alone. For the purposes of memory and performance management, as well as benefiting from OO principles, the goal should be to minimize the use of global functions. A better implementation is to encapsulate functions within objects. PowerBuilder enables the developer to do this. The functions are then kept within the appropriate object and take up memory only for as long as the object in which the functions are encapsulated exists.

Minimize the use of global functions.

In the Window, Menu and User Object painters, a choice is available on the Declare menu called Window Functions, Menu Functions or User Object Functions. Selecting this choice opens the very same Function painter available on the PowerBar, except that the scope of the function is not forced to be public (i.e., global). This method for invoking the Function painter allows you to create functions encapsulated within the respective objects. For example, selecting Window Functions from the Declare menu of the Window painter enables the developer to create functions encapsulated within only that window. Functions encapsulated within menus or user objects can be created in the same manner.

Inheritance in PowerBuilder

PowerBuilder supports single inheritance. Inheritance is accomplished in different ways in PowerBuilder, depending on the object type being inherited. For example, when you open the Window painter, click the New button and begin to develop a window, the new window object type you're creating is actually inherited from the PowerBuilder window base class. Once you've created a window of your own and then want to inherit from it, you click the Inherit button in the Window painter instead of clicking on the New button. There's an Inherit button in the User Object painter as well, for inheriting from your own user objects.

To create a CommandButton on a window, you typically select the CommandButton control from the PainterBar in the Window painter and click on the window. When you do this, PowerBuilder is actually inheriting an object type from the built-in CommandButton class. The process is similar for each of the controls available in the Window painter. You inherit from your own user object controls in a similar manner. For example, assume you've already created a user object CommandButton. You inherit from it by clicking the user object control button on the PainterBar in the Window painter and then clicking somewhere on the window. The user object is drawn on the window and inherited from your user object CommandButton class.

The Mechanics of PowerBuilder Inheritance

The following snippet of code was taken from the definition for a window class called w_de_student_enrollment, which was inherited from an application base class called bw_de. It demonstrates how descendant classes in PowerBuilder reuse their ancestors' code. (This is not code the developer would normally write—we're showing it here for demonstration purposes.)

```
on w_de_student_enrollment.create
call bw_de::create
end on
```

The PowerBuilder internal event called Create is invoked when a window is opened with the Open() function. This code fragment demonstrates that when the descendant window, w_de_student_enrollment, is opened, PowerBuilder first calls the internal Create event for the ancestor window, bw_de. The inherited code is not copied, but is actually called from the descendant object and thus is reused.

Even the standard PowerBuilder object types that you can build upon are descendants of higher-level PowerBuilder object types. You can view the inheritance hierarchy of all object types using PowerBuilder's Class browser. This important tool allows you to see how each object type is *derived* from an ancestor object type. (To say that an object is derived from another object is the same as saying that it has been inherited from an ancestor object.) This is like being able to see the complete genealogy of an object. To use the Class browser:

The Class browser shows how objects are derived.

1. Open the Library painter by clicking on the Library Painter button on the PowerBar.

Figure 1-1: The Library Painter button on the PowerBar.

2. Select Browse Class Hierarchy from the Utilities menu.

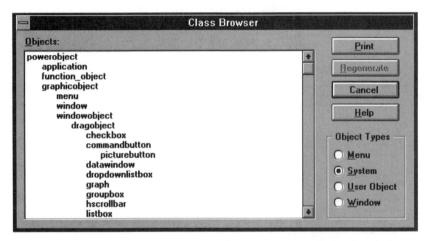

Figure 1-2: Use the Class browser to follow the inheritance hierarchy of all object types.

The Class browser has four radio buttons to the right of the browser box, as shown in Figure 1-2. Click between the four object types to see a tree-structured diagram of the inheritance hierarchy. Click on the System radio button to see where it all begins. The powerobject object type heads the list. It is the highest level of class or object type in PowerBuilder. All other object types in PowerBuilder are derived from this object type.

If you scroll through the list, you see which objects are direct descendants of powerobject. They are as follows:

❒ application

❒ function_object

❒ graphicobject

❒ graxis

❒ grdispattr

❒ nonvisualobject

❒ structure

All other standard object types are ultimately derived from this list of object types. The window object type, for instance, is derived from the graphicobject. Classes that you create will be found in the Class browser in addition to the PowerBuilder classes.

Polymorphism in PowerBuilder

Remember that polymorphism allows the developer to give the same name to functions contained within different objects or to send the same message to different objects. Polymorphism allows for an inherited object to handle the same function or event as its ancestor, but in a way that serves its own needs. In PowerBuilder, we achieve this in one of two ways:

❒ We inherit from an ancestor window, menu or user object, then create a function with the same name as the ancestor's and add new code specific to the descendant. PowerBuilder does not require that we make the argument lists unique among functions of like names. PowerBuilder invokes the first function with the correct name and argument list, beginning with the current object and moving upward through the hierarchy. However, the body of each function can be coded individually. Thus two window objects, for example, could have functions of the same name but containing entirely different code.

❐ We extend or override an inherited event and modify existing code or add new descendant-specific code.

DESIGNING OBJECTS

Object design really consists of asking yourself the following questions about the objects you are creating:

❐ What information should an object contain?

❐ What should an object be able to do?

Though somewhat of a simplification, these two questions form the heart of object design. For instance, in a student registration application, should a student object know the address of the university? Probably not. This would be information a university object might have. Should a student object be able to perform accounting calculations, as with enrollment transactions? Even in real life, a person would probably use a calculator rather than perform calculations by hand. In an object-oriented program, you might design an accounting object that performs account calculations.

An object should only be responsible for "knowing" information and having abilities that you could normally associate with that particular object. This is a principle we call *responsibility-oriented software engineering*. The notion is that an object is only responsible for maintaining itself and information about itself. The student object keeps track of its own address, but not the address of the university. Likewise, the student would not keep information on the calculation formula for enrolling in a course.

There is an entire science growing around the procedures and theory for designing objects and for modeling those objects after real-world entities. There are a number of methodologies for object design. Some are based around theories for approaching object design, and others are based around tools created for helping the developer model the entities of the world. The number and varieties of object design methodologies change often. Below is a list of some of the more popular object design methodologies. Some are methodologies alone, while others are incorporated into design tools.

- ❐ Booch
- ❐ Coad/Yourdon
- ❐ Jacobson/OOSE
- ❐ Martin/Odell
- ❐ Shlaer/Mellor
- ❐ Rumbaugh
- ❐ SOMA

Each methodology comes with its own notation. For example, Figure 1-3 shows a model of part of our student registration application using Rumbaugh notation with ERwin for PowerBuilder.

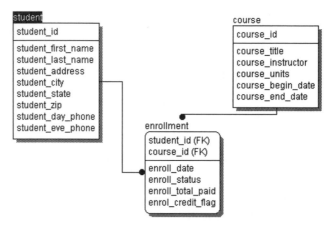

Figure 1-3: ERwin model showing Rumbaugh notation.

As a developer new to OO design, there are a number of angles from which to approach object design and creation. One is to not be overly concerned with the OO concepts on your first project, but to spend the time learning the development tool. When beginning to develop a first PowerBuilder application, don't worry about whether it is object-oriented from day one. Consider your first project experimental. If you find yourself writing the same or very similar code in several places, it is a clue that an object may be useful. As you become more experienced with the tool and the concepts, your object orientation skill set will take shape. You can then take an OO approach from day one on the next project.

If you're writing the same or very similar code in several places, an object may be useful.

Third-Party Class Libraries

A quicker, less painful way to get started in OO development may be to purchase a set of class libraries from a third-party vendor. There are a number available on the market, and we'll talk about some of them in a later chapter. By purchasing class libraries, you can benefit from the OO design of the vendor. However, consider that there is an entirely new learning curve when trying to learn an application base class from a third party, in addition to the learning curve for PowerBuilder alone.

Consulting Services

Finally, an approach that can significantly ease your entry into OO development is to hire a consultant or consulting group for the object design phase of your project. The right consultant can be very helpful in getting off the ground with OO development. Make the training of existing staff a part of the contract, along with designing classes for your project.

BUILDING USER OBJECTS

Often developers think of user objects simply as vehicles to save programming time. They are much more than that. They are necessary elements of a good object-based application. Think back to Dr. Nygaard and his boats. To model his boats in the fjord, he didn't need windows, buttons or checkboxes. He needed boat objects. PowerBuilder 4.0 doesn't include boat objects among its standard object types. In the next few sections, we'll build a user object to meet a real-world requirement, providing a practical illustration of many of the general principles discussed so far in this chapter.

Let's suppose that in our student registration system, we have a requirement to build a clock that will be displayed to the end user. PowerBuilder provides some built-in functions for getting the time from the system clock, but has no object for displaying it. To fulfill our requirement, we'll build a clock user object that will display the date and time more like a physical clock and that can be reused wherever needed. The user object, which we'll call buo_display_date_time, will be a custom visual user object containing one SingleLineEdit control, which will display the time and date in its text attribute.

1. From the PowerBar, click the User Object icon to start the User Object painter.

Figure 1-4: The Select User Object dialog.

2. In the Select User Object dialog, click the New button. The New User Object dialog appears.

PowerBuilder changed the name of its nonvisual user objects to *class* user objects in version 4.0.

Figure 1-5: Use the User Object painter to create both visual and nonvisual user objects.

3. Select the Custom icon under the Visual subcategory, then click the OK button.

4. Change the color of the user object window area to gray by right-clicking the mouse (with the cursor on the window area of the user object) and selecting color from the popup menu, then selecting the color gray.

5. Click on the SingleLineEdit icon on the PainterBar and click on the window area of the user object.

6. Size the SingleLineEdit so it is about 600 PowerBuilder units wide, by dragging the right edge of the SingleLineEdit to the right. 600 units is approximately double the default width of a SingleLineEdit control. (*Note:* The height and width in PowerBuilder units appear in the lower right corner of the User Object painter.)

7. Change the color of the SingleLineEdit to white by right-clicking on the SingleLineEdit, selecting color and then background from the popup menu, and then selecting the color white.

8. Resize the window area of the user object by dragging the lower right corner of the window area up toward the SingleLineEdit, so that the window area creates an evenly spaced frame around the SingleLineEdit. It should look similar to Figure 1-6.

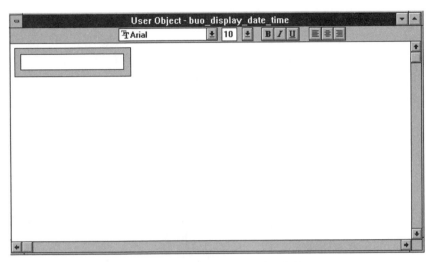

Figure 1-6: Our clock user object of the custom visual class.

9. Name the SingleLineEdit control by right-clicking on it and selecting name. A SingleLineEdit dialog will appear. Type **sle_date_time_display** in the name field. Click OK.

Adding Functionality to the User Object

At this point, we've created only the structure of a user object—that is, we haven't yet given our clock any capabilities. In this section, we'll describe how to add functionality to a user object. We'll create a function that controls how the date and time are displayed in our clock, and we'll create a function for returning the date and time in the format requested.

The clock user object will display time in one of four formats. A string will be passed to the buo_display_date_type object (our clock object) to indicate which format to display. We first need to create an instance variable to store the dis-

Standard visual user objects are derived from the standard PowerBuilder controls.

play state of the clock information. There are four possible states, which are really codes to indicate how the time and date information is to be displayed:

- ❐ 12_hour
- ❐ 24_hour
- ❐ 12_hour_date
- ❐ 24_hour_date

This instance variable will hold the choice used to call the clock user object. Since this instance variable stores information about our clock user object, it is an attribute of it. Instance variables have scope only for the existence of the object in which they are created. So, if there is more than one clock object in our application, each will have its own set of attributes. To declare the instance variable:

1. Right-click the SingleLineEdit control, and select script.
2. Select Instance Variables from the Declare menu, and type the following:

```
protected:
        string    is_display_type
```

Variable Accessibility

PowerBuilder provides a way to specify the scope of the variables stored in an object. The keywords used to describe that scope are known as *member access modifiers*. These modifiers are as follows:

- ❐ **Public**—Accessible by any object within the application. Having public access on a variable or function stored within an object breaks the rule of encapsulation, thus public access should be used minimally.

❏ **Protected**—The object within which the variables or functions are stored and any descendants of that object may access functions and variables declared to be protected.

❏ **Private**—Only the object in which functions and variables are stored may access them.

What does it mean that an object can access a variable or function? In PowerBuilder, the access is achieved when a script in one object references the variables and functions of itself or another object.

You specify the accessibility of functions inside the Function painter. Specify the accessibility of variables using one of two formats. The first format lists the access modifier on the same line as the declaration, and if there are more than one variable of the same datatype, they are separated by commas:

```
protected  string variable1, variable2, etc.
```

The second format places the access modifier on a line by itself followed by a colon. The variables and their datatypes are then placed on lines by themselves:

```
protected:
    string variable1
    long variable2
    etc.
```

The first user object function, buof_get_date_time, retrieves the time or date and time. It takes one argument, a string literal, which determines the display format of the date and time. The function returns the date and time as a single string in the requested format to the calling object. Create this function as follows:

1. Select User Object Functions from the Declare menu. The Select Function in User Object dialog appears.
2. Click the New button to start the Function painter.
3. Type **buof_get_date_time** in the Name field.
4. In the Returns drop-down listbox, select string to indicate that this function will return a value of datatype string.
5. Leave the access drop-down listbox with the default access type public. (Because any object can request the current date and time, we left its access public.)
6. Inside the argument box, we'll define the one argument this function requires. In position one, type **a_date_time_type** in the Name field.
7. Select string from the Type drop-down listbox.
8. Leave Pass By as value. (We'll discuss passing by value versus passing by reference in a later chapter.)

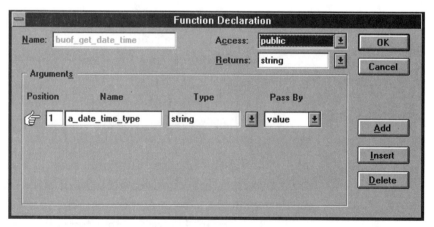

Figure 1-7: Function declaration for user object function buof_get_date_time().

9. Click the OK button to save the function declaration and invoke the PowerScript painter.

10. Type the following:

```
// return time and/or date in requested format
string ls_return_value
CHOOSE CASE a_date_time_type
CASE "12_hour"
   ls_return_value = String(Now( ),"h:mm A/P")
CASE "24_hour"
   ls_return_value = String(Now( ),"h:mm")
CASE "12_hour_date"
   ls_return_value = String(Now( ),"h:mm A/P") + &
   " " + String(Today( ), "m/d/yy")
CASE "24_hour_date"
   ls_return_value = String(Now( ),"h:mm") + &
   " " + String(Today( ), "m/d/yy")
END CHOOSE
RETURN ls_return_value
```

11. Click on the User Object icon on the PainterBar to exit the PowerScript painter, save this user object function and return to the User Object painter.

Our second user object function, buof_refresh_date_time(), resets the displayed value in the text attribute of sle_date_time_display. It uses the instance variable is_display_type to call buof_get_date_time(). This function will be called from a Timer event once per minute, to update the clock.

1. Select User Object Functions from the Declare menu.

2. Click the New button.

3. In the Name field for the function, type **buof_refresh_date_time**.

4. Leave the access as public.

5. Select (None) from the Returns drop-down listbox.

6. Click the OK button. The PowerScript painter will open.

7. Type the following:

```
// refresh the date/time in the text attribute
sle_date_time_display.text = &
          buof_get_date_time( is_display_type )
```

8. Click on the User Object icon on the PainterBar to save this user object function and return to the User Object painter.

9. Invoke the script editor for sle_date_time_display by right-clicking with the cursor on sle_date_time_display and selecting Script.

10. Select the Constructor event from the Select Event drop-down listbox. The Constructor event is common to most of the object types in PowerBuilder. It is automatically triggered once as the object is created, and is analogous to the Open event for a window.

11. In the Constructor event, type the following:

```
// this will retrieve the current time and date
// dependent on the string parm passed from
// an OpenUserObjectWithParm function and put the
// resulting string in the text of the single line
// edit displayed in the object
is_display_type = Message.StringParm
buof_refresh_date_time()
```

12. Click on the User Object icon on the painter toolbar to exit the script editor, save this user object function and return to the User Object painter.

13. Close the User Object painter by double-clicking on the control menu for the painter (not PowerBuilder's control menu).

14. Answer yes to the question "Save changes to (untitled)?" by clicking the Yes button.

Accessing Attributes

PowerBuilder follows OO dot notation syntax conventions in enabling the calling object to access the function (*objectname.functionname*) or attribute (*objectname.variablename*) of the called object.

For example, local_display_date_time.buof_refresh_date_time() is a call to the function buof_refresh_date_time() of the object named local_display_date_time. In the buof_refresh_date_time() function, the reference to sle_date_time_display.text is a reference to the text attribute of local_display_date_time.

A goal of object orientation, although it's not always feasible, is to access the attributes of an object only by calling the functions stored in the object. Technically, accessing an attribute from outside the object using dot notation is a violation of encapsulation. By creating functions to retrieve and change attribute information, you can protect private information, create differing access levels to object information and protect the integrity of an object.

If an object has a large number of attributes, however, it may require an even larger number of functions to manipulate them. There's a balance between only accessing an object's attributes using the dot notation and only using functions to view and change attribute values. One way to achieve this balance is to use functions to access attributes that change the state of an object, and use dot notation to view and change descriptive attributes that will not change the general state of an object. Another approach is to use functions for those attributes that will be changed, and use dot notation to access those attributes that will only be viewed. As you become more comfortable with the idea of objects communicating with objects, you'll naturally tend to create functions to manipulate attributes rather than use the direct access of dot notation.

The Constructor event of sle_date_time_display in the user object assigns the requested display type to the user object instance variable is_display_type from the Message.StringParm attribute of the message object for storage and later use. The Constructor event is common to most of the object types in

PowerBuilder. It is automatically triggered once as the object is created, and is analogous to the Open event for a window. The message object is the vehicle PowerBuilder uses to pass values to a window or user object. If the datatype of the value being passed is character in nature (char, varchar, string, etc.), the value is placed in the StringParm attribute of the message object. If the datatype of the passed value is numeric in nature, it appears in the DoubleParm attribute of the message object. Otherwise, the passed value is placed in the PowerObjectParm attribute of the message object. PowerBuilder handles this passing of values somewhat automatically. The developer calls either OpenWithParm() or OpenUserObjectWithParm(), and PowerBuilder takes care of placing the passed value into the appropriate attribute of the message object. The developer must then retrieve the value from the appropriate attribute of the message object in the called object.

Message Objects vs. OO Messages

It is somewhat confusing that Powersoft has named its vehicle for passing values between objects the "message object." This is unrelated to the OO concept of sending a "message" from one object to another, which, in PowerBuilder, occurs when a script in one object invokes a function call of another object or triggers an event of another object.

Define the Constructor event as follows:

1. Invoke the PowerScript painter for sle_date_time_display by right-clicking with the cursor on sle_date_time_display and selecting Script.

2. Select the Constructor event from the Select Event drop-down listbox.

3. In the Constructor event, type the following:

```
// this will retrieve the current time and date
// dependent on the string parm passed from
// an OpenUserObjectWithParm function and put the
// resulting string in the text of the single line
// edit displayed in the object
is_display_type = Message.StringParm
buof_refresh_date_time( )
```

4. Close the User Object painter by double-clicking on the control menu for the painter (*not* PowerBuilder's control menu).

5. Answer yes to the question "Save changes to (untitled)?" by clicking the Yes button.

6. The Save User Object dialog will appear. Type **buo_display_date_time** in the User Objects field.

7. Click OK to save our user object.

Testing Our User Object

Quite often in development efforts, we need to test a component that is dependent upon other components that may not yet be built. Since we don't want to wait until all relevant components are created in order to test a user object, we can create a test window and add only the code necessary to run that object. This kind of test window is useful when testing many objects in PowerBuilder.

Let's test our new clock user object. We'll create a test window that will open the clock user object, and we'll invoke a timer in the window to refresh the display. We'll use this test window throughout the book. To create it, do the following:

1. Open the Window painter by clicking on the Window Painter button on the PowerBar.

2. Click the New button.

3. First, give the window a title by right-clicking on the new window area and selecting Title.

4. In Title field of the Set Title dialog, type **User Object Test Window**.

5. Click OK.

6. Add a CommandButton by clicking on the CommandButton icon on the PainterBar and clicking on the window.

7. Type **&Close** in the field in the upper left corner of the Window painter, replacing the default title of none.

8. Invoke the PowerScript painter for the CommandButton by right-clicking (with the cursor on the button) and selecting Script.

9. Make sure the Clicked event is the current event by selecting clicked from the Select Event drop-down listbox.

10. Type the following to make our Close button close the window:

```
close( parent )
```

11. Close the PowerScript painter by double-clicking on the painter control menu and responding Yes to the question about saving changes.

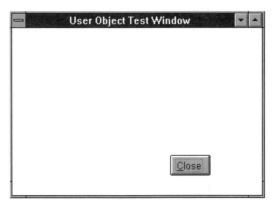

Figure 1-8: Our test window.

Now we'll create an instance variable, local_display_
date_time, which is an instantiation of the user object
buo_display_date_time (our clock user object). In OO
terminology, local_display_date_time is an instance of the
buo_display_date_time class. We're creating an instance for
our test window; if needed, we could create other instances
in the same manner.

1. Select Instance Variables from the Declare menu and
   type the following:

   ```
   buo_display_date_time local_display_date_time
   ```

2. Click OK.

Now we'll add the code to open the clock user object and
refresh the display:

1. Invoke the PowerScript painter for the window by
   right-clicking (with the mouse cursor on the face of the
   window, but not over the CommandButton), and
   selecting Script from the popup menu.

2. Select the Open event from the Select Event drop-
   down listbox.

3. Type the following:

```
// display the current date and time with the time
// in a 24 hour format by creating a user object
// and passing it a parm of the type of date/time
// to display.
this.OpenUserObjectWithParm(local_display_date_time, &
    "24_hour_date", "buo_display_date_time",& 50, 50)
Timer(60)
```

The OpenUserObjectWithParm() function is new to version 4.0 of PowerBuilder. It is used to dynamically call user objects (and display them if they are visual). Previously, the developer had to attach the user object to a window at design time. With the new function, the user objects can be created at run-time. We're using the format of OpenUserObjectWithParm() that requires three arguments and optionally accepts an additional two arguments. The first argument is our window instance variable. The OpenUserObjectWithParm() function stores a pointer to the object in this argument for reference by other objects. The second argument is the value being passed to the user object—in this case,"24_hour_date." The third argument is a string whose contents are the datatype of the first argument. The fourth and fifth arguments are optional and are the X and Y coordinates, measured in PowerBuilder units, that describe where the user object is to be displayed within the window. If the last two arguments are omitted, PowerBuilder defaults them to 0,0, which is the upper left corner of the window.

The Timer() function invokes a timer to run the Timer event every 60 seconds. Now we'll code the Timer event to call the user object function bucf_refresh_date_time() to update the display in our clock user object once per minute with the new current time:

1. Select the Timer event from the Select Event drop-down listbox.

2. Type the following:

```
// refresh the current date and time by using a
// user object function - this event is triggered
// every 60 seconds

local_display_date_time.buof_refresh_date_time()
```

3. Close the PowerScript painter by double-clicking on the painter control menu and responding Yes to the question about saving changes.

4. Select Save from the File menu.

5. In the Save Window dialog box, type **w_bou_test**.

6. Click OK.

At this point, we can test our clock user object by opening the test window from the Open event of the application object. Now that we've coded it, we can use it again as often as we need. (There is a caveat that operating systems have limitations on the number of timers allowed. In Microsoft Windows, the limit is 16.)

INHERITING FROM A USER OBJECT

In this section, we'll use our clock user object as an example to describe how inheritance enables us to reuse user objects in PowerBuilder. Let's assume that we have a new requirement in our student registration application for a clock that beeps at the top of the hour. We'll create a new clock user object by inheriting from our existing clock user object. We'll then modify the descendant object to test whether the time is exactly on the hour and beep if it is.

1. Open the User Object painter. This time, instead of clicking the New button in the Select User Object dialog, click the Inherit button.

2. A dialog entitled Inherit From User Object appears. Select our clock user object, titled buo_display_ date_time.

3. Click OK. The user object appears in the painter, but notice the title of the painter window. It reads "User Object – (Untitled) inherited from buo_display_date_time." This tells us that we're working on a new user object, as yet untitled, that is a descendant of the buo_display_date_time class.

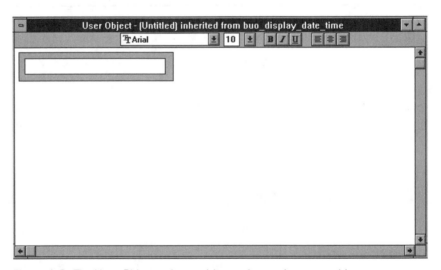

Figure 1-9: The User Object painter with our descendant user object.

Working With Inherited Functions

Recall that when objects are created using inheritance, they inherit the functions and events of the ancestor object. Inherited functions can be used just as if the functions had been created with the descendant. There are times, however, when you want the descendant to provide different functionality from the ancestor. In these cases, you have a couple of choices:

❏ Create new functions in the descendant that have different names from the ancestor's functions.

❏ Create new functions in the descendant that have the same name as the ancestor's. This is called *function overloading*. If you then call the ancestor's function in the overloaded descendant function, the ancestor function can be extended.

O verloading is a form of polymorphism.

In our inherited clock user object, we'll overload the buof_refresh_date_time() function to test whether the time is exactly on the hour and beep if it is.

1. Select User Object Functions from the Declare menu.

P owerBuilder doesn't display the ancestor's functions in a descendant object, but they *are* available to the descendant.

2. Click the New button. Notice that no functions appear in the dialog although we are inheriting from an object that contains functions. (PowerBuilder does not make them visible, though it would be less confusing to the new comer if they were. Perhaps in a future version. . . .)

3. In the Name field of the function, type the same name as in the ancestor for the refresh function: **buof_refresh_date_time**.

4. As before, it does not return a value, so select (None) in the Returns drop-down listbox.

5. When you have an overloaded function, PowerBuilder determines which function to execute at run time by

looking at the function declarations. In PowerBuilder, you do not need to make the argument list for an overloaded function unique, by having either a different number of arguments than the ancestor function or different datatypes of corresponding arguments. (The uniqueness of the function declaration argument list is how languages such as C++ and Smalltalk achieve overloading.) The ancestor user object function buof_refresh_date_time() takes no arguments. To make our overloaded function unique, we'll require one argument. In the Name field of the argument, type **ab_beep_flag**.

6. Select boolean from the Type drop-down listbox.

7. Leave Pass By as value.

8. Click OK. The Function painter appears.

9. In the Function painter, type the following:

```
super::buof_refresh_date_time()
if (minute(now()) = 0) and    &
          (ab_beep_flag = true) then
    beep(4)
end if
```

10. Close the Function painter by double-clicking on its control menu and responding Yes to the question about saving changes.

11. Close the User Object painter by double-clicking on its control menu. Answer Yes to the question about saving changes.

12. Name our new user object **buo_display_date_time_beep** and then click OK.

Although it's compact, there's a lot going on in that script. The first line calls the ancestor's version of our function. Because we gave our function the same name as the ancestor's, we effectively replaced it. But in our overloaded function, we still want to take advantage of the code in the ancestor function, so we call it using the relative reference identifier Super.

Relative Reference Identifiers

A *relative reference identifier* is sort of like a variable you can use to reference objects instead of hard-coding specific object names in a script. In the overloaded buof_refresh_date_time() function in the example, we're using the relative reference identifier Super to call the ancestor's version of the function. (Note that when crossing levels of inheritance, the *scope resolution operator* (::) is used instead of the dot operator to separate the name of the object— or, in this case, the relative reference identifier that represents the object—from the function.) The Super identifier always refers to the immediate ancestor of the current object. Other relative reference identifiers include This, which refers to the current object, and Parent, which refers to the container of the current object (for example, a window is the parent of a CommandButton on that window).

Relative reference identifiers make scripts more dynamic and therefore reusable. You *can* make calls to a specific window, CommandButton, etc., by hard-coding the name of the object. There are times when this is necessary and acceptable. For instance, if you need to refer to an object more than one level removed, such as a grandparent object, Super won't work. You must refer to the grandparent object by name. However, whenever there are hard-coded object names in a script, the ability to reuse the script is diminished: changes have to be made each time you inherit from the object containing the script. Having to make changes each time defeats the benefits of inheritance.

The function argument, ab_beep_flag, serves as a flag to indicate whether to invoke the Beep() function. The IF statement makes use of two built-in functions, Now() and Minute(). Now() returns the current time and takes no arguments. Minute() takes one argument, a time value, and strips off the minute portion of the time argument passed to it. The if statement tests that the minute is zero and that the argument is true. If both parts of the test are true, the Beep() function will be called. Beep() takes one argument, an integer indicating the number of times to beep. If the argument passed to the overloaded function is false or if the time is not exactly the top of the hour, the Beep() function is not invoked.

To test the new overloaded buof_refresh_date_time(), modify the instance variable of our test window, w_buo_test, to read as follows:

```
buo_display_date_time_beep local_display_date_time
```

Modify the Timer event of w_buo_test to include the argument True in the function call to buof_display_date_time, as follows:

```
local_display_date_time.buof_refresh_date_time( True )
```

Open the w_buo_test window to test the new user object.

Working With Inherited Events

Thus far, we've looked at inheriting and overloading functions. At this point, there are no events coded in our user object, but events are inherited along with functions when a descendant is created from an ancestor that has events. The techniques for handling inherited events are slightly different than for functions, although the principles are similar, in that events may be:

❒ Used in a descendant "as is" from the ancestor.

❒ Overridden completely in the descendant event.

❒ Extended to add to the capabilities of the ancestor event.

When you click on the Compile menu item in the PowerScript painter for an inherited object, the last three choices are as follows:

❏ Extend Ancestor Script

❏ Override Ancestor Script

❏ Display Ancestor Script

The Extend Ancestor Script menu item will probably be checked. Extending an ancestor script appends your new code to the end of the ancestor's code. You won't actually see this happening on the screen. When the script in the new object runs, it runs the ancestor script first and then any code in the descendant's script.

To completely do away with an ancestor's script, you can choose to override it. When the object runs the script, only the descendant script will run.

Event scripts that are neither extended with additional script nor overridden operate exactly as they did in the ancestor. You can always choose to view the ancestor script by selecting the Display Ancestor Script menu selection.

It's a good idea to document your objects well so that there are no mistakes with inherited event scripts. As levels of inheritance get deeper, so does the complexity of keeping track of which events are going to be triggered and what script they will run. PowerBuilder keeps track of inheritance hierarchies when it creates a new object type.

Like functions, events at different levels of inheritance can be called using the relative reference identifiers and the scope resolution operator (::). To invoke an event for an immediate ancestor, use the following syntax:

```
call super::event
```

As with functions, you invoke an event of an ancestor at an inheritance level prior to the immediate ancestor by referencing the object by name:

```
call AncestorName::event
```

The previous two examples refer to events in the ancestor object itself. To invoke an event in a control or user object *on* the ancestor object, use a back quote (`) and the control or user object name as part of the call:

```
call AncestorName`ObjectName::event
```

ObjectName refers to either the name of a control, such as a CommandButton or SingleLineEdit, or to the name of a user object. Note that the quote used to precede the object or control name is a back quote (`), *not* a straight single quote ('). The back quote is often found beneath the tilde (~) on keyboards.

APPLICATION DESIGN

When designing PowerBuilder applications using objects, there are many things to keep in mind. The first thing to remember is that as long as you are using a relational database, you won't have a pure object-oriented system.

In fact, it's quite possible to work around almost every object-oriented feature in PowerBuilder. But object orientation was invented to model complex systems, and the more complex an application, the more OO you want to design it. It's easy to miss details in a large system, and overlooked details are much easier to find and correct in an OO application. Making changes to objects is much simpler than attempting to make changes to a program where many of the functions and scripts throughout the entire application need to be modified to effect a change. Forget even one and you have a bug. When code is encapsulated within an object, it isn't necessary to touch code in other parts of the system. This limits the chances of introducing bugs into the rest of your system. Once an object is debugged and working, it can be dropped into any program with the comfort of knowing it will just work.

Here's a quick recap of some of the things you should keep in mind when designing an OO system with PowerBuilder:

- ❐ Make minimal use of global functions.
- ❐ Use global variables only when necessary.
- ❐ Use inheritance. Create new objects only when inheriting from an existing class will not work.
- ❐ Don't reinvent PowerBuilder with objects. Creating your own operations that duplicate PowerBuilder's built-in capabilities doesn't add a lot of value.
- ❐ Don't have one object manipulate another. Have objects communicate with messages.

Once you've been developing applications for a while, you'll develop your own library of objects. It may sound like a complex task to write a communications object or database object. But if they're written well, they only need to be written once and then can be used over and over again. Application development then becomes a task of assembling objects rather than one of intense code-writing. A good question to ask yourself is whether code you are writing for an application will be reusable in other applications. Asking this question forces you to take a look at the bigger picture. With each new application, you'll have to construct objects to perform custom functions. Yet with each application, the number of new objects that need to be developed will decrease. Eventually, all you may need to do to create an application is to create new objects using inheritance, then add functionality to the new descendants.

MOVING ON

In this chapter, we introduced the concepts of object orientation. You'll find that programming in an object-oriented manner will improve the quality of your application. Encapsulation makes your applications easier to debug. Inheritance makes them smaller and more efficient. Polymorphism gives your programs greater flexibility by allowing you to drop in new objects without changing all the other objects. By adhering to the idea of responsibility-oriented software engineering, you can reuse code in application after application. Good application design is your responsibility.

In the next chapter, we'll build upon the concepts we've learned to make some reusable software components.

Chapter 2

Building a Class Library

Think back to when the first PC spreadsheets and word processors were released, in the early 1980s. New versions appeared on the market about every two to three years. In 1996 the turnaround time for new versions of application software is 9 to 18 months. OO software development concepts that focus on creating reusable code have contributed significantly to this trend toward the shortened business cycle of application software. When developers take advantage of base classes (the highest-level classes, classes that have no ancestors) and class libraries, their ability to efficiently develop software increases significantly. If classes are well designed, they can be written once and reused many times. Reusing software saves time, and in business, after all, time is money.

Even though software reuse is a primary goal of OO development, this goal often gets lost in all the details of how to implement an object-oriented language and all the concepts and terminologies surrounding that language. Our goal in this chapter is to emphasize the importance of software reusability and demonstrate techniques for creating reusable software through class and base class development. We'll utilize the PowerBuilder base classes to build a library of reusable classes for our student registration application. We don't want to make classes out of everything—only objects that will be reused. The result will be similar to the kind of class libraries that third-party vendors have built upon the PowerBuilder base classes. (Although, since they do have ancestors, such classes are not technically base classes. They are often referred to as base classes or application base classes because they are the highest-level classes the developer builds.)

There are usually three categories of classes in the hierarchy of reusable classes:

❑ Application base classes.

❑ Application component classes.

❑ Application-specific classes.

The highest level (except for the PowerBuilder built-in classes) are the application base classes. These are classes of atomic or elementary entities that are *simple* in architecture. By simple, it is meant that these classes are single entities—a CommandButton, a window, etc.

The classes of atomic entities are very generic in nature, and should be designed to be used in the majority of applications.

The next, or middle, layer of classes are what we call application components. Application components are usually *complex*. Complex architected classes are classes that consist of multiple entities put together to create a single entity, such as windows with preattached buttons or fields, and spin-controls, which combine a SingleLineEdit control and a vertical scroll bar. Some common examples of application components include login, search and print preview windows. These are still somewhat generic in design and can be used in most applications.

The lowest-level classes are the application-specific classes. Notice we did not say *program*-specific. There is little payback if you spend a considerable amount of time designing a class to be reusable and it's only useful in one program, one time. The OO concepts would have been carried a little too far in that situation. By application-specific classes, we mean those entities that will be used in multiple places but are by definition contained in the application at hand. For example, a window to enter or look up a general ledger number might be used dozens of times in financial modules—accounts payable, accounts receivable, etc. However, such a window would most likely be confined to the financial applications. There's still a benefit from reuse, yet we're getting fairly specific at this point.

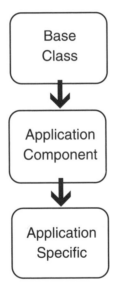

Figure 2-1: Three levels of classes.

These groupings are somewhat broad, but they serve to help us in our design by providing guidelines. For example, the application-specific layer is made up of the application component layer, which is in turn comprised of the atomic elements at the highest level. Knowing which level of class we're intending to create will help us determine whether a particular functionality goes or stays.

APPLICATION BASE CLASSES

Developers new to OO or PowerBuilder often begin an OO project by trying to write a complex class for reuse. It's better to start simple. If we could truly add value to some of the controls that come with PowerBuilder, then we should start there. These simple, atomic controls can be thought of as the building blocks from which other classes are built. We'll begin with these building blocks. How do we know what functionality to add to our base classes? We shouldn't really be trying to make up things to put in a class. Actually, the reverse should occur—when we find ourselves writing the same code over and over in an application, it means that this code would work better as a class.

SingleLineEdit Class

A SingleLineEdit control is used consistently in applications as a "field" control. PowerBuilder supplies its base SingleLineEdit with 11 events. None, however, contain any code. They're merely placeholders for code intended to respond to particular real-world events. Something that we found ourselves constantly coding was the highlighting of text in a SingleLineEdit. For two reasons, we found it better to create a SingleLineEdit user object class with user-defined events to highlight the text rather than to frequently code the same functions to highlight it. First, according to our OO rule of encapsulation, one object should not manipulate another.

And second, the functionality is built into the SingleLineEdit class, so we won't have to code it over and over again—we'll simply send a message to (trigger an event of) the instantiated SingleLineEdit object.

SingleLineEdit Class Events

The text-highlighting functionality could be handled with either an event or a function. A general rule is that if you do not need to send an argument and do not require a value to be returned, make it an event. At this point, let's assume that your applications won't need to know whether there was previously something in the text attribute of the SingleLineEdit. We'll create a user-defined event called ue_select_all_text to handle the functionality. Create it as follows:

*W*rite an event instead of a function when you don't need to send an argument or return a value.

1. Open the User Object painter.
2. In the Select User Object dialog, select New to create a new user object.
3. In the New User Object dialog, select Visual Standard.
4. Click the OK button to accept the choice.
5. In the Select Standard Visual Type list, select SingleLineEdit.
6. Click OK to accept the selection.
7. From the Declare menu, select User Events. The Events - (Untitled) dialog will appear.
8. At the bottom of the list of existing events is a line to enter the new event. In the Event Name field, type **ue_select_all_text** and then tab to the Event ID field.
9. In the Event ID field, type **pbm_custom01** (or select it from the Paste Event ID list).

Cross-Platform Event IDs

When creating a user-defined event, selecting an event ID other than the custom event IDs pbm_custom01 to pbm_custom75 will cause you to lose cross-platform capability. The other event IDs in the Paste Event ID list are Microsoft Windows DLL function calls, which are not cross-platform.

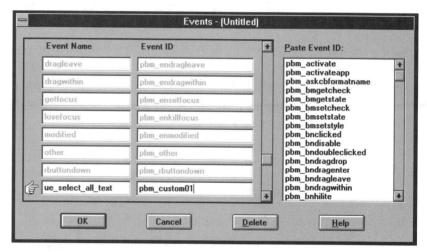

Figure 2-2: Creating a user-defined event.

10. Click OK to accept the new user-defined event.

11. Open the script editor for the SingleLineEdit user object.

12. Make ue_select_all_text the current event in the editor.

13. In the event, type the following:

```
if len(this.text) > 0 then
    this.selecttext(1, len(this.text))
end if
```

14. Close the script editor and save the new code.

15. Save the user object and name it buo_sle.

16. Close the User Object painter.

The SelectText() built-in function takes two arguments. The first is the starting position in bytes of the text to highlight. The second argument is the length in bytes of how many characters beyond the first argument to highlight.

Following are a couple of additional user-defined events for our SingleLineEdit user object. Create them in the same way you created ue_select_all_text. The first event, which we'll call ue_select_start_of_text, places the cursor at the beginning of the text in the SingleLineEdit, but does not highlight the text. Here's the code for the event:

```
// this event places the cursor at the
// beginning of the text in the SingleLineEdit,
// but does not highlight the text

this.selecttext( 1, 0 )
```

The second event, ue_select_end_of_text, places the cursor at the end of the text in the SingleLineEdit, but does not highlight the text. Here's the code:

```
// this event places the cursor at the end of
// the text in the SingleLineEdit, but does
// not highlight the text

this.selecttext( len( this.text ) + 1,  0 )
```

SingleLineEdit Class Function

The same highlighting functionality that we achieved with the ue_select_all_text event can be performed with a function. We'll also take advantage of a function's ability to return values by returning a Boolean value to indicate whether there is a value in the text attribute other than the initialization value of the null string (""). If the

SingleLineEdit is empty, we'll return a Boolean value of false, indicating there was nothing to highlight. If it's not empty, we'll return a Boolean value of true, and we'll highlight the text. Create the SingleLineEdit user object function as follows:

1. Open the User Object painter.
2. Select buo_sle.
3. From the Declare menu, select User Object Functions.
4. In the Select Function in User Object dialog, click the New button.
5. In the Name field, type **buof_select_all_text**.
6. In the Returns field, select boolean.
7. Leave the Access as public.

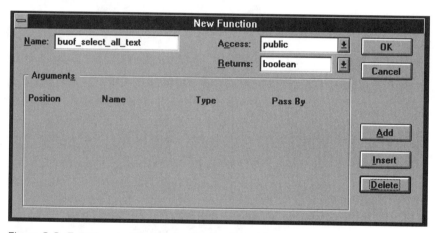

Figure 2-3: Function declaration for buof_select_all_text.

8. Click the OK button to save the function declaration.
9. In the script editor, type the following:

```
boolean lb_return_value
if len(this.text) > 0 then
    this.selecttext( 1, len(this.text))
    lb_return_value = True
else
```

```
            lb_return_value = False
        end if
        return lb_return_value
```

10. Close the script editor and save the changes.

11. Close the User Object painter to save the user object.

If we want to, we can leave both the user-defined event and the function in our class, since a class can contain an event and a function with the same name. Our convention of prefixing the names with type identifiers makes them unique. However, they can be the same.

Using Our SingleLineEdit User Object Class

These are only a few examples of the kinds of functionality we could add to our SingleLineEdit user object class. You can add whatever functionality to your SingleLineEdit class that you find yourself coding frequently. Once we have it in a stable state, we can start using this SingleLineEdit class instead of PowerBuilder's. Instead of choosing the SingleLineEdit icon from the PainterBar in the Window painter and then clicking on the window area SingleLineEdit, select the user object icon from the PainterBar, select our SingleLineEdit user object class, buo_sle, from the dialog and click on the window area. This will cause PowerBuilder to inherit from our SingleLineEdit user object class rather than from PowerBuilder's. As you can see, we can get quite a bit of mileage by simply creating a user object class for each of the controls and then adding events or functions to take care of the administrative kinds of coding.

Specific CommandButton Class

We could create a CommandButton user object class to be generic, as we did with the SingleLineEdit user object class. But let's go a step further and create a CommandButton class that is more specific. Since we often find ourselves creating

Close CommandButtons, we'll create a Close CommandButton user object class.

In Chapter 1, you coded the following line in the Clicked event of the Close CommandButton on the test window:

```
close( parent )
```

With that one line, we're actually breaking our now-familiar rule about one object not manipulating another. In that example, the CommandButton (ObjectA) is invoking the Close() function to close the window (ObjectB). If the only action taken by the Close CommandButton is to close the window, then we're not really gaining much by moving the code to an event on the window.

However, there are many situations where we do house-keeping just before actually closing. Given that, we could accommodate both our rule and the housekeeping by moving the close logic to the Close event of the window and simply triggering the window's Close event from our Close CommandButton. (You may be asking yourself why it's still called a Close CommandButton if it isn't actually closing anything. Well, this kind of situation is not uncommon in OO development.) We don't know what kind of housekeeping we may want to perform for the window; while some windows may require housekeeping, others may only need to be closed. It doesn't matter at this point—we're only interested in coding our CommandButton, and our CommandButton only triggers the Close event of its parent. We can place the button on any window that requires one and then be done. (Something else to consider is that there may be a requirement for a menu item to close the window, in addition to the Close CommandButton. Even with the single call to the Close() function, there would be duplicate code—one call in the CommandButton and one call in the menu—and duplicate code is taboo in OO development!)

Duplicate code is taboo in OO development!

Let's now code our close CommandButton user object class. We've found that often there is something that needs to be done *before* invoking the housekeeping logic on the window, so we'll create one user-defined event, called ue_before_close, as a placeholder for code the developer may want to add to the descendant of our CommandButton user object class. We'll trigger the ue_before_close event from our Clicked event just before we trigger the parent's Close event. Perform the following steps to create our Close CommandButton user object class (if you need some help navigating the painters, refer to the procedures we described when creating our SingleLineEdit class):

1. Open the User Object painter for a Visual, Standard user object.
2. Select CommandButton.
3. Add a user-defined event, called ue_before_close.
4. Add the following code to the Clicked event of the CommandButton:

```
this.triggerevent( "ue_before_close" )
parent.triggerevent( "close" )
```

5. In the upper left corner of the painter window, type **&close** to give the text attribute a default value.
6. Save our new CommandButton user object as buo_cb_close.

Just as with the SingleLineEdit user object, we can inherit from buo_cb_close by selecting the user object icon from the PainterBar in the Window painter.

DataWindow Control User Object Class

Now let's take a look at an atomic user object class that's a bit more complicated than the others. One of the more important areas to focus on when building reusable classes is DataWindow controls. Third-party vendors spend quite a bit of effort on DataWindow control classes. Coding DataWindow controls in applications requires an enormous amount of time. If this code can be written so that it is dynamic and reusable, then we have a good candidate for an application base class.

Follow these steps to begin work on our DataWindow control user object class:

1. Open the User Object painter and select New, then Visual Standard.

2. Select datawindow from the Select Visual Type dialog.

DataWindow controls are complicated to code for several reasons. They have dynamic DataWindow objects on them, which can vary in presentation style and data source. Just with presentation logic alone, there could be freeform, tabular or graph styles. You can add code to handle highlighting a row (as in a tabular presentation style), but it won't apply to graphs or freeforms. The combinations can seem endless. There can also be differing sources of data—multiple databases, flat files, etc. In addition to varying sources, there could be database errors. In the next couple of sections, we'll take a look at some of the principles involved with DataWindows and add a couple of useful events to our DataWindow user object class.

Database Errors

The PowerBuilder DataWindow control class has a built-in event called DBError. It's automatically triggered by PowerBuilder when there's a database error during I/O (input/output) with the database. In this section we'll create a DBError event that will trap some of the more common database errors and present a more user-friendly message to the end user. If you've ever seen the error messages that database vendors put out, you'll agree that this is a service.

The benefit to the developer is that the code needs to be written only once and then reused. The error numbers and corresponding errors vary with each vendor. We'll use the Watcom database for our example, but these trapped error codes will work in the same way for other database vendors, such as Sybase and Oracle. The error numbers and exact verbiage vary by vendor, but the principles are the same.

To code the DBError event, follow these steps:

1. Open the script editor for the new DataWindow control and select the DBError event.

2. In the DBError event, type the following:

```
// this will trap the errors generated from the
// DBMS and redisplay them in a more meaningful
// form it also prevents the display of the
// default error message from DBError

// this will get the error code and message text
// from the DBMS

long    ll_error_code
string ls_error_text

ll_error_code = this.DBErrorCode ( )
ls_error_text = this.DBErrorMessage ( )

// this will look for some of the common DBErrors
// and display more specific messages
// for any other errors, a generic messagebox is
// displayed

CHOOSE CASE ll_error_code

   CASE -100

   MessageBox("DB Error - Database Engine " + &
   "not Running", "The database engine " + &
   "has not been started, possible " + &
```

```
"profile problem" + "~n~r" + &
String(ll_error_code) + " " + ls_error_text, &
Exclamation!)

CASE -304

MessageBox("DB Error - Disk Full", &
"There is not enough free hard disk " + &
"space to store the affected rows for this" + &
" transaction. Transaction has been" + &

" rolled back. Please contact the Database" + &
" Administrator." + &
"~n~r" + String(ll_error_code) + " " + &
ls_error_text, Exclamation!)

CASE -306

MessageBox("DB Error - Deadlock Condition", &
"The row being read or written is in use " + &
"by another user. Your transaction has " + &
"been rolled backed (the changes have not" + &
" been applied). Please retry at a later " + &
"time ~n~r" + String(ll_error_code) + " " + &
ls_error_text, Exclamation!)


CASE -193

MessageBox("DB Error - Duplicate Key", &
"The key value entered is used in an " + &
"existing row, please specify a unique " + &
"value ~n~r" + String(ll_error_code) + &
" " + ls_error_text, Exclamation!)


CASE ELSE

// for all other errors, display a
// general error message with the error
// code and text
```

```
MessageBox("DB Error", &
 "A database error has occurred. " + &
 "Please print this message for debugging, " + &
 "and contact the appropriate personnel." + &
 "~n~r" + String(ll_error_code) + " " + &
 ls_error_text, exclamation!)

END CHOOSE

// don't display the default error message

this.SetActionCode (1)
```

Let's take a look at how this script works. The local variables ll_error_code and ls_error_text are for storing the actual database vendor's error number and error verbiage, respectively. The built-in functions DBErrorCode() and DBErrorMessage() return those database error values when invoked. You can see that our error message is slightly different for each case statement. The default case else message is a catch-all for "other" database errors.

By default, PowerBuilder displays its own message box with database error information. Since we're handling those messages ourselves, we disable PowerBuilder's default behavior. The call to SetActionCode() with an argument of 1 turns off that default behavior. Calling SetActionCode() with an argument of 0 will turn the PowerBuilder default of displaying messages back on.

Selecting DataWindow Rows

Now we'll work on some presentation logic. If the database object is tabular, we can handle the highlighting of a row when the user clicks on the DataWindow control. There are three things we can do when the click occurs:

❏ Highlight the current row.

❏ Unhighlight any rows previously highlighted.

59

❑ Get the key value for the row (if any).

Let's look at the first item, highlighting a row:

1. From the Declare menu, select User Events.
2. Create an event and name it ue_highlight_row.
3. Create an instance variable of type string and name it is_key_value.
4. In the script editor, select ue_highlight_row as the current event and type the following code:

```
long ll_row_number
ll_row_number = this.getclickedrow()
if ll_row_number > 0 then
   this.triggerevent( "ue_unhighlight_all_rows" )
   this.selectrow( ll_row_number, true )
   this.triggerevent( "ue_get_key" )
else
   is_key_value = ""
end if
```

Now we'll create the user-defined event to unhighlight any rows previously highlighted:

1. Create another user-defined event and name it ue_unhighlight_all_rows.
2. In the script editor for ue_unhighlight_all_rows, type the following:

```
this.selectrow( 0, False )
```

3. Save the user object and name it buo_dw.

There are some things to consider when coding functionality to capture a key value. First, not all applications require capturing a key value when the user clicks on the DataWindow control. This point alone suggests that we create only a placeholder for the code to get the key value. To create a placeholder in our DataWindow control user object class, do the following:

1. Create a user-defined event called ue_get_key_value.
2. Add the following code to the Clicked event of the DataWindow user object:

   ```
   this.triggerevent( "ue_get_key_value" )
   ```

3. Save the user object.

It is up to the developer to add the specific code to the descendant of this DataWindow control class to get the key value. A point to consider is whether we know the datatype or the column name of the key value ahead of time (this question assumes there are multiple DataWindow objects used for a single DataWindow control). We would need a case statement that tests the datatype and corresponding column name in the descendant object type.

The last area of this user object class is transaction object coding. Often, developers place the call to the SetTransObject() function in the Open event of the window that contains the DataWindow control. If the DataWindow control is designed to retrieve rows at the time the window opens, that call to Retrieve() also appears in the Open event of the window. This breaks our rule of encapsulation. The window should not be manipulating the DataWindow control; it should send a message to the DataWindow control, telling it to set its own transaction object and retrieve its own data.

In the DataWindow user object class, we can use either an event or a function to meet our needs. If we know that our applications will only ever use one transaction object, then we can go ahead and code that in our ue_set_trans event, as follows:

```
this.settransobject( SQLCA )
```

This assumes that you'll use the PowerBuilder default transaction object SQLCA. If not, then substitute the name of your transaction object.

If your applications will use multiple transaction objects, then we can approach this situation with a function. For multiple transaction objects, perform the following steps:

1. Create a new user object function for buo_dw and name it buof_set_trans.
2. Define buof_set_trans to take one argument of datatype transaction.
3. Set Pass By to reference.

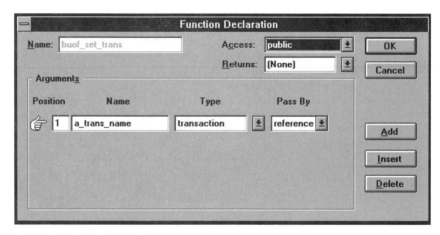

Figure 2-4: Function declaration for buof_set_trans.

When Pass By is set to value, the contents of the argument being passed are copied to the function, and the function operates on the copy of the contents. The contents of the original variable remain unchanged. When Pass By is set to reference, a pointer to the original variable being passed is sent to the function, and the function actually manipulates the value of the original variable. Assume, for example, that SQLCA is passed to this function. There's only one SQLCA, and we want our buof_set_trans() function to manipulate it directly. The same would be true for any transaction object being passed.

Regardless of the method you choose, the user-defined event or the user object function for the user object should be invoked from the Constructor event of the DataWindow control. We cannot make both work in the class. If we use a function, we need a user object variable to store the transaction name. Since the Constructor of the DataWindow control user object class calls buof_set_trans at design-time, we don't know the name of the transaction object. You would think we could create a user object instance variable to store the transaction object and create a function whose argument is the transaction object. The function could then set the instance variable from its argument. This will not work! We want to call the function to set the transaction object name from the window *before* the Constructor of the ancestor DataWindow control class invokes buof_set_trans using the instance variable as its argument. The Constructor event for the DataWindow control is invoked before the Open event of the window. We would have to use a global variable to make it work. It's easier to leave it to the developer to code the call to buof_set_trans in the descendant Constructor event. If your applications are evenly divided between using SQLCA as the transaction object and "other," then you could create a transaction class with the function and not invoke it from the Constructor. This would leave the task to the descendant. Then create a second transaction class, inherited from the first, with the following code in its Constructor event:

```
ue_set_trans( SQLCA )
```

The two classes handle both situations.

APPLICATION COMPONENT CLASSES

Application components are complex classes because they comprise multiple other classes. The other classes can be built-in PowerBuilder controls, your own user objects, or a combination of both. First we'll look at an example of a simple display-only class, and then we'll consider some more advanced components.

Display-Only Classes

A standardized display-only class such as a "splash" screen (see Figure 2-5) or an "about" window is useful for creating commonality across applications or modules. The benefit for these kind of classes is more one of standards enforcement than of time savings.

Figure 2-5: An example "splash screen" window class.

Search Window Class

Now we'll build a search window class that can be used throughout an application. Similar to the Close button we built earlier that does not actually close anything directly, the search window class will not actually search, but will build a text search argument regardless of what is being searched. The search window accepts input of the search argument value and enables the user to indicate whether the item being searched begins with or contains the search argument. Build the search window class with the following steps:

1. Create a new window in the Window painter.

2. On the window, place a SingleLineEdit called sle_search_argument; two CommandButtons, called cb_search and cb_close; two RadioButtons, called rb_begins and rb_contains; and a group box called gb_begin_contains (see Figure 2-6). Don't forget to label the RadioButtons and CommandButtons.

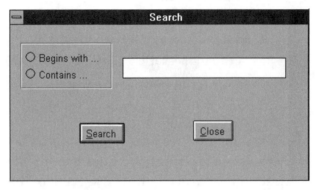

Figure 2-6: Search window class bw_search.

3. Create two window instance variables of datatype string and call them is_begin_char and is_return_value.

4. For the Clicked event of rb_begins, type the following:

```
is_begin_char = ""
sle_search_argument.setfocus()
```

5. For the Clicked event of rb_contains, type the following:

```
is_begin_char = "%"
sle_search_argument.setfocus()
```

6. In the Open event of the window, type the following:

```
rb_begins.triggerevent( "clicked" )
```

7. In the Clicked event of cb_search, type the following:

```
if len( sle_search_argument.text ) > 0 then
    is_return_argument = is_begin_char +
sle_search_value.text + "%"
    parent.triggerevent( "close" )
else
    is_return_value = ""
    messagebox( "Search", "The search argument field
cannot be empty.")
end if
```

8. In the Close event of the window, type the following:

```
closewithreturn( this, is_return_value )
```

9. Make the window type response.

10. Save the window and name it bw_search.

The calling object would call this search window and then check message.stringparm after the call. The call to CloseWithReturn() in the Close event of the window causes the value in is_return_value to be placed in the message object we discussed in Chapter 1. Because the window type is response, the code stops in the calling object until control is returned to it via the close of this search window. The calling object then checks the returned value to determine if its length is greater than 0. If so, the calling object would perform a search using the returned search argument. If the length of the returned value is 0, it indicates that the user canceled the search; therefore, the calling object would not continue to search because there would be no search argument value.

We assume the search value in this window is datatype string. We could check for numbers and convert the text attribute to some numeric datatype, if the need existed. Also, with the Begins With and Contains RadioButtons, we're assuming a partial text search—that is, that the SQL statement performing the search contains the "like" keyword.

There are a number of options that could be added to the search window. For example, we could include case logic to check for an indicator passed to the search window and then set up the window to take specific arguments (which means no Begins With and Contains RadioButtons). We would return numeric, date/time or Boolean datatype search values or accept multiple search arguments.

Login Class

Another common behavior in applications is logging in and out. Like the search window, we could build the login window so that it does not actually log in. It could collect login IDs and passwords and return those values to the calling object. Since the login window is not tied to an application or database, it could be used virtually anywhere. Another approach would be to connect to the database and verify the login ID and password and then return a value indicating whether the login was successful.

1. Create a new window in the Window painter.

2. Make the type of the window "response."

3. On the window, place two static text controls, called st_user_id and st_password; a CommandButton called cb_login; a close CommandButton inherited from our buo_cb_close class (name it cb_close); and two SingleLineEdits, inherited from our buo_sle class, called sle_userid and sle_password (see Figure 2-7).

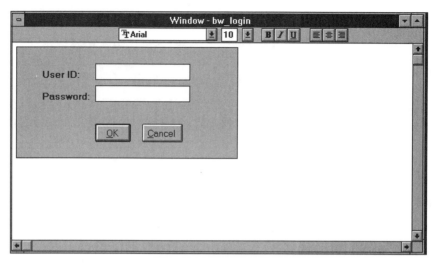

Figure 2-7: An example login class bw_login.

4. Create an instance variable for the window of datatype string and name it is_login_state.

5. In the Close event for the window, type the following:

```
closewithreturn( this, is_login_state )
```

6. In the ue_before_close event of our inherited buo_cb_close button, add the following code:

```
is_login_state =  "NO"
```

7. In the Clicked event for cb_login, type the following:

```
// Did user enter login name?
   if sle_userid.text <> "" then

// Did user enter password?
      if sle_password.text <> "" then

// Declare variable for password
      string ls_hold_password
//
//--- SQL select statement - uses Watcom
//--- database function ucase()
//--- to make the login case-insensitive
```

```
//
            select password
                into :ls_hold_password
                from security
                where ucase( userid ) =
                    ucase( :sle_userid.text );

            if ls_hold_password > "" then
//
//------ If Login was successful,
//------ open first window;
//------ otherwise, give appropriate error
//------ message
//
                if upper( ls_hold_password ) = &
                upper( sle_password.text ) then
                    is_login_state = "YES"
                    parent.triggerevent( "close" )
                else
//
//-------- Password does not match
//
                    sle_password.setfocus()
                    sle_password. &
                    triggerevent( "ue_select_all_text" )
                    MessageBox( "Error", &
                    "Password does not match." )
                end if

        else
//
//------ Login did not match
//
                sle_userid.setfocus()
                sle_userid. &
                triggerevent( "ue_select_all_text" )
                MessageBox( "Error", "Login not found!" )
            end if
        else
//
```

```
//--- Password field was blank
//
            sle_password.setfocus()
            MessageBox( "Error", "Password may not be &
            blank." )
        end if
    else
//
//---- Login field was blank
//
        sle_userid.setfocus()
        MessageBox( "Error", "Login may not be blank." )
    end if
```

8. Save the window class and name it bw_login.

This script assumes a table called security with two columns named userid and password. These three names would need to be changed to match your situation. The calling object invokes a descendant of this window, and when the login window finishes, the calling object checks message.stringparm. As with bw_search, bw_login is of the type "response" and performs a CloseWithReturn() function call in the Close event for the window. The call to CloseWithReturn() places the value in is_login_state into the stringparm attribute of the message object. Its value is either "YES" or "NO," to indicate whether the login was successful. The calling object will check for the value. If it is "YES," it will continue; if it is "NO," it will probably display a message of some type. Even if you'll be using many applications with many databases, you're likely to have only one or two security tables. Since the number of security tables is most likely small, you could have a bw_login class for each security table. Or, you could pass that kind of information to bw_login at run-time. (This example is for the purpose of conveying the concepts; we'll address security issues at length in Chapter 6.)

An Application Base Window Class

We can get a lot of reuse out of a well-designed window class. Ideally, every window in the application would be derived from the application base window class. This window is the generic one. We can create specialized windows as needed, but they, too, would be derived from the application base window class. There is much value that can be added to a window at the general level and reused by all application windows. At the simplest level, we can create a standard look and feel to all the windows in our application by implementing standards in our application base window class. For example, we can set the background to light gray, select border styles or place the company logo in the upper right corner of the window. Following are some examples of useful functionality that can be included.

In a number of applications, we've had to keep track of how many open windows existed at any given time—for instance, in order to warn a user who tried to close an application when there were open windows, or to limit the number of open windows in order to manage memory, as in an MDI application. To accomplish the accounting of open windows, create a new window, then declare a shared variable of type integer and call it si_number_of_open_windows. Create two window functions, called wf_decrement_open_windows and wf_increment_open_windows. Make their access public. They take no arguments and both return an integer. Here's the script for wf_increment_open_windows():

```
si_number_of_open_windows = &
si_number_of_open_windows + 1
```

The script for wf_decrement_open_windows() is as follows:

```
si_number_of_open_windows = &
si_number_of_open_windows - 1
```

71

In the Open event of the window class, invoke wf_increment_open_windows(), and in the Close event, invoke wf_decrement_open_windows().

Often, when we write code to delete something, we display a message of some sort that asks the user to confirm the deletion. We could create a window function for our window class that will provide a common look and feel to displaying the message and interacting with the user. Create a window function called wf_delete_message. The access is protected and there are no arguments. It returns a datatype of string. The script for the function is as follows:

```
string ls_return_value
int    li_user_choice

li_user_choice = messagebox("Delete","Are you
sure?",Question!, YesNo!,2)

if li_user_choice = 1 then
    ls_return_value = 'YES'
else
    ls_return_value = 'NO'
end if

return ls_return_value
```

The code displays a message box titled Delete with two CommandButtons labeled Yes and No and asks "Are you sure?" in the center of the message box. If the user clicks the Yes button, the value 1 is returned to this function, which is then stored in li_user_choice. If the user selects No, the value 2 will be returned. We're trapping for the 1 and 2 and substituting the string values "YES" and "NO," respectively. (It isn't mandatory to do the substitution, but YES/NO seems clearer than 1/2.)

All of the application messages could be standardized in the same fashion—make them functions in the window class, then inherit all windows from it. The message functions are then available to all of the windows, without being global.

Save the new window and call it bw_window.

DataWindow Print Preview Class

Our final example of an application component class is one to preview DataWindows before they are printed. We take advantage of the Describe() and Modify() built-in functions (these were named DWDescribe() and DWModify() in versions of PowerBuilder prior to 4.0). The print preview class takes one argument of datatype DataWindow. The DataWindow to be previewed is passed to the preview object before it is displayed. The user then indicates the viewing ratio and clicks OK to view the DataWindow. The choices for viewing ratio are as follows:

- ❏ 200 %
- ❏ 100 %
- ❏ 50 %
- ❏ Other (user specifies the percentage)

The window consists of four RadioButtons, named rb_50_pct, rb_100_pct, rb_200_pct and rb_other_pct, as well as one group box, named gb_pct. There is one EditMask, named em_other_pct; one CommandButton, named cb_ok; and a descendant of our buo_cb_close CommandButton class, named cb_cancel. Create the print preview class as follows:

1. Create a window of type "response" in the Window painter.

2. Add and label the controls to look like Figure 2-8.

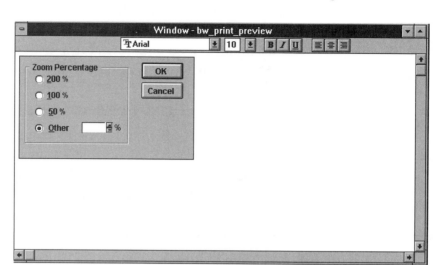

Figure 2-8: An example print preview class bw_print_preview.

3. Create two instance variables for the window:

```
string is_zoom_pct
datawindow idw_dw
```

4. In the Open event for the window, add the following:

```
string ls_print_preview

idw_dw = message.powerobjectparm

ls_print_preview = &
idw_dw.Describe('DataWindow.Print.Preview.Zoom')

CHOOSE CASE ls_print_preview

    CASE '200'
        rb_200_pct.checked = true
        rb_200_pct.triggerevent(clicked!)

    CASE '100'
```

```
            rb_100_pct.checked = true
            rb_100_pct.triggerevent(clicked!)

        CASE '50'
            rb_50_pct.checked = true
            rb_50_pct.triggerevent(clicked!)

        CASE else
            rb_other_pct.checked = true
            em_other_pct.text = ls_print_preview

    END CHOOSE
```

5. Set the EditMask to match the edit style in Figure 2-9.

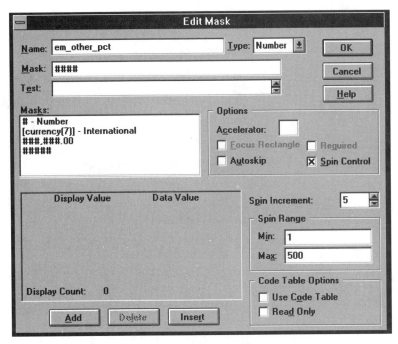

Figure 2-9: EditMask style for em_other_pct.

6. In the Modified event for the EditMask, add the
    following:

```
rb_other_pct.checked = true
is_zoom_pct = this.text
```

7. In the Clicked event of cb_ok, add the following:

```
string ls_print_preview

ls_print_preview = + &
    "DataWindow.Print.Preview.Zoom=" + &
    is_zoom_pct + "DataWindow.Print.Preview = yes"

idw_dw.Modify( ls_print_preview )
parent.triggerevent( "close" )
```

8. In the ue_before_close event of cb_cancel, type the following:

```
string ls_print_preview
    ls_print_preview ="DataWindow.Print.Preview=no"
    idw_dw.Modify( ls_print_preview )
```

9. In the Close event of the window, type: **close (this)**.

10. Each RadioButton has one line in its Clicked event, as follows:

    rb_other_pct:
    ```
    em_other_pct.setfocus( )
    ```

    rb_50_pct:
    ```
    is_zoom_pct = '50'
    ```

    rb_100_pct:
    ```
    is_zoom_pct = '100'
    ```

    rb_200_pct:
    ```
    is_zoom_pct = '200'
    ```

11. Save the print preview window class and name it bw_print_preview.

In the Open event of the window, we're picking up the DataWindow object being passed in with this line:

```
idw_dw = message.powerobjectparm
```

The assignment to ls_print_preview and the case statement are picking up the default preview attributes that were originally assigned to the DataWindow argument, using the Describe() function. In the Clicked event for cb_ok, we're setting the preview mode to yes and the viewing percentage to whatever the user indicated (which is stored in is_zoom_pct), using the Modify() function. If the user cancels by clicking cb_cancel, the Clicked event sets the preview mode to no, using the Modify() function.

APPLICATION-SPECIFIC CLASSES

Application-specific classes are the third layer of classes. Recall that our goal for object-oriented development is to get reuse out of our software. So, candidates for application-specific classes should be components that will be used more than once.

Not all code specific to your application is a candidate for becoming a class. The PBLs you create for this layer of classes should contain code that is more specific than the application components, but still dynamic enough to be reusable. Updating a general ledger table, for example, can be done from many applications or subapplications, such as General Ledger, Accounts Payable, Accounts Receivable, Payroll and Benefits applications. You can likely come up with more candidates for this example. The goal is to create a dynamic class that will update the general ledger table and could be reused by the other applications mentioned.

Compare this type of class with our application component search class. The search class could be used in virtually any application—financial, manufacturing, sales, personnel, etc. By contrast, the general ledger application-specific class in our example would be more restricted to the applications that touch on the financial system.

We're not going to demonstrate the code for these type of classes because they will vary as much as your applications do. Understand the difference between the layers of classes and try to discern the code that falls into each layer. It is not always easy—there will be many classes that fall into the gray area in-between.

A FINAL WORD ON REUSABLE CLASSES

Most developers will tend to write software components for themselves that are dynamic, reusable and therefore beneficial. But the maximum benefit comes when *all* developers can share the same components. Communication between developers is critical to the success or the failure of class usage. Great effort must be expended in communicating what base classes exist and how to use them. If developers rewrite classes that have already been written, there is duplicate effort. And if extra effort was expended to make the classes dynamic in the first place, then that effort will have been wasted as well, since their reusability was never taken advantage of.

MOVING ON

In this chapter, we looked at some examples of the kinds of things you should think about as you develop your own library of simple and complex classes. In the two examples using DataWindows, we glossed over some of the details, particularly with the Describe() and Modify() functions. In the next chapter, we'll look at DataWindows in greater detail.

Chapter 3

DataWindows

Powersoft claims the DataWindow is the most powerful control available in PowerBuilder. DataWindows provide the ability to combine data access code and presentation information in one entity. In addition, the DataWindow painter enables the developer to create DataWindows in an interactive fashion that is straightforward. In this chapter, we will focus on the more advanced features of working with DataWindows. We'll discuss various techniques for manipulating DataWindows in your applications using PowerScript.

We'll discuss the two most powerful functions for manipulating DataWindows—Describe() and Modify(). These functions enable the developer to control the attributes of DataWindows at run-time with PowerScript. In addition, we will look at a number of ways to manipulate the SQL attached to a DataWindow, including the SyntaxFromSQL() function. Multiple DataWindows can share data simultaneously.

SYNTAXFROMSQL()

The SyntaxFromSQL() function is used to generate a DataWindow using an SQL statement as the source code for the DataWindow. DataWindows are composed of data source and presentation style information. The data source is derived from the SQL statement; the function SyntaxFromSQL() also takes an argument to indicate the presentation style.

The presentation style can be one of the following:

❏ Crosstab

❏ Form (freeform)

❏ Graph

❏ Grid

❏ Group

❏ Label

❏ N-up

❏ Tabular

Tabular is the default, and Form is used to indicate freeform. The first argument to SyntaxFromSQL() is the SQL statement passed as a string, the second is the presentation style, and the third is for the purpose of reporting any errors in using SyntaxFromSQL(). This third argument is a string variable, which can be populated with error messages by the function, should any errors occur. The SyntaxFromSQL() function returns a string with all of the attributes for the DataWindow to be created.

You can pass the returned value from the SyntaxFromSQL() function to the Create() DataWindow function, and the DataWindow will be generated at run-time.

Let's discuss an example in detail: we'll use the following student_id–student_ssn cross reference table from our student registration system, which is shown in Figure 3-1.

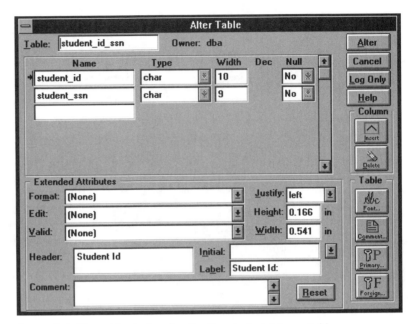

Figure 3-1: The table declaration for the student_id_ssn table.

The data in our table is shown in Figure 3-2.

Student Id	Student Ssn
0000000001	999999999
0000000002	900000000
0000000003	800000000
0000000004	700000000
0000000005	600000000
0000000006	500000000
0000000007	400000000
0000000008	300000000
0000000009	200000000
0000000010	123456789
0000000011	100000000
0000000012	000000001

Ready — Rows 1 to 12 of 14

Figure 3-2: Test data in the student_id_ssn table.

81

To create the example, take these steps:

1. Create a new window in the DataWindow painter.
2. Place the controls listed in Table 3-1 into the new DataWindow, and name them accordingly.

Control	Control Name
1 DataWindow control	dw_1
1 MultiLineEdit control	mle_sql_syntax
1 listbox	lb_columns
3 RadioButtons	rb_less
	rb_equal
	rb_greater
1 SingleLineEdit control	sle_where
1 group box (around the listbox, 3 radio buttons and SingleLineEdit)	gb_where
2 CommandButtons	cb_createsql
	cb_close

Table 3-1: Controls and control names for the example window.

In our example, no DataWindow object should be assigned to the DataWindow control. To simplify the example, we'll break a rule of encapsulation and place all of the code in the Clicked event for the cb_createsql CommandButton. We're going to generate an SQL statement in our script and pass it to the SyntaxFromSQL() function. Part of our SQL statement will be made up of values from the user.

3. Set the text of the radio buttons to <, = and > to correlate with their names—rb_less, rb_equal and rb_greater—respectively.

4. Double-click on the listbox, lb_columns, and type the following two choices (use Ctrl+Enter to create a new line in the choices area).

```
student_id
student_ssn
```

The window should appear as shown in Figure 3-3.

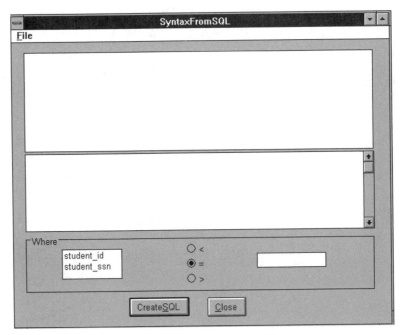

Figure 3-3: The test window for the SyntaxFromSQL() function.

5. To start our script, we must create local variables to hold the different elements of an SQL statement. In the Clicked event for cb_createsql, type the following:

```
string ls_columns, &
         ls_from, &
         ls_where, &
         ls_order, &
```

```
ls_relate, &
ls_sql_statement, &
ls_sql_errors, &
ls_presentation
```

The first four variables—ls_columns, ls_from, ls_where and ls_order—will be used to store the column names and the table name for the FROM clause, the WHERE clause and ORDER BY clause of the SQL statement, respectively. The ls_relate column will be used to store the user's choice for the relation operator (less than, equal or greater than) for the WHERE clause. The last three variables will be used for the SyntaxFromSQL() and Create() functions.

6. In the Clicked event for cb_createsql, type the following code to determine which relation operator the user has selected and to store its symbol in the ls_relate variable:

```
if rb_less.checked = true then
    ls_relate = " < "
elseif rb_equal.checked = true then
    ls_relate = " = "
else
    ls_relate = " > "
end if
```

For this example, we'll supply the column names, table name and ORDER BY clause. We'll demonstrate how to enable the user to generate the WHERE clause.

7. Append the following code to set the values for the elements of the SQL statement:

```
ls_columns = "student_id, student_ssn"
ls_from    = "student_id_ssn"
```

```
ls_where    = lb_columns.selecteditem() + &
              ls_relate + "'" + &
              sle_where.text + "'"

ls_order    = "student_ssn"
```

Notice that the ls_where variable is set to a value based on:

❒ The column name value the user selected from the listbox.

❒ The relation operator radio button the user selected.

❒ The value the user typed in the SingleLineEdit control.

8. Continue appending the following code to build the SQL statement:

```
ls_sql_statement =   "SELECT " + ls_columns + &
                   " FROM "   + ls_from + &
                   " WHERE "  + ls_where + &
                   " ORDER BY " + ls_order
```

A number of options can be supplied for the presentation style. We'll supply the style and column color to demonstrate using the attributes. Appendix A of the PowerBuilder *Function Reference* contains a complete list of the attributes. In this example, we are setting the presentation variable ls_presentation to a string that contains the style and column keywords followed by options in the parentheses. We are setting the type of DataWindow to a grid and the column color to 255 (red).

```
ls_presentation = &   "style(type=grid)column(color=255)"
```

The following code invokes the SyntaxFromSQL() function and assigns the returned value to the MultiLineEdit control, so that we can see all of the attributes of the DataWindow we generate.

```
mle_sql_syntax.text = &
    SQLCA.syntaxfromsql( ls_sql_statement, &
        ls_presentation,  ls_sql_errors )
```

Once we run the SyntaxFromSQL() function, we should test the ls_sql_errors argument for a return code. If it was successful, meaning a string of zero length was returned, we'll invoke the Create() function. The Create() function uses the detailed attribute information returned from the SyntaxFromSQL() function to build a DataWindow at run time. The following code tests the return code, then invokes Create() and retrieves some data into the DataWindow.

```
if len( ls_sql_errors ) > 0 then
    messagebox( "Syntax From SQL" , ls_sql_errors )
else
    dw_1.create( mle_sql_syntax.text,ls_sql_errors)
    if len( ls_sql_errors ) > 0 then
        messagebox( "SQL Create" , ls_sql_errors )
    else
        dw_1.settransobject( SQLCA )
        dw_1.retrieve()
    end if
end if
```

You can supply all of the attributes to the Create() function with PowerScript code. However, it is considerably simpler to use SyntaxFromSQL() and then modify only the attributes you must before passing them to the Create() function. The example assumes that you have already established a successful connection to Watcom database.

THE MODIFY() & DESCRIBE() FUNCTIONS

The Modify() and Describe()—formerly dwModify() and dwDescribe()—functions offer a great deal of access and flexibility in dynamically altering DataWindow attributes. With these functions, you have access to everything you need to control your DataWindows at run-time.

The difficulty of these functions is in the occasionally rigid syntax requirements. PowerBuilder has attempted to relieve these requirements by employing some of the most often-used Modify() and Describe() functions within standard DataWindow functions. For instance, you have full access to alter all DataWindow column attributes with a set of functions that includes GetRow(), GetText(), crosstab, string and computational functions.

For each Describe() and Modify() function, PowerBuilder parses the existing DataWindow attributes and returns the attribute value, for Describe(), or inserts the requested syntax alteration, for Modify(). Because of the significant effort involved, try to minimize the number of Describe() and Modify() functions used within a script. Even though a long Modify string is difficult to debug, the result pays off in performance improvements. Building the string iteratively eases the maintenance burden. As you build each syntax string, add on to the previous string.

Describe()

The Describe() function accepts an attribute or set of attributes and returns the values of these attributes. You use Describe() to determine the current structure or attributes of a DataWindow and use Modify to change these attributes. Describe() can be used to tell you, among a myriad of other things, the DataWindow's SELECT statement, the data types of columns, graph attributes and settings for a DropDownListBox edit style.

The attributes you have access to via Describe(), Modify() and SyntaxFromSQL() are listed in Appendix A of the *PowerBuilder Function Reference* manual. This appendix provides a chart that lists the attributes by grouping, and lists the function—Describe(), Modify() or SyntaxFromSQL()—that is appropriate for the attribute as well as a description of the attribute. The attribute groupings and their meanings are as follows:

❑ **DataWindow Object Attributes**—These are attributes associated with the overall DataWindow, such as Bands, Column Count, QueryMode, and Retrieve as Needed.

❑ **Bitmap Object Attributes**—These are the physical descriptors of the bitmap, including the file name and location.

❑ **Column Object Attributes**—These attributes are useful for determining the makeup of the columns, particularly the database name (dbName), column type (ColType), the edit style and whether you can update the column.

❑ **Computed Field Object Attributes**—This set of attributes provides detail regarding a named computed field. Its primary usage is for determining expressions.

❑ **Graph Object Attributes**—This group gives all the accessibility necessary to understand the graph object. Of primary interest are the graph type, series, category and values.

❑ **Group Keyword Attributes**—These attributes are used with SyntaxFromSQL for determining the effect of a group column change.

❑ **Line Object Attributes**—These attributes are used for determining the x and y coordinates of a line.

❑ **Oval, Rectangle and Rountrectangle Object Attributes**—This set of attributes describes the objects' height, width, placement and visibility.

❑ **Report Object Attributes**—These attributes are specific to *report objects* (not DataWindow objects)—for example, Nest_Arguments, NewPage and TrailFooter.

- **Style Keyword Attributes**—These attributes are used with SyntaxfromSQL and deal with the presentation style.
- **TableBlob Object Attributes**—A TableBlob is a binary large object associated with an OLE application.
- **Text Object Attributes**—These attributes deal with the characteristics of any named text object. The attributes include alignment, font, text and x,y coordinates.
- **Title Keyword Attribute**—This SyntaxFromSQL attribute offers the DataWindow title.

Appendix B of the PowerBuilder *Function Reference* provides the syntax for using the appropriate functions with the attributes. The list of attributes and associated syntax is exhaustive, and it is unlikely you will need most of them. We'll explore some of the more commonly used attributes.

The majority of the attribute groups include an Attribute keyword. Using this keyword with a Describe() returns all the attributes for the current object in a list of objects separated by tab (~t) characters. If the list includes an invalid item, an exclamation point is returned for that item, and the rest of the attribute list is ignored. If there is no value for an attribute, a question mark is returned. If the value of the attribute includes a question mark, the value is enclosed in quotes.

For example, say we want to understand all attributes available to us in a computed field from our Student Transcript DataWindow. The field name is GPA. The necessary code follows:

```
string ls_attributes
ls_attributes = this.describe("gpa.attributes")
```

Figure 3-4 shows the resulting contents of ls_attributes. As you can see, the list provides the attributes, not the associated values. To retrieve the values, you must name the required attributes in a subsequent Describe() statement.

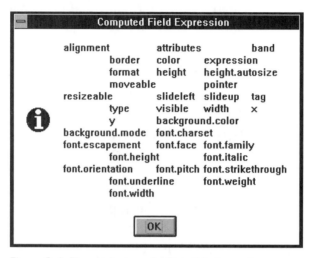

Figure 3-4: The attributes of a DataWindow column.

The general syntax for Describe is:

```
datawindowname.Describe ( attributelist )
```

attributelist is a string with an attribute or a set of attributes separated by blanks. For example, if we wanted to know the expression for the GPA field in the Student Transcript DataWindow, we would code:

```
string ls_gpa_expression
ls_gpa_expression = & this.Describe("gpa.expression")
```

ls_gpa_expression would be set to "sum(integer(grade)) / rowcount()". The following code would return attribute values for the expression and the format:

```
string ls_attributes_requested,& ls_attributes_returned
ls_attributes_requested = "gpa.expression & gpa.format"
ls_attributes_returned = &
this.Describe(ls_attributes_requested)
```

ls_attributes_requested would contain the previously shown expression and the format "0.00". Note that when dealing with column attributes, you can also use the column number in lieu of the name.

A commonly used attribute is the column count. The column count provides us with the number of columns in our DataWindow. It is useful for iteratively making changes for all DataWindow columns via the Modify(). To determine the number of columns in the Transcript DataWindow, we code:

```
string ls_col_count
ls_col_count = & this.Describe("DataWindow.Column.Count")
```

The value of ls_col_count is now 19. Note that the column count is returned as a string. Also, notice that the column count ignores computed fields.

The Describe() function is often used to determine and then Modify the SQL syntax. We will show an example under "Modify()" later in this chapter, which details the addition of a where clause to a SELECT that gets the current syntax by specifying a Describe() function. The type of select you have defined in the DataWindow Select painter has an effect on the returned string from this function. If you have created the syntax graphically, PowerBuilder creates its own version of a SELECT statement called a PBSELECT. This is done to allow for DBMS syntax variations at run-time. If you have not connected to the database at the time your Describe() is executed for this Select, a PBSELECT statement (see Figure 3-5 for an example for our Student Transcript DataWindow) will be returned. If you have connected, a standard SQL SELECT statement is returned. The following code will return the current SELECT for the Student Transcript DataWindow following a connection to the database:

```
string ls_sqlselect
ls_sqlselect =& this.Describe("datawindow.table.select")
```

```
PBSELECT( VERSION(400)
TABLE(NAME="'student_class"')
TABLE(NAME="'student"')
TABLE(NAME="'faculty"') TABLE(NAME="'course"'
) COLUMN(NAME="'student_class.student_id"')
COLUMN(NAME="'student_class.course_id"')
COLUMN(NAME="'student_class.class_id"')
COLUMN(NAME="'student_class.class_term"')
COLUMN(NAME="'student_class.class_year"')
COLUMN(NAME="'student_class.grade"')
COLUMN(NAME="'student_class.instructor_id"')
COLUMN(NAME="'student_class.class_location"')
COLUMN(NAME="'student_class.credits"')
COLUMN(NAME="'student.student_last_name"')
COLUMN(NAME="'student.student_first_name"')
COLUMN(NAME="'student.student_mdl_init"')
COLUMN(NAME="'faculty.last_name"')
COLUMN(NAME="'faculty.first_name"')
COLUMN(NAME="'course.course_title"') JOIN
(LEFT="'student_class.student_id"' OP
="'="'RIGHT="'student.student_id"') JOIN
(LEFT="'student_class.instructor_id"' OP
="'="'RIGHT="'faculty.faculty_id"') JOIN
(LEFT="'student_class.course_id"' OP
="'="'RIGHT="'course.course_id"' )WHERE( EXP1
="'( ( "'"'student_class"'"'.'"'student_id"'"'"' OP
="'="' EXP2 ="':a_student_id ) )"' ) ) ARG(NAME =
"'a_student_id"' TYPE = string)
```

Figure 3-5: The PBSELECT statement for the Student Transcript DataWindow.

The returned string is a standard Watcom SQL statement displayed in Figure 3-6.

```
SELECT ~'"student_class"'.~'"student_id"',
~'"student_class"'.~'"course_id"',
~'"student_class"'.~'"class_id"',
~'"student_class"'.~'"class_term"',
~'"student_class"'.~'"class_year"',
~'"student_class"'.~'"grade"',
~'"student_class"'.~'"instructor_id"',
~'"student_class"'.~'"class_location"',
~'"student_class"'.~'"credits"',
~'"student"'.~'"student_last_name"',
~'"student"'.~'"student_first_name"',
~'"student"'.~'"student_mdl_init"',
~'"faculty"'.~'"last_name"',
~'"faculty"'.~'"first_name"',
~'"course"'.~'"course_title"' FROM
~'"student_class"', ~'"student"', ~'"faculty"',
~'"course"' WHERE (
~'"student_class"'.~'"student_id"' =
~'"student"'.~'"student_id"' ) and (
~'"student_class"'.~'"instructor_id"' =
~'"faculty"'.~'"faculty_id"' ) and (
~'"student_class"'.~'"course_id"' =
~'"course"'.~'"course_id"' ) and ( (
~'"student_class"'.~'"student_id"' = :a_student_id
) )
```

Figure 3-6: A standard Watcom SELECT statement for the Student Transcript DataWindow.

One of the attributes Describe() can report is Objects. This provides a tab (~t)–separated list of all objects in the DataWindow. PowerBuilder creates a default name for all objects in the DataWindow that is decidedly cryptic: obj_ and a string of numbers (see Figure 3-7). You won't see these objects in the DataWindow painter, but Describe will report them in your object list. To alleviate this problem, invoke your naming conventions and give all your DataWindow objects meaningful names.

```
course_id          class_id  class_term
        class_year           instructor_id
        student_student_last_name
student_student_first_name
student_student_mdl_init      faculty_first_name
        student_id            obj_9873867
        class_id_t            obj_9873868
        student_name          obj_9873869
        class_year_t          instructor_id_t
        class_location_t      grade_t   credits_t
        obj_9873870           obj_9873871
        course_class_id
course_course_title           term_year
        faculty_last_name  class_location
        grade     credits  obj_9873872
        obj_9873873           obj_9873874
        gpa
```

Figure 3-7: DataWindow objects for the Student Transcript DataWindow.

Describe() can be used in conjunction with a number of Get DataWindow functions to enable certain user interactions. Consider an example in which we want to allow the user to leave a column after deleting data. For all columns, with the exception of string columns, the user will be given an error MessageBox. To avoid this, we code the following in the ItemError event of the DataWindow script:

```
string ls_col_type
int li_null_num
date    li_null_date
time    li_null_time
ls_col_type = this.Describe(this.GetColumnName() &
    + ".coltype")

CHOOSE CASE ls_col_type
    CASE "date"
        IF Trim(this.GetText()) = "" THEN
            SetNull(ls_null_date)
            this.SetItem(this.GetRow(), &
                this.GetColumn(),ls_null_date)
            this.SetActionCode(3)
        END IF
```

```
CASE "time"
IF Trim(this.GetText()) = "" THEN
    SetNull(ls_null_time)
    this.SetItem(this.GetRow(), &
        this.GetColumn(),ls_null_time)
    this.SetActionCode(3)
END IF
```

Additional datatype checks would follow. Note that SetActionCode of 3 for the ItemError event will reject the data but allow the focus to be changed.

Describe() has an additional function that enables you to determine DataWindow painter expressions. The Evaluate function is primarily used to get data values that are not available through the usual DataWindow control functions. This is the case with a LookUpDisplay. This painter function will return the display value the user sees for a code table. The following code returns the value seen by the user for the location field in our Transcript example.

```
string ls_loc_code
ls_loc_code = & this.Describe("Evaluate('LookUpDisplay &
(class_location) ', " + "1" + ")")
```

The "1" represents the row number of the current row. Our example is a freeform DataWindow, but for tabular DataWindows you could add a GetRow function to determine the current row.

Modify()

The Modify() function is used to alter DataWindow attributes dynamically. You change the DataWindow's definition by specifying a string of instructions. You can change the look, actions and the database activity in the DataWindow as well as add and delete objects (via Create() and Destroy()). The general syntax is:

```
datawindowname.Modify( modstring )
```

datawindowname is the name of the current DataWindow or child DataWindow control. *modstring* is the set of specifications you are using to alter the DataWindow. We'll describe the necessary syntax, from the relatively straightforward to the complex, for *modstring*.

The Modify() function returns a string. If it is successful, an empty string ("") is returned; otherwise, an error message is returned. The error message lists the line number and column number in error. These numbers are counted from the start of the *modstring* text.

Modify() allows you to control the DataWindow object at run-time with access to most of the same capabilities you have when using the DataWindow painter. Modify() is typically executed conditionally, based on other run-time occurrences. Some of the most often-used features affected by Modify() are:

❑ Basic appearance attributes such as borders, font settings, color and visibility.

❑ Print settings and the Print Preview.

❑ Tab sequence.

❑ SQL SELECT statement.

❑ QueryMode on or off (QueryMode is discussed in detail later in this chapter).

❑ Data source.

❑ SQL to and from stored procedures.

❑ Table update status to enable multiple table updates.

❑ Create() and Destroy() objects to allow addition and subsequent deletion of columns, lines, bitmaps, etc.

Modifying Attributes

The easiest application of Modify() is to change a single attribute. We will use the Revenues by Class DataWindow (see Figure 3-8) to demonstrate changing a color attribute. We want to highlight those classes that have a revenue amount of less than $7,500. We will change the text color for the revenue and class name columns to red for the low revenue classes. The following code is in the Constructor event of the DataWindow control:

```
string ls_color_mod
ls_color_mod = "'0 ~t If(revenue_amt<7500,255,0)'"

dw_1.Modify("class_name.color = " + ls_color_mod &
     + "revenue_amt.color = " + &
              ls_color_mod)
```

We declare a local string variable to hold the "if" statement necessary to check the revenue amount value. The variable is useful in debugging. Notice the ls_color_mod value begins with a 0. This represents the default setting defined in the DataWindow painter for the text color value for this column. Because the color attribute requires an expression, we must start the expression with the default for the column. The ~t is a required tab separator. The ~n is used to generate a newline. As we mentioned previously, it is best to place multiple modifications within a single Modify() function to minimize the amount of code that PowerBuilder has to parse.

You'll note that the syntax is somewhat cryptic, particularly with the usage of separators. Generally, PowerBuilder accepts an ~n, ~t or space as a separator. It is preferable to use an ~n character because it generates a newline for each Modify() line. This format is useful in debugging because PowerBuilder returns the line number for Modify() error conditions.

Department Name	Class Name	Term	Year	Revenue Amt
Math	Trigonometry	SP	95	$10,950
Math	Trigonometry	SU	95	$8,850
Math	Trigonometry	FA	95	$9,950
Math	Trigonometry	WI	95	$8,750
Gen Ed	Modern Dance	SP	95	$6,650
Gen Ed	Modern Dance	SU	95	$5,500
Gen Ed	Modern Dance	FA	95	$6,500
Gen Ed	Modern Dance	WI	95	$6,500
Gen Ed	Pottery	SP	95	$9,950
Gen Ed	Pottery	SU	95	$10,950

Figure 3-8: The Revenues by Class DataWindow.

The next example shows a method to change all columns to red if the revenue amount is less than $7,500. We need to determine the number of columns in the tabular portion of the DataWindow so that we can loop through the Modify() to change color. We use the Describe() for the column count attribute to determine the number of columns. Remember that this function returns a string for the number of columns. We'll use the same color attribute modification statement we used in the previous example. The code follows:

```
string ls_color_mod, ls_col_name
int li_col_count, li_idx

ls_color_mod = "'0 ~t If(revenue_amt<7500,255,0)'"
li_col_count =
integer(this.Describe("DataWindow.Column.Count"))

for li_idx=1 to li_col_count
    ls_col_name = this.Describe( "#" + &
        String(li_idx) + ".name" )
    this.Modify(ls_col_name + ".color = " + &
    ls_color_mod)
next
```

The Describe() in the "For...Next" loop returns the name for the column number per the current index value. This name is then used in the Modify() as the column for the color attribute change.

Modify() can be used to alter the visibility of columns conditionally. Although doing so violates CUA(Common User Access) Specifications theories, some user requirements require this type of activity. In our example, we'll change the visible attribute for columns relating to a class that has a lab component. The Class Maintenance window has a DataWindow for the current offering of a class. This DataWindow has a lab indicator that designates if a lab is required with this class (see Figures 3-9 and 3-10). If it is, we need to know the lab fee and the availability of the lab (after hours, on weekend). We want to make these additional fields visible only if the lab indicator is set to Y.

The code is as follows:

```
string ls_col_name, ls_col_text

ls_col_name = GetColumnName()
ls_col_text = GetText()

if ls_col_name = "lab_ind" THEN
    if ls_col_text = "y" THEN
        Modify("course_class_new_lab_fee.visible=1 "
&+"~ncourse_class_new_lab_availability.visible=
    1 " &
                + "~nlab_fee_hdr.visible=1 " &
                + "~nlab_avail_hdr.visible=1")
    ELSE
        Modify("course_class_new_lab_fee.visible=0 " &
                +
"~ncourse_class_new_lab_availability.visible=0 " &
                + "~nlab_fee_hdr.visible=0 " &
                + "~nlab_avail_hdr.visible=0")
    END IF
END IF
```

We have named the column labels with appropriate names to allow their visibility to be modified (compare Figures 3-9 and 3-10).

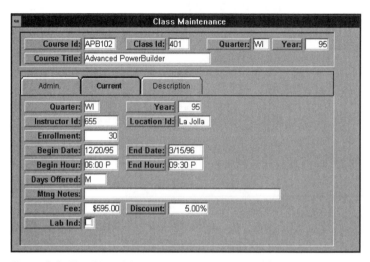

Figure 3-9: The Class Maintenance window, showing the current offering (without lab fields).

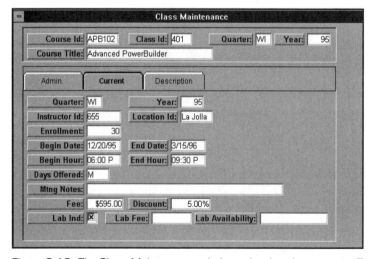

Figure 3-10: The Class Maintenance window, showing the current offering (with lab fields).

Altering the SELECT Statement for a DataWindow

There are two methods for altering the SQL SELECT statement for a DataWindow. You can use the SetSQLSelect() function, or you can use the Modify() function with a SELECT attribute. The SetSQLSelect() function is applicable only to DataWindows that have a data source of SQL statement without an argument. If an argument is present, you must use Modify().

SetSQLSelect validates the new SQL syntax only if the DataWindow is defined as one that can be updated. PowerBuilder invokes the database engine, via a SetTrans or SetTransObject, to do this validation. This function also changes the update capability for a DataWindow for the following conditions:

❒ An updatable column in the old syntax is replaced by a computed column.

❒ The table name for the FROM in the new SELECT changes.

❒ More than one table are in the FROM clause of the new SELECT.

Modify() does not validate the SELECT syntax or alter the update capabilities for a DataWindow; it only changes the SELECT attribute of the DataWindow. This makes the Modify() function much faster but also creates some vulnerability to syntactical errors.

Using SetSQLSelect() to Alter a SELECT

In addition to the limitations mentioned previously for SetSQLSelect(), the new SELECT must contain the same number of columns as the original SELECT. The original definitions of updatable and primary key columns are applied to the columns in the new SELECT.

One of the uses of SetSQLSelect() is to add a WHERE clause to a SELECT statement. Let's look at an example of adding a WHERE clause for the Revenues by Class DataWindow. We want to retrieve only the classes that have revenue exceeding $17,000. The currently defined DataWindow simply retrieves all rows from the table without a WHERE clause. The ls_old_sql is shown only for comparison purposes. The code follows:

```
string ls_new_sql, ls_old_sql
This.SetTransObject(SQLCA)

ls_old_sql = 'SELECT class_revenues.class_name,' &
        + 'class_revenues.term,' &
        + 'class_revenues.year,' &
        + 'class_revenues.department_name,' &
        + 'class_revenues.revenue_amt ' &
    + 'FROM class_revenues'
ls_new_sql = 'SELECT class_revenues.class_name,' &
        + 'class_revenues.term,' &
        + 'class_revenues.year,' &
        +'class_revenues.department_name,' &
        + 'class_revenues.revenue_amt ' &
    + 'FROM class_revenues ' &
        + 'where class_revenues.revenue_amt > &
        17000'

If This.SetSQLSelect( ls_new_sql ) = -1 THEN
    MessageBox("Invalid SQL", ls_new_sql)
ELSE
    This.Retrieve( )
END IF
```

The result is displayed in Figure 3-11. To ease the coding burden, you can obtain the original SQL using the Describe() function and add the appropriate WHERE clause:

```
ls_old_sql = this.Describe("Datawindow.Table.Select")
```

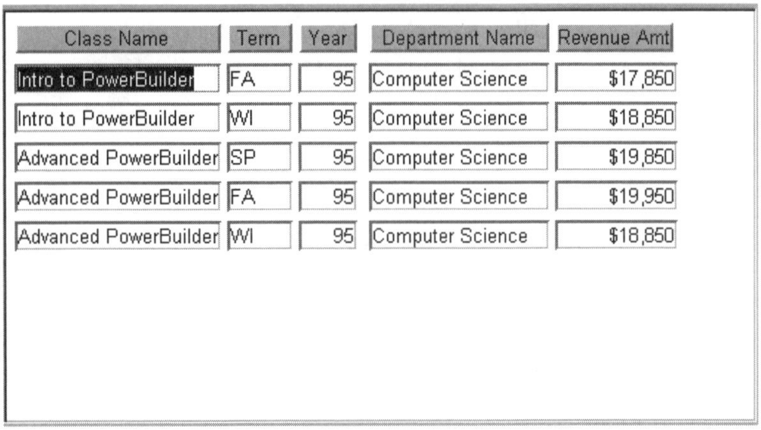

Class Name	Term	Year	Department Name	Revenue Amt
Intro to PowerBuilder	FA	95	Computer Science	$17,850
Intro to PowerBuilder	WI	95	Computer Science	$18,850
Advanced PowerBuilder	SP	95	Computer Science	$19,850
Advanced PowerBuilder	FA	95	Computer Science	$19,950
Advanced PowerBuilder	WI	95	Computer Science	$18,850

Figure 3-11: Classes with revenue of more than $17,000.

Using Modify() to Alter a SELECT

Using Modify() for SELECT changes is preferable in terms of performance, but it can be challenging syntactically. You must be alert to the way PowerBuilder handles single and double quotes. The following code displays the syntax PowerBuilder uses for the simple SELECT in the Revenues by Class DataWindow without a WHERE clause:

```
ls_default_sql = & This.describe("datawindow.table.select")
```

The resulting SELECT is shown in Figure 3-12. Notice the use of tildes (~), double quotes and column names prefaced by the associated table name. The tildes tell PowerBuilder that the next character is a special character. When this statement is used in a Modify() function, PowerBuilder removes the tilde when it finds the double quote. If you place the SELECT statement in a string variable for use in a subsequent Modify(), you have to keep the tildes and double quotes intact. You can use two tildes to represent the two special characters. The resulting first line of your SELECT would look like this:

```
ls_new_sql = "SELECT ~"class_revenues~".~".class_name~",  &
```

```
SELECT ~"class_revenues~".~"class_name~",
~"class_revenues~".~"term~",
~"class_revenues~".~"year~",
~"class_revenues~".~"department_name~",
~"class_revenues~".~"revenue_amt~" FROM
~"class_revenues~"
```

Figure 3-12: The default SELECT statement for the Revenues by Class window.

You can simplify this SELECT. To do so, go to the Data Source in the DataWindow painter. With the SELECT in default mode, remove the double quotes and table name qualifiers (assuming there are no like-named columns from different tables). Building the SELECT for use in the Modify() becomes a much less daunting task. Remember, though, that if the Data Source is changed to "Convert from Graphics", the syntax reverts to the default format.

We'll use the Revenues by Class DataWindow once again to demonstrate the use of Modify() for SELECT changes. In this example, we want to add a Where clause to retrieve classes for only the computer science department. The ls_old_sql is included for understanding of the current SELECT.

```
string ls_new_sql, ls_old_sql

ls_old_sql = 'SELECT class_revenues.class_name,' &
         + 'class_revenues.term,' &
         + 'class_revenues.year,' &
         + 'class_revenues.department_name,' &
         + 'class_revenues.revenue_amt ' &
     + 'FROM class_revenues'

ls_new_sql = "SELECT class_name, " &
         + "term, " &
         + "year, " &
         + "department_name, " &
         + "revenue_amt " &
     + "FROM class_revenues " &
         + "where department_name = 'Computer&
     Science' "


This.Modify("DataWindow.Table.Select='" +&
         ls_new_sql + " ' " )

This.SetTransObject(SQLCA)
This.Retrieve( )
```

We need the tildes to handle the single quotes necessary for the string value of computer science. The resulting DataWindow is shown in Figure 3-13.

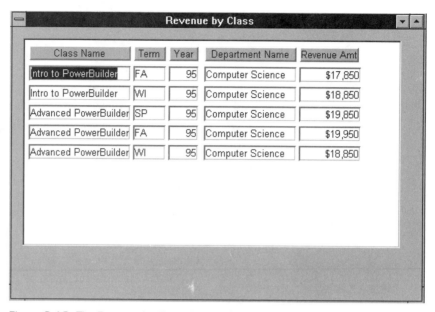

Figure 3-13: The Revenue by Class DataWindow for the computer science department.

Create

You can dynamically create objects within a DataWindow control by using the Create extension of Modify(). This applies to objects such as bitmaps, text and computed fields. Note the difference between this function and the Create function used to create a DataWindow DataObject using SyntaxFromSQL(). The SyntaxFromSQL typically combines SQL with a presentation style to dynamically build the complete DataWindow object. The Create within Modify() is used as a *modstring* to introduce individual objects to an existing DataWindow.

You may want to add objects conditionally based on specific values being entered. For example, we might want to add a bitmap of a phone to our Student Maintenance DataWindow if a student is signed up as a standby in a class and the enrollment for that class becomes open. In the class drop function, we subtract from the class enrollment for the class being dropped. If it is currently below the maximum enrollment number, we check the standby list, and if the list contains the name of a student waiting to enroll in the class, we trigger an event in the Student Maintenance DataWindow name ue_add_phone to add the phone BMP (see Figure 3-14). The appearance of this BMP alerts the user to call the student to determine if he or she is still interested in enrolling in the class. The syntax for the creation of the bitmap follows:

```
string ls_bmp_desc
ls_bmp_desc = 'create bitmap(band=detail & border="6"
filename="c:\pb4\phone.bmp" & height="153" width="183"
x="2268" y="36" & name=phone )'
This.Modify(ls_bmp_desc)
```

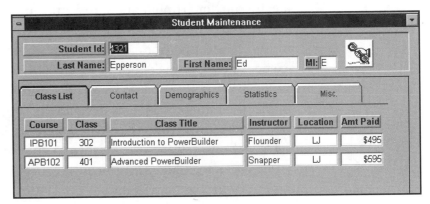

Figure 3-14: The Student Maintenance DataWindow with the addition of a bitmap.

You must provide all the syntax necessary to build the object. In this case, all the attributes listed are required. It is best to create the object initially with the DataWindow painter, so that all the syntax can be understood, and export the syntax to a file. You can then make changes as necessary and import the result into your script.

Query Mode

The Modify() function supports an alternate means for the user to enter selection criteria. You can do this by using the Query Mode attribute. The Query Mode is essentially a Query By Example (QBE) for the user. In this case, you initially retrieve data into a tabular or freeform DataWindow, change the Query Mode attribute to Yes, and allow the user to enter his or her selection criteria. The new criteria is applied in a SELECT when you retrieve the resulting data.

We'll use the Revenue by Class window to demonstrate Query Mode. We initially Retrieve() the data into our tabular-style DataWindow. It displays revenues for all classes in all departments. We subsequently want to allow the user to specify the department and a revenue amount to refine the search. When data is entered in a single row, it is treated as an AND condition (for example, department = computer science and Revenue Amount > $18,000). If data is entered in multiple rows, it is treated as an OR condition. In our example, the initial retrieval is done in the Constructor event of the DataWindow. We have created a Query button and a Retrieve button. If the user wishes to go into QBE mode, he or she clicks the Query button, which triggers a user event in the DataWindow named ue_query_mode. The script follows:

```
this.modify("datawindow.querymode=yes")
```

The user would then enter selection criteria and click the Retrieve button to trigger a user event in the DataWindow named ue_retrieve. The script for this event is:

```
string ls_query_mode
ls_query_mode = & this.describe("datawindow.querymode")
if ls_query_mode = "yes" THEN
    this.Retrieve()
    this.Modify("DataWindow.QueryMode=no")
end if
```

Now add the following code to the Constructor event of the DataWindow:

```
this.settransobject(SQLCA)
```

The retrieval for this code executes a SELECT that includes a WHERE statement specifying a department column = computer science and a revenue_amt > 18000. When the DataWindow's Query Mode is set to No, the results are displayed in the current DataWindow.

We could have displayed the result set of the user's query in another DataWindow. This can be a preferable option if you want to provide a more customized search window (such as our w_student_search). One of the problems in using a DataWindow for both search and retrieval is the edit style. In the previous example, we may have had an edit style for the revenue column that would limit the number of characters we could enter in our search criteria. If you use two DataWindows, you can use the ShareData() function to display data from one DataWindow's primary buffer in another DataWindow.

Prompt for Criteria

Another method for allowing the user to state the retrieval argument values he or she wishes to use is the Prompt for Criteria. This attribute invokes the Specify Retrieval Criteria dialog box (see Figure 3-15). The user is prompted to enter a value for each of the criteria requested. The Specify RetrievalCriteria dialog box is set one column at a time. In the following example, the department_name and the revenue_amt displays in the Specify Retrieval Criteria dialog box when the Retrieve() is invoked.

```
this.modify("department_name.criteria.dialog=yes")
this.modify("revenue_amt.criteria.dialog=yes")
this.Retrieve()
```

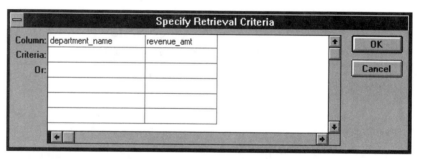

Figure 3-15: The Specify Retrieval Criteria dialog box with the department name and revenue amount.

DataWindow Bands

DataWindows have the following five bands: Header, Detail, Summary, Footer and, for only DataWindows defined with groups, Trailer.

Column headers and generic DataWindow data, such as date and time, are shown in the header band. You can also place in the header static data that does not change throughout the report, such as the department name in a report for a specific department.

The detail band contains data and related labels. The contents of this band can repeat throughout the DataWindow.

The summary band has the total and summary data for the DataWindow. The summary band is displayed only at the completion of the DataWindow.

The footer band has running totals for the DataWindow. You use this band if you need to display intermediate totals for each DataWindow page.

The trailer band applies to groups. It contains running totals and summary data for the defined group. For instance, we could establish a group break by department for our Revenues by Class DataWindow and have summary revenue amounts in the trailer for each department.

You have access to the following band-related attributes in Describe() and Modify():

❒ Color

❒ Height

❒ Height.Autosize

❒ Pointer

Color describes the background color for the band and is specified as a long in an expression. Height specifies the height of the detail area, in the unit of measure in effect for the DataWindow. Height.AutoSize applies to the detail band and tells the band whether to automatically size based on the objects in the band that are autosized. Pointer is a string value to describe the pointer in use when positioned over this band.

Let's suppose that we want to change the pointer in the detail band to the hand pointer. The code in the Constructor event for the DataWindow is:

```
string ls_band_mod
ls_band_mod =& "DataWindow.Detail.Pointer='hand.cur'")
This.Modify(ls_band_mod)
```

Scrolling Functions

PowerBuilder supplies a number of scrolling functions that simplify database navigation. These functions can be used in conjunction with VCR-style buttons to offer an easy visual aid to viewing a table in the specified sequence.

We'll build a user object of VCR-style buttons to understand the scrolling functions. First we'll create a custom visual user object that uses four BMPs—first1, prior1, next1 and last1—to signify the scrolling events. The user object has a function to accept the current DataWindow control name. We will need this to reference the control in the scroll functions. We declare an instance variable of type DataWindow for the DataWindow control name—idw_current_dw. The code for the function named uof_get_dw_name is:

```
idw_current_dw = adw_dw_name
```

adw_dw_name is an argument defined for the function with a type of DataWindow.

We then create scripts for the Clicked events of each of the picture buttons. The script for the last button is:

```
long ll_count
ll_count = idw_current_dw.RowCount()
If  ll_count > 0 Then
    idw_current_dw.ScrollToRow (ll_count)
End If
```

RowCount() returns the total number of rows in this table. We can then scroll directly to the last row by using this number.

```
The script for the "first" button is:
If idw_current_dw.rowcount() > 0 Then
    idw_current_dw.ScrollToRow (1)
End If
```

We check to see if we have any rows in the table, and if so, we set the scroll to row count to 1.

The script for the next button is:

```
idw_current_dw.ScrollNextRow()
```

The script for the prior button is:

```
idw_current_dw.ScrollPriorRow()
```

We now have a user object that can be reused to scroll through a freeform DataWindow (see Figure 3-16). In the window Open event for a window using the VCR-style buttons, the uof_get_dw_name function will be called with an argument of the DataWindow control.

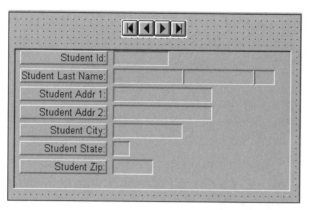

Figure 3-16: Basic student data using VCR-style scrolling buttons.

MOVING ON

In this chapter, we have looked at some advanced techniques for manipulating DataWindows. DataWindows have many capabilities beyond the interactive features that we have focused on thus far. In the next chapter, we will look into the advanced reporting and graphing capabilities of DataWindows.

Chapter 4

Advanced Reporting

In our desire to create more elegant front-end applications, we often overlook one of the most basic objects—the report. From the user's perspective, particularly in corporate environments, the report has always been a reflection of system quality. The time given to report design and development should mirror this importance. Powersoft seems to agree with this notion and has added significant tools to PowerBuilder 4.0 for developing complex reports. In this chapter, we'll discuss a variety of topics that provide a spectrum of approaches to report generation, including

- ❐ Graphs
- ❐ Crosstabs
- ❐ Nested reports
- ❐ Powersoft Report (PSR)
- ❐ Labels

We'll spend a substantial amount of time on graphing, because of the great impact that graph objects can have and the wealth of tools to work with graphs that PowerBuilder provides.

Consider Report Requirements Early

Reporting requirements are an integral part of application design. Typically, these requirements are identified in the latter stages of the design process, and tend to receive something less than the attention necessary to develop a refined reporting mechanism. Consider applying a *reporting classification system* to help in the reporting analysis process. A reporting classification system is a design tool that applies a specific analysis methodology to report definitions. Via an iterative, report prototype–driven method, the developer focuses on the report object and the components of its usage. This system includes the following: a report user list; report security requirements; subject; report description; printing requirements (forms, copies and distribution); and report cycle and volume.

GRAPHING

You've probably learned how to use many of PowerBuilder's graphing features, and have been creating graphs in your applications. But effectively representing data is not always as easy as it seems. This section will help you understand the parts of a graph and how to use various kinds of graphs effectively. We'll also discuss the nuts and bolts of creating graphs dynamically with PowerBuilder's graph object, a powerful feature that lets you create graphs on the fly and display them alongside the data used to create them.

Why Graphs?

Sometimes it takes a picture to actually show how relationships are forming or how subtle trends are occurring. Graphs are very good at showing comparisons between multiple data sets and changes in values over time. Here are some of the reasons to create a graph:

- ❏ They save time for users by interpreting data.
- ❏ They summarize large amounts of data concisely.

❐ They make a quick and lasting impression on the user.

❐ They make complex information simple to see and understand.

❐ They point out regularities or irregularities in the data.

❐ They allow the user to quickly see relationships and trends.

❐ We've become accustomed to viewing information in the easily consumable method that graphing provides. This is particularly true for management.

Interpreting data for the user is an important responsibility. The responsibility includes both interpreting the information correctly and interpreting it in a way that does not lend itself to confusion. When creating a graph, you must be able to explain why you are creating it. What are you trying to show? It's not valid to create graphs just to add color to your application, or to make the user feel like this is a powerful program. If your graph can be interpreted easily and consistently, it will become a successful application component.

Graph Basics

Like object orientation, the world of graphing has many specialized terms that often vary and sometimes conflict depending on who you're talking to. This chapter employs terms commonly used in statistical graphing, as well as terms used in PowerBuilder. Wherever terms conflict we explain the terms in question and then choose the one we feel is "most standard."

PowerBuilder has the ability to create two basic types of graphs: *coordinate* graphs and *circle* graphs. Coordinate graphs allow you to plot information on a rectangular grid.

This is sometimes known as the Cartesian plane. Circle graphs are representations of percentage shown graphically by area and angle.

Coordinate Graphs

A coordinate graph has an x-axis, a y-axis and, in the case of three-dimensional graphs, a z-axis. The x-axis in a two-dimensional graph runs from left to right, and the y-axis runs up and down (see Figure 4-1). The z axis, used only in 3D graphs, is a vertical elevation (see Figure 4-2).

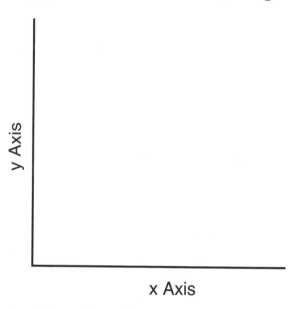

Figure 4-1: x and y coordinates form a 2D coordinate plane.

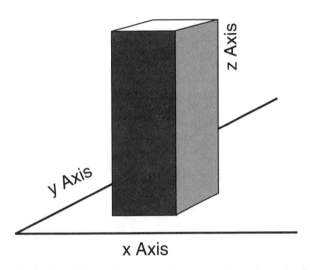

Figure 4-2: The z-axis is a vertical plane rising from the flat x and y plane.

PowerBuilder calls the axes of some coordinate graphs the *category axis* and the *value axis*. These terms don't always correspond to the x-axis and y-axis, and they can sometimes be confusing. The category axis of the graph, whether it's running from left to right or up and down, contains the items being graphed. The value being graphed is plotted in the value axis. In a graph of students enrolled by quarter, the quarter is the category, and the number students enrolled is the value. Each category listed along the category axis is an *independent* variable. It is independent because it wouldn't matter whether the value in our enrollment example said "Fall" or "1st." The value of the information plotted (the *dependent* variable) is still the same.

Here's another example. Graphing the price of several mid-sized cars, the car type would be the category, and the price of the car would be plotted along the value axis in dollars (see Figure 4-3). Values plotted along the value axis are the *dependent* variables. These plotted points are values that "depend" on what is being graphed (the category).

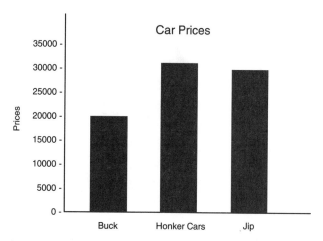

Figure 4-3: Graphing the price of several mid-sized cars.

The set of data points (prices) plotted in Figure 4-3 is known as a *series*. Every graph, no matter what type it is, has at least one series, although you can have more than one series. An example of having more than one series might be graphing the same set of cars over three different years. Figure 4-4 shows how prices increase for each car over a three-year period. Each year's car prices constitute a different series. The graph has three series, one for each year.

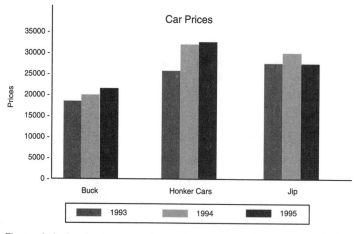

Figure 4-4: A price increase for each car over a three-year period.

A specialized type of coordinate graph is the *scatter graph*. Scatter graphs don't use the value and category axes the way conventional coordinate graphs do. Scatter graphs represent one numerical value plotted against another using the x-axis and y-axis (see Figure 4-5). As in other graphs, you can have multiple series of data points.

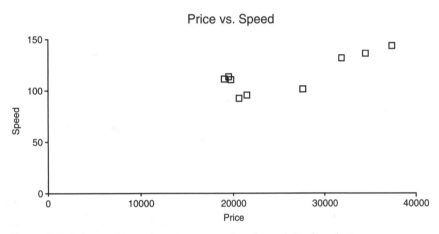

Figure 4-5: Price and speed are two numeric values plotted against one another.

To create a scatter graph, you designate the value you want plotted against the x-axis as the category axis. Notice that for the scatter graph type, you aren't allowed to specify the category as a string type variable. The y-axis variable is plotted as the value axis. For graphs with multiple series, you must click the series checkbox and add the column that specifies the series. Figure 4-6 shows the data from the graph in Figure 4-5, broken out into three different years.

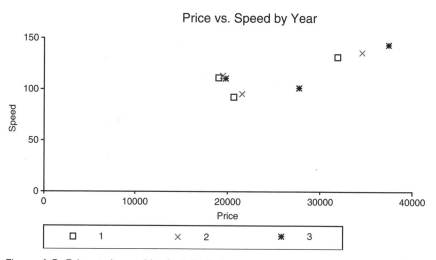

Figure 4-6: Price and speed broken out by year.

Circle Graphs

Circle graphs are used extensively to display relationships and percentages. PowerBuilder includes one of the most common circle graphs: the pie graph. Rather than plotting the values on a coordinate x and y plane, pie graphs represent values as wedge-shaped areas of a circle. Each value plotted on the graph represents a percentage of the whole. This is known as a *part-to-total* relationship. Here's how it works step-by-step:

1. All the values being plotted are summed.
2. Each value is then calculated against the total to find its percentage of the whole.
3. The percentages are expressed as wedges of a circle or "pieces of the pie."

The greatest value has the largest wedge in the pie. The category values (the things being plotted) are listed in legends outside the corresponding wedges of the pie.

In a monthly earnings example, each month would represent a piece of the pie. The whole pie would represent the earnings for the entire year. Providing there were earnings for all 12 months, the pie should have 12 "slices" (see Figure 4-7).

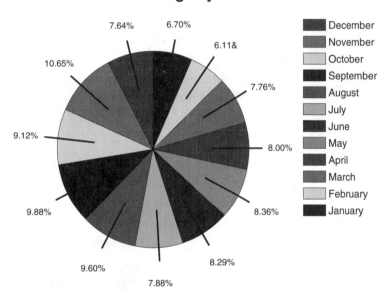

Figure 4-7: A pie graph representing earnings for the entire year.

Pie graphs are limited in what they can represent. Normally they're used to show a single series of data and relatively few data points. Too many data points will make the graph impossible to read. You can create pie graphs with more than one series. Each series is represented as a different concentric ring.

Choosing the Right Graph

It's not always obvious which type of graph will best represent your data. This is one of the reasons why graphing is an experimental process. PowerBuilder makes experimenting with graph types simple. Changing the graph type is as simple as selecting Type from the graph's Object Style popup menu and then selecting a new graph type. PowerBuilder has graph types suitable for most business applications. (For scientific applications that require Fourier transforms or other complex graphing capabilities, you may want to consider a third-party graphing utility.)

Line Graphs

Line graphs are excellent for plotting information that shows a trend. They're also useful where intermediate values can be derived by reading a value on the line between two points. Showing trends is straightforward—just follow the line. Deriving intermediate values is more complex. Both the category and value axes should be numeric or time values. This is similar to a scatter graph. Defining a new point on the line in one axis will allow you to determine its value in the other.

Line graphs lend themselves to text annotation better than most graph types. When you need to explain the data on the graph using annotations, this relatively uncluttered graph is useful. Try and keep annotations out of the graph area. Draw lines and arrows to the points on the graph instead. (See "Graph Labels & Annotations," later in this chapter.)

3D line graphs can also be very useful when viewing multiple series. Often, the lines become crossed and difficult to follow in a 2D line chart. Figure 4-8 is a basic line graph. Notice how the lines cross over and are difficult for the eye to follow. The symbols on the line make it possible to discern which line goes where, but it isn't readily apparent.

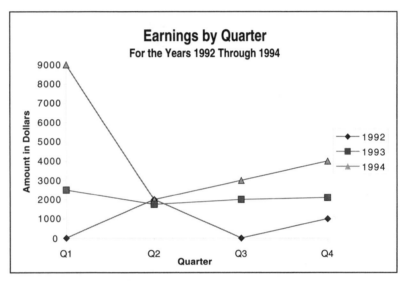

Figure 4-8: Line graphs with more than one series can be hard to read.

Figure 4-9 is a 3D line graph of the same values. With a different perspective, it's possible to see the rise and fall of the values in relation to one another without crossover. It's a trade-off. The simple line graph shows values more accurately. The 3D graph is less confusing and has more impact.

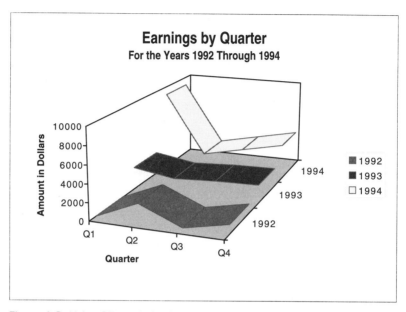

Figure 4-9: Using 3D can help clear up a confusing graph.

Area Graphs

An area graph is similar to a line graph with the area beneath the line shaded. This graph is useful when attempting to give the viewer a feeling for the total of one series over another. For example, suppose you are charting the relative rate at which the student enrollment for two classes differs over a two-month period. If you were to plot the enrollment figures on a daily basis, assuming each of these classes filled its allowable class limits and the classes' limits were similiar, you could readily see the rate differences with an area chart.

In a graph where the differences are small, the viewer may not be able to discern any difference in area. If it's important to show that there *isn't* much difference, this would be a valid graph type to use. Another advantage of the area graph is that the viewer can also view the trends normally seen in a line graph.

Bar & Column Graphs

Bar and column graphs tend to be the most effective and useful of all the graph types. They offer some of the advantages of an area graph. For instance, the differences in area occupied by the bars or columns give viewers a quick, general sense of comparative totals. Bar and column graphs also allow you to take advantage of humans' best visual cue: distance.

Bar charts make use of distance perception.

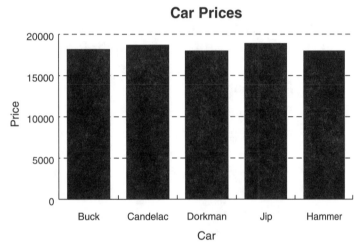

Car Prices

Figure 4-10: Even small differences in a column graph are easy for the eye to see.

Sort bar and column graph information whenever possible.

To make maximum use of the user's ability to discern distance, the values should be sorted. It isn't always possible to sort values, especially in a graph based on a time sequence. Any change-over-time information would be lost. But when graphing information such as the population of major world cities, for instance, ordering the graph from highest to lowest will give the viewer instant access to relative population information.

The only real difference between a bar and a column graph is orientation. The value axis in a column graph is vertical (y-axis). In a bar graph the value axis is horizontal (x-axis).

One reason you may wish to use the horizontal bar graph rather than the column graph is to graph a large number of items. The descriptions in the category axis are written horizontally, allowing more of them to fit on the page.

Using a 3D bar or column graph is especially useful when you are representing more than one series. You can quickly see the series in different rows along the series axis of the graph. The advantage here is the ability to see the values in each series as a group, and each series in comparison with other series. When the values are sorted, this graph can be an extremely valuable source of information.

Pie Graphs

Pie graphs are useful for making an immediate impression of percentages—for example, what proportion of expenses went toward advertising and how much went toward salaries. Pie graphs are most effective when only a few items are being graphed. They become less useful when a greater number of categories are graphed, and when there is a need to discern small differences. The human eye has trouble seeing differences in angle and in area. Unfortunately, these are the two key features of a pie graph. Figure 4-11 is a pie graph of the same five values shown in Figure 4-10. Which graph allows you to instantaneously see which car is most expensive?

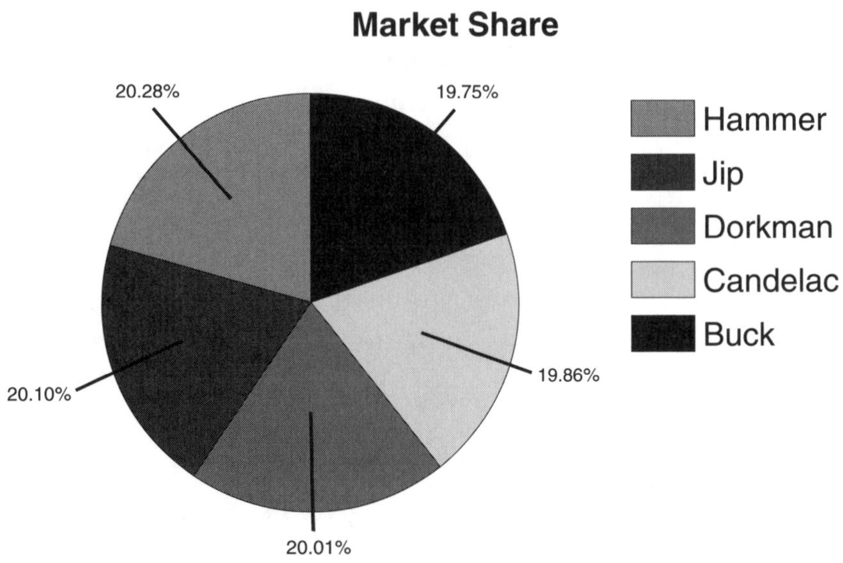

Market Share

Figure 4-11: It's difficult to tell the largest from the smallest wedge in a pie chart when the values are similar.

Anything that can be shown in a pie graph can be shown in a column or bar graph.

You may never want to plot relative car prices on a pie chart. And even when you need to plot percentages of a whole, as you normally would in a pie chart, consider a column or bar graph instead. The eye can discern distances, even small ones, much more easily than area or angle.

When a 3D pie graph is appropriate, it can make a greater impression than a 2D pie graph. And because area and angle are hard to discern, any distortion due to the angle of the 3D pie is meaningless.

Scatter Graphs

Scatter graphs are excellent for plotting one value against another value. This is especially true when there are many values being graphed. Any trends or linear relationships begin showing themselves in the shapes formed by the plotted points.

Scatter graphs are also excellent for spotting exceptional values—points that fall outside the normal distribution of values. You can quickly spot values that appear away from any shapes formed by the majority of the other points. A normal distribution forms a cigar-shaped group of points. Many graphing tools provide the capability to plot a regression line through the points. PowerBuilder does not have the ability to automatically create a regression line, though it is possible to write a utility that creates a regression line object and places it on the graph.

Human Factors

A graph should give the user a rapid visual impression of the information being presented. You can't always count on human perception. Anyone who has ever seen the optical illusions in children's magazines know how easy it is to fool the eye. In the "Pie Graphs" section earlier in the chapter, we saw that pie graphs are not the best choice for contrasting very similar values due to humans' limited ability to perceive small differences in angle and area. In the next couple of sections, we're going to talk about some other typical problems associated with graphs and human perception, and how they can be overcome to make a graph more readable.

Graphing Differences

One of the trickiest things you can do is to graph the difference between two series of plotted points. This is especially true when the graphs are curved. Look at Figure 4-12 to see a graph that attempts to show difference.

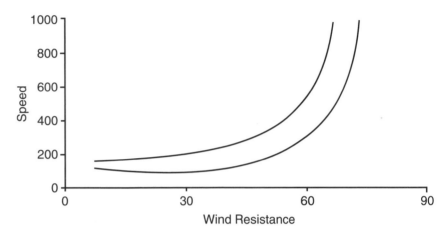

Figure 4-12: Two curves on a graph create an optical illusion.

At first glance, Figure 4-12 seems to be a fairly nice graph. It isn't flashy—it simply plots the differences shown by the two curved lines. However, your eye tends to want to measure the difference between the two lines as if they were curbs on a road instead of vertically and horizontally according to the axes. Figure 4-13 demonstrates how this is a natural thing for the eye to want to do. Hold a ruler between the two points marked "wrong," and then move your ruler vertically along the speed axis. You will see that the first value is quite a bit different from the other value.

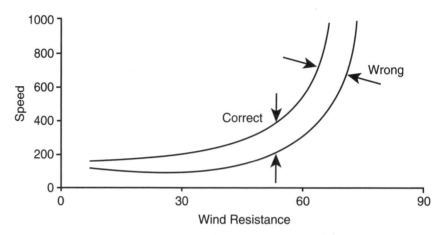

Figure 4-13: Your eye follows the curve, giving the wrong visual impression.

One way around the problem of graphing differences is to create a computed column that subtracts one value from the other, and then graph the result. Instead of seeing the optical illusion in Figures 4-12 and 4-13, the viewer sees a single plotted line that represents the *difference* between the two values. This gives the viewer an immediate impression, with the data correctly interpreted.

Let the graph interpret the data for the user.

Using a Log Scale

The human eye is a tough thing to please. Graphs that present very similar values can become difficult to read. Even the column graph in Figure 4-11 isn't the easiest to read. Scatter graphs will appear cluttered, line graphs will appear flat, column and bar graphs will be difficult to read, and pie graphs will be even worse. One way to effectively present very similar values is by using a *logarithmic* (or simply *log*) scale.

Logarithms are used extensively to represent scientific and engineering data and are not as commonly used in business. There are pros and cons to using a log scale. On the plus side, logarithms make graphs that show the percentage of change much easier to understand. Also, representing data on a logarithmic scale greatly improves resolution. The negative side is that users who are not familiar with logarithmic scales may be confused by the reference on the value scale.

PowerBuilder makes it simple to represent data logarithmically. In the Value Axis box, you'll find a drop-down listbox that allows you to select whether the scale is linear, log 10 or log e. Selecting one of the log entries will automatically convert the scale.

Using Grid Lines

Grid lines can help the viewer determine the value of plotted points. Deciding whether to use them is a matter of taste. Keep in mind that too many grid lines can cause a graph to look cluttered. Also, broken lines will sometimes be easier to distinguish as grid lines than solid lines. You can add grid lines to your graph by clicking the right mouse button over the graph, selecting Name and clicking on either the Category, Value or Series command button.

Graph Labels & Annotations

The text that appears on graphs is just as important as the data being displayed. PowerBuilder allows you to display many standard text descriptions as part of a graph. Table 4-1 lists the different types of descriptive text that appear on a graph.

Text Display Item	Description
Title	The graph title appears along the top of the graph and can be left-, center- or right-aligned.
Category axis label	This label appears along the category axis and describes the items being graphed.
Value axis label	This label appears along the value axis, describing the values and optionally identifying the unit of measure.
Series axis label	In a 3D graph this label would appear next to the series axis (appearing to recede back into the picture), describing the series being graphed.
Legend	This normally appears in a graph with more than one series. It describes the characters or colors used to differentiate the different series. The legend can appear on the bottom or along the side of the graph.

Table 4-1: Descriptive text that appears on graphs.

If a graph requires too much explanation it maybe shouldn't be a graph at all.

All the labels on a graph are optional, and all of them are recommended. But remember that graphs are meant to be pictures, not paragraphs. Place explanatory text in a caption or paragraph that will accompany the graph. If a graph requires too much explanation, you might consider the possibility that it shouldn't be a graph at all. Following are some simple guidelines for adding various kinds of text description to graphs.

Graph Titles

Graph titles should be simple and clear explanations of what the user should expect to see. Don't create long graph titles. If they need to be long to explain the graph, consider creating a simple title and then adding a subtitle to further explain the graph. Here's an example of a bad graph title:

Differences Between the Average Daily Mileage of Southern Canadian Geese Migrating North and South

The following might be a better alternative:

Migration Mileage Variations of Southern Canadian Geese
Variations in Average Daily Mileage Between Northern and Southern Migrations

Presented with a more concise title, viewers can more easily resolve the basic meaning of the graph. They can read the subtitle for additional information. Add subtitles using graphic text objects.

Axis Labels

Each axis should be labeled. Once again, the label should be meaningful, but brief. Make sure when creating labels for the value axis that you include the unit of measure used to create the graph. Remember to label the series axis if you have multiple series. This label is often forgotten. Figure 4-14 is an example of a well-labeled graph.

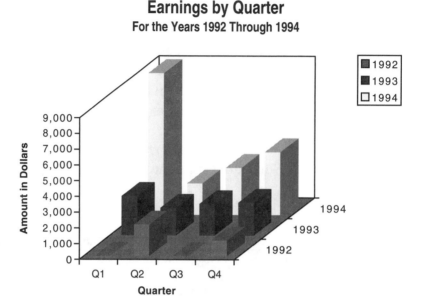

Figure 4-14: Each axis of a graph should have a label.

Adding Annotations

Annotations often add clarity to a graph. An arrow drawn to a low point in a graph with the annotation "Lost Acme as client" can have a great deal of impact. You can add annotations using graphic text objects.

When annotating graphs, keep the annotations out of the graph area. Occasionally it's important to label a plotted data point. But generally, annotations in the graph area tend to clutter the graph and detract from the overall impact. You can always add annotations outside the graph area and draw lines to the region you're annotating. Make sure that your annotations aren't confused with the axis labels. Using a smaller or narrower font will help keep annotations in the background. Use annotations sparingly.

Dynamic Graphing

There are two ways to present graphs in PowerBuilder: in DataWindows and in windows. Using DataWindows you can embed graphs in your data or use the graph presentation style. Graphs in DataWindows normally use the database as their data source. You can manipulate these graphs dynamically using the Modify() function.

The other way to present graphs is by using the graph control in windows and user objects. This is a new feature of PowerBuilder 4.0, and it allows you to create graphs dynamically, using PowerScript to define the data source. Placing a graph control object on a window or user object is just like placing any other control. Click the graph object from the icons in either the Window or User Object painter, and then place the control using the mouse. (If you place a graph object in a user object, you'd use the OpenUserObject() function to tie it to a window.) Using graph controls, you can build a system that allows users to create their own graphs. They can use drag and drop to help build these graphs.

Once you place a graph control object on a window, you have to set its parameters. The graph control uses many other objects to set its parameters. All these parameters are set using PowerScript. You can hard-code the values, create them dynamically based on program values, or allow the users to specify their own graph values and attributes.

For our example, we'll construct a graph control named gr_1. (This is the default name given to a graph control when it's placed on the window.) Our example will not be user-definable. Doing this would fill the book with code. You are encouraged to look at our hard-coded examples and make them user-definable, or interactive. (*Note:* A good idea when allowing users to create their own graphs is to have a popup window that passes back and forth, using the message object, a structure that has the ability to store all the graph parameters.)

Setting the Graph Type & Title

One of the first things you may want to do when creating a graph is to specify the type of graph you're creating. You can either hard-code this or leave the choice up to the users. One of the attributes of the graph control object is GraphType. The data type accepted by the GraphType attribute is GrGraphType, which is an enumerated data type. A complete list of enumerated values can be found in the online help under GrGraphType. Here's an example that sets the GraphType to 3D Column using the Col3DGraph! enumerated data value:

```
gr_1.GraphType = Col3DGraph!
```

This statement can go anywhere after the graph object is placed on the window. In our example, we placed it in the Constructor event of the graph control object.

If you double-click the graph object, you won't find a script button as you do with other controls. Bring up the popup menu to edit scripts. In Windows, this is done by right-clicking the graph control and selecting Script from the menu.

Another of the graph control attributes is Title. Set this attribute with a string containing the title of the graph. Our example graph will represent a distribution of colors, so we'll give it the following title:

```
gr_1.title = "Color Distribution"
```

The PowerScript Graph Functions

When creating and using graph controls you need to use special PowerScript functions specific to graph controls. Don't try to use these on graphs in a DataWindow. These functions are all methods of the graph control object.

AddCategory

The AddCategory method of the graph control appends a category value to the end of the list of categories being graphed. (To insert a category value *within* the list, use the InsertCategory method.) The following code loads our gr_1 graph object with values from an array:

```
integer i
string a_colors[]

a_colors = {"red", "yellow", "blue"}
 FOR i = 1 to UpperBound(a_colors
     gr_1.AddCategory(a_colors[i]

NEXT
```

If you run your window, and press the button with the example script in the Clicked event, you can watch categories being added to your graph.

The categories above are hard-coded and in a button script. In your application, however, these values can come from different locations, such as the following:

- ❐ DataWindow column names.
- ❐ Text values in edit controls.
- ❐ Names of controls that have been dropped onto the graph control using drag-and-drop. Use the Tag attribute to save a more descriptive name.

These are just a few of the many places from which categories can be derived. In all graph types except the scatter graph, categories are normally text descriptions of the values being graphed.

AddSeries

The next step in creating a graph is to add a series. Every graph needs at least one series. The AddSeries function adds a series, giving it the name you pass as a string parameter. The series names must be unique. When you add a series to a graph, PowerBuilder assigns it a sequential number. The AddSeries function returns the number assigned to the new series.

*E*very graph needs at least one series.

Here's an example of creating a new series for the gr_1 graph. Add this code to the Clicked event of the command button that contains the AddCategory function:

```
integer new_series
new_series = gr_1.AddSeries("colors")
```

The variable new_series now holds the number of the empty series. The next task is to add data to the series.

AddData

You can add data points to the graph using the AddData function. The three parameters of the AddData function are the series number, the value of the data point, and the category. One way to find the number of the series is to use the FindSeries method of the graph control. Passing it the name of the series causes it to return the number.

Pass a null string as the third parameter to create a new, unspecified category. In this example we add a numeric value to each category—in this case, colors:

```
integer the_series
the_series = gr_1.FindSeries("colors")

gr_1.AddData(the_series,5,"red")
gr_1.AddData(the_series,7,"yellow")
gr_1.AddData(the_series,9,"blue")
```

We added this script to a button to demonstrate adding data. You might also want to add data from controls, text files or the Windows Clipboard.

ImportClipboard

The ImportClipboard function copies data from the Windows Clipboard to a graph. The data in the Clipboard must be tab-delimited and specially formatted with three columns. The first column must specify the series name, the second column the category and the third, the data value. In the special case of scatter graphs the second and third columns represent the x and y values being graphed.

With the ImportClipboard function you can specify which Clipboard row and column to start reading. A new series will be created for each change in the text in the first column.

Importing data from the Windows Clipboard is a way to move information between different Windows programs in addition to using DDE or OLE. Be aware that using this function in your application may keep you from implementing this code on a Macintosh or UNIX machine.

ImportFile

The ImportFile function is similar to the ImportClipboard function. With the ImportFile function, however, the user can specify the input file name, and the return value is more versatile.

The first parameter of the ImportFile function is a string containing the file name. If this parameter contains a null string PowerBuilder will open the Select Import File dialog. The return values are shown in Table 4-2.

Return Value	Description
0	End of file, too many rows
-1	No rows
-2	Empty file
-3	Invalid argument
-4	Invalid input
-5	Could not open the file
-6	Could not close the file
-7	Error reading the text
-8	Not a TXT file
-9	The user canceled the Import

Table 4-2: The return values of the ImportFile function.

ImportFile is particularly useful if you want to save the values in a DataWindow and then use the saved information as part of a graph. Saving a DataWindow as a TXT file will automatically save it in tab-delimited format.

ImportString

The ImportString function operates similarly to the ImportFile function. Rather than reading from a file, however, you can pass the three parameters one line at a time. It's important that this string end with a carriage return/line feed.

Other Graph Functions

The additional graph functions shown in Table 4-3 allow you to further build and manipulate a graph control dynamically.

Function	Description
InsertCategory	Inserts a category at the specified position within a category list. It can also be used to append to the category list.
InsertData	Inserts a data point in the list of data points. It inserts a new data point before the specified data point.
InsertSeries	Inserts a series into the series list before the specified series.
ModifyData	Changes the value of a data point.
DeleteCategory	Deletes a category.
DeleteData	Deletes a data point.
DeleteSeries	Deletes a series.
Reset	Resets the graph's data.

Table 4-3: Additional PowerScript graphing functions.

Designing Better Graphs

Graphing offers the ability to represent data in a simple and powerful format. The better you understand graphing, the more impact your graphs will have, and there are many books available on effective graphic communications for further study in this area. Designing graphs is an iterative process, like prototyping, where each successive attempt has improvements over the last. It's rare that the first graph you create will be the final version. Here are a few things to keep in mind when creating graphs:

❏ If you're using DataWindows to create your graph, make sure the SQL SELECT statement is correct. Copy the syntax into the Database Administration section of the Database painter and execute the SQL statement. Review the data set returned in the painter to make sure the right data is being retrieved.

❏ Make sure the axes have correct labels.

❏ Make certain the graph is the correct type. Using the wrong graph type can obscure the meaning of your data.

❏ Make certain your graph is makes correct use of the graphic features, such as grid lines and annotations. Some graph features work better than others when displaying certain types of information.

CROSSTABS

Graphs offer a strong, visceral approach to data analysis. Another important, if somewhat less dramatic, approach is *cross tabulation*. Cross tabulations, or crosstabs, present data in a tabular, spreadsheet style. Crosstabs provide an easy way of looking at summary data. They are particular useful for management overviews and for users that have a fondness for spreadsheets. Crosstabs are implemented in PowerBuilder through the crosstab DataWindow presentation style. The crosstab summarizes retrieved data per your DataWindow definition.

Examine the simple crosstab example in Figure 4-15, showing university revenue by department by term.

DataWindow - dw_revenues_by_dept_crosstab				
Term				
	FA	SP	SU	WI	
Department Name	95	95	95	95	**Grand Total**
Biology	$9,550	$8,850	$7,550	$9,250	$35,200
Business	$20,000	$20,100	$18,500	$19,450	$78,050
Computer Science	$37,800	$36,700	$32,600	$37,700	$144,800
English	$21,300	$20,900	$19,300	$23,500	$85,000
Gen Ed	$18,450	$16,600	$16,450	$19,450	$70,950
Math	$19,900	$18,800	$17,700	$18,700	$75,100
Grand Total	$127,000	$121,950	$112,100	$128,050	$489,100

Figure 4-15: Sample crosstab showing revenue by department by term.

You can see that the crosstab displays data in a two-dimensional format. The first dimension, the term (winter, spring, etc.), is shown in the columns. The second dimension, the department, is shown in the rows. Each intersection of the two dimensions is displayed as a value in a cell. Each cell is a summarization of the revenues by class for each quarter. The crosstab also has totals by term and department.

There are two types of crosstabs: dynamic and static. Dynamic crosstabs are the PowerBuilder default and the type used in the majority of cases. The columns and rows are built dynamically as the crosstab is executed. For example, if the university decided to switch to a semester system, we would see these new semesters instead of the current quarters displayed as crosstab columns.

Static crosstabs are constructed from data present in the database at the time the crosstab is defined. PowerBuilder retrieves the data when you use the preview function in the DataWindow painter. Even if data has changed at execution time, the static crosstab will continue to display the data from the original definition. If we change to the semester system, the static crosstab knows nothing about it.

Building a Crosstab

Let's look at the steps necessary to build the crosstab shown in the example above. We'll use the class revenue table that has been built in our sample application, the Student Registration System (for details on the application, see Chapter 16).

1. Open the DataWindow painter and click on New from the Select DataWindow dialog box.

2. Choose Quick Select as the data source and Crosstab as the presentation style.

3. Choose the appropriate table (class_revenues, in this case) and select all.

4. In the Crosstab Definition dialog box, drag department_name to Rows, term and year to Columns, and revenue_amt to Values. (Note that the name revenue_amt changes to sum(revenue_amt for crosstab) when it is dragged.) The Rebuild columns at runtime checkbox should be checked. Click OK to complete the dialog.

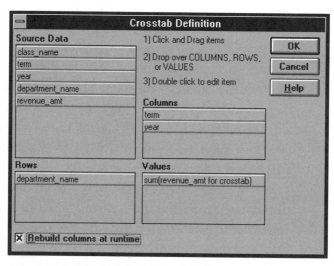

Figure 4-16: Crosstab Definition dialog box for revenue by department.

5. Delete the column named crosstabsum(1,2,"@term"). This was created because we named term and year in the Columns group. It will create an unneeded summary by year.

6. Change the format on all revenue columns to dollar amounts.

7. Preview the DataWindow and resize the columns as necessary (see Figure 4-16).

8. Save the DataWindow with an appropriate name identifying it as a crosstab.

PowerBuilder creates an aggregate function for the revenue value—a sum in our case. PowerBuilder will use Sum for numeric fields and Count for non-numeric fields. Other aggregate functions such as Min, Max and Avg can be used for value fields. If we had a column that used a code table, crosstabs would have to use the displayed value associated with the data.

Modifying Crosstabs

You can enhance crosstabs using the same techniques you use to enhance other DataWindow types. You should follow the general characteristics of your other DataWindows in your crosstabs.

You can determine how grid lines are shown and how the user alters the crosstab during execution by setting grid attributes. To accomplish this, go to the popup menu available below the footer in the DataWindow workspace for your crosstab. This popup provides attributes that affect the presentation of grid lines—on, off and display-only or print-only. It also supports attributes for user interaction with crosstabs at run-time, via the Crosstab Definition dialog box. These attributes include Reorder Columns, Select During Execution, and Resize Individual Rows.

You can rename the column labels to something more meaningful than the database column names by double-clicking on the column name in the Source Data box in the Crosstab Definition dialog. Multiple word names can be entered, and underscores will be replaced by spaces at execution. You can also use a valid PowerScript expression to name the columns. For instance, suppose we had a crosstab that shows the enrollment by class by date for a given time period. We'd like to see the enrollment numbers by day of the week. Define the expression to display the days as DayName(enrollment_date). This returns a string for the day of the week, and the result is columns for Monday through Sunday. The associated data is summarized by these days.

Notice the label crosstabsum(1) under the grand total column. This gives us the totals for each of the classes. CrosstabSum is one of five special crosstab functions:

- ❒ CrosstabSum
- ❒ CrosstabAvg
- ❒ CrosstabCount
- ❒ CrosstabMin
- ❒ CrosstabMax

Each of these functions uses a numeric argument. This argument refers to the relative sequence of the columns defined in the value box of the Crosstab Definition dialog. The functions return the appropriate type of value for each row. The default placement of these functions is in the detail band. Let's add an average of the revenue by class across all terms in our example.

1. Return to the DataWindow painter workspace for the crosstab.

2. Click the Compute button on the PowerBar to create a computed field.

3. Click to the right of the last cell in the detail band.

4. Enter a name for the revenue average by department column in the Computed Field Definition dialog box, and select crosstabavg(1) from the Function drop-down listbox.

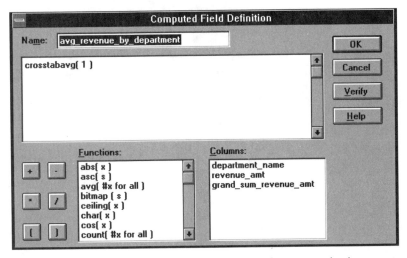

Figure 4-17: Computed Field Definition dialog box for revenue by department with CrosstabAvg function.

5. Select the correct dollar format for this revenue field.

6. Add a title for the revenue average field and click OK.

7. Preview the crosstab and save it.

Crosstabs can also display ranges of values. For example, we could modify our crosstab to display a count of classes that fall within a certain revenue range.

You can also change attributes of crosstab objects conditionally, just as you would with other DataWindow objects. For instance, we could cause the color of those departments with class revenues less than $10,000 to be shown in red. To accomplish this, select the attributes for the revenue_amt field. Double-click on color and enter the following:

```
if ( revenue_amt < 10000, 255, 0)
```

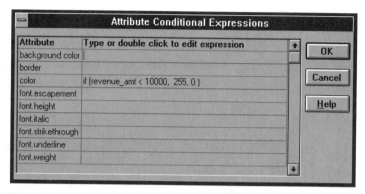

Figure 4-18: The Attribute Conditional Expressions dialog.

Crosstab Execution

The completed crosstab is associated with a DataWindow control and has the same characteristics. The Modify and Describe functions apply. The Modify function will rebuild the crosstab if attributes other than the following list are affected:

- ❐ Alignment
- ❐ Background
- ❐ Border
- ❐ Brush
- ❐ Color
- ❐ Edit styles
- ❐ Font
- ❐ Format
- ❐ Pen
- ❐ Pointer

To minimize the number of crosstab rebuilds, combine all modify expressions in a single entry.

You can offer the user the ability to control the crosstab by using the PowerScript function CrosstabDialog. This function will display the same Crosstab Definition dialog box the developer uses to define the object (see Figure 4-19).

NESTED REPORTS

A *nested report* refers to a report that appears within another report. In PowerBuilder, you can create nested reports in two different ways. One way is to place multiple reports within a *composite* report, a special report that is really just a place-holder or container for other reports. The composite report has no data source of its own, and the reports within the composite container do not communicate with one another via common data. The other way to create a nested report is to place one report directly within another report in a master/detail relationship, where both reports have their own data sources and are related to one another by common data.

Creating a Composite Report

Consider the revenue by department crosstab we discussed earlier in the chapter. In some circumstances it may be important to display related detail information for the crosstab—for instance, revenue broken down by class. You can create a composite report containing both the summary and detail reports. You build composite reports using the Composite presentation style of the DataWindow painter. (You could also use the Report painter. If you're missing the Report PowerBar button, add it from the PowerBar toolbar icons.)

1. Open the DataWindow painter.
2. Click New.

3. Select the Composite presentation style. Since a composite report has no data source of its own, all sources are grayed.

4. Select the reports you want to include from the report list. In our case we'd select the revenues by department crosstab we looked at earlier in this chapter, and a detail report for revenues by class.

5. Review the location of the reports (PowerBuilder places the reports in the sequence selected from the previous dialog box).

6. Preview the report. Notice that you're in a read-only print preview: data changes can only be made to the specific detail report object. Also note that the Filter, Import and Sort menu items are not available from the Row menu item. These functions apply to the individual reports prior to building the composite report.

7. Add additional attributes to the report to standardize its appearance. We'll add a title, a "requested by" field, a date and time and a page number.

8. Save the composite report.

A shortcoming of composite reports is that the data cannot be updated. This means that multiple updatable DataWindows cannot be printed on a single page. To accomplish this, you must use the GetChild and ShareData functions to reference the nested reports. You create a window that holds the updatable DataWindow controls. Then you add a composite report object that includes a report for each updatable DataWindow to the window. The composite report is not visible. After retrieving report data, you use GetChild to build a reference to the nested reports. You call ShareData to link data between the nested reports and associated updatable DataWindows.

Creating a Report Within a Report

Typically, when you create a report within a report, each with its own data source, the reports will communicate with one another via common data values in a master/detail relationship, with the detail (or nested) report depending on data in the master (or base) report. (There's actually no inherent requirement stating that the reports must have an interdependency. In reality, however, there are few occasions where you'd create nested reports of this kind without a stated dependency.) Within a base report showing general student data, for instance, you might want to place a detail report showing classes that the student has taken. The "classes taken" report could be linked to the general student report using a student ID value. This report is used in our sample application, the Student Registration System, which is included on the Companion CD-ROM. The steps required to create this kind of master/detail report are as follows:

Performance Considerations

As you might suspect, there's a price to pay for the connectivity of the base nested reports. With composite reports, PowerBuilder retrieves data one report at a time. For nested master/detail reports, PowerBuilder retrieves all rows for the master or base report and then gets the nested report data for each row in the master report until it's complete with all rows. This more involved retrieval method can become an important performance consideration.

1. Determine the link between the base and detail reports. In our example report, we'd use the student ID to link the basic student information to the classes he or she has taken.

2. Build the nested report with the linked item as a retrieval argument. In our example, we'd build a freeform DataWindow called dw_classes_taken. We'd use the student_id as a retrieval argument and place it in the where clause.

3. Open the base report. For our example, this would be a freeform DataWindow, called dw_nested_student_classes, that contains minimal basic student information. It has a retrieval argument of student_id.

4. Determine the placement for the nested report, then select the nested report, dw_classes_taken, and position it in the appropriate spot in the workspace. A rectangular box with the DataWindow name is returned.

5. Link the base to the nested report by specifying the retrieval argument for the nested report. In the popup menu for the nested report, select the retrieval argument. Select student_id from the base report. This will provide the value for the a_student_id argument in the nested report.

6. Preview the report and customize it as necessary.

Nested reports have some unique characteristics in comparison to other DataWindow or report types. You can see the differences by viewing the selection list in the popup menu for the nested report.

You may have noticed that the Autosize Height attribute was checked. This is required so that the nested report height can change relative to the rows retrieved. This attribute is also on and required for the Detail band of the nested report.

PowerBuilder lets you modify the nested report by selecting Modify Report from the popup menu. Your base report will reflect any changes made and saved to your nested report. You can also use Change Report to select a new report as your nested report.

In our example, we linked the nested report to the base report via a retrieval argument for student ID. The use of a retrieval argument proves to be the most efficient method of connecting the two reports. PowerBuilder will save a compiled version of your Select statement when using a retrieval argument, if your DBMS supports the binding of input variables. ORACLE, for example, supports this functionality. To activate the saving of the compiled version in ORACLE, you must set the SQLCache DBParm to a value greater than zero. A simple guideline for ORACLE 7 is 50 (the maximum number of cursors a process can have open at a time) plus 5 (the number of reserved cursors) plus the number of nesting levels.

USING POWERSOFT REPORTS (PSR)

The PSR feature, new with version 4.0, enables the saving and review of report definitions and associated data. It's particularly useful for looking at reports at particular data points. The PSR is stored as a specific file type with the .PSR extension. PSR files are used extensively in InfoMaker, and they can be attached as documents to e-mail.

Creating PSR Files

PSR files can be created in several fashions. In the Data-Window Print Preview window, you can invoke the Save Rows As dialog box from the File, Save Rows As menu item. This dialog box lets you save the report in a dozen different formats including Excel, Text, CSV, DBF and Report. The Report option saves the data and report definition as a PSR file. The report can also be saved as a PSR file through PowerScript. The Save Rows As dialog box is invoked by simply coding SaveAs() without arguments. Additionally, PowerBuilder will create a PSR file when you send a report to an InfoMaker user via e-mail.

Opening PSR Files

PSR files can also be opened in several ways. InfoMaker opens PSR files using the File Manager or from e-mail. The File menu of the Report painter (this is not available in the DataWindow painter) can be used to open PSR files. To invoke this option, you must set the DefaultFileOrLib variable in the PB.INI file to 1 or 2 (1 is for PSR files; 2 is for DataWindow objects and PSR files, and is the installation default for the Enterprise version). PSR files can also be opened into a DataWindow via the following script:

```
dw_dept_revenue.dataobject = "DEPTREV.PSR"
```

This would display the previewed version of the composite report in the named DataWindow control.

PRINTING LABELS

PowerBuilder provides support for a wide variety of label styles. To create a label, use the DataWindow or Report painter, the appropriate data source, and the Label presentation style. The Specify Label Specifications dialog prompts you to select the label type from an extended list or to specify a custom type. The standard labels are defined in the PBLAB040.INI file. The label with a width of 2.625 and height of 1.000 is adequate for printing the typical name, two-line street address, and city, state and zip lines. You should create computed fields for formatting the name on the first line, and the city, state and zip on the final line, in a smoother format (leave the other address lines as they are). You may want to include a picture object to give the label more corporate identity.

After you've initially defined a label format, you may want to experiment with various types. To select a different type, use the Label menu item from the popup menu in the label object. You can alter label attributes dynamically by changing print attributes through Modify.

MOVING ON

In this chapter, we've discussed a variety of reporting topics. For the sake of brevity, we've limited our discussion to a few of the more meaningful issues, including graphs, crosstabs, nested reports, PSR and labels. PowerBuilder offers a toolbox full of techniques for developing sophisticated reports. The developer's responsibility is to understand the user's reporting requirements and to select the correct tools to meet these requirements.

One of the topics we touched on in this chapter was how to share data between applications. In the next chapter, we'll discuss richer methods for linking and embedding data between applications using OLE 2.0 and, to a smaller degree, DDE.

Chapter 5

OLE & DDE

OLE and DDE are two acronyms that have become ubiquitous in the last few years. Although it is widely understood that they are services for sharing data between applications, the actual definitions of the two concepts are nebulous. In this chapter, we'll define OLE and DDE, and we'll look into the details of working with OLE and DDE in PowerBuilder applications.

OLE DEFINED

Object Linking and Embedding, or OLE, comprises two areas: *linking* objects into documents and *embedding* objects into documents. The term *server* refers to the external application used to create and modify the linked or embedded object. For example, if an embedded OLE object is a Microsoft Word document, then Word is the server; if the OLE document is an Excel spreadsheet, then Excel is the server. The term *container* refers to the objects in which OLE documents are embedded or linked. For our purposes, the PowerBuilder windows and objects retaining OLE documents are the containers. Containers can be embedded or linked documents themselves, creating a hierarchy of containership. Objects that are both containers and OLE documents are called *compound documents*.

The OLE specification provides definitions for linking and embedding. PowerBuilder implements them in slightly different ways. Let's take a look at both the OLE specifications and the PowerBuilder implementations of linking and embedding.

Embedding

OLE maintains two categories of information about an object:

❑ Information about the presentation of the document.
❑ Information about the editing of the document.

In the OLE specification for embedding an object in a document, the contents of an object (its data) together with its presentation information are implanted into a document. When the document is migrated to another destination, the information on how to edit the document travels with the document itself. Since the information about editing the document is stored within the document, an application can access the document and use the relevant editing information in order to modify the document.

PowerBuilder's implementation of embedding is a subset of the OLE specification. PowerBuilder enables the developer to embed an object's presentation information in a document, but the editing capabilities cannot be placed with the document. As a result, the data is displayed in its native format when embedded in the PowerBuilder document. You cannot change that information from within the document without rebuilding the PowerBuilder .PBL or .EXE in which it is stored. If another program changes the document's data, the actual document would be changed, but the presentation information embedded in the PowerBuilder object would remain as it was when originally compiled into the document.

Linking

The OLE specification states that linking is the storing of the presentation information with the document and the storing of a pointer or link to the editing information about the document. The editing information is stored externally to the document, unlike the embedding process.

PowerBuilder implements linking in much the same way as the OLE specification. The presentation information is stored in the document with a link to the actual document's data and editing information. The actual data is external to the PowerBuilder object.

Origins of DDE & OLE

Often, Microsoft is credited as the sole creator of OLE and DDE. This is not true. The proposal for DDE specifications was originated by Microsoft and Aldus in 1988 and 1989. As the acceptance of DDE started to grow, Borland, Lotus, Micrografx, Samna and WordPerfect joined the effort to expand and refine the DDE specifications. This new specification for DDE was briefly renamed the Extensible Compound Document Architecture specification and transformed into what eventually came to be known as Object Linking and Embedding 1.0. The first OLE 1.0-compliant applications shipped in 1991. Afterward, Microsoft immediately worked on the OLE 2.0 specification with an even larger group of third-party vendors. OLE 2.0-compliant products started shipping in 1993.

USING OLE IN POWERBUILDER

PowerBuilder supports OLE in a couple of different ways. You can use DataWindows to support OLE 1.0. blobs (binary large objects) can be used as a column type in the Data-Window to store OLE object data. For example, a Word document can be stored as a blob value for a DataWindow column and contained in the database. When the DataWindow retrieves the blob value from the database, Word can be called to operate as an OLE server application and operate on the contents of the DataWindow.

OLE 2.0 is supported by a feature new to PowerBuilder 4.0: the OLE 2.0 control, available in the Window painter. An OLE 2.0 control is a container that could hold, for instance, a Word document; Word can be invoked in place to operate on the contents of the OLE 2.0 control.

What do we mean when we say that Word can be invoked *in place*? PowerBuilder provides for two types of server application behavior when an OLE object is activated. The activation can be one of two types:

- ❐ In-place
- ❐ Offsite

With in-place activation, the server's menus merge with the menus of your PowerBuilder window. The capability for in-place activation is a new feature of the OLE 2.0 specification. Server applications that are only OLE 1.0–compliant cannot process OLE documents in place.

With offsite activation, the server application opens externally to the PowerBuilder application, and the OLE document in the PowerBuilder object is copied to the server for modification. With offsite activation, the menus of the PowerBuilder window remain unchanged as the server application opens.

Support for OLE 2.0 is new to version 4.0 of PowerBuilder.

The developer does not directly control whether to use in-place or offsite activation. If the server application is OLE 2.0–compliant and can support in-place activation, PowerBuilder will take advantage of this capability and provide in-place document editing. If the server is not OLE 2.0–compliant, or if an object is linked rather than embedded, the activation will be offsite.

In the next several sections, we'll touch on the functional differences between OLE 1.0 and OLE 2.0, and we'll take a look at working with OLE 1.0 and OLE 2.0 objects in PowerBuilder, demonstrating both offsite and in-place activation.

Working With OLE 1.0

OLE 1.0 allows for basic linking and embedding of documents. The only activation method available in the OLE 1.0 specification is offsite. All server applications must start up externally to the container application. A common use of OLE 1.0 in PowerBuilder applications has been to embed word processing documents or spreadsheets in the application's window. The user would then double-click on the OLE object, invoking the appropriate server application, such as Word or Excel. Narrative types of columns, such as comments, descriptions, etc., are good candidates for using Word as an OLE server application. Any window that could use a MultiLineEdit control could be considered a candidate. Following are some sample business uses for storing word processing documents as OLE objects in applications:

- ❐ Employees' resumes.
- ❐ Employees' or applicants' employment applications.
- ❐ Purchase orders (as word processing documents or spreadsheets).
- ❐ Order forms.

❐ Customer profiles.

❐ Customer contact histories.

❐ Product descriptions.

❐ Any specialized forms.

For our example, we'll take a look at the process using a DataWindow as the container, since DataWindows are limited to OLE 1.0. We'll create a table with at least one column of type blob. In that column, we'll store a Word document. The example will be a small test window, but the possibilities for usage are numerous.

We first must create a sample table to store our OLE documents. Our table will have three columns: a document ID column, a document date column and a blob column to store the document.

1. Using the Database painter, create a table with the declaration shown in Figure 5-1. Create a primary key using document_id.

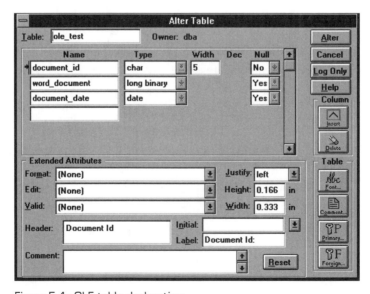

Figure 5-1: OLE table declaration.

2. Create a new DataWindow of type Freeform with a SQL Select data source.

3. In the DataWindow painter, select the document_id and document_date columns and place them on the DataWindow. Do *not* place the OLE blob column word_document on the DataWindow by selecting it with the other columns. OLE blob columns are placed on the DataWindow differently.

4. Click the Design button on the PainterBar to switch to design mode.

5. To place the OLE blob column on the DataWindow, select OLE Database Blob from the Objects menu and click on the DataWindow. The dialog shown in Figure 5-2 will appear.

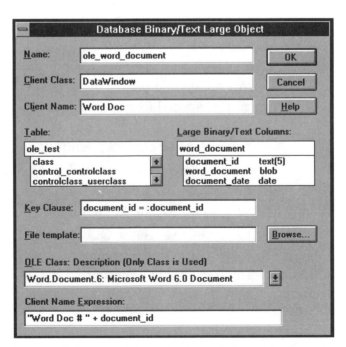

Figure 5-2: Database Binary/Text Large Object dialog is used to describe a blob DataWindow column used as an OLE container.

6. In this dialog, the Name, Client Class, and Client Name fields are optional. The Name field should contain a value only if you intend to reference it with PowerScript. The other two fields are used by OLE server applications to title documents inside the OLE server. We'll be referencing this object with PowerScript, so enter **ole_word_document** in the Name field.

7. Select our OLE test table from the Table drop-down listbox, and select the word_document column from the Large Binary/Text Columns field. Making these choices here causes the blob to be associated with the DataWindow column.

8. The Key Clause field should read as follows: document_id = :as_document_id. PowerBuilder picked up the ID column when you selected a primary key.

9. In the OLE Class drop-down listbox, select Word.Document.6 (or the appropriate version). In the case of special forms, we could choose a particular file as a template by typing its name in the File template field. The two choices are mutually exclusive.

10. In the Client Expression field, enter **"Word Doc #"+ document_id**. This value will be displayed in the server application to identify the file.

11. Click OK to save the OLE column. Control is returned to the DataWindow painter in design mode. There is a small rectangle representing the OLE blob column now on the DataWindow where you last clicked.

The Powersoft documentation warns us to place something behind the blob column, because it will otherwise not be visible on the DataWindow. We can actually take advantage of this situation. There are a number of options we can choose. We could click the border attribute for the blob column and change it from none to box or shadow. Or we can modify its appearance to represent a document. For example, we can place two Rectangle controls over the column and change the color and fill pattern to look like a legal pad.

The width of an OLE column determines the default width of a document in Word.

1. We'll first size the blob column. Be aware that the width of the blob column will dictate the default width of the document inside Word. Drag the corners of the blob column to be approximately 950 PowerBuilder units wide by 1000 PowerBuilder units high. Move the blob column to the upper left corner of the painter area. Temporarily move the other two columns to the right if necessary.

2. From the Objects menu, select Rectangle and click on the DataWindow. Size the Rectangle control to be the exact size of the blob column. Place the Rectangle control over the column so they are exactly on top of one another. If necessary, use Send to Back or Bring to Front to place the Rectangle on top.

3. Change the color of the Rectangle to yellow and change the fill pattern to appear as horizontal lines, as shown in Figure 5-3.

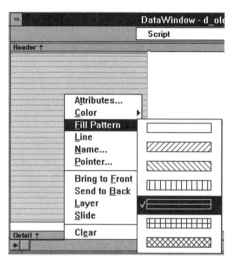

Figure 5-3: Setting the fill pattern for the Rectangle control covering the blob column.

4. Place a second Rectangle control on the DataWindow, with a height of 95 PowerBuilder units and a width of 950 PowerBuilder units. Place it at the top of the other Rectangle as shown in Figure 5-4.

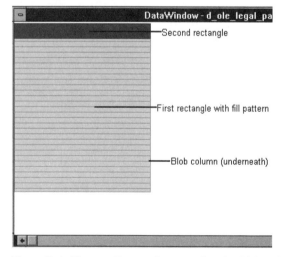

Figure 5-4: The two Rectangles covering the blob column look like a legal pad.

5. Change the font for the document_id and document_date columns to script, to look like hand-writing on the pad. Place these two column headers and columns on the Rectangle as shown in Figure 5-5.

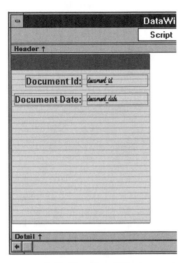

Figure 5-5: The DataWindow columns appear on the legal pad.

6. Set the protection attributes for the two non-OLE columns by typing **1** in the value field for the protect attribute for each column, as shown in Figure 5-6.

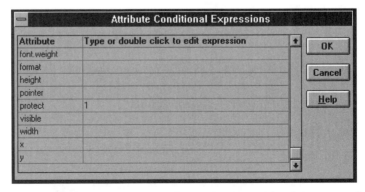

Figure 5-6: Set the protect attributes document_id and document_date to 1.

7. Save the DataWindow by closing the DataWindow painter and name it d_ole_legal_pad.

To test the DataWindow:

1. Place a DataWindow control on a test window and assign d_ole_legal_pad as its DataWindow Object.

2. Run the test window. It should appear similar to Figure 5-7.

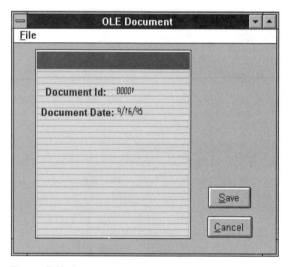

Figure 5-7: A test window with a DataWindow OLE container for Word documents.

3. In the Constructor event of the DataWindow control, type **this.settransobject(SQLCA)**.

4. In the Open event of the window type **dw_1.InsertRow(0)**.

5. Double-click on the open area of the "legal pad," and the OLE server application (Word) will be invoked with our legal pad as the container, as shown in Figure 5-8. Notice that the size of the document is the same as our legal pad.

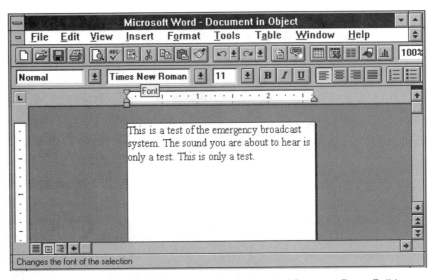

Figure 5-8: Word as an OLE server application invoked from our PowerBuilder application.

Notice that Word's regular File menu changes to accommodate its OLE server status (see Figure 5-9). There's now an Update entry, which will update the document in the DataWindow. (You have to code another mechanism in the PowerBuilder application to save the updated document back to the database.)

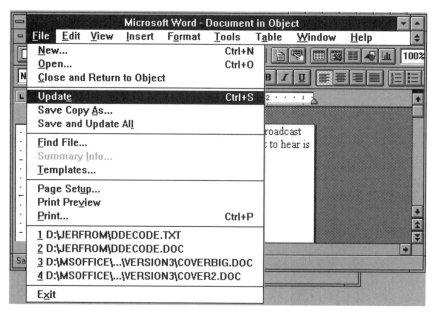

Figure 5-9: The regular Word file menu changes when Word becomes an OLE server.

In this example, the user double-clicks on the OLE container to invoke the OLE server. But you can invoke the server using PowerScript as well. This way the user will not have to "know" to double-click. The OLEActivate() function enables the developer to invoke the OLE server without the user having to double-click on the OLE container (in this case, the DataWindow). It takes three arguments:

❑ The row number of the DataWindow, to indicate which record the OLE server will load.

❑ The column name of the blob column.

❑ An OLE server verb.

The verb is usually an integer that corresponds to an action the server will perform. The values and actions vary by OLE server application. For Word, 0 is the Edit verb, which indicates that we'll open Word to edit the OLE document. Each OLE-compliant application will have information on the verbs it supports in its documentation.

Add the OLEActivate() function to our sample DataWindow as follows:

1. Add a user-defined event to the DataWindow control in the test window. Name the user event ue_ole_activation. In the ue_ole_activation script, type the following:

   ```
   this.oleactivate( this.getrow(), &
                     "ole_word_document", 0 )
   ```

2. Add a CommandButton to the test window and change its text to **Word**. In its Clicked event, type the following:

   ```
   dw_1.triggerevent( "ue_ole_activation" )
   ```

3. Save the changes and run the test window again. This time, click the CommandButton labeled Word, instead of double-clicking on the legal pad. Word will run as an OLE server, just as before.

Although PowerBuilder now supports OLE 2.0, there are still plenty of opportunities to use OLE 1.0. Many software applications are still only OLE 1.0–compliant. We can code OLE 2.0 containers that use offsite activation, which will look and act very much like OLE 1.0 applications.

Working With OLE 2.0

OLE 2.0 is backward-compatible to OLE 1.0.

The OLE 2.0 specification provides a number of new features over 1.0. (OLE 2.0 remains 100 percent backward-compatible to the OLE 1.0 specification, however. OLE 1.0 is now a subset of OLE 2.0. So documents created with OLE 1.0–compliant applications will work without modification with programs that are OLE 2.0–compliant.) Following are some of the features new to OLE 2.0:

❑ *In-place editing.* We've briefly discussed in-place activation. This area includes in addition to in-place editing the complementary features of in-place re-cording and playing (such as audio or video documents) and in-place displaying of documents.

❑ *Drag-and-drop.* This feature is common to a number of visual development environments. Applications can be developed to allow the dragging of objects with a mouse to other destinations, such as other applications' windows or objects, or to different objects within the same application and then dropped inside that destination.

❑ *OLE automation.* OLE automation allows for commands in server applications to be invoked from within the container applications in order to manipulate the OLE document(s). (We'll discuss how to implement this feature within PowerBuilder later in this chapter.)

❑ *Object conversion.* This feature enables an object created with one vendor's server application to be converted and accessed by another vendor's server application. For example, if we embed a Word document in a PowerBuilder container object, we could convert that embedded document to WordPerfect format.

❑ *Component object model.* This is the feature that allows for the existence of compound document types.

❑ *Memory management.* OLE 1.0 documents were forced to load the entire object into memory all at once if the object was used. The OLE 2.0 specification allows for incremental swapping of an object from disk to memory and vice versa.

PowerBuilder provides a new control in version 4.0 to take advantage of OLE 2.0 features. This OLE 2.0 control is available in the Window painter along with the other controls on the PainterBar. In this section, we'll look at using an OLE 2.0 control, accessing OLE 2.0 controls from PowerScript, including OLE automation, and using storages and streams.

Using an OLE 2.0 Control

OLE 2.0 controls are actually quite simple to get up and running. The first thing we'll do is create a basic OLE 2.0 test window:

1. Create a test menu with one menu entry, &File, and under File, create the single entry E&xit. In the Clicked script for Exit, type the following:

   ```
   parentwindow.triggerevent( "close" )
   ```

2. Save the menu as m_test.

3. Create a new test window in the Window painter and assign m_test as this window's menu. In the Close event for the window, add the following code:

   ```
   close( this )
   ```

4. From the Controls menu, select OLE 2.0 control and click on the window area. The Insert Object dialog will appear. This dialog is used to specify the document to embed or link into our OLE 2.0 control. There are options for either creating a new OLE object or

A new object is always embedded into an OLE 2.0 control—it cannot be linked.

using an existing file as a template. When you select New, the object must be embedded into the OLE 2.0 control. When you select Create from File, you can choose between linking or embedding.

5. Select the Create New radio button. The Object Type listbox will appear.

6. From the Object Type listbox, select Microsoft Word 6.0 Document.

7. Click OK. The OLE server application (in this case, Word) will be invoked in order to enable you to create a document to embed.

8. What you type in the document at this point will be the value that becomes stored in the PowerBuilder PBL. Whatever you type in will not change in the PowerBuilder object unless you revisit this process. Think of this value as a representation of the document. For now, just type the following: **Word OLE Document**.

9. Select Update from Word's File menu and then close Word. The value you typed in the Word document now appears in the OLE 2.0 control in the PowerBuilder window.

That's it for a basic use of an OLE 2.0 control! Now you can run an application with the test window. When you double-click on the OLE 2.0 control, Word will be invoked.

Notice that Word runs inside our PowerBuilder test window and the menus for Word merge with our window's menu. This is a default behavior that is an example of in-place activation. PowerBuilder determines based on the server application's capabilities whether to attempt to activate in place or offsite. We can demonstrate how the same procedures can lead to offsite activation by using a different server application:

1. Open the same test window in the Window painter.

2. Right-click on the OLE 2.0 object that currently contains embedded Word data. From the popup menu, select Object, and then select Insert. The Insert Object dialog appears.

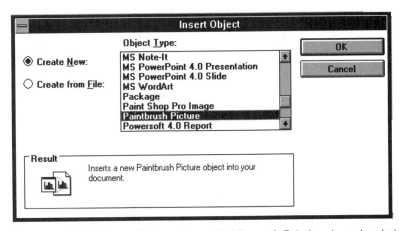

Figure 5-10: The Insert Object dialog with Microsoft Paintbrush as the choice for server application.

3. The Insert Object dialog enables us to change the OLE object type. From the drop-down listbox, select Paintbrush Picture and click OK.

4. Paintbrush will open. Draw a picture in Paintbrush, and then select Update from the File menu. Close Paintbrush. Just as the Word document did, the Paintbrush object we just drew becomes embedded into the OLE 2.0 object of our PowerBuilder window.

5. Close the Window painter and save the changes to the test window.

Now run the application to test the changes we made. The window opens with the Paintbrush object in the test window. When you double-click on the OLE 2.0 Paintbrush object,

Paintbrush will open as an offsite application with our OLE 2.0 document loaded into it. We used the very same container as in the Word example, but this OLE server application opens differently. This behavior is an example of how PowerBuilder determines, based on the server's capability, how to attempt to activate the server. Paintbrush is only capable of supporting OLE 1.0 features, and since OLE 1.0 servers cannot process OLE documents in place, the server application (Paintbrush) for our OLE 2.0 object is opened offsite.

There are some additional options we can use to further control our OLE 2.0 document. Double-click on the OLE 2.0 control in the Window painter and the dialog shown in Figure 5-11 will appear.

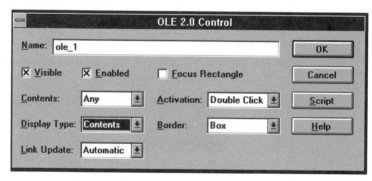

Figure 5-11: The OLE 2.0 Control dialog.

The selections you see at this point are the defaults for the various OLE 2.0 control options. The Contents drop-down listbox allows you to select Embed, Link, or Any. Any is the default and indicates that both embedding and linking are allowed.

Display Type determines whether to use the server application's icon or the embedded document as the indicator for the OLE object.

Link Update is an option available only when linking. It's used to handle broken connections. If you select Automatic, PowerBuilder will try to reconnect the OLE container with the server application. If you choose Manual, PowerBuilder will leave the connection broken. You'd have to write code to reconnect.

The Activation drop-down listbox is used to control how the user invokes (activates) the server application. The default, Double Click, enables the user to double-click on the OLE 2.0 control (or icon, depending on the Display Type choice) to activate the server application. Choosing Manual requires the activation to be coded by the developer.

The Get Focus option activates the server application when the OLE 2.0 control is tabbed to or clicked upon. Be careful with this option. If the activation for an OLE 2.0 control is set to offsite, either manually by the developer or because the server application cannot support in-place activation, then selecting Get Focus will cause a nice little loop. The offsite server application opens, the user edits the document and closes the server application. Control is then returned to the OLE 2.0 control in the PowerBuilder window and the server application is activated again. Loop! The solution is to add a line to the GetFocus event of the OLE 2.0 control to set the focus to another object. The OLE server application will still activate when the OLE 2.0 control is tabbed to, then the script in the GetFocus event of the OLE 2.0 control will run, setting control to something else. For example, if we have a CommandButton on the test window named cb_close, we can type the following code in the GetFocus event of the OLE 2.0 control:

```
cb_close.setfocus()
```

Using Get Focus can create a loop.

Accessing OLE 2.0 Controls From PowerScript

In the previous section we mentioned that if you choose Manual as the Activation choice in the OLE 2.0 Control dialog, you have to code for the activation yourself. Let's look at how this is done:

1. Open our test window in the Window painter.
2. Add a new CommandButton and name it cb_activate. Set its text attribute to &Activate.
3. Add a new user-defined event for the OLE 2.0 control and call it ue_self_activate. In the ue_self_activate event, type the following:
   ```
   this.activate( OffSite! )
   this.doverb( 0 )
   ```
4. In the Clicked event for cb_activate, type the following:
   ```
   ole_1.triggerevent( "ue_self_activate" )
   ```
5. Double-click on the OLE 2.0 control and change its Activation choice to Manual.
6. Save the test window and run the application. When you click the &Activate CommandButton, the OLE server will invoke as it did previously when you double-clicked on the OLE control.

Step 3 in the above example uses two functions that PowerBuilder provides for manipulating OLE objects in scripts. The Activate() function invokes the server application for the OLE 2.0 container and activates the server application based on the argument passed to Activate(). The choices for arguments are OffSite! and InPlace! (Note that an OLE 1.0 server application will still open offsite, even if you pass the InPlace! argument.) The DoVerb() function invokes the integer value representing the server application verb. In this example, 0 indicates Edit.

Following are additional functions that PowerBuilder provides for manipulating OLE objects inside OLE controls:

- InsertObject()
- InsertClass()
- InsertFile()
- LinkTo()
- Open()

Let's look at the InsertFile() function. It's used to embed an object from an external file into the OLE 2.0 control. It takes one argument: the full path to a file to be inserted into the OLE 2.0 control. The function returns a 0 when successful, −1 when the file is not found, and −9 when another error occurs. Consider the following example:

1. Create a file in Paintbrush and save it as C:\OLE.BMP.

2. Open our test window in the Window painter.

3. Add a new CommandButton to the window named cb_ole and change its text to Change&OLE.

4. In the Clicked event for cb_ole, type the following:

```
if ole_1.insertfile( "c:\ole.bmp" ) <> 0 then
    messagebox( "OLE InsertFile", &
        "An error occurred when trying to " + &
        "insert the OLE object" )
end if
```

OLE Automation

With OLE 2.0, the concept of *automation* was introduced. OLE automation is the procedure of coding PowerScript to use commands available within the OLE server application to manipulate the OLE document.

Each server application has its own set of commands for automating functionality to manipulate documents. These commands can be invoked from PowerBuilder and used in conjunction with PowerScript. You cannot create server application variables or use server-side flow control statements from within PowerBuilder. As a result, you use PowerScript statements for flow control and then call the server application commands for manipulating the document.

In our example we'll use OLE automation to manipulate an Excel document inside the Excel server application. The OLE 2.0 control, when activated, will open Excel, and then our automation will create a calendar for the current month inside the spreadsheet in Excel. It will also change the color for the current day to red. Modify our test window as follows:

1. Open your test window in the Window painter.

2. Right-click on the OLE 2.0 control, and select Object and then Insert from the popup menu. The Insert Object dialog will appear.

3. Select Microsoft Excel 5.0 Worksheet from the drop-down listbox and click OK. Excel will open to edit the embedded document.

4. Type the letters **A**, **B**, **C** and **D** in cells A1, A2, A3 and A4, respectively.

5. Close Excel to update the OLE container in our PowerBuilder window.

6. In the ue_self_activate event, replace the old code with the following:

```
//
// This script activates the attached OLE 2.0 object
// (Excel document) and uses OLE Automation to create a
// calendar in the spreadsheet for the
// current month.  The calendar is created in the
// spreadsheet inside the OLE server application.
//

//
// Declare variables and constants
//

string ls_this_month, ls_week, lsa_months[12]

int li_week, li_this_month, lia_max_days[12], &
    li_max_this_month, li_constant=1

lia_max_days[] = &
    {31, 28, 31, 30, 31, 30, 31, 31, 30, 31, 30, 31 }

lsa_months[1]  = "January"
lsa_months[2]  = "February"
lsa_months[3]  = "March"
lsa_months[4]  = "April"
lsa_months[5]  = "May"
lsa_months[6]  = "June"
lsa_months[7]  = "July"
lsa_months[8]  = "August"
lsa_months[9]  = "September"
lsa_months[10] = "October"
lsa_months[11] = "November"
lsa_months[12] = "December"

// Determine the integer (1-12) indicating current month
li_this_month = month( today() )

// Use the current month integer to extract the
// corresponding month name
ls_this_month = lsa_months[li_this_month]
```

```
// Use the current month integer to extract the total days
// in this month
li_max_this_month = lia_max_days[li_this_month]

//
// Begin activation
//

this.activate( InPlace! )

//
// Create the template for the month
//

this.object.cells(1,1).value = ls_this_month
this.object.cells(1,2).value = ""
this.object.cells(1,3).value = ""
this.object.cells(1,4).value = ""
this.object.cells(2,1).value = ""
this.object.cells(2,2).value = "Sunday"
this.object.cells(2,3).value = "Monday"
this.object.cells(2,4).value = "Tuesday"
this.object.cells(2,5).value = "Wednesday"
this.object.cells(2,6).value = "Thursday"
this.object.cells(2,7).value = "Friday"
this.object.cells(2,8).value = "Saturday"

For li_week = 3 to 7
    ls_week = "Week " + string( li_week - 2)
    this.object.cells( li_week, 1).value = ls_week
next

//
// Start filling the calendar for the current month
//

// Determine the day of the week (1-7) for the first day of
// this month
int li_day_of_first
li_day_of_first = daynumber(date(string(li_this_month)+ &
```

```
                      "-1-" + string(year(today())))))

        int li_row, li_col=0, li_col1, li_col2

        for li_row = 1 to 5    // Loop once for each week
            if li_row = 1 then
                for li_col = li_day_of_first to 7  //Loop for each
                                                   //day
                    li_col1 = li_col1 + 1
                    this.object.cells(3, li_col + 1).value = li_col1

                    // Set the current date to red
                    if li_col1 = day(today()) then
                        this.object.cells(3, li_col+1).font.color = &
                        rgb(255,0,0)
                    end if
                next
            else
                for li_col2 = 1 to 7   // Loop for each day
                    li_col1 = li_col1 + 1
                    if li_col1 <= li_max_this_month then
                        this.object.cells(li_row + 2, &
                          li_col2 + 1).value = li_col1
                    end if

                    // Set the current date to red
                    if li_col1 = day(today()) then
                        this.object.cells(li_row + 2, &
                           li_col2 + 1).font.color = rgb(255,0,0)
                    end if
                next
            end if
        next
```

7. Save the test window and run the application. When you click the &Activate CommandButton, Excel will open with a calendar in the document.

In this code we take advantage of the Visual Basic language contained in Excel. Each of the Excel commands must be called as a function from PowerBuilder. For example, the calls to the Cells() function invoke the Visual Basic Cells command inside Excel. Check the documentation for each server application you use to determine what commands are available.

Storages & Streams

Using storages and streams enables the developer to take more control of OLE applications. Storages and streams are analogous to the OLE containers and OLE documents we've previously discussed. You create storages as containers for OLE objects. The OLE objects themselves are stored in streams, and the streams are stored in storages. We can save OLE information, both document and container information, as operating system files, as an alternative to storing OLE documents in a database. The mechanism for managing OLE storages and streams on disk is different than when coding for OLE in a PowerBuilder application.

You create the OLE streams from within PowerBuilder. OLE server applications, such as Word and Excel, create OLE files for their own use. You should not access those OLE files from within PowerBuilder. Instead, you load an OLE document into an OLE 2.0 control and then save the document as a PowerBuilder OLE file—a stream. Assume for the following example that we've created a Word document from within Word and saved it as an operating system file called OLE_TEST.DOC. We can create a PowerBuilder OLE storage by replacing the code in the ue_self_activate event of the OLE 2.0 control with the following:

```
this.insertfile( "c:\ole_test.doc" )
this.saveas( "c:\ole_test.stg" )
```

The InsertFile() function will place the Word document into the OLE 2.0 control. Then it is written to disk as a PowerBuilder OLE storage with the SaveAs() function.

The PowerBuilder datatype OLEStorage is used to create a variable for holding storages for the purpose of manipulation with PowerScript. In the following example, we'll retrieve our OLE storage file into an OLEStorage variable:

```
OLEStorage lo_local_storage
lo_local_storage = create OLEStorage
lo_local_storage.open( "c:\ole_test.stg" )
```

We can now retrieve an OLE document into the storage that we've created inside our PowerBuilder application. Consider the following code for retrieving the OLE document:

```
// inserts the OLE document into the OLE
// 2.0 control
ole_1.insertfile( "ole_test.doc" )

// saves the OLE document from the OLE control
// to our storage
ole_1.saveas( lo_local_storage, "ole_test.doc" )

// closes our OLE storage variable and returns
// control of the memory back to the operating
// system
lo_local_storage.close()
```

This code is a small example of the ways in which we can manipulate with PowerScript the same kinds of OLE objects that we manipulated earlier within the OLE 2.0 control.

DDE DEFINED

Dynamic Data Exchange, or DDE, allows for the sharing of data between applications. It was the predecessor to OLE 1.0 and has many features of OLE 1.0 in terms of data-sharing, but not embedding. With DDE, both the server and the client applications must be running beforehand in order to share data. The server application cannot be invoked from within the document. The server application can, however, be invoked from within the PowerBuilder application.

Note that we used the term *client* instead of container. There's no notion of embedding in DDE, so there is really no containership. The application making the request for shared data from another application is considered the client application. The application servicing the client's request for data by sharing its data with the client application is known as the server application. PowerBuilder provides for developing applications that are either DDE clients or DDE servers.

Vendor support is focusing away from DDE toward OLE. Regardless, DDE still provides great benefits. Once the channel (the connection between DDE client and DDE server) has been established, the two applications can continue to run, saving overhead of application startup.

USING DDE IN POWERBUILDER

To enable you to use DDE from within a PowerBuilder application, PowerBuilder provides a number of DDE-specific functions. The PowerBuilder DDE functions are grouped in the form of DDE client functions and DDE server functions. The DDE client functions are as follows:

- ❏ CloseChannel()
- ❏ ExecRemote()
- ❏ GetDataDDE()

- ❏ GetDataDDEOrigin()
- ❏ GetRemote()
- ❏ OpenChannel()
- ❏ RespondRemote()
- ❏ SetRemote()
- ❏ StartHotLink()
- ❏ StopHotLink()

Following are the PowerBuilder server DDE functions:

- ❏ GetCommandDDE()
- ❏ GetCommandDDEOrigin()
- ❏ GetDataDDE()
- ❏ GetDataDDEOrigin()
- ❏ RespondRemote()
- ❏ SetDataDDE()
- ❏ StartServerDDE()
- ❏ StopServerDDE()

Let's look at an example of DDE that uses Microsoft Excel as a server application to populate a DataWindow in a PowerBuilder client application. The first thing we want to do in our application is test to see whether Excel is available to us. We can make this determination using the FileExists() function.

```
//
// Can we find Excel ?
//
if fileexists("excel.exe") = false then
    messagebox( "Sorry! This process requires" + &
        "Microsoft Excel", "Check that " + &
            "EXCEL.EXE is available and in the " + &
            "current directory or path")
    return
end if
```

The FileExists() function returns either True or False to indicate whether the Excel executable was located. If not, we return out of this script.

If Excel was located, we can then run Excel by calling the PowerBuilder Run() function. The Run() function takes one mandatory argument, the name of the executable, and an optional enumerated datatype argument to indicate the state of the called executable. The enumerated data type choices are as follows:

❏ Maximized!

❏ Minimized!

❏ Normal! (default)

These options indicate to the called executable how to display once up and running. For example, we would continue our script with the following code, which calls Excel and passes a particular spreadsheet (CLASSAGE.XLS) to be opened within Excel:

```
//
// Bring up Excel with normal window size
//
run( "excel classage.xls" )
```

Using the ExecRemote() function, we can invoke commands in the server application to operate on the document. The arguments to ExecRemote() are the command to be executed, the application name and the topic name. The command name is specific to the server application software: Word will have Word-specific commands, Excel will have its own commands, etc. The application name is the name you assigned to the DDE server application. The topic name is an indicator of what area of the application the commands apply to. For Excel, you can address a specific spreadsheet by name, or use the topic "system" to refer to the application itself. In this example, we'll position the DDE server application on the window, size the window and size the spreadsheet to fit the window:

```
execremote( "[APP.MOVE(300,20)]", "Excel", &
         "system" )
execremote( "[APP.SIZE(175, 280)]", "Excel", &
         "system" )
execremote( "[ARRANGE.ALL()]", "Excel", "system" )
```

We can now use the SetRemote() function to place values in a specified location within the DDE server application. The arguments to SetRemote() are a location in a format specific to the application, the value to be placed at the location, the application name and a topic name. For Excel, the location is in the format r#c#, where # is a number corresponding to either the row (r) or the column (c). For example, r3c4 is row three, column four of the spreadsheet. In the following example, we'll set the column headings in row one for our spreadsheet server application:

```
setremote( "r1c1", "Class Name", "Excel", &
         "classage.xls" )
setremote( "r1c2", "Year", "Excel", &
         "classage.xls" )
setremote( "r1c3", "18-25", "Excel", &
         "classage.xls" )
setremote( "r1c4", "26-33", "Excel", &
         "classage.xls" )
setremote( "r1c5", "34-41", "Excel", &
         "classage.xls" )
setremote( "r1c6", "42-49", "Excel", &
         "classage.xls" )
setremote( "r1c7", "49-56", "Excel", &
         "classage.xls" )
setremote( "r1c8", "57+", "Excel", &
         "classage.xls" )
```

Assume we have a tabular DataWindow in our application that's formatted like our spreadsheet. We can loop through the rows and columns of our DataWindow and set the value in the corresponding cells of the DDE server spreadsheet to place the DDE client and DDE server in sync. The following code demonstrates this synchronization:

```
string  ls_cell, &
            ls_cell_row, &
            ls_cell_col, &
            ls_current_value,&
            ls_current_string_value

int     li_current_value, &
            li_row=1, &
            li_erow=2, &
            li_ecol=1

decimal{2} ld_pct_decimal

// Loop through rows of datawindow and assign
// values in the array qty. This algorithm is
// limited by upper bound of qty array.

do while li_row <= dw_1.RowCount( )
   do while li_ecol < 9
      if li_ecol = 1 then
          ls_current_string_value = &
             dw_1.GetItemString(li_row, li_ecol)
          ls_cell_row = "r" + String(li_erow)
          ls_cell_col = "c" + String(li_ecol)
          ls_cell = ls_cell_row + ls_cell_col
          SetRemote(ls_cell, &
             ls_current_string_value, &
             "Excel","classage.xls")
          li_ecol = li_ecol + 1
      else
          ls_cell_row = "r" + String(li_erow)
          ls_cell_col = "c" + String(li_ecol)
```

```
                ls_cell = ls_cell_row + ls_cell_col
                ld_pct_decimal = &
                    dw_1.GetItemDecimal(li_row, &
                        li_ecol)
                SetRemote(ls_cell, &
                    string(ld_pct_decimal), &
                    "Excel", "classage.xls")
                li_ecol = li_ecol + 1
        end if
    loop
    li_ecol = 1
    li_erow = li_erow + 1
    li_row = li_row + 1
loop
```

Once the DDE client (our PowerBuilder application) and the DDE server (Excel) are in sync, we can keep them in sync using the StartHotLink() function, which triggers the HotLinkAlarm event in the client. In the HotLinkAlarm event, you won't have to traverse all rows and columns as we did to get them in sync. You can call the GetDataDDE() function to obtain only the data that changed and then update the DataWindow. If you have more than one spreadsheet or more than one server application running, you can call GetDataDDEOrigin() to determine in which application the change occurred. (The two GetData... functions assume that a hotlink has been established.)

MOVING ON

In this chapter, we looked at OLE objects and at mechanisms for manipulating them within our PowerBuilder application. We also looked at DDE, which, while older and less sophisticated than the OLE specification, is still a useful tool in those situations where its capabilities are all that an application requires.

Up to this point in the book, we've focused on how to perform certain tasks in PowerBuilder. We haven't concerned ourselves with control and access to the objects we've manipulated. In the next chapter, we'll discuss security and various ways to access both data and controls in our application.

Chapter 6

Security

Mention the topic of security and you will wreak havoc in the minds of application developers! As client-server development becomes more widespread, security takes on greater importance and even greater complexity. In the days of mainframes, security was certainly important, but it was more easily achievable. Users could log in only through a common interface, which usually included a security package such as Top Secret or RACF. If they didn't get past the security package, they couldn't log in to the mainframe; there was no way around it. With mainframes, the single point of entry enables security to be implemented at that point. With today's "open" systems and client-server architecture, however, the number of variables relating to security has increased significantly.

The days of having a single point of entry into a system are gone. The two-tier client-server architecture has application programs and logic on one machine and a database on another machine, connected by a network. All of these elements—network, database and application—are variables in terms of points of entry to the data in the system. With a two-tier client-server architecture, the database, the network and the application programs all can be accessed directly. Each point of access exposes data to vulnerabilities. In addition, there is exposure to damage—for example, flooding a network, corrupting a database, deleting all or part of application programs. Complicating the issue further, there is significant work being done to move toward a *three*-tier client-server architecture, where the database or data layer is separated from the business rules, or logic, layer, which is separated from the presentation layer. These three elements are connected by a network, effectively doubling the number of variables, and therefore further increasing the system's vulnerability. In both the two- and three-tier client-server architectures, there are at least three categories of security involved, with varying degrees (or levels) of security within the categories. In general, the categories are as follows:

❒ Network security
❒ Database security
❒ Application security

These categories indicate the areas in which there is potential exposure. As a result, these are the areas where security must be applied. What must be secured? The bottom line is that the data must be protected. Data are the assets of an organization. An organization doesn't want its capital equipment to be pilfered. In the same way, it doesn't want its data stolen. And in addition to safeguards against data theft, there must be safeguards against damage. The most secure and robust solution is to provide security at all three levels—the network, the database and the application. In this chapter, we'll look at each of these security categories.

NETWORK SECURITY

A network is probably the most difficult area to protect. As client-server implementations grow, the number of network exposures grows. If an organization has wide-area networks installed, the exposure is magnified. For example, cellular, microwave and satellite links in the wide-area network permit anyone with similar equipment to pick up the signals being transmitted. With the proliferation and recent explosion of the Internet, having your site connected exposes your communications to the weakest links on the Internet. You have little control over those weak links because the Internet is so vast. Even with no Internet connectivity, there are still exposures to individuals conducting *packet sniffing*. Packet sniffers are software programs that can pick up communications in transit over networks in their binary state (packets) and decipher them. Thus, someone with a packet sniffer could "listen in" to telecommunications of your network interactions, and any sensitive corporate data the interactions contained could find itself in the hands of those doing the sniffing.

There are continuing efforts toward solving the issues of network security. Most recently, there has been a resurgence in encryption and authentication. The idea is that encrypted data becomes theoretically indecipherable by an outsider, so it really wouldn't matter much if someone got at the packets—they couldn't understand or decipher them anyway. There are public-key and private-key protection schemes for the encryption and dissemination of data. A key pair is purchased from a certification agency, such as RSA. The public and private keys are mathematical algorithms that use prime factors of extremely large numbers. When you want to send encrypted data to someone, you get his or her public key and encrypt the data with it. When you send the data to the destination, the recipient uses his or her private key to decrypt the message. You distribute your public key to anyone you choose to receive protected data from. You give your private key to no one. It's used only to decrypt data that has been encrypted with the corresponding public key.

A Security Benefit

Not all network security issues are liabilities; networks can also help *enforce* security for your applications. Instead of loading PowerBuilder applications on individual workstations, you can store them on a network drive and reference them from the desktop machine. In this configuration, the security privileges within the network can be set to allow only the appropriate users to get to the application executables. Thus, if users do not have a valid network ID or proper permissions in the network, they cannot run the application.

Another network security concern is the point of entry into networks—that is, logging in to networks. For example, NetWare from Novell recently changed with its new version 4.0 to log individuals in to "trees" of trusted servers. The servers are designated to be "trusted" by the central server. An individual logs in to the central server, which automatically connects him or her to the other trusted servers. Effectively, you log in to the network and not the server.

While an exhaustive discussion of network and telecommunications security is well beyond the scope of this book, this section has provided a thumbnail sketch of some of the issues surrounding network security. We introduced these issues here to make you aware of them and at least get you started in thinking about them. Network security is a critical factor in the overall security scheme of your client-server implementations. Even if a PowerBuilder application has a pretty good security implementation and there is tight security on the database, if the network is exposed, then data is exposed.

DATABASE SECURITY

Protecting data at the database is mandatory in client-server implementations, because that's where data is stored. When we talk about databases, we're referring to relational database management systems (RDBMSes). They are used in the majority of client-server applications, so we'll focus on them. (Other systems, such as imaging databases, OO databases, geographical imaging systems, etc., are growing in market penetration, however.) RDBMS vendors such as Oracle, Sybase and IBM do an excellent job of providing security with their respective products. The ANSI SQL standard provides for permissions such that data can be protected down to specific columns and/or rows in a table for client-server applications that use RDBMSes. RDBMS products typically provide augmented SQL functions that enhance this level of security, but in general, you can use SQL to define security by creating predefined views of the data, establishing user privileges, creating stored procedures and regulating login access.

Using Views for Security

One way to provide security is to create predefined views of the data and allow users to access only the view that they need to see. For example, suppose you have a requirement to provide student information in an application, but some of the information, such as ethnic background, is sensitive and should be accessed only by supervisors. A view could be created to show only the columns that were not as sensitive—name, address, etc. Although a table would hold all of the columns of information, including the ethnicity information, the view is the database mechanism to show only those columns that you choose. So our PowerBuilder application could access the view for nonsupervisors and access the table directly for supervisors. Without knowing about the database mechanism of views, this would require considerably more programming effort on the application side and leave the exposure at the database level, assuming you left the table open and programmed around the ethnicity code with your application. PowerBuilder can interact with a view as if it were a table.

For another example, suppose that all of the columns in a table were allowed to be seen by users, but certain rows (or records) of data were limited to those users who created them. This occurs frequently in accounting systems where departmental users can see only the general ledger transactions for their department. We could use a view again, but in a different way. Many of the larger-scale databases provide proprietary functions to get the login ID of the connected user at run-time. So if you store a table that cross-references login IDs with department codes, you can create a dynamic view, as follows. (*Note:* Watcom SQL does not provide a function such as username(). This code is generic to demonstrate the point. The syntax will vary from vendor to vendor.)

```
CREATE VIEW dept_gl_view
AS
SELECT gl_col1, gl_col2, gl_col3, etc.
FROM      general_ledger_table, cross_ref_table
WHERE  general_ledger.dept_code =
          cross_ref_table.dept_code
AND    cross_ref_table.user_id = username()
```

In our PowerBuilder application, we can then create a DataWindow that contains the following SQL:

```
select * from dept_gl_view
```

The result set from this query will provide only the rows for our user. This assumes that we connect the application to the database with a login ID that is stored in cross_ref_table. You could certainly program this row restriction into an application, but the same issues apply as with the columnar view. The users could go around your application and get at all the data if the security existed only in the application.

SQL Privileges

The SQL language provides the keywords GRANT and REVOKE to add or remove privileges to users, groups of users and aliased users. The privileges allow or disallow access to whole databases, tables, views, stored procedures, rows and columns. SQL privileges can be granted or revoked on the following SQL keywords:

- ❏ SELECT
- ❏ INSERT
- ❏ UPDATE
- ❏ DELETE
- ❏ EXECUTE
- ❏ ALL

The first four keywords apply to tables and views. EXECUTE applies to stored procedures, for those databases that support them. ALL applies to SELECT, INSERT, UPDATE, DELETE and EXECUTE.

Assume you want to define database security so that users can see the data, but none can modify it. In that case, you would do the following:

```
REVOKE ALL ON <table|view> FROM <login_ID>

GRANT SELECT ON <table|view> TO <login_ID>
```

Most logical combinations are possible. You could enable a user to create rows but not update or delete them, as in accounting transactions. In this case, you would type this:

```
GRANT INSERT ON <table|view> TO <login_ID>
```

Stored Procedures

Stored procedures, for those databases that support them, are very powerful in terms of applying security. Stored procedures are SQL transactions stored in a binary state inside the database. (SQL that is not a stored procedure is interpreted and stored with the application.)

One of the advantages of using stored procedures as a security layer is that the user must explicitly be granted rights to execute the stored procedure. This is useful if you want to limit the view of certain data in a specific format. To accomplish this, remove all user rights from the sensitive table and grant users rights to the stored procedure. Users can then view the data only through the stored procedure. We'll discuss the use of stored procedures in complete detail in Chapter 7, but for now, let's look at how we can use them with regard to security.

We can create a stored procedure called sp_login(), for example, and use it to verify login IDs that are stored in security tables in a database. The sp_login() stored procedure would take two arguments: the login ID and password of the individual logging in. It would then verify the two arguments against the values in the security tables and return a value indicating whether the login was successful. The syntax for the stored procedure might look like this:

```
CREATE PROCEDURE sp_login( IN login_id VARCHAR(7),
        IN pass_word VARCHAR( 11 ) )
BEGIN
   DECLARE local_password VARCHAR( 11 ) ;

   SELECT password INTO local_password
   WHERE login = login_id ;

   IF local_password = password THEN
       RETURN 0
   ELSE
       RETURN -1
   END IF ;
END
```

The application would prompt the user for a login and password, then call the stored procedure passing the entered values as arguments. The application would then check the return code and proceed accordingly.

There are a number of benefits to using a stored procedure in this way. We're taking a more object-oriented approach, in that we have only one copy of the code used to verify login IDs. If there is maintenance to be done on the login procedure, it needs to be done in only one place—the stored procedure. If the structure of the security tables changes, it will not affect the applications, since they're only calling a stored procedure and not accessing the tables directly. From a security perspective, the stored procedure is the only entity that requires access to the security tables. The application developers and the application require access to only the stored procedure, not the underlying tables. By narrowing access to the security tables, the DBAs maintain control over them.

Advanced Login Security

Storing database login IDs and passwords in tables is somewhat of a duplication of effort. The database or server already requires some type of login ID and password in order to get to the server at all. By creating login data and storing it in tables, we're not taking advantage of the security already supplied with the server. There's a reason for this. A stored procedure would have to query the system tables (or catalog) and retrieve the login and password values and then compare those values to arguments. The server passwords stored in system tables are stored in their encrypted format. So, the viability of a stored procedure that queries system tables instead of user tables would depend on whether the database vendor provided the encryption algorithm.

There may be occasion in large installations that users acting as security officers will maintain application security for their own department, division, etc. In this situation, DBAs would most likely prefer that users not have the ability to modify database accesses. Also, there would probably be an application built enabling the security officers to perform the user maintenance. The security application would then access the rows in security tables, rather than modify the server logins.

Another approach is to create only an application login ID in the server. The application would prompt the end user for a login and password, then log in to the database server with the application login ID. Once connected, the application would either pass the user's login and password to the sp_login() stored procedure or query the system tables directly and verify the user. If the permissions are limited to an application login ID, then users cannot go around the application and get to the database.

The benefit of this configuration is that the number of database server IDs is kept small and manageable—one per application. There's a potential exposure, however, in distributing the application login ID and password with each application. Even if encrypted, the embedded login ID and password could be derived by reverse-engineering or disassembling the application. Do not misunderstand. These security tactics are not bulletproof—they are additional layers to deter the would-be infiltrator.

Using login IDs either at the database level or as rows in security tables gives us the flexibility to actually keep different login IDs for a given user for different purposes. Perhaps users need to query data once it's entered into a transactional application. If so, another way to apply security is to provide two login IDs per user, one with only SELECT privileges and another with INSERT, UPDATE and/or DELETE privileges. The login ID with update capabilities is created as an encrypted, scrambled, modified or otherwise changed version of the read-only login ID. The password is encrypted in the same way. Users log in to the application with what they think is the only ID they have. The application then encrypts their entry to match the update-capable login ID and logs in to the database server with the encrypted ID. Should a user go around this application with a query tool and log in with his or her same login ID, the query tool would not do any encryption. The user is effectively logging in with the read-only ID. Many third-party query tools and development tools enable users to retrieve a list of user names, so this is not going to fool them for long. However, since the passwords are encrypted with the application, it still prevents their logging in with an update-capable login ID.

APPLICATION SECURITY

Up to this point, we've talked about providing security at the network level and the database level, but PowerBuilder, being a client application development environment, provides numerous methods for applying security from within the application. We'll take a look at some of these methods now.

Suppose we allow a user to enter data into the application, then click the appropriate button to send the transaction to the database. If we try to ascertain the database connection at the time the user dispatches the transaction, we could have some frustrated users. They'll spend the time to enter the data and then find out via a message back from the database that they don't have proper privileges. A better approach would be to design the application to pick up the security privileges at the time they start the application. We could then display the controls and windows within the application according to their privileges (or choose not to display controls and windows, according to privileges).

Suppose, as in our earlier example, we have a sensitive data element, such as an ethnicity indicator in our student registration application. Only supervisors are allowed to view or change the indicator. We could acquire the privilege level of the user as the application is loading and store that value or values in volatile memory inside the application. Since we would have the value as the application starts, if the user is a supervisor we could then display one SingleLineEdit or DataWindow object that contains the ethnicity code. If it wasn't a supervisor logging in, we would not show the SingleLineEdit or DataWindow with the ethnicity code.

. . . .

Get Rid of That Gray-Out

We once worked on an application that required certain users to have retrieve capability within the application, but not delete or modify capability. In that situation, we placed similar code in the Constructor event of Update and Delete CommandButtons. The capability for deleting and updating simply did not exist for the users without the proper level. A general note on GUI design is that it's better to not display an object such as a CommandButton if the user will never be able to use it, as opposed to displaying it and having it eternally grayed out.

. . . .

The Constructor events work perfectly for this type of application behavior. For simplicity, assume we obtain the security level for the user in the application object and place its value in a global string variable called gs_security_level. The security level for supervisors is an arbitrary value of 40. We could have the following code in the Constructor event of a SingleLineEdit control that is supposed to display the ethnicity code:

```
if gs_security_level >= "40" then
    this.show()
else
    this.hide()
end if
```

This code will work in any PowerBuilder control with a Constructor event. The example is a little simple in design—we typically store the values to be compared (the value 40, in this case) in a table as well. We could then load the security-level values for all the relevant PowerBuilder controls at application startup, along with the security level of the user. Also, we use variables instead of hard-coded values when comparing for security level. We want to have an internal table loaded inside the application so that we don't have all these hard-coded numbers (30s, 40s, etc.) embedded in controls throughout the application.

Let's demonstrate how the controls would check security as the controls are created in order to determine whether they should be visible. We'll create three security tables to store the appropriate security data for users, controls, classes of controls and classes of users. (In this situation, we refer to a *class* of users or controls as a category or a group—not the OO concept of class.) We'll create a security window that contains one DataWindow. The DataWindow will retrieve the control_controlclass table in full. We'll create a window function for the security window that takes a control name as its argument, then searches the DataWindow and returns the corresponding control class. Then, we'll write the code for the Constructor event of a control to call the security window's function to determine the control's security class. The control will compare its class to the class of the current user (which is obtained separately) and determine whether it should be visible.

Security Tables

The three security tables in our database are shown in Figure 6-1.

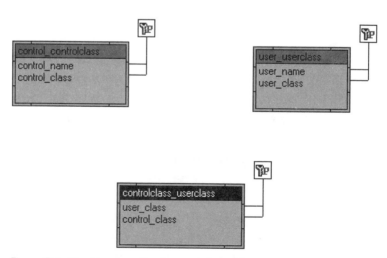

Figure 6-1: Our three application security tables.

Our first table, user_userclass, is defined as follows (see its declaration in Figure 6-2):

```
create table user_userclass
(   user_name varchar( 7 ) not null,
    user_class char( 10 ) not null        )
```

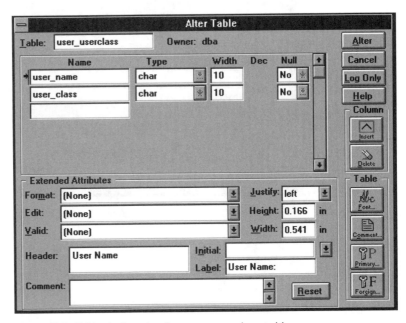

Figure 6-2: Table declaration for user_userclass table.

Here's the definition for the second table, control_controlclass (Figure 6-3 shows its declaration):

```
create table control_controlclass
(   control_name varchar(40) not null,
    control_class char( 10 ) not null )
```

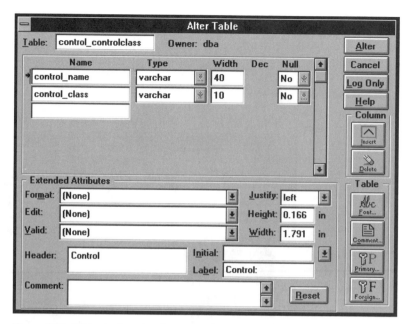

Figure 6-3: Table declaration for control_controlclass table.

And finally, here's the third table, controlclass_userclass:

```
create table controlclass_userclass
(   user_class char( 10 ) not null,
    control_class char( 10 ) not null )
```

Figure 6-4 shows the table declaration for controlclass_userclass.

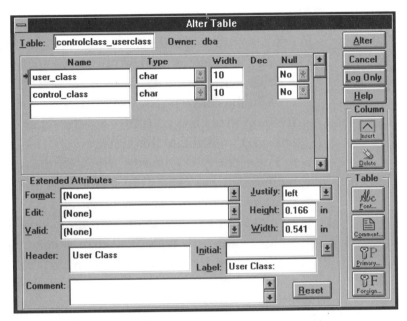

Figure 6-4: Table declaration for controlclass_userclass table.

The tables are used to maintain values that enable the combination of user and user class to be matched with the combination of control and control class. The classes are used to store controls or users in groups. For example, there are probably a number of users who do similar work and therefore have similar security privileges. Data entry clerks, for example, might all have the same privileges. All supervisors might have a common set of privileges that are different than the clerks'. Similarly, all Delete CommandButtons might be considered to have the same security level.

Having classes of users and controls enables the DBAs to make global changes without having to reassign codes to each control or user. For example, if a user with the login ID Jerry was promoted to supervisor from clerk, the DBA would have to change only the class code in Jerry's security record in the user_userclass table to SUPVR from CLERK, and all application privileges would be set. Jerry would now receive the same access as each of the other supervisors without the DBA having to recode any controls. Conversely, if it were decided that clerks should now have authority to delete records, which we'll say is security level 40, then the control class in the controlclass_userclass would simply be changed to 40 for user class CLERK. No other changes would be required to facilitate this change.

The security-level numbering scheme we're using here is deliberately simple for the sake of discussion. You can create your own types of security levels and classes of security levels as appropriate. Also, you may want these security tables to hold this type of security level data for numerous applications. If so, you probably need a column in the control_controlclass table to signify the application.

Security Window

Our security window, w_security, is a regular window of type main. (It will work with an MDI application as well. Although there will be an MDI frame, the MDI frame can still open a window in addition to its typical behavior of opening sheets.) It will contain the DataWindow to retrieve the contents of the controlclass_userclass table. The security window will actually remain hidden from the user in the application. To the developer, it will look like the window shown in Figure 6-5.

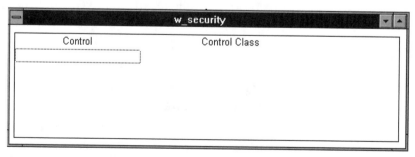

Figure 6-5: View of the hidden application security window, w_security.

We're inheriting the DataWindow from our buo_dw class, created in Chapter 2, so it already has the following function call in its Constructor:

```
this.buof_set_trans( SQLCA )
```

We'll add the following line to the Constructor of our descendant DataWindow to retrieve all rows:

```
this.retrieve()
```

Since the window is hidden, there's no use placing a Close CommandButton on it. Instead, add the following line to the Close event of the window, so that we may trigger the Close event from our application in order to close the security window as the user shuts down the application:

```
close( this )
```

Create a window function called bwf_get_control_class to return the class of a control, based on the class name passed to the function as an argument. Its one argument is datatype string, and it returns a datatype string. Create the window function with the declaration shown in Figure 6-6.

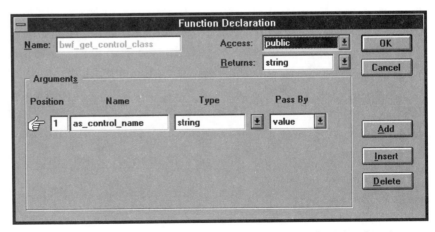

Figure 6-6: Function declaration for bwf_get_control_class() window function.

In the script of the function, add the following:

```
long ll_row_number
string ls_control_class

ll_row_number = &
    dw_security.find( "control_name = '" + &
    as_control_name + "'" , 1, &
    dw_security.rowcount() )

if ll_row_number > 0 then
    ls_control_class = &
        dw_security.getitemstring( ll_row_number, &
        "control_class" )
else
    ls_control_class = "-1"
end if

return ls_control_class
```

Security-Aware Controls

The entries in the control column of the control_controlclass are in the form *windowname.controlname*. For example, assume we have a CommandButton called cb_test on a window called w_test. The entry in the control_controlclass table would be w_test.cb_test. We need to know this so that in each control, we pass the argument in the correct format to the bwf_get_control_class() function. Assuming the same example with cb_test on a window w_test, the following code would go in the Constructor for cb_test:

```
string ls_control_name, ls_control_class

ls_control_name = parent.classname() + "." + &
    this.classname()

ls_control_class = &
    w_security.bwf_get_control_class( ls_control_name )
```

```
if ls_control_class > "30" then
    this.hide()
end if
```

The two local string variables are for holding the control name and control class. We populate ls_control_name by calling the classname() built-in function for the parent and for the current control and concatenating their names with a dot (.). This format causes the value to match the entry in the security table. We call the security window function bwf_get_control_class() and pass it the name of our control as the argument. The function returns the class level for our control, and we store the returned value in ls_control_class. We then compare ls_control_class with the security class level of the user. In this example, it is the value 30. The numbering scheme assumes a hierarchy of security in which the higher the number, the more access allowed. So, if our control's class is greater than that of the user, we hide the control.

In this code, we've hard-coded the value 30 to represent the security class level of the current user. This value would actually be a variable containing the user's security level. The user's security level would be retrieved at application startup, just as the control information was retrieved. We would create an instance variable in the window w_security and create a window function to return the value of that variable to the caller.

We could create a mechanism such as this for checking the security level and build it into each of our control user object classes—buo_dw, buo_sle, buo_cb, etc. The code in the above example would be added to each control user object class in the Constructor event. If we then inherit from each of those control classes instead of PowerBuilder's, we have the security code in place. The only task left is to populate the tables with appropriate data.

It's most likely that at least half of the controls in an application would always be displayed, regardless of the user. If so, then there is no need to invoke the security code needlessly. There are a number of ways to handle the different types of controls. You could create two sets of control classes—one with security in the Constructor, one without. Another approach would be to have an IF statement in the security code in the control that checks a flag variable to determine whether to run the security code. These are only a couple of examples.

CREATING A TOTAL SECURITY SOLUTION

There are many ways to implement security and many points along the client-server path where security can be applied. Data protection is of paramount importance. The three types of security—application security, network security and database security—all need to be applied and synchronized for data to be completely secure, from the client across the network to the server.

In a transactional application, the data is entered through the application software. So there must be security at the application level. But security at the application level is insufficient if implemented alone. Because client-server systems are open systems, users can simply go around your application software if there's no database security. They can purchase their own copy of PowerBuilder or a myriad of query tools and connect to the database directly, bypassing your application programs and application security.

Neither can one rely solely on database security. If data is traveling across the network both to and from the database, the network exposure is a factor—database security cannot help in this area. If an application developed in PowerBuilder relied only on database security, then the application would provide messages that came directly from the database. As mentioned in Chapter 2, there's a benefit to trapping these error messages and interpreting them for the user. Database error messages and warnings can look unfriendly, and in many cases, incoherent, to the user. However, the situation can become even less friendly when there's security on only the database. Depending on how your PowerBuilder application is designed, it's conceivable that users could run the application, spend a fair amount of time entering data, click a button to save the data and then find out (via an ugly database message) that they don't have access to the data. This is more a nuisance than a security risk, but it's not acceptable behavior in most organizations.

All users should have a database login or password. Passwords should be changed often. As a courtesy to users, we might want to display some type of security indicator in the title bar for each of the windows, or in some other way, so that users can identify their security level. If security data is stored in a table inside the database and the user is trying to log in to the application, the application has to read the table. The options are to:

- ❐ Create a separate application ID so that the application itself can go out and look at the security table in order to compare it with the security of the person logging in.
- ❐ Allow a read-only right to the security table itself for the individuals.

With the latter option, the users could read the data but not change it. The worst thing that could happen is they could see the security level of other users. This is not a security breech.

MOVING ON

In this chapter, we discussed application security, network security and database security, and illustrated that all three types need to be implemented to achieve an acceptable level of security. In the next chapter, we'll address some advanced techniques for working with databases.

Advanced Database Techniques

The software created with PowerBuilder interacts with databases via a number of methods, as is typical in client/server development. In this chapter, we'll take an in-depth look at the techniques for manipulating databases from within PowerBuilder.

What do we mean when we say "database?" The overwhelming majority of client/server applications interact with relational database management systems (RDBMSes), although there is no technical reason it must be that way. SQL (Structured Query Language) is the primary language used when interacting with RDBMSes. SQL can be used with other databases as well, but it's not as prevalent. For instance, there are "wrapper" technologies that encompass databases other than relational ones with software that enables SQL to be used with hierarchical or network databases. An example is EDA/SQL, which enables a developer to use SQL against an IDMS network database. Similarly, there are wrapper software programs being developed today that will enable RDBMSes to behave as object-oriented database systems (OODBMSes).

PowerBuilder has the capability to work with flat files, and, via function calls, virtually any other type of data source. However, PowerBuilder excels when working with RDBMSes. As a result, we will focus on this area. (For convenience' sake, we'll use the terms "database" and "RDBMS" interchangeably. Whenever we say "database," assume that we're referring to an RDBMS, unless otherwise specified.) We'll discuss some general database topics, in addition to the following areas as they relate to PowerBuilder:

- ❏ ODBC and native drivers
- ❏ Transaction objects
- ❏ Stored procedures
- ❏ Triggers
- ❏ Cursors
- ❏ Remote procedure calls (RPCs)

CONNECTING TO DATABASES

There are a number of places to connect to databases within PowerBuilder. However, the software connectivity occurs via one of two ways: either through native database drivers created by the RDBMS vendor, such as Sybase Open/Client, Oracle SQL*Net, etc., or via Open Database Connectivity (ODBC) drivers.

ODBC is a common software interface specification proposed as a standard by Microsoft. Although ODBC did not become an explicit standard, it has become a de facto standard for the *application interface layer* of software that connects to databases. What does "application interface layer" mean? To understand ODBC, let's look at the way a native driver is constructed. Sybase, the vendor that created SQL Server, has its own native connectivity software called Open/Client. Open/Client comprises two separate software pieces, called CT-LIB (prior to System 10, it was called DBLIB) and NetLIB. CT-LIB and NetLIB each represent a "layer" between PowerBuilder and the back-end RDBMS—in this case, Sybase SQL Server. (Note that the network software layers that complete an OSI model are beyond the scope of this book.) Consider a typical PowerBuilder application connected to the following layers:

- ❑ Application interface layer (CT-LIB)
- ❑ Database interface layer (NetLIB)
- ❑ RDBMS

Figure 7-1 is a graphical representation of this connection.

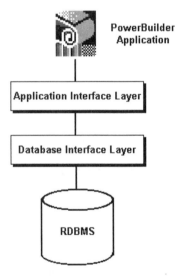

Figure 7-1: Application interface and database interface layers of database connectivity software.

The application interface layer enables an application development vendor, such as Powersoft, to write its internal code to a common database interface and not concern itself with which RDBMS the developer will be using. The database interface layer translates the application interface layer to communicate with the RDBMS via the network layer. ODBC is really an Application Programming Interface (API) specification for application software vendors to easily write software to communicate with RDBMSes. ODBC effectively replaces the application interface layer. The connection using ODBC is represented in Figure 7-2.

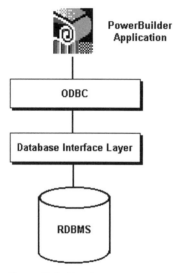

Figure 7-2: Database connectivity software with ODBC as the application interface layer.

As you can see from Figure 7-2, ODBC takes care of only one of the requisite layers. Some vendors choose to handle both the application interface and database interface layers within a single program. In the case of Sybase, they pull out the user interface layer and separate that into CT-LIB for certain platforms. On Macintosh computers, Sybase's Open/ Client connectivity software is only one program. On a PC running Intel or equivalent CPU chips, Open/Client consists of two programs. The reason is that Macintosh has only one user interface—the Macintosh interface. PCs could have a

DOS character user interface, Microsoft Windows user interface or OS/2 Presentation Manager user interface. Oracle's SQL*Net works in a similar fashion.

ODBC Vendors

Microsoft is no longer the sole vendor of ODBC connectivity software. For example, Microsoft chose not to support the System 10 version of Sybase SQL Server, so companies such as Open Link and Intersolv, among others, came to market with their own versions of ODBC that did support Sybase System 10.

We're often asked whether there's a need to purchase database vendor-specific (native) drivers if the application development environment uses ODBC. This depends on the database vendors' connectivity software. Turn the previous discussion around and look at the connectivity software from the database vendors' perspective. Some vendors, such as Sybase, Oracle and IBM in the case of DB2, have developed their own proprietary database interface API and connectivity software. In those cases, ODBC alone would not solve the connectivity problem because the database interface layer isn't handled by ODBC. Other vendors, however, have created their database interface layer from the ODBC specification. Thus, they don't have an additional native database interface layer to deal with. Such products as Watcom SQL, FoxPro, dBASE and Access fall into the latter category. They have no proprietary connectivity layer. They require only ODBC for connectivity to their databases.

The inclusion of database native drivers is one of the distinguishing features between the Desktop and Enterprise versions of PowerBuilder. The Desktop version comes with ODBC only. The Enterprise edition comes with ODBC and the native database interface layer drivers for top-selling databases, such as Oracle, Sybase, Informix and DB2.

PowerBuilder supports both ODBC and native drivers directly. You can build client applications that connect to RDBMSes with any of the following combinations, depending on the RDBMS:

❒ ODBC only.

❒ ODBC and the native database interface drivers.

❒ Vendor-specific application interface and database interface drivers (no ODBC).

POWERBUILDER TRANSACTION OBJECTS

To connect your PowerBuilder client applications with the back-end RDBMS (through ODBC or native drivers), PowerBuilder uses built-in non-visual (class) objects called *transaction objects* to pass values back and forth. Transaction objects communicate with ODBC and native drivers in the same way. Being non-visual, they have no graphical interface component that you can see, such as a window or menu. We've discussed transaction objects briefly in previous chapters; in the following sections we'll look at them in considerably greater detail.

Transaction Object Attributes

Transaction objects have 15 attributes that are used to send and receive data values. The attributes are as follows:

❒ DBMS

❒ Database

❒ UserID

❒ DBParm

❒ DBPass

- ❏ Lock
- ❏ LogID
- ❏ LogPass
- ❏ ServerName
- ❏ AutoCommit
- ❏ SQLCode
- ❏ SQLNRows
- ❏ SQLDBCode
- ❏ SQLErrText
- ❏ SQLReturnData

The 10 attributes whose names do not begin with "SQL" are used to pass data from the application to the RDBMS. The 5 whose names begin with "SQL" are used to receive data back from the RDBMS. By data, we mean more than the end-user data values. These attributes are used to hold parameters, status codes and error message information.

Not all attributes of a transaction object apply to all databases. Nor do the same attributes necessarily apply to different connections to databases from the same vendor. Powersoft has done an excellent job documenting the differences in attribute use by the various database vendors. If you have questions, check the Powersoft manual entitled *Connecting to Your Database* or the specific database vendor's documentation.

Let's take a closer look at each of the attributes of the transaction object.

DBMS

The DBMS attribute is a string that should match the values in the list of database profiles. The database profile names are created when you install either ODBC drivers or native drivers. The values in the Database Profiles list within the

Database Profile dialog are also listed in the [Database] section of the PB.INI or IM.INI file. (IM.INI is used if you're using the Powersoft InfoMaker product.) If you're unsure of the string to assign to the DBMS attribute, check the Database Profiles list or the PB.INI file to determine under what name your database was created.

Database

The Database attribute is straightforward. Supply a string value that matches the database name within the DBMS to which you wish to connect. For those databases that are case-sensitive, the database name must match case as well as name.

UserID

UserID is a string attribute often confused with the LogID attribute. For most of the database types supported by PowerBuilder, the UserID and LogID attributes are mutually exclusive. Some RDBMSes are architected to have the user log in to the database *server*, with individual databases as a subset of the server. They use the server login as the user name for each individual database (assuming the login ID has been allowed user access to a given database). Some examples of server-based RDBMSes are Oracle and Sybase. These RDBMS vendors will not use UserID. Other RDBMSes, such as Gupta's SQLBase, Informix and Hewlett-Packard's AllBase, enable login IDs per database, rather than per database server. These databases use the UserID attribute rather than LogID. Check the RDBMS documentation or consult with your DBA to determine how your RDBMS is architected.

DBPass

DBPass is an attribute that holds the database login password. It's used in conjunction with UserID and follows the same usage criteria described in the "UserID" section above. DBPass also has a datatype of string.

Lock

The Lock attribute of a transaction object is used to set the value corresponding to the configuration of the RDBMS. *Locking* is a mechanism for enforcing data integrity in a database. If two users try to write to the same record or page of records at the same time, they could step on each other's transactions (this is known as *colliding*). Some databases enable locking of a specific row, while others lock in pages (blocks of rows usually in increments of 2k or 4k bytes) in order to prevent collision. Database vendors have spent great effort designing locking schemes to prevent collision of database transactions. The intent of locking is to ensure that if one user retrieves a record for update, the record is locked by the database so that no other user can retrieve it. After the first user completes the transaction, the lock is released.

You can imagine that if one user could lock a row or block of rows, other users might get frustrated waiting for the record(s) to be released. The challenge RDBMS vendors face with locking schemes is to try to reach a desirable point within a sliding scale with data accessibility at one end and data integrity at the other (see Figure 7-3). Vendors' locking schemes vary considerably. PowerBuilder does no locking. It simply supplies locking configuration values to the RDBMS, via the Lock attribute.

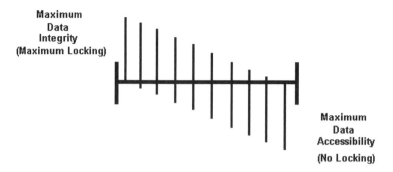

Figure 7-3: Scale representing the tradeoff between data availability and data integrity of locking schemes.

LogID & LogPass

LogID and LogPass are used in place of UserID and DBPass for some servers. LogID and LogPass are strings used for database *server* login ID and password, respectively. (See the "UserID" section for more information on when these are used.)

ServerName

For the most part, the use of the ServerName attribute correlates with use of LogID and LogPass. It's used with these attributes and contains the name of the server in which the database resides.

AutoCommit

AutoCommit is used by those databases that permit turning on and off of transaction processing recovery. Not all RDBMSes support this feature. A transaction is the grouping of one or more SQL statements treated as one entity. For example, assume two tables are to be updated for a single enrollment in our student registration system. One table, the student_class table, is updated with a new record containing the ID of the student and the ID of the class, at the time a student enrolls in the class. For the same enrollment transaction, an accounting record is created that details how the student paid for the class, and the record is inserted into the enrollment table. Because both SQL transactions relate to the one student enrollment transaction, they would be committed or rolled back together, as one entity. The two logically related SQL statements are considered one logical SQL transaction by the database.

If recovery is turned on for a database, the two SQL transactions could be treated as one entity and rolled back together. (Note that not all databases support transaction recovery.) If recovery is turned off for the database, the individual SQL statements are either committed or rolled back individually. With the latter, PowerBuilder automatically commits each statement as it is finished. So, one half of the enrollment transaction could be committed automatically by PowerBuilder. If a database error occurs, the second SQL statement would never complete. The database would be out of sync.

The confusing part of the AutoCommit attribute is that when it is set to True (its datatype is Boolean), the database recovery is turned *off*. When the attribute is False, recovery is *on*. An important thing to remember is that you cannot roll back a transaction when AutoCommit is set to True!

You cannot roll back a transaction when AutoCommit is set to True.

DBParm

The DBParm attribute is the last of the attributes used to pass data *to* the RDBMS. It's also the most complex. This attribute is used to set database-specific parameters. There are over three dozen parameters that can be set with DBParm. You set the string attribute with the following syntax:

```
<transaction object>.DBParm = &
          " parameter, parameter, etc."
```

The entire list of parameters is surrounded by double quotes. Each parameter is in the form of the parameter name followed by an equal sign and then the value of the parameter within single quotes, as follows:

```
<parameter> = '<value>'
```

Sometimes, the individual value for a parameter could be a series of options with their corresponding values. For example, the ConnectString parameter has a number of options:

```
<transaction object> = &
        "ConnectString='DSN=test,UID=dba,PWD=sql' "
```

The entire series of options appears between a set of single quotes. Each option for the parameter is listed in the following format:

```
<option> = <value>
```

In the above example, DSN=test is one option for the value for ConnectString.

The syntax rules for DBParm are a bit confusing at first, but they become clearer with use. The parameters and their use vary widely from vendor to vendor. Consult the RDBMS documentation and the PowerBuilder manuals for parameters and values specific to your database.

SQLReturnData

SQLReturnData is used by a subset of the supported databases. It is not used consistently from database to database. Its use is not as simple as containing the result set of a query. For Informix, it contains the rowid of the result set and is invoked only from embedded SQL statements, not DataWindows. It's also used by Oracle and ODBC. Its datatype is string.

SQLCode

PowerBuilder sets the SQLCode attribute upon completion of a database transaction, whether successful or unsuccessful. It places in the attribute its own return codes of datatype long, shown in Table 7-1.

Code	Meaning
0	Successful transaction.
100	Successful transaction, but no rows were returned in the result set or end of rows when using a cursor.
-1	Unsuccessful transaction. (The SQLDBCode attribute would have to be checked for the database-specific reason for the unsuccessful transaction.)

Table 7-1: Return codes for the SQLCode attribute.

These values are set by PowerBuilder for all databases regardless of the back-end database being used. A return code of 0 may not necessarily mean that your query worked as you intended—this is the difference between syntax errors and logic errors. When the return code is –1, you must check the SQLDBCode attribute (described later in this section) to get database-specific information as to why the transaction failed. Note that the meaning of a return code of 100 depends on whether you are using cursors.

SQLNRows

SQLNRows is also of datatype long. It contains the number of affected rows after a transaction completes. It may be the number of rows in a result set or, in the case of database updates, the number of rows that were actually changed (whether added, updated or deleted). The attribute is used by all the supported databases, and its value could have different meaning depending on the vendor.

SQLDBCode

SQLDBCode is of datatype long and contains the vendor-specific return code after a database transaction completes (whether successfully or unsuccessfully). This attribute is the value that the DBErrorCode() function returns in a DataWindow. When the SQLCode attribute contains –1, indicating a database error, this SQLDBCode should be checked to obtain the specific reason for the error. Consult your RDBMS documentation to interpret the results in this attribute.

SQLDBErrText

This attribute is type string and contains the vendor-specific explanation of the error condition in freeform text. It correlates with the SQLDBCode attribute and explains the value in SQLDBCode. Quite often, these error messages are not suitable for end users. The corresponding error codes must be trapped and a meaningful error message text displayed to the user. In Chapter 2, we demonstrated code in the DataWindow control user object to trap certain codes in SQLDBCode and display our own messages.

Using Transaction Objects

PowerBuilder preallocates one instance of a transaction object for us. It is called SQLCA (Structured Query Language Communications Area) and is the default transaction object. Unless you specify another transaction object to use in your code, PowerBuilder will connect to the database using SQLCA.

The main reason to create transaction objects in addition to SQLCA is to connect to multiple databases simultaneously in your application. If your application connects to only one database at a time, there's no need to forego SQLCA. To use transaction objects, populate the appropriate attributes and then connect to the database via the SQL CONNECT statement. Always test the SQLCode attribute after each transaction with the database, including CONNECTs.

PowerBuilder Preferences

Setting values in the PowerBuilder Preferences painter is not the same as setting attributes within PowerScript code. The Preferences painter sets the values for database connection information. These preferences are for your interactive development process while running PowerBuilder to develop client applications. You code transaction object attributes for use in the client application. The database preferences for your default database can sometimes be misleading. The application can run successfully in the development environment, but not as a standalone application.

Multiple Transaction Objects

If your application will connect to more than one database at the same time, you'll need to create transaction objects to handle the additional connections. You can still use SQLCA for one of the connections. Each transaction object will contain connection parameters, return codes and other information for its respective database connection. Consider the following example, where we require a connection in addition to SQLCA to connect to Sybase SQL Server. We'll create an instance of datatype transaction and then populate its attributes before connecting, as follows:

```
// Create an instance of type transaction
// and name it ltran_sybase_tran
//
transaction ltran_sybase_tran
ltran_sybase_tran = CREATE transaction

// Populate the attributes of our new
```

```
// Transaction Object
//
ltran_sybase_tran.DBMS = "SYB"
ltran_sybase_tran.LogID = "Fred"
ltran_sybase_tran.LogPass = "abracadabra"
ltran_sybase_tran.DBParm = "release = '4.2' "

// Connect to the database with our
// Transaction Object (If you are not
// using SQLCA, you must use the USING
// keyword and specify the Transaction
// Object name. If you don't, PowerBuilder
// assumes SQLCA).
//
CONNECT USING ltran_sybase_tran;

// We are testing whether the connection
// worked. You should always test SQLCode
// after interacting with the database
//
if ltran_sybase_tran.SQLCode <> 0 then
   MessageBox( "Database Error - " + &
       string( ltran_sybase_tran.SQLCode ), &
          "Connection Error:  " + &
       ltran_sybase_tran.SQLErrText )
end if
```

Notice the semicolon following the line containing the CONNECT statement. It's there because CONNECT is considered an SQL command, and we always terminate an SQL statement with a semicolon. The following SQL statements also require that you specify the transaction object with the USING keyword:

- ❐ COMMIT
- ❐ CONNECT
- ❐ DECLARE
- ❐ DELETE

- ❑ DISCONNECT
- ❑ INSERT
- ❑ PREPARE
- ❑ ROLLBACK
- ❑ SELECT
- ❑ SELECTBLOB
- ❑ UPDATE
- ❑ UPDATEBLOB

Recall from Chapter 1 that you must DESTROY an object that you created with the CREATE command, in order to return the memory back to the operating system. DESTROY the object as soon as you no longer need it to maximize memory use. (Note that you cannot CREATE or DESTROY the SQLCA transaction object. PowerBuilder handles that for you.) To continue our example, we would destroy the above transaction object as follows:

You cannot CREATE or DESTROY the SQLCA transaction object. PowerBuilder does that for you.

```
DESTROY ltran_sybase_tran
```

Adding Value to Transaction Objects

Since the details of transaction object attributes are a bit tedious, you might consider creating a custom user object transaction class to handle each type of database to which you usually connect. We'll add user object functions to populate the attributes of the transaction object for each type of database we'll connect to. We'll also create a function to test the SQLDBCode attribute and filter for common errors, similar to the code we added to the DataWindow user object class in Chapter 2. This function will perform the same processes as the code in the DataWindow class, but will be in the new transaction object. If we use embedded SQL statements, the code in the DataWindow class will be of no use. So, if we place similar functionality in the transaction object, we can trap common errors for both situations.

Create our new user object transaction class as follows:

1. In the User Object painter, create a new non-visual (class) standard user object.
2. Select transaction as the user object type.
3. Create a new user object function with the declaration shown in Figure 7-4.

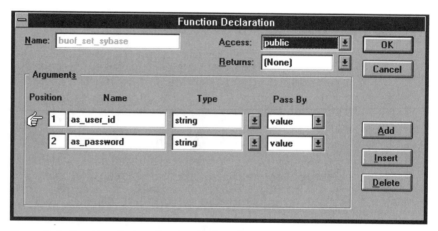

Figure 7-4: Function declaration for the function buof_set_sybase().

4. Add the following code to the function:

```
// Set the applicable attribute values to connect
// to our Sybase database. (Your values may be
// different to connect to your Sybase database).
//

this.DBMS      = "SYB"
this.LogID     = as_user_id
this.LogPass    = as_password
this.ServerName  = "syb_server"
this.DBParm     = "release='4.2'"
```

5. Save the user object and name it buo_transaction.

Instead of using SQLCA as our transaction object, we'll create a descendant of our buo_transaction class. After we create it, we'll then call buof_set_sybase() to populate the attributes with Sybase-specific values. If we know we'll also be using an Oracle database, for example, we can create a similar function called buof_set_oracle() to set the attributes for Oracle-specific information. To use our new transaction class function, consider the following example:

```
buo_transaction ltran_sybase_tran
ltran_sybase_tran = CREATE buo_transaction
ltran_sybase_tran.buof_set_sybase( "MyLoginID",
                                   "MyPassword")

CONNECT USING ltran_sybase_tran;

...< your code > ...

DESTROY ltran_sybase_tran
```

These types of functions will work if you have a stable group of servers that you use consistently. If the server, database or attribute values change frequently, these types of functions probably will not be as beneficial.

STORED PROCEDURES

Stored procedures are precompiled SQL transactions stored in a binary state inside the database. SQL that is not a stored procedure is interpreted and stored with the application. SQL is entered at run-time either with a tool or by the user typing in SQL commands. One of the advantages to procedures being stored in the database in a binary state is improved performance of a given query. The number of steps involved in the internal processing of SQL statements is significantly reduced when processing the SQL as a stored procedure than when processing the same SQL statements within the client application software. When the SQL is not a stored procedure, the application has to parse, compile, etc., at run-time. When the same SQL statement is a stored procedure, it is already in a compiled, parsed state. Therefore, it only has to resolve any arguments passed to it and then run. Table 7-2 compares the processes that occur when processing SQL statements in the client application software versus the processing of SQL statements as stored procedures in a RDBMS.

Client-Side Processing	Server-Side Processing
Parsing	Argument binding
Variable substitution	Execution
Compiling	
Optimization	
Binary code generation	
Argument binding	
Execution	

Table 7-2: Client-side processing vs. stored procedure processing.

Table 7-2 is general in nature. The actual steps vary from vendor to vendor, but the idea is the same. The processes of parsing, variable substitution, compilation, optimization and code generation take place only on the client-side processing of SQL statements. The reduced number of steps required on the RDBMS side for stored procedures translates into overall faster execution of the SQL transaction.

In Chapter 6 we touched on using stored procedures for security. Security was the first benefit derived from stored procedures. Another area where stored procedures are invaluable is input/output (I/O) with the database. By I/O, we mean that any interaction with the database (Select, Insert, Update or Delete) could be handled by using a stored procedure. Putting certain other performance considerations aside, stored procedures could be used for all database I/O. Doing so would have a number of benefits to both application developers and to DBAs. Benefits to the DBAs include:

- ❏ Centralized control of table interaction.
- ❏ Improved database integrity.
- ❏ The benefits we've already discussed that come with the OO principle of reuse.

Benefits to application developers include the following:

- ❏ The ability to use a callable "black box" module for I/O rather having to code I/O.
- ❏ Easier maintenance of I/O coding, since it's stored in only one place.
- ❏ Faster application development.

The procedures that interact with the database, whether on the server side or client side, are frequently referred to as *business rules*. These business rules define the parameters and logic for successfully updating a database table. If this logic is spread throughout application code, then changes to the logic would require changes to the code in all places that database updates exist. Using a stored procedure in a database enables changes to be made in a single location. Unless the parameter list changes, the existing application code that calls the stored procedures would not require changing.

DBAs will be supportive of having the update logic stored in only one place. The potential for errors is reduced. Once the stored procedures are coded and debugged, the chances for data problems will be reduced since the only way data gets into or out of the database is via the stored procedures.

You must balance the use of stored procedures with various other performance considerations, however. Although a given stored procedure is faster than its interpreted counterpart, a database tends to bog down if its stored procedures are run frequently and concurrently. There are a number of reasons for this. One is that the RDBMS is burdened with running application logic in addition to servicing SQL transactions. At a point, it is doing twice the work compared to having the stored procedure transactions at the application level. The database server's normal operation consists of some of the following actions:

- ❒ Reading/writing of data pages.
- ❒ Reading/writing of index pages.
- ❒ Reading/writing of transaction logs.
- ❒ Reading/writing of system catalog tables.
- ❒ Internal connection and process management.
- ❒ Memory management.

When you add the processes for executing stored procedures, the number of tasks increases and at some point affects the above processes. Also, stored procedures tend not to be reentrant. So, if 10 users invoke the same stored procedure at the same time, there are 10 copies of that stored procedure in the server's memory. (Of course, these issues vary by database vendor.) The user perceives this as a performance degradation. The DBA's job is to help the developer manage this balance. Include the DBA in system design in order to get help with this and other issues.

Database performance is a real issue that should be dealt with. If a server is overloaded with stored procedures, the performance will go down. The "breaking" point for a database or server depends on a number of criteria, including the following:

❐ Database size

❐ Database memory size

❐ Machine throughput capability

❐ Machine memory

❐ Disk space

❐ Swap space

❐ Network throughput capability

Network load must be considered along with application and database server performance.

Recall that each time a request is made of a database server or a server responds back to the application, this communication takes place over a network. A very important matter to consider in addition to database server performance is network traffic. Network load must be balanced in the equation along with application performance and database server performance. As you design large-scale client/server applications, you must also include your network administrator when weighing the issues involved.

Despite potential performance degradation, stored procedures still provide great benefit and should be used as much as possible. However, stored procedures are not portable. This means that you cannot take a stored procedure written for Sybase SQL Server and move it unchanged to Oracle. There are efforts under way to standardize stored procedure language across RDBMS vendors.

Not all RDBMSes support stored procedures, but most of the major ones do. PowerBuilder provides mechanisms to work with stored procedures for the supported databases. In addition, stored procedures are used as resources in a few contexts within PowerBuilder. For example, they can be used:

❐ With embedded SQL in PowerScript code.

❐ As a data source for DataWindows.

❐ As a data source for reports.

In the next few sections, we'll look at various ways of working with stored procedures, both within the database server and within PowerBuilder.

Using Stored Procedures With Embedded SQL

The code we discussed in the "Stored Procedures" section in Chapter 6 demonstrated how to create stored procedures from within the database server. In order to use the stored procedures, we must write some PowerScript code to reference them. The PowerScript code creates a conduit between the client application and the database stored procedure. The PowerScript code looks similar to the SQL code used to create the stored procedures on the server, but it is different. The PowerScript code is actually creating a variable of type procedure.

Stored Procedures in the Database

Let's first look at the database SQL code to create a stored procedure on the database server. The Watcom syntax for creating a stored procedure is as follows:

```
CREATE PROCEDURE <procedure_name>(
    <IN | OUT | INOUT> <parameter> <datatype>,
    <IN | OUT | INOUT> <parameter> <datatype>,
    ..., etc.)
        <SQL code> ;
```

The words CREATE PROCEDURE begin the declaration. Then comes the procedure name, followed by an opening (left) parenthesis, the keyword IN or OUT or INOUT, followed by the parameter name, followed by the datatype of the parameter. If there's more than one parameter, then a comma follows the first parameter and the parameter options repeat until finishing with a closing (right) parenthesis.

For example, the following SQL code creates a stored procedure in a Watcom database called usp_insert_user_userclass():

```
create procedure usp_insert_user_userclass(
        IN user_value  varchar(7),
        IN class_value varchar(11))
BEGIN
   Insert into user_userclass
   values (user_value, class_value)
END;
```

Within the database, we drop stored procedures with the keywords DROP PROCEDURE and the procedure name. For example:

```
drop   procedure usp_insert_user_userclass ;
```

Also within the database, the procedure is executed with the CALL command followed by the procedure name and then data values in the parentheses matching by position the arguments defined in the stored procedure. For example:

```
call usp_insert_user_userclass( 'NewUser',
                                'CLERK' );
```

Stored Procedures in PowerBuilder

Within PowerBuilder, you must create a procedure variable matching the database stored procedure. Then you must call the PowerScript procedure variable and supply values to match the arguments defined for the stored procedure.

Below is a script that declares some local variables to be used as arguments to the stored procedure. The script then declares a local PowerScript variable called lsp_update_proc for the database stored procedure usp_update_proc(). Finally, the script invokes the stored procedure via the PowerScript procedure variable using the Execute PowerScript command.

```
string ls_arg1, ls_arg2
ls_arg1 = 'Ed'
ls_arg2 = 'CLERK'

declare lsp_update_proc procedure for
usp_update_user_userclass
    @user_value=:ls_arg1, @class_value=:ls_arg2;

EXECUTE lsp_update_proc;

If sqlca.SQLCode <> 0 then
    messagebox( string( sqlca.sqldbcode ),
sqlca.sqlerrtext )
End If
```

As with other SQL statements embedded in PowerScript, the DECLARE PROCEDURE and EXECUTE commands end with semicolons. And as we do with other SQL statements, we test SQLCode following the Execute statement.

The code that created the above stored procedure is as follows:

```
drop    procedure usp_update_user_userclass ;

create procedure usp_update_user_userclass(
    IN user_value varchar(7),
    IN class_value varchar( 11) )

    BEGIN
        update user_userclass
        set user_class = class_value
        where user_name = user_value
    END;
```

The previous example showed SQL update and insert logic in a stored procedure. Below is sample code to drop, create and call a stored procedure with delete logic:

```
drop    procedure usp_delete_user_userclass ;

create procedure usp_delete_user_userclass(
```

```
    IN user_value varchar(7) )

BEGIN
    delete from user_userclass
    where user_name = user_value
END;


call usp_delete_user_userclass( 'Ed' );
```

Stored procedures within PowerScript can also be declared with the same scope options available to other variables. To declare a PowerScript stored procedure with global, shared or instance scope, select the scope from the Declare menu as when declaring global, shared and instance variables. Similar to the CONNECT PowerScript SQL statement, you can indicate a transaction object to use with the stored procedure. You add the USING keyword and the transaction object name following the DECLARE PROCEDURE statement. If no USING statement is coded, the default transaction object for the PowerScript stored procedure is SQLCA.

Using Triggers

Triggers are a specialized type of stored procedure used for maintaining tables in databases. One of the primary benefits and uses of triggers is for controlling *referential integrity*—that is, ensuring that related records in different tables are either inserted, deleted or updated in unison, so the data tables do not get out of synchronization with one another. (Since triggers are a type of stored procedure and not all database vendors support stored procedures, triggers also are not supported in every RDBMS.)

Like the syntax for creating stored procedures, the syntax for creating a trigger varies by database vendor. The body of the trigger is the same as that for stored procedures. The syntax for creating Sybase triggers is as follows:

```
CREATE TRIGGER <triggername>
        FOR
        <INSERT | UPDATE | DELETE>
        AS
            < ... code ... >
```

Here's the syntax for creating a Watcom trigger:

```
CREATE TRIGGER < triggername>
        < BEFORE | AFTER >
        < INSERT | UPDATE | DELETE >
        REFERENCING
        < OLD | NEW >
        FOR EACH ROW
            < ... CODE ... >
```

You can see that the syntax differs somewhat between Sybase and Watcom. However, the syntax accomplishes similar things, such as naming the trigger and assigning it to a particular database action (Insert, Update, Delete).

Once a trigger is attached to a table, it's invoked whenever the action to which the trigger was attached has been invoked. For example, assume the following trigger, which is attached to the delete action for the user_userclass table:

```
CREATE TRIGGER utrig_delete_control_class
    AFTER DELETE ON user_userclass
    REFERENCING OLD as lrow_deleted
    FOR EACH ROW
        BEGIN
            delete from controlclass_userclass
            where  lrow_deleted.user_class =
                controlclass_userclass.user_class
        END
```

Whenever a SQL transaction attempts to delete a row or rows from the user_userclass table, the trigger is automatically invoked by the database *after* the original row is deleted from the user_userclass table. The trigger will then delete a corresponding row from the controlclass_userclass table. Thus, the trigger keeps the two tables in sync.

Be aware of two caveats. First, since triggers are a type of stored procedure, the same concerns about database server performance that apply to all stored procedures apply to triggers. The potential for degraded performance increases because triggers are invoked automatically with each table transaction associated with the trigger.

The second caveat is that triggers can cause a looping situation. For example, assume one table has a trigger that creates a transaction on a second table that also contains triggers pointing back to the original table. In this situation, the possibility for the database to automatically loop is very high. This potential pitfall must not be overlooked!

Beware of looping when using triggers.

Using Stored Procedures as DataWindow Data Sources

We've seen that stored procedures and triggers can be created and invoked on database servers. In addition, we've seen that stored procedure calls can be embedded into PowerScript code. In this section, we'll discuss another way stored procedures can be used: as a data source for DataWindows.

We're now getting more into working with stored procedures from within PowerBuilder, as opposed to working with them from within database servers. The common use of a DataWindow is to tie its presentation logic to one or more tables in a database. Another option is to tie the presentation logic to a database stored procedure, which is used for the purpose of retrieving data into the DataWindow.

In order for the DataWindow to work with a stored procedure, the stored procedure must return a result set. The previous examples of stored procedures demonstrated database I/O and did not return a result set. The following Watcom stored procedure returns a result set:

```
CREATE PROCEDURE usp_get_class(
    IN as_user_name varchar(7),
    OUT as_user_class varchar(11) )

RESULT (ls_user_class varchar(11) )
BEGIN
    select user_class from user_userclass
    where user_name = as_user_name
END
```

This stored procedure can now be used with a DataWindow. The procedure for creating such DataWindows is similar to the procedure for creating a DataWindow that accesses database tables directly. The general steps are as follows:

1. Create a new DataWindow in the DataWindow painter.
2. In the New DataWindow dialog, select stored procedure (see Figure 7-5).

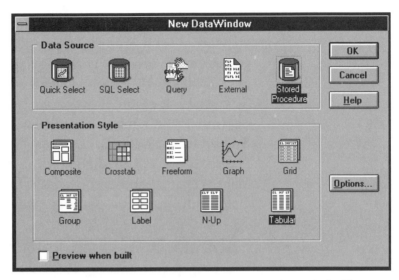

Figure 7-5: Selecting the data source and presentation style for New DataWindow.

3. Click OK. The dialog shown in Figure 7-6 will appear.

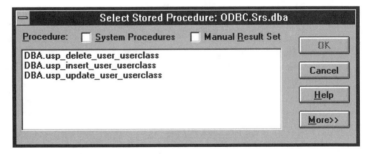

Figure 7-6: The Select Stored Procedure dialog.

4. Click on the appropriate stored procedure. (Click the System Procedures checkbox to display stored procedures provided with the database.)

5. Select the Manual Result Set checkbox to create your own layout for the result set returned from the stored procedure. If you don't click this checkbox, PowerBuilder will create a default result set based on the query in the stored procedure. (*Note*: Stored procedures that do not return a result set will not work as a data source for DataWindows unless you select the Manual Result Set checkbox.) If you do select the Manual Result Set checkbox, the Result Set Description dialog will appear, as shown in Figure 7-7.

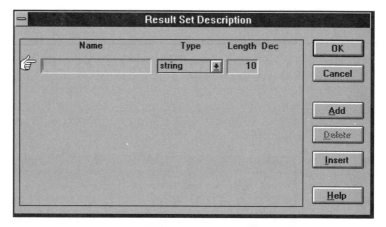

Figure 7-7: The Result Set Description dialog.

6. The Result Set Description dialog is similar to the argument declaration area for functions. Type in a name and select the datatype and length for each column in your result set. The order of columns in this dialog must match the order of the columns being returned. Click OK when finished.

7. The Presentation area of the DataWindow painter will appear. From here, the procedures are the same as for any other DataWindow.

Understanding Database Cursors

SQL is known as a *set-processing* language. That is, it operates on sets or groups of rows at once. When you code an SQL update statement, for example, you don't have to code for it to loop through the rows in order to update each row. SQL processes the whole set of applicable rows with one statement. In fact, you have to go to extra effort with SQL to *not* process all rows at once. If you need to process one row at a time, you use a *cursor*. Cursors are attached to an existing SQL SELECT statement and enable the developer to process each row of the SQL SELECT result set one at a time.

As in the case of stored procedures, support for cursors and the syntactical details vary by vendor. The syntax for a Watcom cursor is as follows:

```
DECLARE <cursorname> CURSOR FOR
    SELECT ... ;
```

The keyword DECLARE followed by the cursor name and then the keywords CURSOR FOR precedes a valid SQL SELECT statement. For example,

```
DECLARE lcur_class CURSOR FOR
    select user_class
    from   user_userclass;
```

PowerBuilder provides for the creation of cursors with PowerScript. It's a little different than declaring stored procedures in PowerScript. As we've discussed, the PowerScript procedure variable is only a variable to interact with the database stored procedure. With PowerScript cursors, we're actually creating a cursor and not just a variable.

The PowerScript syntax for creating a cursor is as follows:

```
DECLARE <cursorname> CURSOR FOR
    <SQL Select>
{ USING <transaction object name> } ;
```

The optional USING keyword applies to PowerScript cursors as it applies to PowerScript procedures. We can actually use the same Watcom syntax to declare a PowerScript cursor:

```
DECLARE lcur_class CURSOR FOR
    select user_class
    from   user_userclass;
```

How do we process a value once we've declared a cursor? In PowerScript, we use the FETCH command. The PowerScript syntax to use a FETCH statement is as follows:

```
FETCH <cursor name> INTO :<host variable> ;
```

The FETCH statement, because it is an SQL command, ends with a semicolon. The colon before the variable name indicates to the SQL parser that the identifier following the colon is a host variable and not a table column name or variable local to the SQL script.

Consider this example script that processes each row in the above cursor:

```
STRING ls_class_name
INT x

DO WHILE SQLCA.SQLCode <> 100

    FETCH lcur_class INTO :ls_class_name ;

    IF SQLCA.SQLCode = 0 THEN
        IF ls_class_name = 'SUPVR' THEN
            ... code ...
        ELSE
            ... code ...
        END IF
    END IF

LOOP
```

We have a DO...LOOP to repeat calls to the FETCH command. After the FETCH command, we test SQLCA.SQLCode for return codes. Recall that a return code of 100 indicates end of rows for a cursor. Thus, the SQLCode of 100 is the test argument for our loop. The rest is standard PowerBuilder script.

Some databases support variations of FETCH commands. In the above example, the default is FETCH NEXT. For those databases that support other FETCH options, PowerBuilder can support the following:

- ❏ FETCH FIRST
- ❏ FETCH PRIOR
- ❏ FETCH LAST
- ❏ FETCH NEXT

In some situations, multiple SELECTs may run more quickly than a FETCH.

FETCH statements can also be a performance burden to database servers. Additional buffers and connections must be maintained in order to keep the connection between the client and server, for the purpose of going back and forth to read a row at a time. Involving a DBA in the system design will help determine proper use of FETCH.

Multiple SQL SELECTS on the same table can achieve the same results as a FETCH. For example, assume you have a PowerBuilder script to loop through rows in a result set and test a column for a particular value. The script's processing will then vary depending on the value in the column. If the number of possible column values is small, two SELECT statements, each with a WHERE clause testing for one of the two value conditions, might run more quickly than a FETCH loop. You'd make two passes through the database, but in some instances, this may perform better than one pass with a FETCH loop. The additional overhead maintained by the server for FETCH statements sometimes outweighs the overhead of running multiple SELECT statements. We're not suggesting that multiple-pass SELECT statements are preferable to FETCH statements, but we are offering this approach as an option. There's no quick and easy way to determine which statements will run faster—you may have to test them.

Remote Procedure Calls

Remote procedures are precompiled external functions or subroutines that are called from the application. Remote procedure calls (RPCs) enable developers to access separate platform-specific programs from platform-independent applications. A typical use of RPCs is depicted in Figure 7-8.

Figure 7-8: A common configuration of remote procedures.

PowerBuilder enables us to call a database stored procedure as an RPC. This configuration is a variation of a typical RPC. We can create a new transaction user object and an external function that calls the database stored procedure. To PowerBuilder, the call to the external function that in turn calls a stored procedure is a form of RPC. We'll create one as follows:

1. Open the User Object painter and select New.
2. Select a Class, Standard, Transaction user object.
3. From the Declare menu, select Local External Functions. The Declare Local External Functions dialog will appear.

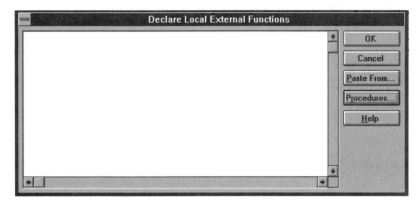

Figure 7-9: The Declare Local External Functions dialog.

4. Click the Procedures button. The Remote Stored Procedure(s) dialog will appear.

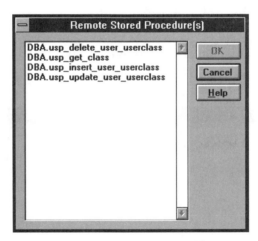

Figure 7-10: The Remote Stored Procedure(s) dialog.

5. Select the usp_insert_user_userclass stored procedure and click the OK button. The Declare Local External Functions dialog will appear with the database stored procedure declaration in the dialog.

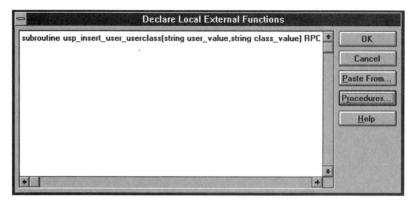

Figure 7-11: PowerBuilder uses the stored procedure declaration to create the external function declaration.

6. The declaration appears on one line and continues to the right. You can edit the declaration in the dialog at this point. Insert an ampersand to the left of the RPCFUNC keyword, and press Ctrl+Enter after the ampersand to achieve a new line in the declaration, as shown in Figure 7-12.

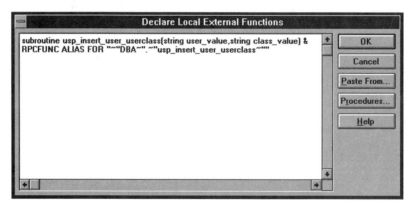

Figure 7-12: The declaration continued to the following line.

Functions vs. Subroutines

Notice the keyword "subroutine" that begins the declaration shown in Figure 7-12. With the term "subroutine," PowerBuilder indicates that no values are returned from the RPC. If values are returned from the stored procedure, then the declaration is preceded by the keyword "function." To PowerBuilder, a subroutine is a function that doesn't return any values. This is why there's only a Function painter, and not an additional subroutine painter.

7. PowerBuilder automatically retrieves the database owner ID and appends it to the stored procedure when it is returned as an RPC declaration, as shown in Figure 7-12. You can edit this out, as shown in Figure 7-13.

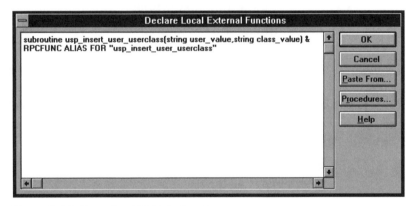

Figure 7-13: The edited RPC declaration.

8. Click OK.

9. Save the transaction user object and name it uo_rpc_tran.

We can now use our new transaction user object class to create an instance for our application. (We've done this kind of inheriting previously.)

```
uo_rpc_tran luo_rpc_tran
luo_rpc_tran = create uo_rpc_tran
```

Once the attributes of our transaction object have been set and we connect to the database, we can use the RPC as follows:

```
string ls_arg1, ls_arg2
ls_arg1 = 'Ed'
ls_arg2 = 'CLERK'
luo_rpc_tran.usp_insert_user_userclass( ls_arg1, ls_arg2 )
```

Third-party vendors offer RPC programs as well. These could be called in a similar manner to the stored procedures we've described as external function RPCs.

MOVING ON

In this chapter, we've looked at some advanced topics for working with RDBMSes, including transaction objects and various kinds of stored procedures. There's much work that can be accomplished on the database server side, in addition to the work that client applications perform. In the next chapter, we'll examine SQL, the language for manipulating RDBMSes, more closely.

Advanced SQL

In 1986 most of the computer world adopted Structured Query Language (SQL) as the standard language for information update and retrieval in a database. PowerBuilder is no exception. But despite SQL's wide acceptance and use, many database programmers don't take advantage of some of its more advanced features. In this chapter, we're going to take a look at some of SQL's most useful advanced capabilities. Although implementations and grammars vary among database vendors, the concepts discussed in this chapter should generally apply to your specific project. You will, however, have to consult the SQL reference manuals for your particular database to get the correct implementation syntax.

OUTER JOINS

One of the most common tasks a database programmer faces is to retrieve information from more than one table where the rows are related on a linking field. This kind of retrieval is called a *simple join*. The general form for this operation is as follows:

```
SELECT table1.field1, table2.field2
    FROM table1, table2
    WHERE table1.field3 = table2.field3
```

This syntax retrieves field1 from table1 and field2 from table2 where the rows have the same field3. Here's a more practical example of the procedure:

```
SELECT employee.last_name,  employee.first_name,
department.dept_name
FROM employee, department
WHERE employee.ssn = department.ssn
```

This example retrieves the first name, last name and department name for each person in both the employee table and the department table, as shown in Figure 8-1.

Last Name	First Name	Department
Jones	Cheryl	Accounting
Anderson	William	Info Systems

Figure 8-1: Result set of a simple join.

A simple join is fine for many cases, but it contains a sweeping assumption: *The value of the linking field in one table must exist in the other table, or no fields will be displayed.* In other words, if employee John Smith exists in the employee table with a social security number of 123456789, he must also have a record in the department table in order for his name to appear in the result set. If there is no record in the department table that contains the value 123456789 in the ssn field, the values John and Smith will not appear in the result set. This means employees who are not yet assigned to a specific department will not appear in the query.

An outer join retrieves all records from a master table and any corresponding records in a child table.

Fortunately, this problem is solved by using a retrieval type called an *outer join*. An outer join lets you retrieve all records from a primary table as well as any corresponding records in a secondary table. Records in the primary table need not have corresponding records in the secondary table in order to be retrieved. The general format for an outer join is as follows:

```
SELECT table1.field1, table2,field2
    FROM table1, table2
    WHERE table1.field3 = table2.field3 (+)
```

(*Note:* While this specific syntax is common to many DBMSes, you'll need to refer to the SQL reference manual for your particular system for the correct syntax.)

This syntax retrieves all records from table1 and any corresponding records from table2. If a particular record in table1 has no associated record in table2, the field2 column for that row will contain a NULL value. The previous example would then look like this:

```
SELECT employee.last_name, employee.first_name,
department.dept_name
    FROM employee, department
    WHERE employee.ssn = department.ssn (+)
```

Even though John Smith still hasn't been assigned to a specific department, he now appears in the result set, as shown in Figure 8-2.

Last Name	First Name	Department
Jones	Cheryl	Accounting
Anderson	William	Info Systems
Smith	John	

Figure 8-2: Result set of an outer join.

THE HAVING CLAUSE

The HAVING clause is like a WHERE clause at the group level.

Nearly all SQL statements require the use of a WHERE clause to discriminate between records. The nice thing about this clause is that it applies a condition to each record in order to decide whether or not the record should be included in the result set. Many programmers, however, are unaware that such a tool also exists at the group level.

You can use the HAVING clause with the GROUP BY statement to discriminate between entire groups in the same way you might use the WHERE clause to discriminate between individual rows. Here's the general format:

```
SELECT fields
    FROM tables
    WHERE recordLevelConditions
    GROUP BY fields
    HAVING groupLevelConditions
```

In general, your DBMS will process this statement in the following stages:

1. It retrieves all records that meet the criteria in the WHERE clause.

2. It groups the retrieved records according to the specifications of the GROUP BY clause.

3. It eliminates from the result set all records belonging to groups that don't meet the criteria in the HAVING clause.

The following example should help make the processing clear. Suppose you want to retrieve a list of all departments that have more than 10 employees who are managers. You would use the following syntax:

```
SELECT distinct dept_no, count(*)
    FROM employee
    WHERE job = 'MANAGER'
    GROUP BY dept_no
    HAVING count(*) > 10
```

This SQL performs the following logic:

1. Retrieves all the department numbers of employees who are managers.
2. Groups the records together by department number.
3. Removes all groups that have 10 or fewer records in the result set.

USING CURSORS

For many programmers, using a cursor presents a dilemma. On the one hand, they can perform many database operations without having to create a new DataWindow object. On the other hand, cursors can be unwieldy to use. One of the biggest complaints about cursors is the general inability to address a specific row. If, however, you are using a DBMS that supports the WHERE CURRENT OF CURSOR clause in its SELECT grammar, you can work around this problem.

WHERE CURRENT OF CURSOR lets you update a specific row in a table from an open cursor.

The WHERE CURRENT OF CURSOR clause allows the programmer to update a specific row in a table from an open cursor. (Most DBMSes that support this feature require that the cursor be opened with the FOR UPDATE clause.) The syntax of this statement is as follows:

```
UPDATE table
    SET field = value
    WHERE CURRENT OF cursor_name
```

This statement updates the value of *field* for the row in the *table* corresponding to the current row in the cursor *cursor_name*.

Here, we update salary information for a specific record in an employee table:

```
UPDATE employee
SET salary = 100000
WHERE CURRENT OF emp_cursor
```

This code updates the value of the field salary in the employee table for the row corresponding to the current row in the cursor emp_cursor.

Each row of a defined cursor corresponds to a specific row in a table. Figure 8-3 shows this relationship.

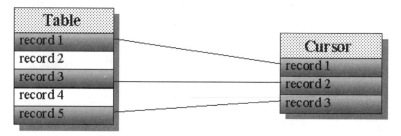

Figure 8-3: How selected rows from a table correspond to rows in a cursor.

As each record is stepped through in the cursor using the FETCH statement, a pointer is updated to reflect the new row associated in the table. Therefore, the WHERE CURRENT OF CURSOR clause causes the UPDATE statement to act on only the row in the table being referenced by the current cursor record.

DYNAMIC SQL

In Chapter 3, you learned how to alter the SQL of a Data-Window at run-time to accommodate dynamic changes in data needs. In this section, you'll learn how to perform similar functions without a DataWindow. You'll do this using *dynamic SQL*. Dynamic SQL simply refers to programmers' ability to determine their SQL statements at compile-time, execute them and read/manipulate the results.

Necessary Components

All dynamic SQL statements require the use of one, two or three special variable types:

- ❒ Transaction objects.
- ❒ Dynamic staging areas.
- ❒ Dynamic description areas.

You've already learned that a transaction object represents a connection to a database. A *dynamic staging area* is a place in memory where the components of an SQL statement are prepared for execution. A *dynamic description area* is a place in memory where certain key aspects of the prepared SQL statement and its result set are described. PowerBuilder predefines three global variables for dynamic SQL operations:

- ❒ SQLCA, the default transaction object.
- ❒ SQLSA, the default dynamic staging area.
- ❒ SQLDA, the default dynamic description area.

SQLCA

SQLCA is the default transaction object provided by Power-Builder. Like all transaction objects, it is used to transfer data to and from a database, as well as store critical information needed for successful DBMS interaction. Much of this information is available to you via publicly accessible data members. These data elements store such information as the database server type, lock isolation level, user name and so on. Because the syntax for these data members varies with the DBMS, you'll have to refer to your SQL reference manual for specific information.

What is important to stress here is not what data you must provide to SQLCA, but what information you can get from it. Table 8-1 describes the data members you can use to check the results of your SQL statements.

Data Member	What it Reports

SQLCode	The success or failure code of the most recent operation:
	   0 Success.
	  100 No result set returned.
	  −1 Error (use SQLDBCode or SQLErrText to get details).

SQLNRows	The number of rows affected. The database vendor supplies this number; therefore, the meaning may not be the same in every DBMS.
SQLDBCode	Database vendor's error code.
SQLErrText	Database vendor's error message.

Table 8-1: Data members for testing SQL statements.

The following example shows how to use these codes:

```
int counter

SELECT count(*) into :counter FROM employee;

if (SQLCA.SQLCode = 0) then
    messagebox("Hurray","It worked!!")
else
    string errorText
```

```
errorText = "The SQL statement failed with an error code" + &
" of " + string(SQLCA.SQLDBCode) + " and an error text of '" + &
SQLCA.SQLErrText + "'"

messagebox("Uh Oh!",errorText)

end if
```

This code executes a simple SQL statement, checks the result and tells the user whether or not it worked.

SQLSA

A dynamic staging area, in this case SQLSA, is a place in memory where PowerBuilder assembles critical components of an SQL statement, including:

❏ The SQL statement to execute.

❏ The number of parameters needed in the statement.

❏ The transaction object used for each subsequent SQL statement.

This information is used internally by PowerBuilder and cannot be accessed by the user. SQLSA is no longer needed once an EXECUTE statement has been completed for it.

SQLDA

A dynamic description area, in this case SQLDA, is an area of memory that PowerBuilder uses to store information about the input parameters and result-set elements of a particular SQL statement. PowerBuilder uses SQLDA only when either the input parameters or the result-set elements are not known at compile-time. SQLDA's publicly accessible data members are shown in the following table.

Data Member	Description
NumInputs	Number of input parameters.
InParmType[]	Array of input parameter types.
NumOutputs	Number of output parameters.
OutParmType[]	Array of output parameter types.

Table 8-2: SQLDA's publicly accessible data members.

These parameters are especially helpful when the data types of the result set are not known. We'll take a closer look at the use of SQLDA and variables like it in the "Format 4: Possibly Some Inputs/Possibly Some Outputs" section, later in this chapter.

Types of Dynamic SQL

In general, PowerBuilder identifies four types of dynamic SQL:

❑ Format 1: Non-result-set statements, no input parameters.

❑ Format 2: Non-result-set statements, input parameters.

❑ Format 3: Result-set statements, known input parameters and result-set columns.

❑ Format 4: Result-set statements, unknown input parameters and/or result-set columns.

In the next few sections we'll take a detailed look at each of these categories of SQL statements.

Format 1: No Inputs/No Outputs

Use dynamic SQL format 1 when you want to execute a dynamic SQL statement that requires no parameters and returns no values. All you need to do is compose an SQL statement and execute it using the EXECUTE IMMEDIATE statement, as shown in the following example:

```
string mysql

mysql = "DELETE FROM employee WHERE salary > 100000"

EXECUTE IMMEDIATE :Mysql USING SQLCA;
```

You may wonder why you should bother using this technique, since the same SQL could have easily been done in one line of code:

```
DELETE FROM employee WHERE salary > 100000;
```

The real value of this method comes when programmers want to use SQL commands supported by their DBMS but not by PowerBuilder. A good example of this is the PACK statement that is prevalent in many database systems based in xBASE. This command removes all records marked for deletion from a specific table. The PACK statement, however, is not recognized by PowerBuilder. Thus, the following code would yield an error:

```
PACK employee;
```

The following code, however, would work:

```
string foo
foo = "PACK employee"
EXECUTE IMMEDIATE :foo USING SQLCA;
```

To see if a particular SQL statement is supported by your DBMS, try running it in the Database Administrator painter. If it works there, but not as embedded SQL, then it's a good candidate for this method.

Format 2: Some Inputs/No Outputs

Use dynamic SQL format 2 when the statement returns no result set but requires some dynamic parameters. The general format for this method is as follows:

```
PREPARE DynamicStagingArea FROM SQLStatement  {USING
TransactionObject};

EXECUTE DynamicStagingArea  USING {ParameterList};
```

The following example removes all records with the last name Rensin or the first name Ted from the authors table:

```
String lname, fname, sqlStatement

lname = 'Rensin'
fname = 'Ted'

sqlStatement = "DELETE FROM authors WHERE &
last_name = ? OR_" + "first_name = ?"

// Prepare the dynamic staging area with the
// following SQL.

PREPARE SQLSA FROM :sqlStatement;

// Execute the contents of the dynamic staging
// area with the parameters :lname and :fname

EXECUTE SQLSA USING :lname,:fname;
```

Use a question mark to reserve a place for parameters in your SQL statement.

Format 3: Some Inputs/Some Outputs

Dynamic SQL format 3 is used when both the input parameter types and output column definitions are known at compile-time. It's useful when you need to perform basic data modifications dynamically but don't need all the power of a DataWindow. The general format of this procedure is as follows:

```
DECLARE CursorName DYNAMIC CURSOR
FOR DynamicStagingArea;

PREPARE DynamicStagingArea
FROM SQLStatement
{USING TransactionObject};

OPEN DYNAMIC Cursor
{USING ParameterList};

FETCH Cursor
INTO HostVariableList;

CLOSE Cursor;
```

The following steps show the required order of processing for this type of dynamic SQL:

1. Declare a new dynamic cursor that is linked to a specific dynamic staging area.
2. Assemble and compile the elements of an SQL statement into a dynamic staging area and link to a specific transaction object.
3. Execute the staged SQL and retrieve its contents into the defined dynamic cursor.
4. Fetch each row of the cursor and do some processing.
5. Close the cursor.

The following example further illustrates this process. This code prints all names from the employee table.

```
String fname, lname

// Step 1

DECLARE my_cursor &
DYNAMIC CURSOR &
    FOR SQLSA;
```

```
// Step 2

PREPARE SQLSA
FROM "SELECT lastname, firstname from &
employee" USING SQLCA;

// Step 3

OPEN DYNAMIC my_cursor;

// Step 4

do while (SQLCA.SQLCode = 0)

    FETCH my_cursor
        INTO :fname, :lname;

    messagebox("Name",fname + " "  + lname)

loop

// Step 5

CLOSE my_cursor;
```

The WHERE CURRENT OF CURSOR syntax will *not* work with a dynamically declared cursor.

Format 4: Possibly Some Inputs/Possibly Some Outputs

Dynamic SQL format 4 is the most complicated form of dynamic SQL. Use it when the input parameter types, the result-set column definitions or both are unknown. This method makes use of SQLDA, and variables like it, to describe these parameters. The general format for this type of dynamic SQL is as follows:

```
DECLARE CursorName
    DYNAMIC CURSOR
    FOR DynamicStagingArea;

PREPARE DynamicStagingArea FROM SQLStatement   {USING
TransactionObject};
```

```
DESCRIBE DynamicStagingArea  INTO DynamicDescriptionArea;

OPEN DYNAMIC Cursor   USING DESCRIPTOR
DynamicDescriptionArea;

EXECUTE DYNAMIC Cursor   USING DESCRIPTOR
DynamicDescriptionArea ;

FETCH Cursor
    USING DESCRIPTOR DynamicDescriptionArea ;

CLOSE Cursor;
```

The following steps show the required order of processing for this type of dynamic SQL:

1. Declare a new dynamic cursor that is linked to a specific dynamic staging area.
2. Assemble and compile the elements of an SQL statement into a dynamic staging area and link to a specific transaction object.
3. Link the dynamic staging area with a dynamic description area.
4. Open the cursor for processing.
5. Execute the staged SQL and retrieve its contents into the defined dynamic cursor.
6. Fetch each row of the cursor and do some processing.
7. Close the cursor.

As mentioned earlier, SQLDA has several publicly accessible data members that describe both the input parameters and the output rows for a particular dynamic cursor. PowerBuilder provides several functions to read these data members:

- ❐ GetDynamicDate
- ❐ GetDynamicDateTime
- ❐ GetDynamicNumber
- ❐ GetDynamicString
- ❐ GetDynamicTime

The syntax for these functions is as follows:

```
data = DynamicDescriptionArea.Function (index)
```

If, for example, you determine that the second column of the cursor contains a string, the following code will retrieve it:

```
String data
data = SQLDA.GetDynamicString(2)
```

This script retrieves the value in the second column of the current row of the dynamic cursor attached to SQLDA. The complete script for this function looks like this:

```
string data, sql

sql = "SELECT * FROM employee"

// Declare a new cursor

DECLARE my_curs &
    DYNAMIC CURSOR &
    FOR SQLSA;

// Prepare the staging area

PREPARE SQLSA
    FROM :sql
    USING SQLCA;

// Describe the input parameters into the
// description area.
```

```
DESCRIBE SQLSA &
    INTO SQLDA;

// Open the cursor

OPEN DYNAMIC my_curs &
    USING DESCRIPTOR SQLDA;

// Execute the SQL bound to the cursor.

// Populate the output data members of the
// description area and process the results.

do while (SQLCA.SQLCode = 0)

    FETCH my_curs &
        USING DESCRIPTOR SQLDA;

    data = SQLDA.GetDynamicString(2)

    messagebox("Data is...", data)

loop

// Close the cursor.

CLOSE my_curs;
```

At this point, you may be wondering why you would ever use such a complicated method to retrieve data. The truth is that, in most cases, you don't. There are, however, a few special times when this method comes in handy. Consider the following scenario.

You're writing a reporting system in which the table structure is fixed, but the table names are not. In other words, the users will be able to specify what table to run the report against. As long as the table they choose has the correct structure, the report will run fine. If it doesn't, however, your DataWindows will complain bitterly. Given this possibility, you decide that it would be a good idea to check the table structure before trying to report against it. This is where dynamic SQL format 4 is useful. You can retrieve the table structure into SQLDA and use the values in its OutParmType array to check the table structure. Assume, for the sake of this example, that the structure of the table must be String, Number and Date. In other words, there are three columns. Column 1 must be a string, column 2 a number and column 3 a date. The following code performs this check:

```
String tableName, sql

tableName = "authors"
sql = "Select * from " + tableName

// Declare cursor and attach to a staging area

DECLARE my_curs &
    DYNAMIC CURSOR &
    FOR SQLSA;

// Prepare the staging area from the SQL and
// attach to a transaction object.

PREPARE SQLSA
    FROM :sql
    USING SQLCA;

// Describe input parameters into the
// description area

DESCRIBE SQLSA &
    INTO SQLDA;
```

```
// Open the cursor described in SQLDA

OPEN DYNAMIC my_curs &
   USING DESCRIPTOR SQLDA;

// Execute the cursor described in SQLDA

// Close the cursor. It's not needed anymore
// since the table structure has been
// described.

CLOSE my_curs;

// Check to see if the format is correct

if (SQLDA.NumOutputs = 3 AND &
SQLDA.OutParmType[1] = TypeString! and &
SQLDA.OutParmType[2] = TypeInteger! &
and SQLDA.OutParmType[3] = TypeDate!) then
   messagebox("Hurray!","Table OK.")

else

   messagebox("Uh Oh!","Table not correct.")

end if
```

The Right Tool for the Job

Many PowerBuilder programmers believe that it's more effective to use dynamically created DataWindows to perform cursor operations than it is to declare a cursor directly. Others disagree. We have discussed both ways. The long and the short of it is to use your best discretion. A good rule of thumb, though, is to use dynamic SQL formats 1 and 2 when you can, and dynamic DataWindows instead of formats 3 and 4. No matter which you choose, though, comment your code diligently, as both methods can quickly become convoluted.

WRITING DBMS-INDEPENDENT SQL

In an ideal world, all DBMSes would use exactly the same SQL grammar. This way, a programmer could write the fastest, most efficient SQL without worrying about portability. However, the unfortunate truth is that SQL syntax can vary tremendously among vendors. The only sure way to keep your code portable is to write purely ANSI-compliant SQL. By doing so, however, you forego many nice, time-saving features specific to one database system or another. Given this dilemma, more and more programmers are opting for a hybrid approach.

OO purists often point to the problems associated with SQL portability as a prime example of the advantages of a good object-oriented design. Programmers, they argue, should write user objects that handle all database communication. This way, when they need to use a new DBMS, the only thing that needs to be recoded is the communication object. One of the key problems with this approach is that the overall complexity and initial development time of your system rise.

OO design or damage consolidation?

Other programmers, however, take a slightly different approach. They write functions that return the correct SQL for the situation and keep these functions in a single PBL. When the DBMS changes, only these functions need to be rewritten. Here's an illustration of the technique, which is often referred to sarcastically as "damage control" or "damage consolidation."

```
String result
SELECT substr(name,6,10) INTO :result FROM authors WHERE
ssn = '123456789';
```

This code would thus become simplified and easier to use:

```
String result
result = GetSubstrName()
```

The function GetSubstrName() returns the correct SQL syntax to perform the function. If all embedded SQL were replaced with function calls and those functions were placed in a central PBL, migration would be a lot easier. This approach, like the OO approach, adds a level of complexity to the overall system development that many programmers find unnecessary.

No matter which way you decide to do it, keeping your SQL portable is a difficult task. The implications of your decision affect the entire scope of the system's life cycle, so be sure to address this issue as soon as the functional requirements for your system are established.

MOVING ON

SQL is a primary tool when developing applications in PowerBuilder. In this chapter, we've taken a look at some of the more advanced ways to use SQL. In the next chapter, we'll take a look at some other programming techniques that you can use when developing PowerBuilder applications.

Advanced Programming Topics

●
●
●

Human beings are a curious species. Something within us compels us to understand our place in the world. Not surprisingly, most programmers behave much the same way in writing their programs. Once programmers become comfortable with the applications they're writing, they usually try to figure out a way to broadcast their applications to the rest of the computer world. This chapter shows you how to make connections between your application and other applications, how to connect to the underlying operating system and how to talk to a network.

WRITING TO THE WINDOWS API

Microsoft Windows is more than just an interface to MS-DOS: from a programmer's perspective, Windows is a more flexible development environment than MS-DOS. The reason for this is that all low-level system functions are contained in dynamic link libraries (DLLs) located somewhere in an application's search path. Programmers can call these routines from their applications without having the source code for them.

For example, you can call a system function to determine how much memory is free in order to decide whether to open another window. To do the same thing in DOS, you have to write your own routine. This ready accessibility to system functions makes interfacing with the operating environment easier. This section discusses some basic reasons why you may want to interact directly with the operating environment and offers some practical examples.

The Basics

Before discussing all that you can do by writing to the Windows API (application programming interface), it helps to know how PowerBuilder provides this capability.

Declarations for functions not internal to a PowerBuilder application are contained in the Global External Functions section of an application or in the Local External Functions section in the Window painter, Menu painter and User Object painter.

Getting to the External Functions
You can get to the Global External Functions section of an application from any script painter by selecting it from the Declare menu option. You can get to the Local External Functions section of the Window painter, Menu painter and User Object painter from the script painter in these objects.

For example, there might be a function called Time() that returns the system time as a number of seconds past midnight. If this function is contained in a DLL and you want to access it, you have to declare it first so PowerBuilder knows where to find it. The general format for declaring a function is as follows:

```
Function return_type FunctionName([Ref] Parm_type
parm_name, ...) Library "library name"
```

The declaration for Time() would look something like this:

```
Function integer Time() library "stuff.dll"
```

The following is an example of a more complicated function requiring parameters:

```
Function integer SomeOtherThing(String param1, ref String
parm2, integer parm3) library "c:\dlls\mylib.dll"
```

Note: Using the Ref keyword in a function declaration means that the parameter is being passed by reference rather than by value.

Task Management

PowerBuilder makes it easy for you to launch other Windows applications from your application. You can do this via OLE or by using the Run() function. This section shows you how to verify that a particular Windows application is running and how to run multiple instances of an application. You'll also learn how to delete a particular application window from your PowerBuilder program and make a particular window a child of the MDI frame.

How to Determine If an Application Is Running

Many applications don't allow you to have more than one copy of the application running simultaneously on a given machine. Some programs such as Windows Notepad have no such restriction. The number of instances of NOTEPAD.EXE that you can run at one time is limited only by the memory of your computer. For applications that don't have this capability, you need a way to check whether an application is already running before you launch it to avoid making errors.

Checking to see if a particular executable is running is a relatively simple matter. It involves two Windows system functions: GetModuleHandle() and GetModuleUsage().

GetModuleHandle() returns a unique integer that represents the program in memory. Windows uses this number to uniquely reference the program for all system task management operations.

GetModuleUsage() returns the number of programs that have caused a given *module* to be loaded into memory. A module is any executable code that can be loaded into memory. This can include DLLs and device drivers. For example, if seven separate applications are making calls to functions in a particular DLL, a call to GetModuleUsage() for that DLL returns a 7. When the module in question is an executable, GetModuleUsage() returns the number of copies of the application currently running. This number is called a module's *reference count*. If a program has a reference count greater than zero, at least one copy is running.

When a program has a reference count greater than zero, at least one copy is running.

To use GetModuleHandle() and GetModuleUsage() in a PowerBuilder application, the following declarations have to be made in either the Global External Functions or Local External Functions section of the application.

```
Function uint GetModuleHandle(String ModuleName) library
"krnl386.exe"

Function int GetModuleUsage(uint ModHandle) library
"krnl386.exe"
```

The following code shows you how to check if NOTEPAD.EXE is already running, how to limit the number of instances of the application to one, and how to post an error message to the user and end the routine if NOTEPAD.EXE is already running.

```
uint handle
int usage

// Get the handle for notepad.exe

handle = GetModuleHandle("notepad.exe")
```

```
// Get the reference count

usage = GetModuleUsage(handle)

if (usage > 0) then
    messagebox("Error","Still going.")
else
    Run("notepad.exe")
end if
```

The following code shows you how to check if the user is trying to run a second instance of your application. You can also use it in the Open() event of a PowerBuilder application to ensure that only one copy is running at a time.

```
uint handle
int usage

// Get the handle for myapp.exe

handle = GetModuleHandle("myapp.exe")

// Get the reference count

usage = GetModuleUsage(handle)

if (usage > 1) then
    messagebox("Error","App is running.")
    halt
end if
```

When an application checks to see if another copy of itself is already running, its reference count must be greater than one. This is because at least one copy of the program must be running in order to perform the check. It's also important to mention that this code does not work in development mode. It works only in a running executable, and your application executable file doesn't exist until you compile it. This is a common mistake that has caused many programmers to try to debug code that was not intended to work in development mode.

One copy of your application must be running before you can check for a second instance.

Running Multiple Instances of an Application Simultaneously

Sometimes a developer *wants* several instances of the same application running as long as they don't interfere with one another. Editing text files is an example: when a programmer writes an application that generates several text files, the user may want to edit all of the files at the same time. The developer can accommodate the user by launching several copies of NOTEPAD.EXE.

All is well as long as two or more copies of NOTEPAD.EXE are not operating on the same file. The Windows function FindWindow() allows you to distinguish between two instances of the same program. The FindWindow() system call returns the handle of the window with a title matching a given string. The syntax for FindWindow() is as follows:

```
Function uint FindWindow(String class, String title)
library "user.exe"
```

In Chapter 1 you learned that all Windows objects (windows, menus, etc.) are actually instances of a base type. This base type is also known as a *class.* The FindWindow() function allows the user not only to search for all windows that have title text matching a given string, but to also search for windows that belong to a specific class. If the string that represents the *class* parameter is NULL, all windows are searched.

For example, the following block of code checks to see if there is an open window that has the title "Microsoft Word - CHAPTER8.DOC":

```
String NULL
SetNull(NULL)
uint handle

handle = FindWindow(NULL,"Microsoft Word - CHAPTER8.DOC")
```

All window manipulation functions discussed in this chapter are contained in USER.EXE.

```
if handle = 0 then
    messagebox("Error","Not Found")
else
    messagebox("Success","Window Found.")
end if
```

A programmer can use this technique to determine whether a *specific* copy of Word is already running. For example, if two copies of Word are running and one copy contains CHAPTER7.DOC and the other contains CHAPTER8.DOC, this code finds the copy of Word that loaded CHAPTER8.DOC.

If the title text does not match *exactly*, the call to FindWindow() fails.

In our example, because the *class* parameter is a null string, all windows are searched. If the string contains the name of a specific class, only windows belonging to that class are searched.

Terminating an Application

In Windows, when the main window of an application is destroyed, the application is terminated. This process is accomplished with a call to DestroyWindow(). The syntax for this function is as follows:

```
Function boolean DestroyWindow(uint window_to_close)
library "user.exe"
```

You can use PowerBuilder's Run() command to open an application, the FindWindow() command to get its window handle, and the DestroyWindow() command to terminate it. Here's an example of this sequence:

```
// Launch notepad.exe

String NULL
SetNull(NULL)
uint windowhandle
```

```
Run("notepad.exe")

// Get its window handle

windowhandle = FindWindow(NULL,"Notepad - (Untitled)")

// Do some processing...
// etc...
//Terminate the application
```

Integrating Your PowerBuilder Application With Other Applications

The ability to launch, control and close other applications at will makes integrating your PowerBuilder program with other applications much easier. The ability to make a window from another application a child of your MDI frame is also important. Why? Consider the following scenario.

Your PowerBuilder program MYAPP.EXE launches XYZ.EXE so the user can do something. While XYZ.EXE is running, the user minimizes MYAPP, but the main window for XYZ.EXE is still active! All of a sudden, things don't look quite so integrated. If, however, XYZ's main window were a child of MYAPP's MDI frame, XYZ.EXE would be minimized as well. The system call you need to establish this link is called SetParent(), and its syntax is as follows:

```
Function uint SetParent(uint child_window, uint new_parent)
library "user.exe"
```

The unsigned integer returned by SetParent() is the handle of the window that was previously the parent of child_window. This function call would be made after a call to FindWindow(). When the pieces are all put together, the code looks like this:

```
// Launch notepad.exe

Run("notepad.exe")
string s_null
setnull(s_null)
uint windowhandle
uint previous

// Get its window handle

windowhandle = FindWindow(s_null,"Notepad - (Untitled)")

// Set our MDI frame as the parent

previous = SetParent(windowhandle,handle(main_window))

// Do some processing...
// etc...

// Terminate the application
```

PowerBuilder's Handle() function returns the handle to a particular object.

Talking to a Network

Not long ago, if a computer was part of a network, it was part of only one network. Computers didn't have to connect simultaneously to multiple networks. As the need for interconnecting multiple networks has grown, so has the set of available Windows API calls. Depending on which version of Windows a user is running (Windows 3.1, 3.11, NT, Workgroups or 95), any number of system-level function calls may be available to perform sophisticated network operations.

This section shows you how to view, add and change network connections. The ability to dynamically change network drive mappings is especially useful in a database application. This allows a programmer to write a program that looks for data on a particular drive and simply change where that drive points to in order to change the data set. This kind of operation requires the use of three API calls: WNetGetConnection, WNetAddConnection and WNetCancelConnection.

For a complete list of the networking functions available in your version of Windows, consult the programmer's reference for that version.

Viewing a Network Connection

Use WNetGetConnection to view the network connection for a computer drive or printer port. The syntax for this function is as follows:

```
Function uint WNetGetConnection(ref String local_name, ref
String remote_name, ref int buffer_size) library "user.exe"
```

Table 9-1 describes the function parameters.

Parameter	Description
local_name	A string containing the name of the local resource to check. This may be either a drive letter (A:–Z:) or a printer port (LPT1– LPT*x*). The string contained in local_name must end with a colon (:), or the call to WNetGetConnection() will fail.
remote_name	A string into which the name of the network resource attached to local_name will be copied.
size	The size, in characters, of the remote_name string.

Table 9-1: The WNetGetConnection() function parameters.

The following code looks for the network resources attached to drive F:.

```
String local_name, remote_name
int size

local_name = "F:"

// Reserve room for 256 characters of data

remote_name = space(256)

// Set to the number of available characters
// in remote_name

size = 256

// Get connection information

WNetGetConnection(local_name, remote_name, size)

// Check if local_name is connected to
// anything

if (len(trim(remote_name)) > 0) then
    messagebox("Connected to", remote_name)
else
    messagebox("Error","Not Connected.")
end if
```

You can make a few minor changes to the previous block of code to find the network resource connected to any given drive or printer port. Declare a global function called GetResourceName that takes a single string parameter (local_name) and returns a string. Insert the following code into the newly created function:

```
String remote_name
int size

remote_name = space(256)
```

```
size = 256

// Get connection information

WNetGetConnection(local_name, remote_name, size)

if (len(trim(remote_name)) = 0) then
    SetNull(remote_name)
end if

return remote_name
```

This function returns the name of the resource connected to a given local device, or it returns NULL if the local device is not connected to anything. Using this function, a programmer could easily check all local drives and printer ports with two FOR loops, as follows:

```
int counter
string local_name, remote_name

// Check all local drives

for counter = Asc('A') to Asc('Z')

    local_name = String(counter) + ':'
    remote_name = GetResourceName(local_name)

    if (IsNull(remote_name)) then

        // Do some processing..
        // etc...

    else

        // Do some other processing
        // etc...

    end if
```

```
next

// Check all printer ports

for counter = 1 to 3

    local_name = 'LPT' + String(counter) + ':'
    remote_name = GetResourceName(local_name)

    if (IsNull(remote_name)) then

        // Do some processing..
        // etc...

    else

        // Do some other processing
        // etc...

    end if

next
```

Adding a Network Connection

Use a call to WNetAddConnection() to connect a network resource to a local device. The syntax for this function is as follows:

```
Function uint WNetAddConnection(ref String remote_name, ref
String user_password, ref String local_name) library
"user.exe"
```

Table 9-2 describes the function parameters.

Parameter	Description
remote_name	The name of the network device receiving the connection.
local_name	The name of the local resource that connects to the network device (remote_name).
user_password	The password used to make the connection. If this parameter is NULL, the user's default password is used. If this parameter is empty, no password is used.

Table 9-2: The WNetAddConnection() function parameters.

A complete call to this function looks like this:

```
String local_name, remote_name, password

local_name = 'F:'
remote_name = '\\file_server\vol1\homes\smith'
password = 'smithisgreat'

WNetAddConnection(remote_name, password, local_name)
```

Deleting a Connection

A programmer can disconnect a local device from a network resource using the WNetCancelConnection() API function. The syntax for this is as follows:

```
Function uint WNetCancelConnection(ref String local_name,
boolean force) library "user.exe"
```

Table 9-3 describes the function parameters.

Parameter	Description
local_name	The name of the local device to disconnect.
force	If this parameter is TRUE the local device will be disconnected even if the device is in use. If the parameter is FALSE, the local device will not be disconnected if it is in use.

Table 9-3: The WNetCancelConnection() function parameters.

The following is a brief example of how to use this function:

```
String local_name
boolean force

local_name = 'F:'
force = TRUE

WNetCancelConnection(local_name,force)
```

MAIL-ENABLING A POWERBUILDER APPLICATION

Communicating with other applications running on the *same* machine allows programmers to more fully integrate their applications into the current working environment. Communicating with other applications running on *other* machines, however, allows programmers to be more fully integrated into the network community at large. One of the simplest ways to conduct this kind of communication is through electronic mail. PowerBuilder has many built-in functions and data structures to facilitate the use of e-mail in an application. Although these features were written for the Microsoft Mail API (MAPI) standard, you can also use them with the Lotus Vendor Independent Mail (VIM) standard.

Creating a mailsession Object

All transactions in PowerBuilder involving mail revolve around an object type known as a *mailsession*, which is analogous to all DataWindow transactions revolving around a transaction object. The mailsession object is in a special class that contains all the information about a specific connection to a mail server. The mailsession object type is as follows:

❏ **SessionID**—A protected long integer that uniquely identifies the particular connection to a mail server.

❏ **MessageID**—A string array that contains the unique message IDs for each message in the current mailbox.

A̲ll mail commands in PowerBuilder are member functions (methods) of the mailsession class.

Like all other PowerBuilder object types, a mailsession object is instantiated using the CREATE statement.

```
mailsession MyMail
mymail = CREATE mailsession
```

Beginning a Mail Session: mailLogon()

After you have created a valid mailsession object, use the mailLogon() command to connect to a mail server. This command uses three optional arguments, which are listed in Table 9-4.

Parameter	Description
UserName	The user name of the account being connected to the mail server.
Password	The account password.
LogonOption	One of three enumerated types that describe how the mail session is started.

Table 9-4: The mailLogon() function parameters.

After you connect to the mail server, you can start a new mail session using the following code:

```
mailsession MyMail
MyMail = CREATE mailsession

MyMail.mailLogon('JSMITH','JOHNGUY',mailNewSessionWithDownLoad!)
```

This code creates a new mailsession object called MyMail and logs on to the mail server as account JSMITH. If the username and password options are omitted, a logon dialog appears for the user to enter the information.

Once a valid mail session has been established, a call to mailGetMessages() is made to populate the MessageID[] array of the mailsession object.

Reading Mail: mailReadMessage()

After you've made a valid connection to a mail account, you can read the contents of the mailbox using the mailReadMessage() function. This command has the following syntax:

```
mailSession.mailReadMessage (messageID, mailMessage,
readOption, readFlag)
```

Table 9-5 describes the function parameters.

Parameter	Description
mailSession	A valid mailsession object.
messageID	The message ID string that identifies the message to be read.
mailMessage	A variable of type mailmessage. The contents of the mail identified by messageID are copied into this variable.
readOption	An enumerated type specifying how the message is to be read.
readFlag	A Boolean that specifies whether only unread messages are displayed.

Table 9-5: The mailReadMessage() function parameters.

The following script is an example of how to use the commands in this section to make a valid connection to a mail server and read all of the mail headers in your inbox:

```
// Create a mailsession object and connect.

mailsession mymail
mymail = CREATE mailsession

mymail.MailLogon(mailNewSessionWithDownLoad!)

// Retrieve mail messages.
mymail.MailGetMessages()

// Loop through and read.

int ctr, ctr2
mailmessage mmes
string current
```

```
ctr2 = upperbound(mymail.MessageID[])
for ctr = 1 to ctr2

    current = mymail.MessageID[ctr]

    mymail.mailReadMessage(current, mmes, &
    mailEnvelopeOnly!, False)

    messagebox(current, mmes.Subject)

next
```

Sending Mail: mailSend

So far you've learned how to establish a valid mail session, retrieve messages and read them. Now you're going to learn how to send a message.

Follow these steps to send a mail message in PowerBuilder:

1. Establish a valid mail session.
2. Create a variable of type mailmessage and populate it.
3. Send the new message.

You've already learned how to perform steps 1 and 2. Step 3 involves a simple call to the mailSend() function. The syntax of this command is as follows:

```
mailSession.mailSend(mailMessage)
```

The following is an example of the entire process of sending mail:

```
// Create a new session and connect

mailsession newmail
newmail = CREATE mailsession

newmail.mailLogon()

// Create a new mail message and populate it

mailmessage newmessage

newmessage.Subject = 'This is a test'
newmessage.NoteText = 'My test message body'
newmessage.Recipient[1].Name = 'John Smith'

// Send the new message

newmail.mailSend(newmessage)

// Logoff

newmail.mailLogoff()
```

This code logs on to the mail server, creates a new message, sends it to user John Smith and, finally, logs out of the account.

Using the Mail Commands With VIM Products

PowerBuilder's built-in support for electronic mail complies with the MAPI standard. Many sites, however, use Lotus Notes, cc:Mail or some other VIM-compatible package. Fortunately, users of these VIM packages can easily use the MAPI mail commands.

Microsoft ships a DLL called MAPIVIM.DLL with the Microsoft Office suite. Excel and Word use this library to access VIM-compliant messaging systems with MAPI-compliant function calls. If you copy this file to the \WINDOWS\SYSTEM directory and rename it MAPI.DLL, any program that attempts to complete a mail function via MAPI will, in fact, use the resident VIM mail system. This includes PowerBuilder applications. The downside to this technique is that if you replace MAPI.DLL with MAPIVIM.DLL, you won't be able to use Microsoft Mail or any other MAPI post office. This procedure is useful only if you need to attach to only one kind of mail server. If you want to operate on a MAPI server and a VIM server simulta-neously, you'll have to either use DDE to talk to a VIM package (such as cc:Mail) or write directly to the VIM API with a special SDK.

Submitting SQL Requests in Batch

By combining the information you've learned in this chapter with what you learned in Chapter 2, you can create a mail server that accepts incoming SQL queries via e-mail and sends back the results. This process is actually a lot easier than it may seem. The tricky part is settling on a format for the submitted request and its subsequent reply.

The Request

The format of the requesting message consists of two compo-nents:

❑ A subject line consisting of the word *Query*.
❑ Body text that is valid SQL.

The following is an example of how to create a valid request message and send it:

```
mailsession sqlmail
sqlmail = CREATE mailsession

// Connect

sqlmail.mailLogon('sqlmail','sqlpass')

// Create new request

mailmessage newrequest

newrequest.Subject = 'Query'
newrequest.NoteText = 'SELECT name FROM people WHERE' + &
' salary > 50000'

newrequest.Recipient[1].Name = 'SQLMAILSERVER'

// Send request and logoff

mailsession.mailSend(mailmessage)
mail.session.mailLogoff
```

The Response

The format of the query response is also composed of a specific subject and message body. The query response includes:

❑ A subject line consisting of the word *Response*.

❑ Body text containing the original SQL request and the result set.

The original SQL is included in the response so that the sending client can construct a DataWindow using the SyntaxFromSQL() and Create() functions to update the data.

A Basic Mail Server Routine

A basic mail server routine consists of the following steps:

1. Get the requesting SQL from the current message.
2. Use the SQL to construct a DataWindow.
3. Retrieve the result set.
4. Construct and mail the reply.

The following code shows how to accomplish these four steps.

```
// Create session, logon, and populate
// MessageID[]

mailsession servermail
servermail = CREATE mailsession

servermail.mailLogon('SQLMAILSERV','SQLPASS')
servermail.mailGetMessages()

string rSQL, dSyntax, resultSet, IDString
mailmessage SQLRequest

// Read 1st message

IDString = servermail.MessageID[1]

servermail.ReadMessage(IDString, SQLRequest, &
mailEntireMessage!, True)

// If it's query ...

if (SQLRequest.Subject = 'Query') then

    // Create and retrieve a DataWindow
    // based on the request SQL

    DataWindow dwResult
```

```
rSQL = SQLRequest.NoteText
dSyntax = SyntaxFromSQL(rSQL)

dwResult = Create(dSyntax)
dwResult.SetTransObject(SQLCA)

dwResult.Retrieve()

// Get result data

resultSet = dwResult.Describe("DataWindow.Data")

// Construct and send the reply

mailmessage SQLReply

SQLReply.Subject = 'Response'
SQLReply.NoteText = 'SQL: ' + rSQL + '~r~n' + &
'Data: ' + resultSet

SQLReply.Recipient[1].Name = &
SQLRequest.Recipient[1].Name
servermail.mailSend(SQLReply)
end if
// Logoff and destroy the mailsession object
servermail.mailLogoff()
DESTROY servermail
```

This kind of client-server interaction via e-mail can be very useful if your application needs to get data from a source without a physical data source or network connection. Although this process is done in batch, it could be used for the following operations:

❏ Nightly data mirroring.

❏ Daily updates to a central database.

❏ Other batch-style operations.

THE POWERBUILDER API

You've already learned that one of the advantages of programming in the Windows environment is that you can call system-level functions simply by knowing how they are defined and knowing the DLL in which to find them. This is true not only for Windows system DLLs, but for any dynamic library that has been built to allow external references.

Most DLLs have been built to allow external references, including DLLs that PowerBuilder uses. If you know how the PowerBuilder system functions are defined and the DLLs in which they are located, you can write C code to call them. Luckily, Powersoft provides just such a mechanism through its Open Repository CASE API (ORCA).

ORCA is a set of functions contained in PBORC040.DLL that allows developers to access most of PowerBuilder's Library painter functionality, session management functions, library entry compilation functions and object query functions. (If you're using PowerBuilder 3.0a, the name of the ORCA API is PBORC030.DLL.) The entire development kit consists of three files (see Table 9-6) found on Disk 3 of the PowerBuilder Enterprise installation disks.

File Name	Description
PBORCA.H	ORCA include file
PBORCA.LIB	ORCA import library
PBORCO40.DLL	ORCA run-time dynamic library

Table 9-6: Files in the ORCA development kit.

All functions in ORCA belong to one of four categories:

- ❑ Session management
- ❑ Library management
- ❑ Compilation
- ❑ Object query

Using ORCA DLLs

Most PowerBuilder developers will never use the ORCA library calls because most PowerBuilder applications don't need the functionality that ORCA provides.

It's important to know that you cannot freely distribute the ORCA DLLs. Anyone receiving your PowerBuilder application must own a licensed copy of PowerBuilder Enterprise in order to have the DLLs required to run your program. Remember, ORCA works only with the development system. It can't operate on its own.

Session Management

All of ORCA's library functions operate within the context of a *session*. A session is similar to a file pointer. Programmers can operate on more than one file at a time by referencing different file pointers. Similarly, they can operate on different PowerBuilder library sets using different sessions.

Table 9-7 shows the five functions ORCA uses to manage sessions.

Function	Description
PBORCA_SessionOpen()	Opens a new ORCA session.
PBORCA_SessionSetLibraryList()	Sets the library list for a given ORCA session.
PBORCA_SessionSetCurrentAppl()	Sets the current application for the session.
PBORCA_SessionGetError()	Gets the last error for a given session.
PBORCA_SessionClose()	Closes a given ORCA session and frees any related resources.

Table 9-7: ORCA session management functions.

The following code is a brief example of how to start, configure and close an ORCA session:

```
#include <windows.h>
#include "pborca.h"

void main() {

    HPBORCA session;
    LPSTR appname, lib_list[2];

    appname = "pb40orca_example";
    lib_list[1] = "dave1.pbl";
    lib_list[2] = "dave2.pbl";

    /* Get session handle. */

    session = PBORCA_SessionOpen();

    /* Set library list for session to the
       values in lib_list[]. */
```

```
PBORCA_SessionSetLibraryList( session, lib_list, 2)

/* Set the application for session,
  ('pb4Oorca_example'), which is
   contained in the library pointed
   to by lib_list[1]. */

PBORCA_SessionSetCurrentAppl( session, lib_list[1],
appname)

/* Close session and free any resources
   that the ORCA functions may have
    allocated. */

PBORCA_SessionClose(session);
}
```

Appendix D contains a
detailed list of all function prototypes and data
structures.

Appendix D contains a detailed list of all function prototypes
and data structures.

Library Management

The core of the ORCA standard deals with the ability of
programmers to access PowerBuilder's Library painter
functions. Although some processes are not yet available (for
example, the creation of PowerBuilder Dynamic Libraries, or
PBDs), most are. Table 9-8 lists all of ORCA's library management functions.

Function	Description
PBORCA_LibraryCommentModify	Modifies the comments for a given library.
PBORCA_LibraryCreate	Creates a new library.
PBORCA_LibraryDelete	Deletes an existing library.
PBORCA_LibraryDirectory	Retrieves a list of all objects in a library and a user-specified callback function for each.
PBORCA_LibraryEntryCopy	Copies an entry from one library to another.
PBORCA_LibaryEntryDelete	Deletes an entry from a library.
PBORCA_LibraryEntryExport	Exports an entry from a library to a string.
PBORCA_LibraryEntryInformation	Gets information about a particular entry in a library.
PBORCA_LibraryEntryMove	Moves a library entry from one PBL to another.

Table 9-8: ORCA's library management functions.

One common operation a programmer may want to perform is viewing information about all the entries in a particular library. This involves three basic steps:

1. Opening and configuring a new ORCA session.
2. Calling the PBORCA_LibraryDirectory() function.
3. Closing the new session.

You've already learned how to perform steps 1 and 3. Step 2 is not complicated, but requires some attention. The PBORCA_LibraryDirectory() function is defined as follows:

```
Function int PBORCA_LibraryDirectory( session, libName,
commentsBuffer, bufferSize, callbackPointer, userdata)
```

Table 9-9 describes the function parameters.

Parameter	Description
session	A valid session created with PBORCA_SessionOpen().
libName	A string containing the name of the library to examine.
commentsBuffer	A string into which the comments for the library are copied.
bufferSize	The number of characters commentsBuffer can hold.
callbackPointer	A pointer to a function called for each entry in libName. The function is called a *callback function*.
userdata	Any data that the programmer may want to pass to the callback function.

Table 9-9: Parameters of the PBORCA_LibraryDirectory() function.

The *callback function* listed in Table 9-9 is a segment of code that has a *void* return type and is passed as a parameter to another function. The callback is then executed by the function to which it is passed.

All ORCA callback functions must be declared in the following form:

```
void FAR PASCAL fnName(type parm1, type parm2, ...)
```

The following is a complete code example of using the PBORCA_LibraryDirectory() function to examine the contents of a PBL.

```
#include <windows.h>
#include "pborca.h"
#include <alloc.h>
#include <stdio.h>
```

```
#include <time.h>


/* Global defs */

char *days[7], *types[8];
LPSTR appname, libname;
HPBORCA session;

/* Prototype for the callback function */

void FAR PASCAL entry_details(PPBORCA_DIRENTRY entry,
LPVOID userdata);


/* main routine */

main() {

    /* Declare variables */

    LPSTR comments;
    LPVOID userdata;
    int rval;
    PBORCA_DIRENTRY fooz;

    appname = "pb40orca_example";
    libname = "PBORCA.PBL";
    comments = (LPSTR) farmalloc(1000);

    /* Fill days[] array */

    days[0] = "Sunday";
    days[1] = "Monday";
    days[2] = "Tuesday";
    days[3] = "Wednesday";
    days[4] = "Thursday";
    days[5] = "Friday";
    days[6] = "Saturday";
```

```
         /* Fill types[] array */

         types[0] = "Application";
         types[1] = "DataWindow";
         types[2] = "Function";
         types[3] = "Menu";
         types[4] = "Query";
         types[5] = "Structure";
         types[6] = "UserObject";
         types[7] = "Window";


         /* Open Session */

         session = PBORCA_SessionOpen();

         /* Set the library list, application name,
             and get information for the library
     directory. */

         PBORCA_SessionSetLibraryList(session,&libname,1);

         PBORCA_SessionSetCurrentAppl(session,libname,appname);

         PBORCA_LibraryDirectory(session, libname, comments, 250,
     entry_details, userdata);

         /* Close session */

         PBORCA_SessionClose(session);

         return (0);
     }


/* entry_details() - The callback function
     for PBORCA_LibraryDirectory(). */

void FAR PASCAL entry_details(PPBORCA_DIRENTRY entry,
```

```
LPVOID userdata) {

    struct tm *footime;
    int rval;
    PBORCA_ENTRYINFO foo;

    /* Fill a PBORCA_EntryInformation structure
       for the current entry */

    PBORCA_LibraryEntryInformation(session, libname, entry-
>lpszEntryName, entry->otEntryType, &foo);

    /* Translate lCreateTime from the number of
       seconds since Jan. 1 1970 to a tm struct.
    */

    footime = localtime(&foo.lCreateTime);

    /* Print the results. */

    printf("Object Name: %s\n",entry->lpszEntryName);

    printf("Object Type: %s\n",types[entry->otEntryType]);

    printf("Object Size: %ld\n",foo.lObjectSize);

    printf("Source Size: %ld\n",foo.lSourceSize);

    printf("Comments: %s\n",foo.szComments);

    printf("Last Modified On: %s, %d/%d/%d\n",days[footime-
>tm_wday],footime->tm_mon+1,footime->tm_mday,footime-
>tm_year);

    printf("At: %d:%d:%d\n\n",footime->tm_hour+1,footime-
>tm_min,footime->tm_sec);
}
```

Compilation

The ORCA compilation functions allow the programmer to import and regenerate library entries. They are listed in Table 9-10.

Function	Description
PBORCA_CompileEntryImport	Imports and compiles an entry.
PBORCA_CompileEntryImportList	Imports and compiles a list of entries to a list of libraries.
PBORCA_CompileEntryRegenerate	Regenerates an entry.

Table 9-10: ORCA's compilation functions.

The current application and library list *must* be set before calling the ORCA compilation functions. The following code is a simple example of regenerating a library entry:

```
#include <windows.h>
#include "pborca.h"
#include <alloc.h>
#include <stdio.h>

/* Global defs */

LPSTR appname, libname;
HPBORCA session;

/* Prototype for the callback function */

void FAR PASCAL CompError(PPBORCA_COMPERR error, LPVOID
userdata);

/* main routine */

main() {
```

```
    /* Declare variables */

    LPSTR comments;
    LPVOID userdata;

    appname = "pb40orca_example";
    libname = "PBORCA.PBL";
    comments = (LPSTR) farmalloc(1000);

    /* Open Session */

    session = PBORCA_SessionOpen();

    /* Set the library list, application name,
        and regenerate the application object. */

    PBORCA_SessionSetLibraryList(session,&libname,1);

    PBORCA_SessionSetCurrentAppl(session,libname,appname);

    PBORCA_CompileEntryRegenerate(session, libname, appname,
PBORCA_APPLICATION, CompError, userdata);

    /* Close session */

    PBORCA_SessionClose(session);

    return (0);
}


/* CompError() - The callback function
    for PBORCA_CompileEntryRegenerate(). */

void FAR PASCAL Comperror(PPBORCA_COMPERR error, LPVOID
userdata) {

    printf("Error: %s\n",error-> lpszMessageText);

}
```

Object Query

A final area addressed by the ORCA API deals with references to and from a particular PowerBuilder object. These functions are listed in Table 9-11.

Function	Description
PBORCA_ObjectQueryHierarchy	Calls a user-defined function for all objects in an object's ancestor tree.
PBORCA_ObjectQueryReference	Calls a user-defined callback for all objects referenced by a particular library entry.

Table 9-11: ORCA's Object Query functions.

Why Use the ORCA Library Calls?

The majority of PowerBuilder developers will never use the ORCA library calls because the majority of PowerBuilder applications don't need the functionality that ORCA provides. Nevertheless, the library is included with PowerBuilder Enterprise Edition and is not documented in the online help or the user documentation.

It's important to know that you cannot freely distribute the ORCA DLLs. Anyone receiving your PowerBuilder application must own a licensed copy of PowerBuilder Enterprise in order to have the DLLs required to run your program. Remember, ORCA works only with the development system. It can't operate on its own.

The ORCA DLLs cannot be distributed freely.

Maybe someday you'll want to write your own CASE tool for PowerBuilder. At the very least, this discussion of ORCA should give you a better understanding of how closely you can control all aspects of your computing environment.

MOVING ON

In this chapter, you learned about the many ways to interact with other computer applications, the Windows API and networks from your PowerBuilder application. The key point to remember is that anything is possible, given enough effort. The examples in this chapter can be used and modified to create an environment in which the central application is a PowerBuilder program that controls the flow of all information within an entire network of machines. The possibilities are endless! It's only a matter of imagination and persistence.

Because of the client-server model running on some networks, clients may be on different platforms. In the next chapter, we'll discuss how to prepare for cross-platform applications. You can take steps now in your development efforts to be ready for cross-platform application development when PowerBuilder becomes available on UNIX and Macintosh platforms.

Developing Cross-Platform Applications

PowerBuilder has become the leading development tool for the Windows environment. It won't be long before the Macintosh and UNIX versions of the software hit the market. We're including this chapter because you can make preparations now so your program can be built in Windows and recompiled to run on other platforms.

OPERATING SYSTEMS

Operating systems are the foundation for developing applications. More than that, operating systems provide graphical user interfaces (GUIs). Knowing how an operating system handles file names, paths, users, security, multitasking and executables is essential for a developer who wants to create an application to run on that operation system.

UNIX

The rapid growth of the Internet has helped fuel a new interest in UNIX. UNIX used to be the domain of intellectual types in academia who thought nothing of commands like "grep" and "awk." Now, UNIX is in the hands of the average user. X Windows has come a long way in providing a friendly GUI to shield the user from the command-heavy UNIX. Until recently, there was more than one X Windows standard. Motif has won out over OpenLook as the standard for X Windows development.

The UNIX operating system has won the hearts of developers for years. Even users willing to venture into just a few of the UNIX capabilities are reluctant to switch to another operating system. Two of the major advantages of UNIX are its multitasking and multiuser capabilities.

Multitasking Miracles

Microsoft Windows developers have been able to give users the impression that they can run multiple applications in different windows. UNIX, on the other hand, does true multitasking: UNIX programs truly can run simultaneously in different windows.

While the user works in one application, a query performed in another window runs as fast as the microprocessor allows. The applications don't even have to be in separate windows. Some UNIX programs can run in the background while other applications operate in the same window.

This ability is based on two important concepts: the *process* and the *shell*.

UNIX processes

Every program running in UNIX is considered to be a process and is given a process ID number. The next time you are sitting at a UNIX machine, type the **ps** command to see which processes are running. Add the parameters **-aux** after the command, and you'll see a complete list of all the processes running on the machine. The command-line option -aux may actually be -ef depending on your version of UNIX.

The -aux and -ef options list all the processes currently running. Running the ps command by itself shows only the processes running on your workstation. Plenty will be running. In the UNIX environment, most processes can operate in the foreground or in the background. The amount of CPU time they demand can be adjusted by changing the *niceness* of the program. The term *niceness* refers to the priority of the process within the CPU. Processes can be allocated disproportionate amounts of CPU time.

Because of UNIX's multitasking ability and the ability of multiple users to be logged on to a UNIX computer at the same time, rebooting a UNIX computer is definitely a last resort if you're having problems with an application. However, if you have the correct user privileges and the process ID number, you can stop individual processes from running by issuing the kill command.

Processes can be built to intercommunicate using *interprocess communication (IPC)*. For MS Windows programmers, IPC is a little like DDE. The way the different parts of the UNIX operating system work together is even simpler than Windows's IPC.

One example of IPC in UNIX is the ability to send the output of a UNIX command to the input of another UNIX command, allowing you to string one command after another. This is done using a pipe or a redirect symbol. For example, you can type the contents of a file using the cat command and pipe the output into the UNIX mail command, as shown below:

```
cat myfile.text | mail joe@schmoe.net
```

The text from myfile.text is piped into the mail command and sent to Joe through a machine named schmoe, which resides on a network connected to the Internet.

UNIX shells

The shell is a work environment. When a user logs in to a UNIX machine, he or she is given a shell in which to work. In the X Windows environment, each window is a separate shell. The beauty of having different shells is that each can be totally different from the next. There are different shell types that allow the differentiation. Some of the more common shell types are:

- ❏ C shell
- ❏ Bourne shell
- ❏ Korn shell
- ❏ Bourne-again shell (bash)

We won't describe them here. Suffice it to say that each type allows different activities or programs. Each has its own scripting language, its own environment variables and, in some cases, a slightly different command set. The most common, by far, is the C shell.

We just mentioned environment variables. UNIX depends far more on environment variables than do DOS and Windows. Most of a shell's environment variables are set automatically when the user starts a new shell. Environment variables are somewhat global variables used by the operating system to store information about your particular login session. The variables themselves can store login information, your personal operating environment configuration information and application program information. In the UNIX X Windows system, a new shell is started each time you open a new window. See Figure 10-1.

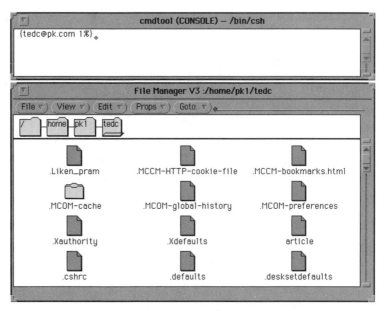

Figure 10-1: The X Windows File Manager and Console.

Multiuser Machines

UNIX allows several people to work on one machine at the same time. Individual users can log in to a UNIX machine and be given their own *virtual machine*. To individual users, whether they're using a dumb terminal, an X terminal or a network connection from another machine, it appears as though the entire machine is theirs. There are a few clues along the way that this is not actually the case, but for practical purposes, they have their own machine within a machine.

When users log in to a UNIX machine, they are given their own shells. Each shell has its own environment, which is determined by the users' login files. For users logging in to a C shell, these are the .login and .cshrc files. The Bourne shell uses the .profile file. The dot that precedes these file names causes them to be hidden while the most common UNIX commands are in use. Hiding the files reduces clutter when files are listed and in similar activities.

Individual users can log in to a UNIX system more than once: that is, they can have more than one login *session*. When using X Windows, each window is a different shell and therefore a different login session. UNIX requires the user to enter a login ID and password for only the first shell. Each session is similar to having a new virtual machine. The user can start a new shell of any type, set up different environment variables and run different programs without affecting the other shells. The only effect they have is in the overall usage of the CPU. In a RISC machine, this usage is usually fairly negligible.

DOS & Windows

In DOS, you can run multiple programs as long as all the programs running in the background are of a type known as TSR, or *terminate and stay resident*, programs.

Windows brought graphics and a windowing environment to the PC, which shielded users from the text-based, command-based DOS operating system. Windows also offered the ability to extend the operating environment using DLLs, or dynamic linked libraries, and to share information among programs through OLE, Object Linking and Embedding. As much as it extended DOS and made computers easier to use, Windows was still restricted to the constraints of the DOS operating system.

Windows is changing. Windows promises to free the PC windowing environment from DOS. PowerBuilder 4.0 currently runs under Windows 3.1. Its applications are also developed to run under Windows 3.1, even if they are talking to client-server databases running on another platform.

You can run several applications at the same time in Windows. However, only one of those programs actually operates at full capacity in the foreground. All the others are put into "suspended animation" until they are brought to the foreground. This behavior is also called *time-slicing*. Some programs can receive messages while operating at a diminished level and can even be "brought to life" to let you know that something has happened that requires your attention. For example, an e-mail program that has just received new mail can notify the user and then fade into the background until the user activates it. Rather than having each process running separately, Windows activates an application when the user clicks in an open window or uses keyboard shortcuts to bring an application to the foreground.

Windows is the only windowing environment for the PC. Other windowing environments such as Geoworks can run Windows programs, but none has gained the complete market success of Microsoft Windows. Emulation packages are available that allow you to run Windows programs on a UNIX machine or Macintosh computer.

Until a few years ago, DOS/Windows was the only operating system that would run on PC-compatible computers. Now several versions of UNIX are available for this platform, and several object-oriented operating systems are in the works.

Windows, like DOS, can be run only by a single user. Only one DOS session can be run at one time, and since Windows runs on DOS, there can be only one Windows session. Some products running under DOS have tried to overcome the single-user/single-threaded capabilities of DOS. Products such as Carousel emulate multitasking. dBASE for Windows permits multiple sessions, each distinct from the others, but they are still single-threaded. Only one session can be active at a time.

Microsoft's advanced operating system called Windows NT gives users enhanced operability, especially in the area of seamless network connectivity. This is also true of the Windows 3.1 enhancement known as Windows for Workgroups.

Macintosh

The Macintosh computer is the only machine that never had a text-based interface. Until recently, it was difficult to discuss this machine apart from its operating system. This simple-to-use graphic interface has attracted millions of users. Despite the limited number of software applications written for this machine, it has continued to grow in popularity. The current operating system shipped with the Macintosh computer is System 7.x. The Macintosh can now also run UNIX.

The Macintosh didn't benefit from the windfall of shareware products available for the UNIX and DOS/Windows platforms. Consequently, application development products and compilers for the Macintosh remained costly, and improvements were slow. In spite of this, the Macintosh continued to be popular because of its enhanced graphic and sound capabilities. It still is the preferred tool of desktop publishers and many graphics developers, especially those who can't afford the high cost of a Silicon Graphics workstation.

Aside from these business and artistic benefits, the Macintosh remains the most user-friendly of all the user interfaces. The Mac's programs all have the same look and feel, and most have been designed to read many of the file formats generated by other Macintosh applications. This allows you to easily move information between programs.

Long before Microsoft invented OLE, you could include graphics from the Mac's drawing programs in your Mac word processing file or Mac spreadsheet. Just as OLE files remain associated with the applications that created them, files on the Macintosh are associated with their applications. Simply clicking on a file activates the program that created it.

The Macintosh is strictly a visual environment. Until recently, developing an application using a visual development tool was impossible. Now, with the impending release of PowerBuilder for the Macintosh, you will be able to develop powerful client-server applications on the Macintosh.

HANDLING USER INTERFACE DIFFERENCES

As you have seen, each operating system handles applications and manages files differently. There are also visual differences in the windowing interfaces to the operating systems. The rest of this chapter gives you a head start in preparing your application to handle these differences so that applications developed in one environment can run on other platforms with little or no changes to the program code.

Differences in File Management

Probably one of the most obvious differences among operating systems is how they store files. This includes everything from the delimiters in a path statement to the number and type of characters allowed in the file name. The good news is, other than the differences in file names, the way a file is stored and conventions for executable files, a file is a file. It contains either text or binary data and can be either executable or nonexecutable.

UNIX

The UNIX operating system allows long file names with multiple extensions. The following is a valid UNIX filename:

```
This.is.a.valid.UNIX.filename
```

Although UNIX file names allow spaces, most shells don't interpret spaces as part of the file name, and it's best not to use them. UNIX file names are case-sensitive. The following file names are actually for two separate files:

```
File.of.Text
file.of.text
```

The delimiter for UNIX file names is the forward slash (/). It's important to recognize that drives, whether they are floppy, hard or CD-based, are *mounted* into the file system as part of the directory structure. Unlike DOS/Windows or the Macintosh, UNIX doesn't use drive names. Instead, when you access part of the directory structure that physically resides on a different drive, UNIX accesses that drive.

Because UNIX has one big file system, it makes healthy use of the slash separator. It's not unusual to access files using a path name like this:

```
/usr/local/etc/mybin/yourbin/remotebin/file.hi
```

A UNIX file type isn't determined by an extension but by its *mode*. Each file has three modes:

❒ Read

❒ Write

❒ Execute

You can change the mode of a file with the cryptic chmod command. You can make any file executable provided that it contains certain commands. It's possible to make data files and graphics executable even if they don't contain the proper commands to execute anything.

You can create batch files in UNIX using a UNIX editor (such as vi) or the cat command (similar to the DOS copy con command) to enter commands into a text file. The following text file changes directories and then lists the file names in the directory:

```
cd /home/me
ls -l
```

To make this file executable, you would use the chmod command as follows (the file name is mydir):

```
chmod 777 mydir
```

The mydir file is now executable. The chmod command also sets the read, write and execute security attributes for the owner, any groups set up in the UNIX system and the general public.

DOS/Windows

Windows currently follows the DOS file naming scheme, so in the following discussion, anything we say about DOS file names also applies to file names in Windows. Windows 95, however, allows long file names.

A DOS file name has the following characteristics:

- ❏ Is eight characters or less in length.
- ❏ Can have an optional three-letter extension preceded by a dot.
- ❏ Cannot contain spaces.
- ❏ Is not case-sensitive.
- ❏ Can contain underscores.

A DOS file name could look like this:

```
my_file.txt
```

Generally, the file extensions identify the file type. Executable files must have one of the following file extensions: .COM, .EXE or .BAT.

The delimitor in DOS path names is the backslash (\). The backslash is often preceded by the letter name of the disk drive on which the file resides. For example:

```
c:\mydir\my_file.txt
```

The attrib command in DOS allows you to add or remove read and write security attributes to or from a file. To remove the write access attribute from a file, you would use the attrib command as follows:

```
attrib +r my_file.txt
```

Because there is only one user and one session in DOS, you can specify additional security only through the network operating system. In UNIX, the network operating system is built-in. In DOS, the network operating system runs either on top of or external to DOS.

Macintosh

Files on the Macintosh are stored in *folders*. As operating systems become more similar, the concept of folders has migrated to both the Windows and X Windows graphic environments. A folder is similar to a directory in both Windows and UNIX. Folders organize information stored on the different disk drives and appear in separate windows.

Since file names on a Macintosh can include spaces, the following file name is valid:

```
My File
```

File names can be up to 32 characters in length, allowing them to be descriptive. Since a user rarely has to type a file name in the Macintosh environment, there is little reason not to make Mac file names as descriptive as possible.

In keeping with the user-friendliness of the Mac system, disk drives have real names. You can call them George, Friend, MyDrive, Earth or anything else that suits your fancy. To refer to a file on a specific disk drive, you can precede the file name with the name of the disk like this:

```
Friend:My File
```

Files on a Macintosh do not include an extension to indicate if they are executable. Nevertheless, the Mac operating system is not like UNIX, in which any file can be made executable. On a Mac, if the file is executable, it runs; if it's not executable and you attempt to run it, the Mac attempts to run the application that created it.

Macintosh System 7.x is a single-user, single-tasking system. In this way, it is very much like using the Windows environment. You can have many programs active in different windows, but only one of the windows is active and running. One of the great features of the Macintosh system is that you can easily move information between applications by simply dragging it from one application and dropping it in another.

Resolution

Resolution is the number of pixels and colors your monitor, video card and software graphics driver support. The difference in resolution between (1) a Sun Microsystems workstation monitor with a graphics card and (2) a PC running in 16-color mode with a pixel resolution of 640 X 480 is astronomical. This difference is because of the two extremes your applications may have to cover. Macintosh machines come with a wide variety of graphics capabilities. The Windows drivers can be set up to handle millions of colors and super VGA resolutions of 1024 X 768 pixels.

If you're a developer who likes to run Windows with a resolution of 800 X 600 or higher, you'll find that your applications won't fit on a monitor running in 640 X 480 mode. This situation worsens if you develop your application on a Sun and then port it over to run on a PC. The rule of thumb is to develop the application in the lowest resolution to be sure it can run on all the other machines.

Controls

One visual effect that is becoming more common among platforms is three-dimensional controls. Both Windows and X Windows support 2D and 3D controls and graphics. In fact, the 3D look of X Windows is quite impressive. Until very recently, 3D on the Mac was unheard of, but the platform that has boasted superior graphics has moved into the world of three dimensions. Three-dimensional graphics are available through third-party software library vendors for the Macintosh.

PowerBuilder controls appear in 3D if you specify a 3D border attribute. This is true across platforms. If you want a Macintosh application to have the traditional 2D appearance, use the default border. Even controls that are 3D by default correctly map to 2D on the Mac if you specify the default border.

The border around a default CommandButton in Windows and UNIX is heavy. On the Macintosh, it is much heavier. In fact, the border on the Macintosh is so much heavier than the heavy border in either Windows or X Windows that you have to leave extra room around the CommandButton if you expect your application to run on the Macintosh.

Behavioral Differences

Most of the behavioral differences among the platforms concern the use of the mouse. DOS, UNIX and Mac platforms use three types of mice. The Macintosh uses a single-button mouse. The PC uses a mouse with two or three buttons. Most PC applications use only the left and right mouse buttons. A UNIX workstation usually has a three-button mouse, but only the left and right mouse buttons are generally used.

Menu Operation

Menus on an X Windows system (see Figure 10-2) appear when you click on the menu name with the right mouse button. You select menu commands with the left button. Clicking on a menu name with the left mouse button automatically selects the default command in the menu. For example, if Edit is the default command in the File menu, clicking on File with the left mouse button selects the Edit command.

Figure 10-2: An Informix Wingz menu in X Windows.

In Windows, you select menu commands using the left mouse button. You select the menu name with the left mouse button to display the drop-down menu, then select the command by clicking on the left mouse button.

Additionally, UNIX and PC software often allows you to display a popup menu by clicking on an object or window with the right mouse button. You choose commands from these menus by clicking on them with the left mouse button. This feature is not available in X Windows.

You select commands on a Macintosh by selecting the menu bar and then selecting the command by clicking on it with the single mouse button. PowerBuilder uses the Command key instead of the Ctrl key and the Option key instead of the Alt key for menu shortcuts. Ctrl+click simulates the click of the right mouse button. However, this action is clumsy for the user, so it's best to avoid writing a program that uses the right mouse button if the application is going to run on a Mac.

Tab & Focus

X Windows convention allows you to tab from edit control to edit control, but not to CommandButtons or menus. This is very similar to the behavior on a Macintosh. Keep this in mind when planning applications that will eventually run on either X Windows or Macintosh computers.

In Windows, you can use the Tab key to move from object to object, whether the objects are edit fields or CommandButtons. In PowerBuilder, you can control which objects you can tab to by setting the tab order.

The Macintosh computer has no concept of focus, so it's not a good idea to write scripts for any of the GetFocus or LoseFocus events if your application is expected to run on a Mac.

Window Behavior

Windows behave differently depending on the platform. In the X Windows environment, you can close windows completely by selecting Quit from the control menu in the upper left corner of the window. To minimize or iconify a window, you select Close from the control menu. In X Windows you can also increase the size of a window to the length of the screen by double-clicking within the title bar. You can do the same thing by selecting the Full Size option from the control menu. You can resize a window by grabbing the corners of the window with the mouse and dragging it to a new size.

In the Windows environment, the design of the window determines whether you can minimize (iconify), maximize or resize it. You can add minimize and maximize arrow buttons to the upper right corner of the window. The control menu in the upper left corner of the window allows you to restore, move, size, minimize and maximize the window using a menu selection. These options are available only if the developer has enabled them. Selecting Close from the Windows control menu actually closes the window instead of minimizing it, as in X Windows.

You can resize Mac windows using the Zoom option, and you can close Mac windows completely, but you can't minimize a Mac window. As a result, if you specify a minimize box in your PowerBuilder application, it will be ignored when running on a Macintosh. The Mac size box is in the bottom right corner of the window, so do not place controls in this corner if you want the user to be able to resize the window.

MDI

MDI, the Windows Multiple Document Interface, is an application style unique to Windows. All child windows of the MDI frame must remain inside the frame. In both the Macintosh and X Windows environments, all of the windows share the master window. In these environments, you can move a window beyond the edge of its parent.

If you use MDI windows in an application that will run on a Macintosh, it's important not to place controls directly on the MDI frame window because they won't display.

DDE

Even though it has largely been replaced by OLE 2.0 automation, DDE can still be used to exchange data between PowerBuilder applications running on the UNIX platform. Remember that applications other than PowerBuilder running on a Mac or in UNIX will ignore your efforts to exchange data using DDE.

OTHER CONSIDERATIONS

If your application is going to run on multiple platforms, here are some additional considerations:

❐ Calling external functions from a DLL in Windows is a powerful way to extend your application. If you want to run your application on another platform, you'll have to make sure that the same function is available on the new platform. The Macintosh supports a shared library file in which these functions can be placed. UNIX supports shared libraries in a .SO file.

❐ Don't use VBX controls. They are supported only in Windows.

❐ Don't use the Win.ini file to access information. This is a Windows-specific file.

❐ Don't write code that uses Windows message IDs: these are Windows-specific and are not available on other platforms.

❐ Be aware of the fonts available on each platform and how they will map before using them.

❏ To run applications on other platforms, you need to own the PowerBuilder development system for that platform so you can recompile your PowerScript code on that platform.

❏ .PBL and .PBD files are supported across all platforms.

MOVING ON

PowerBuilder applications are composed of objects. You can make your PowerBuilder application more object-oriented by saving your data in an Object Database. The next chapter explains how to use an Object Database with PowerBuilder.

Handling Group Development

There's something magical about creating something from nothing. The ability to make an otherwise useless pile of silicon and metal do something useful is intoxicating. One result of this intoxication is that programmers tend to get personally attached to their code and to their methods of doing things, which is not necessarily bad. These feelings of ownership tend to make the quality of work outstanding and the features plentiful.

In a system in which there is a single programmer, the amount of excess code due to the rapid addition of new features tends to be relatively small. As you add programmers to the group, however, the amount of excess code (or "code bloat") and source corruption tends to increase. These are the two major problems in group development today and are especially problematic in a GUI development environment. Because GUI development tools enable rapid application development, code bloat occurs more quickly. This chapter discusses techniques for reducing the impact of these problems without sacrificing individual creativity and a robust feature set.

REDUCING CODE BLOAT

Code bloat is the natural effect of team development and usually increases as deadlines approach. This problem can be especially bothersome in a PowerBuilder project because excess code and unused objects can greatly increase the size of an executable while dramatically reducing its performance. Fortunately, you can use a few techniques to avoid such ailments:

- ❏ Data modeling
- ❏ Object-oriented design
- ❏ DataWindow warehousing
- ❏ Communication

Data Modeling

You might be surprised by how much extra code can creep into your projects when the data isn't modeled efficiently. The unfortunate paradox is that modeling data to reduce code also results in reduced development speed. Data modeling can be one of the most time-consuming tasks in any development project.

Consolidating tables can be an effective way to reduce the number of DataWindows needed by an application. If records in one table tend to have a one-to-one relationship with records in another table, consider combining the two.

TIP

Combining tables without careful consideration can result in excessive data redundancy.

You also should check whether your tables are in third, second or even first normal form. If the concept of normalization is not familiar to you, you might consider further research on relational theory. If you find that your tables have a lot of redundancy, but have minimal linking, you may have poorly normalized data. It would be worth your while to review the first, second and third normal forms for a database in a basic database book. (Boyce and Cobb normalization is great in theory, but slow in practice.) To paraphrase Einstein, "Keep things as simple as possible, but no simpler."

Watch out for data bloat, too.

Object-Oriented Design

Take 30 minutes one day and look through all the windows you've developed for your application. Notice how many are similar but how few are inherited. Solid object-oriented design tends to be sacrificed when multiple developers are working on the same project. Establishing an intelligent inheritance hierarchy early in the project can greatly reduce the amount of excess code, as well as the time spent coding.

Before any coding begins, your development team should establish an efficient data model and define the basic system objects for your application. It is well worth the time to take a few days and establish basic inheritance trees, as well as common procedures. If you spend the extra time, the number of global functions and variables in your system will decrease dramatically.

Keep your inheritance trees shallow for better performance and ease of management.

Be careful to keep your inheritance trees reasonably shallow. Try to limit your trees to no more than four levels. The reason for this limitation is simple: if the application tries to instantiate an object that is four levels deep on the inheritance hierarchy, it must create an object at each level of the tree. That's four separate constructor events! This undoubtedly causes serious degradation in system performance. PowerBuilder 4.0 has provided a significant performance improvement in this area.

DataWindow Warehousing

Programmers often don't realize what a tremendous gain in system resources they can achieve by constructing data entry forms with DataWindows. The reason for this is that a DataWindow control is just one object on the window, while SingleLineEdit controls that do the same could require more than 20 controls on the window. The DataWindow controls can begin to make a difference when the user opens five or six sheets at the same time. The savings in system resources, in addition to a robust ability to control the information contained in the window, makes the DataWindow an easy choice over a window with individual SingleLineEdit controls.

DataWindows can be warehoused in a database.

DataWindows also hold another advantage that most programmers never realize: they can be *warehoused* in a database. To put it simply, a DataWindow's syntax can be stored as a string in a table (or warehouse) and then retrieved and used to create the object dynamically. Warehousing offers the following advantages:

❑ The original object doesn't have to be compiled into the executable or a .PBD.

❑ Fewer objects mean less time for PowerBuilder to search for objects.

❑ The executable or .PBD is smaller.

All of this translates into increased application performance.

Report preview windows offer a great example of the benefits offered by DataWindow warehousing. Many developers write applications with a single print preview window for reports. Depending on which report needs to be viewed, they change the DataWindow object associated with the DataWindow control. If 12 reports are in the system, the executable or .PBD must have 12 separate DataWindow objects. This requirement most definitely increases the size of executables and .PBDs. The alternative is warehousing. Store the name of the DataWindow and its syntax in a special table. When you need a specific report, you can retrieve the syntax and dynamically create the DataWindow object (see Chapter 2). The following code example highlights the differences between the two approaches.

This example provides code that optionally loads different DataWindows into a DataWindow control, depending on an indicator passed via a message object:

```
String report_name

report_name = message.StringParm

choose case (report_name)
    case ('Inventory')
        dw_1.dataobject = "dw_inv_report"
    case ('Employee')
        dw_1.dataobject = "dw_emp_report"
    case ('Salary')
        dw_1.dataobject = "dw_salary_report"
end choose

dw_1.SetTransObject(SQLCA)
dw_1.Retrieve()
```

The following example performs the same behavior, but uses passed SQL syntax to load the appropriate DataWindow into the DataWindow control:

```
String report_name, dwsyn

report_name = message.StringParm

SELECT syntax into :dwsyn FROM datawindows WHERE &
report_name = :report_name;

dw_1.Create(dwsyn)
dw_1.SetTransObject(SQLCA)
dw_1.Retrieve()
```

The second approach has several advantages:

❏ DataWindow objects are not compiled into the executable.

❏ The code is shorter and easier to read.

❏ More reports can be added to the system without changing the code. All that is needed is a new record in the DataWindows table.

The Blob Variable Type

To overcome string length limits, use the blob variable type.

When creating your warehouse table you should consider using the blob variable type if your database supports it. This allows you to overcome any string length limits you have. (The syntax descriptions for DataWindows tend to be fairly lengthy.)

Blob data types are not directly supported by most relational DBMSes. Table 11-1 is a list of the some of the ways the blob data type is stored on the database server.

RDBMS	Data Type
Watcom	Long Binary
SQLServer	Image, Binary, VarBinary, Text, Long
Informix	Byte, Text
MDIDB2	Long Varchar
SQLBase	Long Varchar

Table 11-1: Ways the blob data type is stored on the database server

Warehousing isn't optimal for every DataWindow in your application, but it's a good idea for DataWindow controls with DataObjects that change frequently.

Speed vs. Size

You may be wondering how slowly your system will run if it has to dynamically create many of its DataWindows from stored syntax. The answer depends on your particular operating environment. On fast machines (486 DX2 or better) running the executable from a local disk, this method of DataWindow storage is likely to decrease overall performance. If, however, the machine is slower or the executable is being run from a network drive, you may actually see system performance jump. The following example illustrates this point.

A client named Joe had a PowerBuilder application consisting of an 800K executable and a 300K .PBD containing 30 report DataWindows. This application ran on a 486 DX/33 with 8MB of memory, and it loaded the .EXE and .PBD from a NetWare server. A Watcom 4.0 database was running as an NLM on a Pentium 90 server with 64MB of memory. Joe wasn't happy with the performance of his application and asked the consulting firm that wrote the program to restructure it to increase speed. When ACME Software House, Inc.

moved all the DataWindows in Joe's .PBD to a table on his Watcom server, the application speed increased by 30 percent, and the code in the affected sections became easier to read, maintain and extend.

Although it has been simplified to make a key point, this story is true. The particular configuration of Joe's environment was conducive to data warehousing. This won't always be the case. If Joe had been using .DBF tables that resided on the same NetWare server as his application, he probably would have seen the performance decrease. The trick is to evaluate your environment before trying data warehousing.

Reading From the Same Page

It's very important to keep your entire development staff "on the same page" during the application life cycle. Most problems with excess code occur when members of the same team don't know what the other members have already implemented. A manager or senior developer can keep this from occurring by getting the development staff together on a regular basis to talk about outstanding issues. The challenge is to make sure that programmers don't spend too much time in meetings and not enough time developing.

Isn't This a Programming Book?

It is. Good time and code management are essential aspects of good programming, especially in PowerBuilder. Some languages are minimalist in nature. They have built-in mechanisms to help reduce excess code. Other languages and tools take a "kitchen sink" approach. They give the developer wide latitude in implementation schemes but also increase the risk of redundant programming. PowerBuilder is in the latter category. It is therefore most important in this kind of environment to establish good time management practices early and to maintain them throughout the system life cycle.

The Two-Meeting Plan

To efficiently resolve technical issues without wasting a lot of time, many large development efforts follow a two-meeting schedule. The first meeting is usually held relatively early in the week and concentrates on system architecture, future design and weekly milestones. This is the "architecture" meeting, and it sets the tone for the week. Bugs are not discussed in this meeting unless the bug fixes require a modification or addition to the system architecture. This meeting is the place where you and your team establish inheritance trees, method names and calling conventions. This time is spent making decisions about how the different system components will interact.

The architecture meeting sets the tone for the week.

The second meeting occurs late in the week (Fridays are recommended), and concentrates on system bugs. The purpose of the meeting is to build the executable and run through it to catch bugs in the compiled version that didn't show up during individual application development. (If it takes more than 15 to 20 minutes to build the executable, you may wish to schedule the build during lunch hour.) As each bug is found, the team talks about how to fix it and how to prevent others like it.

This meeting, often called the "fire-fighting" session, usually lasts longer than the architecture meeting, but the extra time is always worth it. Avoid architecture discussions in this meeting unless you find a bug that requires a major system change. It's important not to allow the content of the two meetings to overlap, or you will be tempted to combine the two sessions into one long weekly staff meeting.

Why Not a One-Meeting Approach?

Some people wonder why the architecture and fire-fighting meetings can't be combined into one weekly staff meeting. Here are a couple of good reasons not to do this:

- ❏ A combined meeting will most likely run too long to hold anyone's interest. No one wants to spend three or four hours in a meeting.
- ❏ Bug-fixing and system-planning require two different kinds of skills. Fixing bugs requires attention to the small details of the application, while planning a module requires a much broader and more general outlook. Most people cannot easily change gears between the two perspectives in the same meeting.

Why Even Have a "Fire-Fighting" Meeting?

Some people (especially nontechnical managers) wonder why the development staff should waste valuable time on bug-fixing meetings during the development stage of the application life cycle. They ask, "Isn't that what system testing is for?" Think carefully about the following question: At what stage of the project do you spend most of your overtime hours? The answer is that you spend most of your overtime hours at the end of the project. This is usually because the system testers have found many more bugs than you anticipated. After all, who anticipates writing faulty code?

After all, who anticipates writing faulty code?

   A good system is tested incrementally. Incremental testing ensures that bugs can be fixed while the code is fresh in the minds of the programmers. This approach spares all concerned from many long, frantic hours spent getting the product to market on time and is the most compelling reason to have a weekly fire-fighting session.

AVOIDING SOURCE CORRUPTION

Nothing is more frustrating than getting a bug report on a piece of code that you *know* worked the last time you looked at it. Any time multiple programmers work on the same set of .PBLs, the chance for source corruption is enormous. This section explores various options for a team considering a version control mechanism.

Third-Party Tools

Third-party version control packages that allow development teams to check system objects in and out are becoming more popular. A few, such as PVCS, RCS, CCC, LBMS and ENDEVOR, interface directly with PowerBuilder. Depending on the package, you can set access rights for individual developers or groups of developers. Rights can be granted to access individual .PBLs or even individual objects within a .PBL. An effective version control package can give a team peace of mind. The one obvious downside to using a third-party tool is the additional cost to your project. It may also add too much complexity to your development process by lengthening the learning curve for developers and thus increasing time spent on the project, which translates to monetary costs.

Object Responsibility

Many teams are opting for a home-grown approach to source management.

Because of the cost and complexity associated with third-party version control tools, many teams are opting for a homegrown approach to source management that revolves around the concept of *object responsibility*. At its most basic level, object responsibility means that each developer or group of developers is responsible for maintaining a particular object or group of objects. Those responsible for a particular object or group of objects take steps to ensure that critical changes aren't lost. This is done with some kind of check in/ check out system. Specific implementations of this method are up to the development team. The following sections discuss a few options.

Use the Phone

If you're a team leader for a group of developers working on a particular object, you need a system that tells you who has the object at any given time. The surest way to do this is to require the developers to call and ask you for permission to modify the object. If you know that programmer A currently has the object open, you can tell programmer B that he or she will have to wait. This method, although thorough, has some serious problems. If you happen to be out of your office, all development on a particular object has to wait until your return. If the work is on your system's critical development path, you may be jeopardizing the team's ability to meet its deadlines.

Excel as an Object Broker

One development team faced with source management problems devised a clever solution using an Excel spreadsheet with a list of all the objects in the application. If a developer wanted to edit an object, he or she had to consult the spreadsheet to see if the object was available. If it was available, the developer inserted his or her name in the cell next to the desired object. This method would work just as well with a common text file instead of a spreadsheet, but the point is the same: the object owner never has to be consulted.

Object Ownership

Like any other model, object responsibility can be taken to an extreme. You could always mandate that only the owner of an object can edit the object. This means that each owner is responsible for all changes to his or her objects, but it also means that an owner knows exactly what's going on with his or her code and that there is no risk of the work being lost or overwritten.

This idea is especially applicable to object-oriented application design. If you're responsible for the *base class* (a class used to build other objects), any changes you make to the base class affects all the derived objects. Making the base class owner solely responsible for changes is known as *base class protection*. This centralized control of the base code helps to maintain the integrity of the base classes.

CONFIGURATION MANAGEMENT

So far, this chapter has discussed specific issues you have to address in a team PowerBuilder development environment. Many projects have configuration or architecture managers to coordinate these activities. This person is usually a senior developer and has the last word about changes to any base objects. This section briefly discusses the following essentials for effective configuration management:

- ❐ Identification
- ❐ Control
- ❐ Accounting

Identification includes specifying basic system requirements and objectives such as data, process and object modeling. Good identification procedures can save months of development time. This book identifies many third-party products that can help you with this process.

Control includes formulating and managing mechanisms for altering the code base. Source control and meeting schedules fall into this category. Be aware that source code control has a point of diminishing returns. Developers can get so bogged down in source control mechanisms that they lose valuable programming time. Control is the most important part of good PowerBuilder configuration management but is also the most hazardous.

Having control mechanisms in place to ensure that only one developer is working on an object at a time is desirable. Having an audit trail of changes is better. *Accounting* is the formation and administration of mechanisms that log all configuration changes. One accounting method is entering change records as comments in the source code. Although adding comments to the source code should always be encouraged, you need to discourage too much commenting to prevent the size of the associated object from growing too large. A good rule of thumb is to comment only on what the script is doing, not on what it has done. Put the comments *before* the actual code the comments describe.

Alternatively, you can separate the change logs from the source code, which keeps the source code files from becoming too large. One important benefit of third-party version control products is they are able to keep "versions" of any one specific object during the course of its development. Therefore, the object in PowerBuilder contains only the latest code, but the third-party control product keeps a record of all changes made to that object. Some tools even support being able to "take" from a previous version of an object in case recent changes were rejected by end users.

Keep change logs out of the source code.

MOVING ON

Development projects can lose their luster if you and your team don't plan ahead. The following is a summary of techniques that ensure the success of your project:

- ❏ DataWindow warehousing reduces code bloat.
- ❏ Organize data and objects in the beginning of a project.
- ❏ Establish controls for the source code and libraries.
- ❏ Most importantly, talk to the other team members regularly in a structured setting. Too many projects have failed for no other reason than a lack of planning or communication.

Now that you know how to effectively manage development projects, you can move on to making your PowerBuilder applications more powerful. Chapter 12 shows you how to create DLLs to enhance your applications.

Tips for Creating a Windows 3.1 DLL

Creating a DLL is an excellent way to incorporate more power and flexibility into your PowerBuilder applications. This chapter gives you concrete DLL coding tips, including step-by-step instructions on building a Windows 3.1 DLL using the Watcom compiler.

ANATOMY OF A WINDOWS 3.1 DLL

Building a DLL is a relatively simple process once you know the basic elements involved. If you can write a simple C program, you can create a DLL using the Watcom compiler. This section covers the basic anatomy of a Windows 3.1 DLL. DLLs for other Windows platforms such as NT are quite different from DLLs for Windows 3.1, and they are not covered here.

Every function in a Windows 3.1 DLL is either exported or nonexported. Exported functions can be called from inside or outside the DLL. Nonexported functions can be called only from inside the DLL. In Windows 3.1, a DLL consists of the following components:

- ❏ An assembly language module named LibEntry.
- ❏ A nonexported startup function named LibMain().
- ❏ An exported Windows Exit Procedure named WEP().
- ❏ Exported Programmer-Defined DLL Functions.
- ❏ Optional Nonexported Programmer-Defined DLL Functions.

The LibEntry assembly language module, LIBENTRY.OBJ, is provided for you in the Watcom \LIB286\WIN directory. A copy is also available with the Windows SDK. Basically, LibEntry is the Windows entry point into a DLL. Windows calls LibEntry immediately upon loading a DLL into memory. LibEntry then calls your LibMain() function to perform any DLL-specific initialization.

The LibMain() and WEP() functions are executed once by Windows every time the DLL is loaded and unloaded. LibMain performs any initialization required for the DLL, such as memory preparation, and WEP performs any cleanup required. In many DLLs, LibMain and WEP don't actually do anything, but they are required nonetheless.

When you install the Watcom C/C++ compiler provided with PowerBuilder Enterprise, the following source code is provided in the DLLSAMP directory under the file name LMAIN.CPP:

```
/* This file is generated by PowerBuilder.
 * You may modify it in any way you wish but do not remove
 * Libmain and WEP.  Without them you will be unable to
```

```
link your DLL.
 */

#include <windows.h>
#include "pbdll.h"

int PB_EXPORT LibMain( HANDLE hmod, WORD dataseg, WORD
heap, LPSTR cmdline )
{
    hmod = hmod;            // these assignments
                            // generate no code
    dataseg = dataseg;      // but prevent compiler
                            // warnings about
    heap = heap;            // unreferenced variables
    cmdline = cmdline;
    return( 1 );
}

int PB_EXPORT WEP( int res )
{
    res = res;
    return( 1 );
}
```

Unless you have a specific reason to add code to the LibMain and WEP functions, the LMAIN.CPP file provides satisfactory source code for both functions. The LMAIN.CPP file is also generated automatically when you use Power-Builder Enterprise Class Builder to create a new user object DLL in C++.

The PBDLL.H file referenced in the beginning of LMAIN.CPP can be found in the Watcom compiler's H directory. It looks like this:

```
#define PB_EXPORT       __pascal __export
```

The only remaining components of a DLL are the functions that you create. Some and possibly all of the functions must be exported in order for your PowerBuilder applications to access them. Any function that is not exported will be available only to functions within the DLL, meaning that you can't access them directly from your PowerBuilder programs.

BUILDING A DLL

This section shows you how to use the Watcom compiler to build a DLL. Before you begin, make sure that the Watcom compiler is installed on your system and that your path and environment are configured correctly. You should be able to execute the Watcom C++ compiler (wpp), the Watcom make utility (wmake) and the linker (wlink) simply by typing their associated commands at the DOS prompt. If you can, your system is ready to build a DLL.

The Watcom Make Utility

The Watcom make utility is a useful tool for managing the files in a project. If you've never used a make utility before, there isn't too much to learn. A file named makefile is used to track the project files and the commands to use when compiling and linking. Since the format of the makefile is somewhat complex, it may take a while before you become comfortable with it. This section contains the steps you must follow to create a makefile, compile and then link it:

1. Create a file named makefile, and type the following text in the file. *Note:* Do not insert a space between the $ and the (when typing variable references like **$(LDFILES)**.

```
CC = wpp
LD = wlink
```

```
CFLAGS = -i=C:\WATC\H;C:\WATC\H\WIN -ml
LIBPATH = C:\WATC\LIB286\WIN
LDFILES = mydll.obj,lmain.obj
LF = NAME mydll.dll FILE $(LDFILES)
LDFLAGS = LIBPATH $(LIBPATH) libf libentry.obj

mydll.dll: mydll.obj lmain.obj
 $(LD) SYS WINDOWS DLL $(LDFLAGS) $(LF)

lmain.obj: lmain.cpp
 $(CC) $(CFLAGS) lmain.cpp

mydll.obj: mydll.cpp
 $(CC) $(CFLAGS) mydll.cpp
```

2. Be sure to copy LMAIN.CPP into the directory with your makefile.

3. If the path to your Watcom compiler is other than C:\WATC\, replace these paths in the makefile with the correct paths for your system. For the purposes of this example, leave everything else in the makefile as it is.

4. Create the file MYDLL.CPP. This is the primary source code file for your DLL. Type the following in this file to declare and define a single exported DLL function:

```
#include "pbdll.h"

extern "C" {
int PB_EXPORT testfunc(int a);
}

int PB_EXPORT testfunc(int a)
{
 a = a * 2;
 return(a);
}
```

5. Save the file, and return to the DOS prompt.

6. Type the command **wmake**, and press Enter.

This invokes the Watcom make utility, which reads the MAKEFILE and follows the instructions found there to compile and link MYDLL.DLL. If an error occurs, you'll see an error message. If the Watcom compiler is installed correctly and the files LMAIN.CPP, PBDLL.H, MAKEFILE and MYDLL.CPP all exist in the current working directory, you should see a number of messages scroll by, ending with:

```
creating a Windows 16-bit dynamic link library
```

After you see this ending message, the DLL MYDLL.DLL is complete.

The major advantage of using a make utility is that any time you change your source code, you can recompile and relink it by simply issuing the wmake command. The make utility detects the changes you've made to your source files, recompiles them and relinks the compiled source files.

ACCESSING YOUR DLL USING POWERBUILDER

To access the testfunc DLL function, you must first copy the DLL into a directory in your DOS path and declare an external function as shown in Figure 12-1. This allows Power-Builder to locate your DLL when needed.

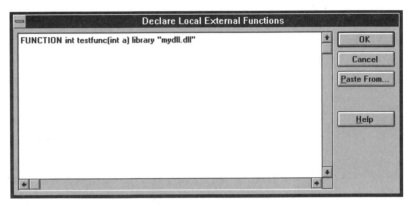

Figure 12-1: External function declaration in PowerBuilder.

Now testfunc() can be called just like any other function.

WHAT EVERY DLL AUTHOR SHOULD KNOW

If you write DLL functions for use in PowerBuilder, you need to know about working with memory in a DLL. This section assumes that you are knowledgeable about pointers and memory. If you aren't, we suggest that you skip this section.

Declaring DLL Functions

Each of your exported DLL functions including WEP() should be declared using PB_EXPORT. By immediately preceding the function name with PB_EXPORT, you tell the Watcom compiler that the function will be called by external programs using the Pascal calling convention. Both of these settings are necessary to ensure that your PowerBuilder program can call the DLL function.

When using the C++ compiler to create a DLL, you must use the extern C directive to tell the compiler the particular code object is defined elsewhere. If the C++ compiler is allowed to decorate an exported function's name, other programs will have trouble calling the DLL function.

Many DLL functions must return a result to the caller.

361

When the result is other than a simple numeric value (like a string value), this becomes a little tricky. The easiest way to do this so that you don't need to know anything other than how to write good C code is to accept a pointer to a buffer as one of the DLL function's parameters. The function can store the result in the memory buffer referenced by the pointer, and the calling procedure will be able to use the result without any problems.

To pass a pointer as a parameter to an external function, the parameter must be declared using the ref symbol in the external function declaration. Figure 12-2 shows a sample function declaration for a DLL function that accepts several pointers as parameters.

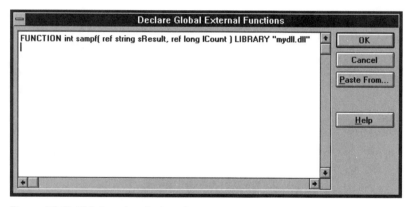

Figure 12-2: DLL function declaration.

This sample function can use the pointers to store values. When the function is called from within PowerBuilder, it must have two variables passed to it, like this:

```
string sTmp
long lTmp
int iRet

sTmp = space(20)
```

```
iRet = sampf(sTmp,lTmp)
```

It is absolutely essential that the string variable sTmp be filled with something before calling sampf(). This is because sampf() is going to try to copy several bytes of memory (in this case, no more than 20 bytes) into the address pointed to by the string pointer.

When you declare a string in PowerBuilder, what you're actually doing is declaring a *char far **, a pointer to an array of characters. Until you store something in the string, no memory is set aside in PowerBuilder's memory manager for a string, and the string pointer points to nothing. If sTmp is passed to sampf() without first being filled with spaces, a general protection fault (GPF) occurs as soon as sampf() tries to copy characters into sTmp.

Long variables are different because longs have a fixed length. Since a long value is stored as 4 bytes of computer memory, those 4 bytes are allocated as soon as a long variable is declared. To store a long value in the lTmp variable, sampf() simply sets the variable pointed to by the lCount parameter equal to a long value, like this:

```
int PB_EXPORT sampletwo(long far *lCount)
{
 *lCount = 84000;

 return(1);
}
```

When writing DLL functions that accept pointers from PowerBuilder code, it is very important to know how many bytes of memory a particular variable represents. If necessary, fill your PowerBuilder variables with data before passing them to these DLL functions. This is important because if your DLL functions attempt to access memory that isn't properly allocated or try to store too many bytes of data in a memory buffer, it generates a GPF.

Arrays & Structures

PowerBuilder structures and C structures can be used interchangeably provided they have the exact same format. Remember that a C structure involves no overhead beyond the bytes required to store each one of its elements. PowerBuilder structures are the same. A C structure containing two integers has the same format as a PowerBuilder structure containing two integers. This makes it convenient to pass PowerBuilder structures to your DLL functions. All you have to do is declare a similar structure in your DLL source code.

Our recommendation has one caveat: we've discovered that passing a pointer to a PowerBuilder structure often leads to erroneous GPFs by the PowerBuilder memory watchdog. If you have trouble with pointers to structures, you'll have to pass each structure element as a separate pointer parameter instead of passing one pointer to your PowerBuilder structure.

Don't forget about *pointer arithmetic*. If you pass a pointer to a PowerBuilder array, you're actually passing a pointer to a pointer. In C, you can step through each of the array elements by adding a 1 to the array pointer. Instead of adding the actual value 1, the pointer is incremented to the beginning of the next array element. If your C programming is rusty in this area, it's worth a review.

The Undocumented Alias Option

The *alias* option for function declarations is a very important yet undocumented PowerBuilder feature provided with the undocumented PowerBuilder reserved words. If you've ever tried to declare a connect() or select() function in Power-Builder or any of a number of other functions that happen to use PowerBuilder reserved words, you know that it won't work. Usually, it's no big deal once you figure out what's going on: you simply change the name of your function and continue.

What happens if you need to access a function in someone else's DLL and the function name ends up being a PowerBuilder reserved word? You use the alias option. Figure 12-3 shows an example function declaration using the alias option.

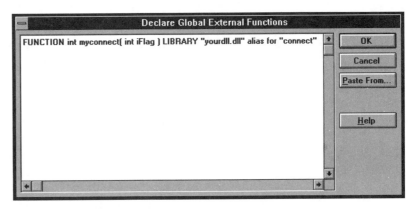

Figure 12-3: A DLL function declaration using the alias option.

The alias option tells PowerBuilder to declare the function but to give it a different name. This is the only way to work around the abundance of PowerBuilder reserved words that may conflict with DLL function names.

Accessing External DLL Functions From a DLL

Sometimes it's necessary to call functions in another DLL from within your DLL. The steps required to accomplish this are no different than those required for any C or C++ program that needs to call functions in a DLL. Of course, if you don't know how to access a DLL from a normal program, this information doesn't help you much. This section shows you how to call functions in a DLL from another DLL or from any C or C++ Windows program.

To call the functions in another DLL from within your DLL, you need to #include a header file containing the DLL function declarations. Doing so keeps the compiler from complaining about unrecognized symbols. Then you should link your compiled source code with an *import library*. The import library convinces the linker that the functions declared in the header file actually exist, or at least will exist at run-time. Without an import library, the linker won't build your DLL as long as it contains references to external functions.

For example, to build a DLL containing calls to functions in a Winsock DLL using the Watcom compiler, add the following #include to your source code:

```
#include <winsock.h>
```

Also add the following import library directive to your linker parameters:

```
libf winsock.lib
```

Both WINSOCK.LIB and WINSOCK.H are available from your Windows programming repository. If you need to build your own import library for a DLL, use an import library creation utility. They're commonly named IMPLIB.EXE and are included with most compilers. An import library creation utility creates an import library for the DLL that you specify. You can then use this import library when linking.

MOVING ON

Now that you've worked on creating your own DLLs, the next chapter shows you how to take advantage of some of the work being done for you. Chapter 13 discusses some of the related software you can use to enhance or extend your PowerBuilder applications.

Related Software Tools

PowerBuilder provides a rich and flexible tool set for building applications. However, there are some areas that PowerBuilder, by either omission or commission, does not address. In this chapter, we'll look at some of the software that has been developed to fill the void.

Because of the success of PowerBuilder and the aggressiveness of its user community, there has been a big demand for add-on software. The niches created have been filled nicely by entrepreneurial developers. Perhaps the most significant category of the add-on tools is Base Classes. Dozens of robust Base Classes are commercially available, including:

- ❏ PowerClass
- ❏ PowerBase
- ❏ Object Start
- ❏ SEI ObjectClass Library
- ❏ ObjectFrame
- ❏ PowerTool

In addition to commercial Base Classes, a number of areas that are closely coupled to PowerBuilder have generated some significant software development efforts. Version control systems, such as ENDEVOR and PVCS, have direct links to PowerBuilder objects. Add-on security systems, such as PowerLock and PowerFrame, provide mechanisms to build security tables and related objects. Help development applications, such as RoboHELP and VisualHelp, provide tools for building context-sensitive Help systems tied directly to a PowerBuilder application. Third-party CASE tools, such as EasyCase, Evergreen, ERwin and S-Designor can generate DDLs for Watcom tables.

Powersoft has decided to leap into the breech as well. It has provided, with the Enterprise version 4.0, a number of utilities to enhance PowerBuilder and Watcom. These utilities fall into two general categories: analysis utilities and development utilities. The analysis utilities are:

- ❏ Cross Reference
- ❏ DataWindow Extended Attribute Synchronizer (DWEAS)
- ❏ DataWindow SQL Verifier
- ❏ DWSyntax
- ❏ PowerBuilder Extended Attribute Reporter (PEAR)
- ❏ Interactive SQL (ISQL) for Watcom

The development utilities are:

- ❏ Image Editor
- ❏ Install Diskette Builder (IDB)
- ❏ Stored Procedure Update (SPUD)
- ❏ RoboHELP

ANALYSIS UTILITIES

Analysis utilities provide information about the state of various pieces of your application. Some of the utilities provide values of variables, whereas others describe relationships between components, as in the Cross Reference utility. In this section, we'll discuss a few of them.

Cross Reference

Cross Reference provides a view of the relationships between PowerBuilder objects. Cross Reference is a useful analysis tool that assists the developer in determining the "where-used" of objects. Objects that Cross Reference deals with include:

- Windows
- Menus
- DataWindows
- User Objects
- Global Variables
- Shared Variables
- Instance Variables
- Global Functions
- Window Functions
- User Object Functions
- PowerScript Functions

The Library painter offers the developer a view of the objects in use in a PBL. The Class browser gives a view of the object hierarchy by object. Cross Reference extends the perspective of the developer to a view of the full usage of an object. This view can be useful in determining change impact, particularly for heavy uses of inheritance.

Cross Reference can be used to determine the usage scope for objects. For example, you can determine if a variable is used in enough objects to warrant its declaration as a global variable. You can analyze the usage of functions that are similar in nature in order to move them, if applicable, to a higher ancestor level.

Cross Reference builds its reporting from the application level. It can provide you with a list of all applications from all directories. If you select an application with multiple PBLs, you are shown a selection list to choose the PBLs you want to use in your cross reference reporting.

A two-phase reporting process is used to build the analysis report. The first phase finds all objects contained in the application. The second phase looks for relationships between the found objects. Cross Reference reviews the attribute and variable declarations and the PowerScript contained in events and functions. The second phase generates a grid-style DataWindow that lists all objects found and their references (see Figure 13-1).

Cross Reference Report

Company : SS Solutions   Report [
Project : SRS Cross Reference Reporting
Application : c:\pb4\srs.pbl(pbptk_srs)
Options : Report global and object level references , List all events, List all PowerScript function refer
Sorted By : Object Asc., Script/Declared Asc., Parent Object Asc.

Scope	Object	Type	Script/Declared	Parent Object	Parent Ob
0	accepttext	PS function	cb_1:clicked event	bw_search	Window
			wf_updatedb function	w_dept	Window
				w_emp	Window
	arrangesheets	PS function	m_genapp_sheet.m_wind m_genapp_sheet event		Menu
			m_genapp_sheet.m_wind m_genapp_sheet event		Menu
			m_genapp_sheet.m_wind m_genapp_sheet event		Menu
			m_genapp_sheet.m_wind m_genapp_sheet event		Menu
			m_genapp_sheet.m_wind m_genapp_sheet event		Menu
			m_main.m_window.m_ca m_main event		Menu

Figure 13-1: A Cross Reference report.

Cross Reference can generate two types of report: the Un-Referenced Objects report and the Cross Reference report. The Cross Reference report can be displayed in either Referenced Object form or parent object form. The form type determines the starting point of the report. The user can also select the sort order for the report. There are four sort sequences, and each includes a radio button selection for scope, object, type, script/declared, parent object and parent object type.

The Un-Referenced Objects report lists those objects that are not referred to in any other objects. These objects are orphans and are good candidates for deletion.

The Cross Reference report is a grid DataWindow consisting of modifiable header data and cross reference detail. Table 13-1 shows the detail columns and descriptions.

Column	Description
Scope	Global (G) means that the item is visible and accessible throughout the application. Object (O) means that the item is an object or a component of an object.
Object	The name of the item being referenced.
Type	PowerBuilder datatype such as window, menu, DataWindow object.
Script/Declared	The name of the event or attribute in which this item is declared. This column can also contain "is inherited from."
Parent Object	Name of the object that is the parent of the current item or the object that contains the script or declaration of the item.
Parent Object Type	The PowerBuilder data type of the parent object.
Parent Object Library	The PBL of the parent object.

Table 13-1: Cross Reference report, detail columns and descriptions.

Cross Reference reporting results can be saved to a database named XREF. These saved results can be displayed later by reloading the report from the database. Any report that is not saved will be deleted. The XREF database contains three tables: the App_info table, the App_objects table and the Xref_info table. The App_info table includes application and report parameter information. The App_objects table contains a row for each object in the application. The Xref_info table has all the cross reference information for each application object listed in the App_objects table. This table includes the object type, the event and a Referenced In column.

DataWindow Extended Attribute Synchronizer (DWEAS)

DWEAS provides the developer with the ability to update DataWindow objects with the current extended attributes that are stored in the catalog. Extended attributes—such as validation rules, display formats, edit styles and text for column headings and labels—can be defined for columns with the Database painter. As the DataWindow is painted, these extended attributes are referenced. If the attributes are subsequently changed, the changes are not directly reflected in the associated DataWindows. DWEAS provides a method to synchronize the changed attributes in the DataWindows. DWEAS is a useful tool for developers who make significant use of extended data attribute definitions.

DWEAS creates a new DataWindow object using dynamic DataWindow facilities. The creation of the DataWindow includes the most recent attribute definitions. After the DataWindow is created, DWEAS compares the new DataWindow to the previously defined DataWindow. The differences are highlighted (the user can specify the color to use for highlighting). The user can determine any or all of the extended attributes to change. After changes are made to the DataWindow, the developer can save the updated object.

DWEAS looks only at the DataWindow's logical attributes, such as:

- ❏ Column ID
- ❏ Edit Style
- ❏ Validation Information
- ❏ Format
- ❏ Initial Value

The physical attributes, such as font size, text color, visibility and location, are not dealt with by DWEAS and are dependent upon the standards in the developer's environment. DWEAS allows changes to the following column attributes (each attribute is preceded by the column name in a dot notation):

- ❏ BitMapName
- ❏ ColType
- ❏ Edit.Case
- ❏ Format
- ❏ Initial
- ❏ Validation
- ❏ ValidationMsg

As you enter DWEAS, the developer is presented with a response window that is built from the DWEAS INI parameters. It includes the company name, project, SQL constants and profile (connect parameters). The SQL constants are dummy variables that can be replaced with valid retrieval arguments as required. These parameters can be changed by altering the INI file or via the System Options menu item under Options in the menu bar. Clicking OK invokes a Database connection.

After the connection, the developer is presented with a selection window of PBLs. After selecting a PBL, you are shown a selection list of DataWindows that includes the DataWindow name, the date and time of last update and a comment. Selecting a DataWindow from this list initiates the creation of the dynamic DataWindow that DWEAS uses to determine the differences between the repository definition and the definition in the PBL.

At this point, the DWEAS workspace contains a report that shows the current (PBL version) and repository (DWEAS dynamically built DW) attributes (see Figure 13-2). The display is scrollable and includes attributes for the following:

- Column ID
- Logical and/or Physical Column Name
- SQL Data Type
- Display Format
- Edit Style Data
- Validation Data
- Initial Value
- Edit Case
- Bitmap

The attributes that differ are highlighted in the specified color (the default is red).

Changes Between Current And Repository

Col. ID	Logical Column Name/ Physical Column Name		SQL Data Type	Display Format	Edit Style Style
1	course_id	Current:	char(10)	[general]	edit
	course_class.course_id	Repository:	char(10)	[general]	edit
2	class_id	Current:	char(5)	[general]	edit
	course_class.class_id	Repository:	char(5)	[general]	edit
3	term	Current:	char(3)	[general]	edit
	course_class.term	Repository:	char(3)	[general]	edit
4	year	Current:	number	[general]	edit
	course_class.year	Repository:	number	[general]	edit
5	location_id	Current:	char(10)	Hidden	
	course_class.location_id	Repository:	char(10)	**[general]**	**edit**
6	instructor_id	Current:	char(10)	Hidden	
	course_class.instructor_id	Repository:	char(10)	**[general]**	**edit**

Figure 13-2: Changes Between Current And Repository report.

The developer can apply the repository attribute values by double-clicking on the highlighted value. Double-clicking changes the attribute to the marked color (the default is green). After you have completed selecting the changes to apply, you save these changes via a menu item or a toolbar item. Then you are presented with a dialog box asking if you want to overwrite the existing DataWindow or create a new version (Save As). If you overwrite the DataWindow, DWEAS reloads and reanalyzes the updated DataWindow object.

DataWindow SQL Verifier

The DataWindow SQL Verifier is an analysis utility that validates SQL created for a DataWindow. It is particularly useful for applications that either are being migrated between DBMSes or must connect to multiple DBMSes. It is also effective for validation in cases in which tables have been altered.

DBMSes have varying SQL syntax requirements. For example, the DBMS used to initially develop a DataWindow may have a requirement that single quotes be used in all SQL statements. The target DBMS in a migration may require double quotes. SQL Verifier highlights these differences.

SQL Verifier begins by supplying a selection list of applications. Selecting an application initiates a connection to the database. Following this, SQL Verifier analyzes all DataWindows for an application. The analysis goes through the following steps:

1. Log on to the database.
2. Display an empty results window.
3. Retrieve the SQL statement for each DataWindow object.
4. If any retrieval arguments are specified, they are replaced with the constant values specified in the INI file.
5. Send the SQL statement to the DBMS for verification.
6. Check the result for errors.
7. Display the status in the results window.

This process is repeated for each DataWindow object.

The resulting report displays rows for each DataWindow object analyzed (see Figure 13-3). Three columns are displayed:

❏ **Library**—The name of the PBL that contains the referenced DW.

❏ **DataWindow Object**—The referenced object.

❏ **Status**—A result of a check of the SQL statement for the DataWindow.

The Status column displays the determination that SQL Verifier has made regarding the transportability of the SQL. The status statements and their meanings are:

- ❐ **DataWindow SQL is Valid**—No error was produced during verification.

- ❐ **Script Source DataWindow**—The DataWindow was created from SQL source within a script.

- ❐ **Missing Column**—A column referenced in the DataWindow is no longer present in the database.

- ❐ **Unable to Create DataWindow** —A DataWindow mismatch prevented generation.

- ❐ **Incomplete Update Message** —The DataWindow updates the database but doesn't access all columns.

- ❐ **DBMS-specific error message**—The specified DBMS returned an error condition when processing the SQL.

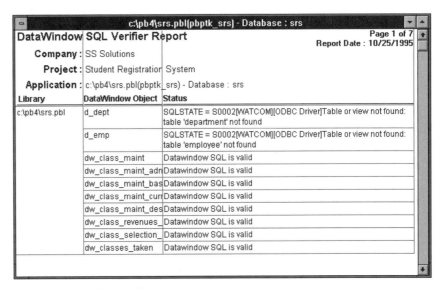

Figure 13-3: A SQL Verifier report.

The report can be viewed or printed. The developer can also alter the report heading (company or project).

DWSyntax

DWSyntax is a utility that assists in the creation of dynamic DataWindow syntax. It includes support for Describe, Modify and SyntaxFromSQL. The primary goal of this utility is to ease the developer's burden of creating the dynamic DataWindow syntax. This syntax can be very exacting, and this utility enables the user to save created syntax to the Clipboard to paste into PowerScript later.

DWSyntax initially displays two windows (see Figure 13-4). The 'Modify' Syntax window displays the syntax as it is being built. The 'Modify' Objects/Attributes Selection List window lists the objects and associated attributes for each syntax type. As you select from the 'Modify' Objects/Attributes Selection List, the connected syntax is generated in the 'Modify' Syntax window.

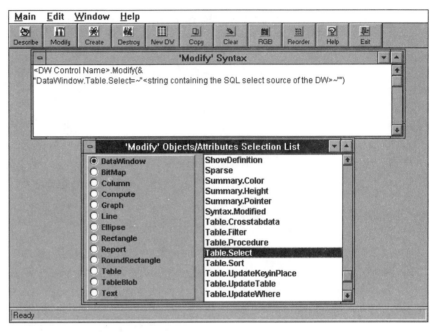

Figure 13-4: Two work areas in DWSyntax.

You begin by selecting Describe, Modify or SyntaxFromSQL from the toolbar. Let's first look at SyntaxFromSQL (the New DW icon is the equivalent in the toolbar). DWSyntax builds some of the necessary syntax based on choices you make from the SyntaxFromSQL Parameters Selection List (see Figure 13-5). The parameters include selections for the following:

❑ **Title**—The title of the error message box with the errors that are generated as a result of the execution of the SyntaxFromSQL statement. (You must declare the string variable to hold the errors elsewhere.)

❑ **Style**—The primary choice here is Type. When you select Type, DWSyntax asks if the type will be Group, and if you respond "Yes," it provides another response window to select the grouping attributes. If you do not want a group, the syntax is built to allow you to select from the five style types. Note that in the syntax, you are responsible for supplying any values between the open angle bracket (<) and the close angle bracket (>) characters. In the case of Type, DWSyntax provides a list of choices.

❑ **DataWindow**—Attributes affecting the overall presentation of the DataWindow, such as color, label attributes, print margins and timer interval.

❑ **Text**—Presentation attributes of the text such as color, background color and font.

❑ **Column**—Presentation attributes affecting all columns in the DataWindow, such as background color, border, scrolling and font.

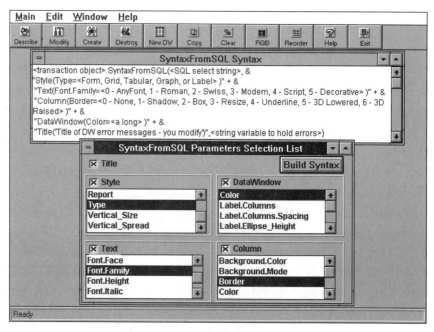

Figure 13-5: The SyntaxFromSQL window in DWSyntax.

Notice that no facility to build the SQL is necessary. DWSyntax strictly deals with the syntax for attribute definition. After you complete the syntax selections, you may copy the resulting syntax to the Clipboard for pasting in your PowerScript.

The Describe option gives you all the objects appropriate for the Describe() function such as DataWindow, Column, Graph and Report (see Figure 13-6). For each of these objects, a long list of associated attributes is provided. As you select an object and attribute, the syntax is built in the window above the selection list. It is best to consult Appendix A of the PowerBuilder *Function Reference* manual for a description of the attributes. The MicroHelp in DWSyntax is contextual and provides some assistance in explaining the meanings of attributes.

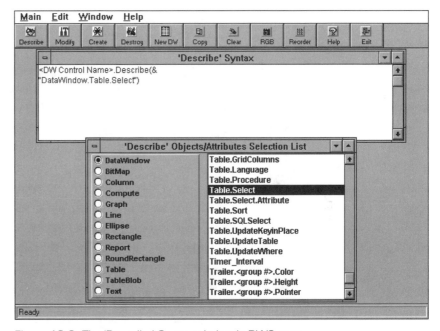

Figure 13-6: The 'Describe' Syntax window in DWSyntax.

The Modify option acts in the same fashion as the Describe option, building the appropriate Modify() syntax as you select the objects and attributes (see Figure 13-7). DWSyntax provides some meaningful comments that describe the string that makes up the attribute value. You must build this value in your script after pasting the DWSyntax-built Modify statement.

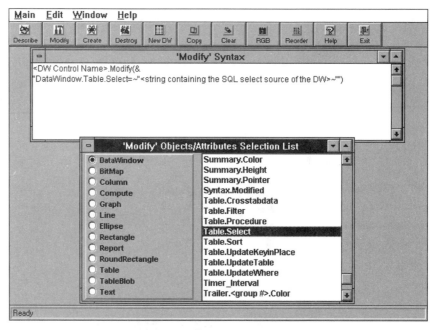

Figure 13-7: The 'Modify' Syntax window in DWSyntax.

DWSyntax also provides support for creating DataWindow objects. Selecting the Create option from the toolbar gives you the windows you see in Figure 13-8. If you select Column, a selection list is provided for the column type. This feature is useful for building columns because of the extended Create syntax required for column attributes. DWSyntax also supports the generation of Destroy syntax.

By selecting the Destroy button from the toolbar and the required object, the Destroy subcommand of Modify() is built. As you can see in Figure 13-9, the syntax requirement for Destroy is limited.

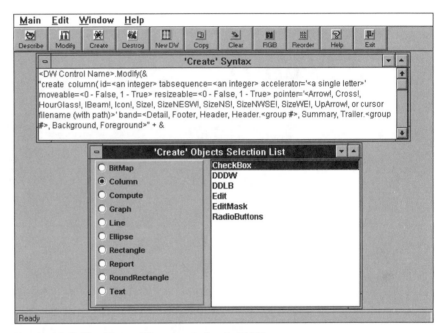

Figure 13-8: The 'Create' Syntax window in DWSyntax.

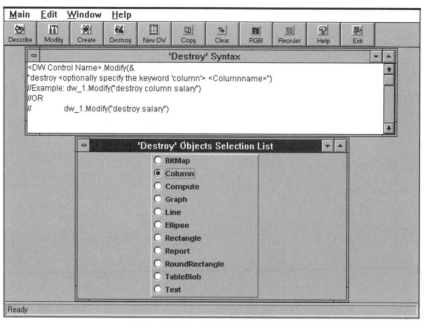

Figure 13-9: The 'Destroy' Syntax window in DWSyntax.

A miscellaneous feature of DWSyntax is the RGB Calculator, shown in Figure 13-10. This feature assists in the tedious task of determining the RGB value for a particular color. It runs as a popup window and includes a sliding scale for red, green and blue values. As you scroll through the scales, the color change is reflected in the associated rounded rectangle object and the RGB calculated value is returned. The calculated value can be copied to the Clipboard for use later in your scripts. You can also enter specific values for the RGBs.

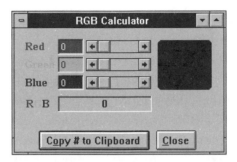

Figure 13-10: The RGB Calculator in DWSyntax.

PowerBuilder Extended Attribute Reporter (PEAR)

The PowerBuilder Extended Attribute Reporter (PEAR) utility offers reporting on the extended attributes contained in the PowerBuilder repository. When you initially connect to a database with PowerBuilder, it builds the default attributes for the tables in the repository. The extended attributes can be altered via the Database painter. In the case of Watcom, you can build the attributes initially when you create the table.

The repository is a set of five tables that hold the extended attributes. These tables and their contents are:

❏ **pbcatcol**—This table stores column information including names, comments, headers, labels, case, initial values and justification.

❏ **pbcatedt**—Editing styles are contained in this table.

❏ **pbcatfmt**—This table has display format names and definitions.

❏ **pbcattbl**—This table has table data such as table name, owner, default fonts and comments.

❏ **pbcatvld**—Validation rules and definitions are contained in this table.

You can view these tables in the Database painter by clicking on the Show System Tables checkbox.

When you run PEAR, it initially attempts to connect to the Database profile you have named in the PEAR.INI file. The INI file contains headers for the profile, the repository and the SQL SELECTs necessary for your DBMS to retrieve a list of tables and related columns (typically the catalog tables). The INI file settings can be changed by selecting the Configure Profile menu item from the Options menu. You can specify the company name and project name and select a different profile. You can, additionally, specify the Connect profile parameters by clicking the Set Profile button from the Configure Profile dialog box.

After connecting to your database, PEAR displays a selection list of tables. You can select one or more tables from this list. After selecting the appropriate table, PEAR accesses the repository to retrieve the extended attributes. PEAR builds the report you see in Figure 13-11. The report has stacked columns with the following information:

- ❐ **Column Name**—The name of the column.
- ❐ **Bitmap**—If the column is defined as a bitmap type, this is the name of the associated bitmap file.
- ❐ **Label**—For use in freeform DataWindows.
- ❐ **Header**—For use in tabular style DataWindows.
- ❐ **Justify**—Left, Right or Center.
- ❐ **Case**—Any, Upper or Lower.
- ❐ **Display Format**—This is the name of the display format.
- ❐ **Validate Rule**—This is the name of the validation rule.
- ❐ **Edit**—The edit style.
- ❐ **Initial Value**—The initial value.

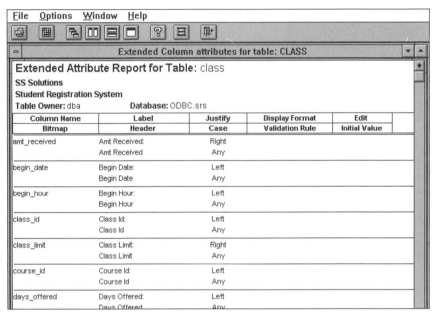

Figure 13-11: A sample Extended Column attributes report.

A summary level of the report simply lists the display formats, validation rules and edit styles used in the table. You can preview the report prior to printing via the preview option from the File menu.

Interactive SQL (ISQL) for Watcom

ISQL provides support for building and executing SQL statements interactively. ISQL runs against the Watcom DBMS. This utility is an excellent tool for testing SQL, examining data and building stored procedures.

To run ISQL, you should initially connect to the appropriate Watcom database. When you select the connect menu item from the Command menu, you are prompted for the necessary connect parameters. They include the User ID, Password, Connection Name, Database Name, Database File, Server and Start Line. The necessary parameters for connection are User ID, Password, Database File and Server (see Figure 13-12). The Database File is the full name of the database being connected to. The Server is the name of the database engine to start (db32w, in Figure 13-12). You can also create Connect SQL that can be saved as a SQL file (see Figure 13-13) and then reuse this when connecting to various databases.

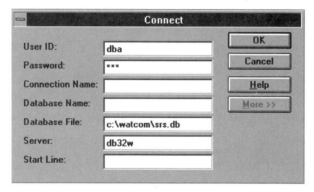

Figure 13-12: Connect parameters.

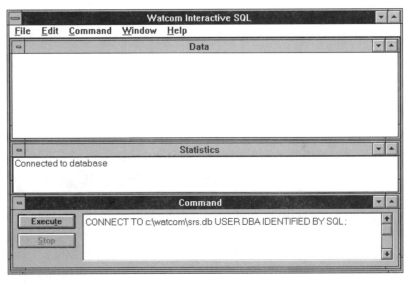

Figure 13-13: An ISQL connect statement in ISQL.

After connection is complete, you can generate any supported SQL statement. ISQL supports all standard SQL statements including DDL, DML, Database options and ISQL options. Database options include date and time formatting, command delimiter and precision. The ISQL options include a variety of commands that affect ISQL execution, including INPUT and OUTPUT commands.

INPUT allows the importation of data into a database table. The data can be imported from either a file or the keyboard. If the PROMPT keyword is specified with INPUT, you are prompted to provide input into a freeform window. The input requires comma delimiters and an END statement at completion. If you use the FROM file name format, the file must be one of the following formats:

❏ **ASCII**—Comma delimited.

❏ **DBASE**—Either dBASE II or dBase III (ISQL determines this based on file information).

❏ **DBASEII**—dBase II.

❏ **DBASEIII**—dBase III.

❏ **DIF**—Data Interchange Format.

❏ **FIXED**—Column width can be specified by the COLUMN WIDTHS command.

❏ **FOXPRO.**

❏ **LOTUS**—WKS format.

❏ **WATFILE**—A tabular file management tool from WATCOM.

The OUTPUT command copies data in the current retrieval set to the specified file. OUTPUT supports all file types available to the INPUT command plus the SQL and TEXT types. SQL type is an ISQL INPUT command required to rebuild the table data. TEXT is a file type that lists the results in a columnar format with the column names on top and vertical lines separating the columns.

SQL has three text windows that support your SQL entry and execution. These windows are:

❏ **Command**—The entry area for your SQL statement.

❏ **Statistics**—The number of rows acted upon and related statistical data (which is explained later in this section).

❏ **Data** —The returned set from your SQL statement.

The Statistics window includes a plan feature. This feature displays the optimized method ISQL will use to execute your SQL statement. The optimizer makes an educated guess at the best method for data retrieval. For example, in Figure 13-14, we are joining the student table and student_class table over the student_id column. You can see the plan reads student_class(seq), student(student). The student_class table's primary key is a composite key of student_id, course_id and class_id, so that the DBMS must walk through the primary key index sequentially looking for the partial key we wish to join over (the student_id). The primary key for the student table is student_id, so the DBMS can go directly to a student occurrence. Use the plan to make determinations on the "better" method to retrieve data.

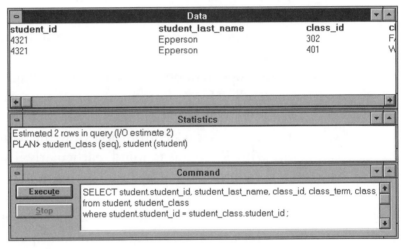

Figure 13-14: A sample join in ISQL.

The Statistics window has a line that displays the number of rows retrieved for a query and the number of estimated I/Os. ISQL determines the number of estimated I/Os based on the type of reads/writes you are doing. For example, if you are not ordering your result or you are using the primary key or a portion of the key, the number of estimated I/Os is significantly reduced as compared to when you use a sort order based on nonindexed columns. The I/O count is affected by the number of rows retrieved and the buffer size.

ISQL retains your SQL statements in a temporary log that is initiated when you begin your ISQL session. You can review this log by selecting Recall from the Command option on the menu bar. Double-clicking on any of the commands brings the line into the Command window for re-execution. You can also walk through the commands sequentially by using the Previous Command and Next Command menu items. There are also menu items for connecting and disconnecting from the database and executing your SQL command.

An important point to remember is that ISQL will be contending for resources with other concurrent database users. ISQL issues requests that result in row locking, which prevents other users from accessing the data you are working with. Keep this in mind, particularly if you're viewing data that is accessed by multiple users.

You can change ISQL run-time options by selecting Options from the Command menu. The options include groupings for Commit, Data and Commands, Command Files and Input/Output (see Figure 13-15). The default for Commit is When Exiting ISQL. You may want to change to After Every Command to free resources and to mitigate the impact of a system failure when making multiple changes. If you don't specify a name in the Log ISQL Commands to File field, ISQL uses the temporary command log discussed previously. You may want to assign it a file name so you can review your SQL commands later. You can change the Input/Output file format by selecting from the drop-down lists. ISQL uses your selection as the current file type when using the Input or Output ISQL commands.

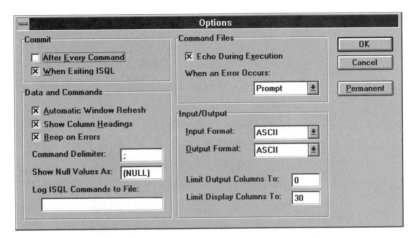

Figure 13-15: The Options window in ISQL.

A useful feature of ISQL is the Insert Table function. This function is available as a menu item from the Edit menu. It provides a list of tables for the currently connected database. If you double-click on a table, the table name is inserted into the current cursor location in your Command window. You can also display the columns for the table by clicking the Columns button from the Tables list. You can click on the column desired and click the Insert button, and that column name is returned to your Command window.

You can save and retrieve your SQL commands by using the Open, Save and Save As options from the File menu. Files are saved with an SQL suffix. If you retrieve a SQL file and try to re-execute the statement, you must first be connected to the database to properly execute your SQL.

The Help feature of ISQL is very robust. It includes complete information about the Watcom DBMS, including all supported SQL commands. Of particular interest are the discussions of database design and performance.

DEVELOPMENT UTILITIES

The Image Editor utility assists in the creation and update of graphic images. You can use it to develop bitmaps, icons and graphics for cursors. It is primarily used to alter a previously created bitmap that you are using in your application.

The default file type is BMP, although Image Editor supports ICO and CUR (cursor file) file types. Opening the file brings the image into two windows, the smaller full-image window and a grid-square window. The full-image window gives you a macro view of the image as it currently exists. The grid-square window gives you an enlarged view of the image. The enlarged view is your workspace.

You are given a toolbox and a Colour Palette to help in altering the image (see Figure 13-16). The Colour Palette gives you the ability to assign draw and fill colors to the left and right mouse buttons. You can customize the 14 basic color sets by editing the current color (selectable as a menu item from the Palette menu). The toolbox includes the following tools:

- **Select region**—Lets you select a rectangular grid region.
- **Pencil**—Draws pixel by pixel.
- **Lines**—Creates lines pixel by pixel.
- **Brush**—Draws in a brush size specified in the options. (The default is 2 X 2 pixels.)
- **Ellipse outline**—Allows you to draw outlines of circles and ellipses.
- **Ellipse fill**—Fills circles and ellipses.
- **Rectangle outline**—Enables you to draw the outlines of rectangles.

□ **Rectangle fill**—Fills rectangles.

□ **Fill area**—Fills the bounded area beneath the cursor with the current fill color.

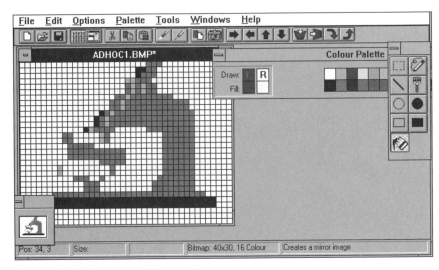

Figure 13-16: The ImageEditor workspace.

Image Editor gives you the ability to move the image in preset ways. You can shift the image right, left, up or down. The image shifts two pixels per your shift direction. You can flip the image over a horizontal or vertical axis. Flipping over a vertical axis changes the direction the image faces; flipping over a horizontal axis flips the image 180 degrees along a horizontal axis. You can rotate your image clockwise or counter-clockwise. This moves your image 90 degrees in the direction selected.

You can build cursors with Image Editor. A cursor can be used as a pointer in your application to communicate a specific activity within an application. For instance, you may want to create a cursor of a truck that the user moves to drag and drop an object between windows. The cursors can be created only in black-and-white images. An additional toolbox item for the cursor is Select Hot Spot. This tool allows you to select the pixel you want to place the hot spot image for the cursor. Cursor images are saved with the .CUR suffix.

Icon images can also be created and altered by Image Editor. Icons are saved with the .ICO suffix. You can create these images as 16-color, 32 X 32 pixel images; 2-color, 32 X 32 pixel images; or 2-color, 32 X 16 pixel images.

At this writing, Image Editor may have limitations on support for higher video resolutions. You may have to reduce the resolution support to 16 colors.

Install Diskette Builder (IDB)

One of the most time-consuming and error-prone portions of application development is deployment. PowerBuilder is certainly no exception to this rule. Including the correct EXEs, PBDs, INI files, ODBC settings, database components, etc. can be a daunting task. IDB eases this burden. Of all the development and analysis utilities, IDB has the most value.

The IDB utility helps the developer include the proper components in the deployment package. There are five components involved in an IDB definition. They are:

❑ **Configuration file**—This is the primary file used by IDB. It contains application components (a logical breakdown of the application), the files used for each component and INI file settings.

❐ **Reusable components**—These are base components that can be reused in other deployments. The typical examples are PowerBuilder and DBMS executable files.

❐ **Program group**—This prompts the setup utility to create a Windows Program Group and allows you to name the items in the group.

❐ **Diskette images**—Images can be created on your local drive or a network drive for later copying to diskettes.

❐ **Installation diskettes**—A copy of the images created in the previously listed component. The diskettes are used directly by the user for installation.

The installation configuration shown in Figure 13-17 defines the components to use for the installation process. The definition is held in a configuration file (with the .CFG suffix). The configuration file is used only within IDB.

When defining the configuration, you are prompted for a Caption, which is the title displayed as the setup process is executing. Use the application name for the Caption. You can also include a Read Me File component. The Read Me File displays as the installation process is running. You can specify a name for the Read Me File window and name the Read Me file. You can create the Read Me file as a text file in any word processor. This file should contain any information about the installation process or about the application in general that is not in other documentation. You could also point the user to additional documentation to review prior to initially running the application.

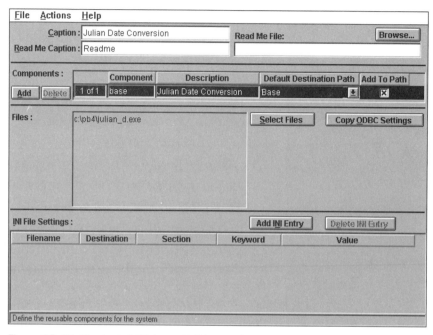

Figure 13-17: The Install Diskette Builder workspace.

IDB employs the concept of application components. The purpose of application components is to allow the modularization of your application. This theory fits generalized software such as spreadsheets, word processors, application development tools and database management software that have multiple add-on options. Most business applications tend to focus on a specific functional area, although exceptions do exist. You may be deploying a complete accounting application, for instance, that includes Accounts Payable, Receivables and General Ledger. By defining application components, you provide a configurable installation to your users.

IDB has an identifier for each application component. The first is called base. You define a description for this component and a default destination path. If you use BASE as the default destination path, the destination will be overridden by the user's selection of the installation path at install run-time. Each component is given an individual name and will be displayed as an option selection during installation.

If your application uses an ODBC database, include the ODBC.INI file. When you request the ODBC.INI file, you are prompted to select the database name in a response window. The settings, including the appropriate driver DLL, are listed in the response window. You can alter the settings as necessary. For instance, you may want to change the directory name for the database. After selection, the settings are displayed in the INI File Settings area of the primary workspace. This area shows each INI header with the associated keywords and values. You can change any of these values in the workspace.

You can include any additional INI files necessary for the application or add entries to an existing INI file. Again, all the settings can be altered within the workspace.

Reusable components are entities that will be used across multiple applications. They are typically PowerBuilder and/or DBMS executables. To add a reusable components, follow these steps:

1. Name the directory to be used for the compressed files. Reusable components use DOS file compression to reduce file size.

2. Add a description for the component's files.

3. Add a default directory for the component's files. The same convention used for the application components is applied here. Use BASE if you want the reusable components to use the same directory as the other application components.

4. Select the drives, directories and file types for the files to be included with the reusable components.

5. Include the necessary files by selecting from the file list.

401

You can also include INI files with reusable components. The same rules as specified in the previous section apply to handling INI files with reusable components.

You can have the installation execution create a Program Group and specify the files to be contained within the group. You must add a name for the group and then specify the group item name, the associated directory, the file name and a description.

You can use the PowerBuilder project object as the source for inclusions in your component list. By selecting the project object for the application you're deploying, IDB includes the EXE and PBDs named in the project.

After you have completed naming the installation components, any reusable components, and program groups, you must save the configuration file and build a diskette image. You place the image in a stand-alone subdirectory. You specify the subdirectory name, the components to include (this list should be complete from your previous activity), and the disk size (1.2 or 1.44mb). IDB builds subdirectories within your named subdirectory—one for each component.

After you finish building the diskette image, you can create the actual installation diskettes. IDB tells you the number of diskettes required. It copies the images created previously to the necessary number of diskettes. The output of this step includes the creation of a SETUP.EXE on your first installation diskette. At the completion of this step, you have a deployable application.

The resulting diskettes can be run as any standard Windows application installation. The user can double-click on the SETUP.EXE or use File, Run from the Program Manager. The resulting setup allows the user to select from the components you have defined. The user will see the README.DOC you have named and will be prompted to select the destination path for the application's files. The user also will see the file sizes and the amount of disk space available. This process is a seamless and polished installation procedure.

Stored Procedure Update (SPUD)

The Stored Procedure Update (SPUD) utility creates PowerScript statements that override the default DataWindow update processing. The stored procedures are invoked in lieu of the standard DataWindow updates. The stored procedures created as a result of SPUD can be pasted into the SQLPreview event of the DataWindow control.

You should not create stored procedures until you have completely tested all your DataWindows because of the potential maintenance necessary if errors are found. The stored procedures should contain WHERE clauses naming all table columns. This provides some protection from incomplete updates.

SPUD works by associating DataWindow columns with stored procedure arguments. The three basic functions that SPUD accomplishes are:

❑ Maps DataWindow fields to stored procedure arguments.

❑ Links database actions (update, insert, delete) to the stored procedure via mapping specifications.

❏ Generates PowerScript statements to allow the DataWindow to update the database via the stored procedure.

SPUD initially provides a list of applications. After selecting the application, a selection list of associated DataWindows is displayed. After you select the DataWindow, SPUD connects to the associated database, and the SPUD work area is displayed (see Figure 13-18). The work area consists of the action group, a list of DataWindow columns with associated attributes, and stored procedure information with arguments and associated attributes. The stored procedure used in this process must be predefined.

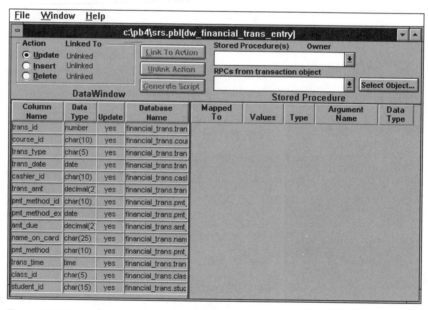

Figure 13-18: The Stored Procedure Update workspace.

The following steps are necessary to generate the PowerScript statements to use stored procedures to update the database:

1. Select an action (update, insert or delete).
2. Select a stored procedure from the selection list of all stored procedures for the current database. This stored procedure should apply to the action you chose in step 1.
3. Link the DataWindow fields to stored procedure arguments by dragging and dropping the Data-Window fields onto the stored procedure arguments.
4. Repeat steps 1–3 for each action.
5. Generate the script.
6. Save the generated script to a file or the Clipboard for later insertion into a script.
7. Update the SQLPreview event of the affected DataWindow by pasting the generated script from the Clipboard or importing it from the saved file.
8. Modify the script if necessary, and save it.

After completing this procedure, you can execute stored procedures to update your database instead of the DataWindow update.

RoboHELP

RoboHELP is a complete authoring tool used for creating Windows Help systems. RoboHELP is one of a number of support tools that assist in the time-consuming job of building Windows Help files and integrating those files into your PowerBuilder applications.

RoboHELP works with Microsoft Word for Windows version 2.x or version 6.x. Within Word are two document templates that offer a convenient mechanism for building the necessary file structure. Also included in RoboHELP is a Help compiler from Microsoft.

Windows Help systems require three files—the Help Project (HPJ) file, a Rich Text Format (RTF) file and the HH file or map file. The HPJ file tells the Help compiler how to build the Help system. The RTF file is a text file that includes formatting information. RoboHELP provides a template to make the job of creating a RTF easier. The HH file forms the interface between your Help system and the PowerBuilder application. The HH file contains an address for each Help system topic.

The Help Project

You begin creating a Windows Help system by creating the Help Project. A project, in RoboHELP, provides a structure for organizing the files that are necessary to build a complete Help system. Several sections within a Help Project file specify which files to include, such as graphics files, RTF files and context-string mapping files. It also contains compiler-directive statements, such as how to perform compression. RoboHELP builds the actual content of the Help Project file based on options selected by maintaining a Project Document.

To create a project in RoboHELP, initiate the starter program. RoboHELP displays the Create New Help Project dialog box, shown in Figure 13-19, which includes a Development Environment selection window. You can select PowerBuilder from this window. RoboHELP creates a project document and an RBH file from the selections you make.

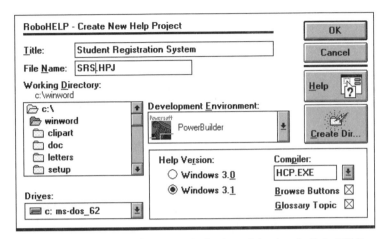

Figure 13-19: The Create New Help Project dialog box in RoboHELP.

You can compose, edit and format the Help document in a standard Word document. Each Help document is attached to a template that allows RoboHELP to do the following:

❑ Alter Word menus to add Help authoring commands.

❑ Automatically load and unload RoboHELP DLLs that are responsible for project management and the Floating Tool Palette.

❑ Provide a single, consistent, formatting style throughout a Help project.

❑ Provide a structured method of editing and formatting Help text.

The Help document is a temporary file that exists until the Help file is compiled (a make) and the document is closed.

Each Help document stores a private list of formatting styles. When the document is created, the style is inherited from the base document template. You can change the styles in RoboHELP document templates.

Help Topics

The Help Topic is the basic unit of organization in the Help system. Help Topics can contain formatted text, graphics and phrases linked by hypertext links and popups. Help Topics in RoboHELP can be newly created, or you can create Help Topics by selecting existing text. Each Help document is composed of a series of Help Topics. Each topic is separated by a hard page break. After each hard page break is a series of footnotes. The footnotes provide directives to the Help Compiler regarding attributes of the Help Topics (see Figure 13-20).

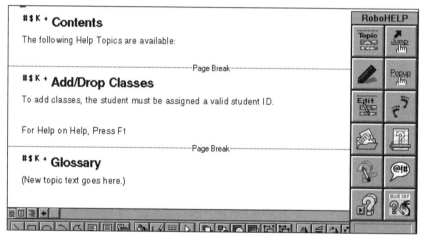

Figure 13-20: Building RoboHELP Help Topics.

You can add Help Topics by selecting the insertion point within the Help file and clicking the Topic icon. The topic separators (hard page breaks) and footnote characters are generated by RoboHELP. Enter a topic title, and follow it with explanatory text. You can subsequently edit the Help Topic and do things such as change the standard topics to popup topics. You can also move the relative location of the Help Topic or copy or move it to another Help file.

Hotspots

A *hotspot* is a phrase, text or graphic that is a link to either hypertext or a term definition. Hotspot links provide a framework for navigating within the Help system and bind related Help Topics.

The three kinds of hotspots are:

- ❑ Jump
- ❑ Popup
- ❑ Macro

A *jump* hotspot is similar to a cross reference in printed documents. It causes the Windows Help Viewer to display the destination topic in the main or secondary Help window. A *popup* hotspot is similar to a glossary entry. It causes the Windows Help Viewer to display a popup window. A *macro* hotspot is coded in the source Help document as a double underline, followed by an exclamation point and command script. The macro link goes directly to the mark specified by the macro.

To create a jump hotspot, you select the insertion point and select the Create Jump tool. You then select the destination for the jump or create a new Help Topic as your destination (see Figure 13-21).

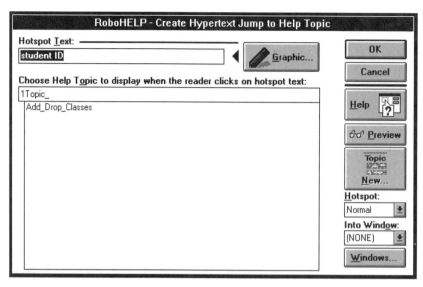

Figure 13-21: Building a RoboHELP Hypertext Jump.

Adding Graphics

RoboHELP provides four tools to assist in creating and altering graphic images for use in the Help system. They are the Graphic Placing Tool, the InWord Graphic Image Converter, the Screen Capture Utility, and Paintit for Small Images. You can place bitmap, metafile, hypergraphic (multiple hotspots) and multiresolution bitmap files within the Help text.

RoboHELP includes utilities to convert embedded images into metafiles and bitmaps for inclusion in the Help file. It also has a utility to convert icon and cursor images into bitmap files.

Graphic images can be pasted into the Help document from the Clipboard. Pictures can be inserted into the Help file using the Word Insert Picture command. OLE objects represented as bitmaps and metafiles can also be inserted into the Help file. Additionally, any picture embedded in a Word document can be converted into a Help graphic object.

Compiling

The elements of the Help file the help author deals with in Word are called the *source files*. The result of the authoring process is the compiled Help file. The compiler included with RoboHELP is Microsoft's latest Help compiler (HC30.EXE).

The Help compiler is invoked by selecting the Make Help File option from the Project menu. RoboHELP assists in the process of compilation by using a Graphical Help Debugger. If compilation is successful, a Rich Text Format (RTF) file is created, and you can run your Help project to test the results.

Advanced Help Features

You can automatically create a glossary that provides a popup for each item included in the glossary. You should add a button next to each section. While reading one topic, a user can jump to other topics by pressing the button.

RoboHELP supports the conversion of an existing RTD file into a RoboHELP file. It also supports the conversion of Help files into standard documentation by stripping out the help-specific formatting.

Adding Context-Sensitive Help

The basic notion of context-sensitive help is to provide entry points that the associated application program can call. A developer should always strive to provide accurate and complete contextual reference points to the Help system.

The WinHelp function provides your interface to Windows Help. By altering the parameters to the Win Help function, you can control the following:

☐ The file and topic to be displayed by Windows Help.

☐ Displaying the topic in a secondary Help window.

☐ Displaying the topic in the main Help window or in a popup window.

RoboHELP includes a standard Visual Basic control, the VBX Help button, to invoke context-sensitive Help from an application. In PowerBuilder, you add a VBX user object for the hypertext help button. You associate with the button the Project file for the Help system and a destination topic to link to, which provides context-sensitive Help at the object level.

MOVING ON

In this chapter, we have examined some PowerBuilder Developer's Toolkit utilities. We have given brief synopses of these tools—when to use them, their advantages, their disadvantages and the methods of using them. Of particular value are RoboHELP, primarily because of its ease of use in building a robust Help system, and Install Diskette Builder, because it standardizes application deployment.

In the next chapter, we'll discuss another important utility for extending PowerBuilder functionality—a method of TCP/IP programming using the WinSock library.

Winsock TCP/IP Programming in PowerBuilder

TCP/IP and Windows 3.1 have had a long, frustrating relationship. For years, dozens of companies sold dozens of Windows 3.1 TCP/IP networking products—all based on proprietary programming interfaces. While these products were great for adding your Windows-based PC to a TCP/IP network, they failed to provide a single standard interface for Windows TCP/IP programming. This meant that software developers writing TCP/IP applications for Windows had to accommodate several conflicting APIs to appeal to the entire Windows TCP/IP software market.

Further, developers wanting to create programs to work with a particular vendor's TCP/IP API had to purchase another proprietary development kit. The introduction of the Winsock specification changed all that. The creators of the Winsock standard took an existing, proven TCP/IP API and implemented it in Windows.

Winsock is based on the Berkeley sockets standard for TCP/IP programming in UNIX, sometimes referred to as BSD (Berkeley Software Distribution) sockets, a well-documented API. Once Winsock was available, anyone who purchased a Winsock-compliant TCP/IP networking package could also begin writing his or her own Winsock applications without buying a separate TCP/IP development library. And, anyone who had already written a TCP/IP application for UNIX could easily port his or her code to Windows.

As with any new standard, it took a while for Winsock to get off the ground. Companies had already invested a lot of time, energy and money purchasing their existing Windows TCP/IP networking products and were understandably reluctant to scrap it all and start over again. For many companies, there was simply no reason to switch: they weren't directly affected by the lack of a Windows TCP/IP standard because they weren't in the software development business, and their existing software did everything they needed.

Or so they thought. The growth of the Internet and the hype over the "Interactive digital revolution" and the "Information Superhighway" placed the Winsock standard in the right place at the right time. Suddenly, Internet TCP/IP applications for Windows were being written by people around the world, and the lack of a standard was no longer acceptable. Winsock became the de facto standard for Internet application programming in Windows, and therefore became the standard for Windows-based Internet TCP/IP networking. This gave individuals and companies a simple choice if they wanted to connect their Windows-based PCs to the Internet: switch to Winsock, or miss out on all the action.

Winsock is one of the most significant add-ons to Windows 3.1 in recent history. This chapter shows you how to use the library for PowerSocket, a Winsock programming interface for PowerBuilder, and how to use sockets to write TCP/IP client and server programs.

SOCKET PROGRAMMING

The idea of a socket is simple: it is a virtual communications link created over a real communications link. More precisely, a socket is the *potential* for a virtual communications link, since two sockets are required in every virtual link. Socket programming is used to create and manage the virtual links, allowing many sockets to exist simultaneously over a single real communications link. The real communications link can be a modem connection over a telephone line, a satellite uplink, an RS-232 cable connecting two computers or anything in between.

Socket technology was designed to shield programmers from the technical details of the network and give them a simple, standard way to write network software. In practice, socket programming is primarily used to write TCP/IP applications. In fact, Winsock 1.1 supports only TCP/IP, but future versions of the Winsock specification will support additional network protocols.

The PowerBuilder/Winsock Predicament

You're sold on Winsock programming, and you really like PowerBuilder as your Windows application development tool. You decide to write a Winsock application in PowerBuilder, thinking that PowerBuilder will be able to call any of the functions in your Winsock DLL once you know the function syntax. A quick search on the Internet reveals just the thing you need: complete Winsock 1.1 API documentation.

You test your theory by declaring a few of the Winsock functions as global external functions and calling them in your PowerScript code. It works! Then you try a few more and discover that you can't manipulate all of the Winsock data structures, perform certain data type conversions or read the data that Winsock puts in your string buffers. In other words, you find out that PowerBuilder is not C and that Winsock was designed by C programmers. We have built a library that contains the Winsock DLL function calls. It is the PowerSocket Library for PowerBuilder.

The PowerSocket Library for PowerBuilder

The PowerSocket Library is a Winsock programming interface for PowerBuilder. It gives your applications access to the Winsock DLL functions that PowerBuilder is usually unable to use. The PowerSocket Library also provides an intuitive PowerBuilder Winsock programming interface based on user objects.

As the PowerSocket Library is a shareware product, you can find a copy on the CD-ROM included with this book, and there is a per-programmer charge to purchase a license. Without a license, you can:

❏ Write programs for the purpose of evaluating the PowerSocket Library.

❏ Use the PowerSocket Library for your own education.

❏ Write programs for personal (noncommercial) use.

POWERSOCKET LIBRARY PROGRAMMING

Every PowerBuilder application that uses the PowerSocket Library needs the dynamic library WINSOCK.PBD in its Library Search Path (see Figure 14-1). This dynamic library is the heart of the PowerSocket Library for PowerBuilder.

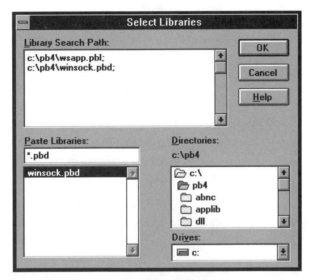

Figure 14-1: Include WINSOCK.PBD in your application's Library Search Path.

When you purchase a license for the PowerSocket Library, you receive the WINSOCK.PBL file. This gives you a choice between using the PBD in your applications or simply using the PBL as you would any other PBL. Programming with the PowerSocket Library involves four PowerSocket user objects:

- ❐ socket
- ❐ socketstream
- ❐ socketdgram
- ❐ winsock

The socket, socketstream and socketdgram user objects give you three ways to create and manipulate sockets. The socket user object is a generic socket type providing a user object wrapper around a socket descriptor. The socket user object must be initialized before you use it. The socketstream and socketdgram user objects are both inherited from the socket user object. They automatically create a new socket and don't require initialization before you can use them.

417

The winsock user object is meant to exist as a global variable within your PowerBuilder application. It contains code that automatically registers your application with the Winsock DLL when you create the winsock user object and automatically de-registers your application when you destroy the winsock user object. It also contains important Winsock functions and constants that your entire application will need to access after your program is registered with the Winsock DLL.

You can create a global winsock object variable by adding the following to the Declare Global Variables window (see Figure 14-2):

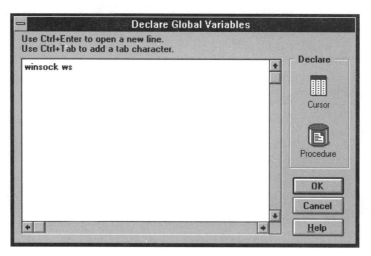

Figure 14-2: Declare a global winsock object variable.

This winsock object variable is global so you can access the winsock user object and its associated functions and attributes from anywhere within your application. You can declare a winsock user object variable in a specific location within your application, but that would prevent any component of your application that doesn't have access to the winsock variable from using the PowerSocket Library.

The next step is to create a winsock user object and store it in the winsock user object variable that you just declared. This is usually done in the application object's open event (see Figure 14-3) so every part of your application can access the object and use the PowerSocket Library. Use the following PowerScript code to create a winsock user object:

```
ws = create winsock
```

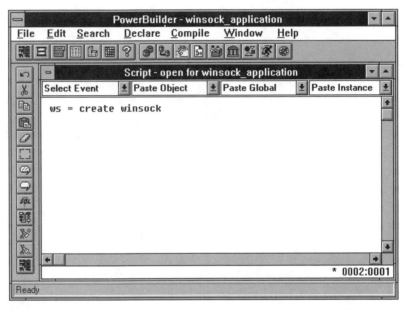

Figure 14-3: Use the PowerScript create command to create a winsock user object.

When your application is closed or when you're finished with the PowerSocket Library, you must destroy the winsock user object using the destroy command. This is usually done in the application object's Close event (see Figure 14-4) and looks like this:

```
destroy ws
```

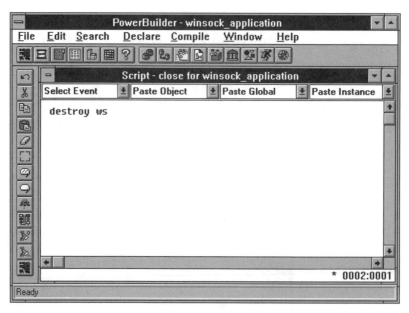

Figure 14-4: Destroy the global winsock user object when you no longer need it.

Now that you understand the basics of the PowerSocket Library, you can use sockets to create TCP/IP client and server programs. The rest of this chapter assumes that you've followed the instructions in this section and have the global winsock variable ws declared in your application.

WRITING A TCP/IP CLIENT PROGRAM

Writing a TCP/IP client program is a simple matter of creating a socket and instructing it to talk to another socket that is waiting to have a conversation. Any program that originates a socket conversation with another socket is considered to be a *client program*. Some client programs have very complex user interfaces or perform lengthy calculations, but they're all trivial when it comes to socket communications.

The following sections show you how to:

❐ Create a socket.

❐ Address a socket.

❐ Send and receive data over a socket.

❐ Create a socket that can detect errors and respond to other conditions.

Creating a Socket

Two socket types are available:

❐ Stream

❐ Datagram

Stream sockets are connection-based, meaning that the first step in using a stream socket for data communications is connecting the socket to another stream socket listening for connections. Datagram sockets are connectionless, meaning that datagram sockets don't have to be connected to other datagram sockets before they can communicate.

Datagram sockets are less reliable and less common than stream sockets. One drawback to datagram sockets is that there is no way to know whether data sent over a datagram socket actually arrives at its destination. Datagram sockets also provide an unreliable data stream that has the potential to duplicate or lose information. Conversely, stream sockets have built-in data integrity checking. If data is mangled in stream socket communications, your program reports the error. Datagram sockets work well in certain applications: for most Winsock programs, stream sockets are the socket of choice.

To create a new socket, do the following:

1. Declare a socket variable.
2. Use the PowerScript create command to create a new socket object.
3. Call the socket object's Socket() function to initialize the socket and determine the socket's type: stream or datagram.

The following code illustrates these three steps:

```
socket sockTestSocket // declare variable

sockTestSocket = CREATE socket  // create
sockTestSocket.Socket(ws.SOCK_STREAM)  //init

sockTestSocket.closesocket()
DESTROY sockTestSocket
```

The socket object's Socket() function accepts a single parameter identifying the type of socket. The two possible values are:

❏ ws.SOCK_STREAM (stream socket)
❏ ws.SOCK_DGRAM (datagram socket)

In the example, ws.SOCK_STREAM is used to initialize the socket object as a stream socket. Notice that both SOCK_STREAM and SOCK_DGRAM are defined within the winsock user object. This is one of the reasons that the winsock user object ws is declared as a global variable. The closesocket() function is required when your program is finished with the socket. After closing the socket, the PowerScript destroy command is used to destroy the socket user object sockTestSocket.

You can simplify the creation of sockets by using the socketstream or socketdgram user objects instead of the generic socket. For example, the following code accomplishes the same as the previous example, with one less step:

```
socketstream sockTestSocket // declare

sockTestSocket = CREATE socketstream  //create

sockTestSocket.closesocket()
DESTROY sockTestSocket
```

Creating a datagram socket is very similar to creating a stream socket: just replace ws.SOCK_STREAM with ws.SOCK_DGRAM if you're using a socket user object, or use a socketdgram user object instead. Whether you create a stream socket or a datagram socket, the next step is determining the address of the socket with which your socket has to communicate.

Understanding Socket Addressing

By default, sockets don't have addresses, but a socket can acquire one in many ways. For example, a socket is given an address automatically whenever an action is performed on the socket that requires it to have an address. When a stream socket is connected to another stream socket, the originating stream socket is given an address if it doesn't already have one. You can also give a socket an address explicitly, but in most client programs, it's okay to let the Winsock DLL choose the address for a socket when needed.

The address of a TCP/IP socket consists of two parts: the unique IP address of the computer on which the socket exists and the port number to which the socket is bound. There is really a third part to a socket's address: the protocol understood by the socket. Stream sockets understand TCP, and datagram sockets understand UDP. The primary concern you should have regarding a socket's protocol is to decide whether to use a stream socket or a datagram socket.

When writing a client application, you generally know the port number of the socket with which your program must communicate. This is because server applications use a socket to listen to a predefined port number. Requiring a client program to guess the port number to which a server is listening would make network programming a horrible game of socket hide-and-seek. As you'll see in the next chapter, standard port numbers have been assigned, for this very reason, to the most common server programs.

Assuming that you know the port number and the protocol, the only element left to determine is the IP address of the computer with which your program needs to communicate. This can be done in several ways, but first you need to know something important about IP addresses in Winsock: they aren't strings. Instead, Winsock uses unsigned long values to represent IP addresses.

Using Unsigned Longs to Represent IP Addresses

The reason that Winsock uses unsigned longs instead of strings is quite simple. To you, it makes sense to express a four-part unique number in the form:

```
128.64.32.16
```

To a computer, this format is sloppy. Why should a computer store 12 bytes of data (one byte for each character) when it can store the same IP address using a 32-bit binary value? That's 4 bytes (8 bits per byte) in binary form compared to 12 bytes or more in character form. To see how this works, first convert each of the four numbers in the IP address to binary form (see Figure 14-5). The sample IP address 128.64.32.16 looks like this in binary:

```
10000000.01000000.00100000.00010000
```

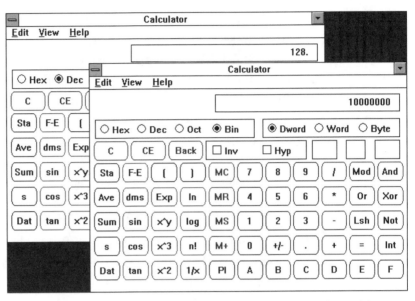

Figure 14-5: Use the Windows calculator to convert each number to binary.

If the world were a perfect place, you would simply remove the periods separating each of the binary values to get 32 bits, just the right size for an unsigned long. Instead, you must start from the right-hand side and work your way to the left, effectively switching the order of the bytes in the IP address. This is called *network byte order*. Normal order is called *host byte order* of all IP addresses in Winsock. Continuing with the example, the final binary representation for the IP address 128.64.32.16 in network byte order is:

00010000001000000100000010000000

Or, converting this to a decimal value, it's also:

270549120

This is the number you must use instead of the IP address 128.64.32.16, but don't worry: there are functions to handle this conversion for you. All you need to think about is which of several functions to call to obtain the unsigned long network byte order IP address.

The simplest way to obtain an unsigned long version of an IP address is to call the inet_addr() function in the winsock user object. The inet_addr() function accepts a single parameter that is the string version of the IP address and returns the IP address as an unsigned long in network byte order. Here's an example:

```
ulong ulAddr

ulAddr = ws.inet_addr("128.64.32.16")

messagebox("ulAddr equals",string(ulAddr))
```

Figure 14-6 shows the result of this script. The inet_addr() function works very well if you already know the IP address, but that's not always the case.

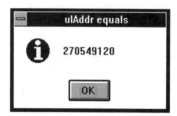

Figure 14-6: The inet_addr() function returns an unsigned long value in network byte order.

If you only know the host name of a computer and not its IP address, the winsock user object function GetHostByName() can help you. This function performs a domain name lookup for the specified name and returns a pbhostent structure containing the result of the lookup. If the pbhostent structure is equal to NULL, an error occurred. The following script illustrates the use of the GetHostByName() function:

```
pbhostent pbheTmp
string sMessage

pbheTmp = ws.GetHostByName("science.org")
if isnull(pbheTmp) = TRUE then
    // an error occurred, do something about it
else    // no error
    sMessage = string(pbheTmp.h_addr_list[1])
    messagebox("Address",sMessage)
end if
```

Figure 14-7 shows the result of this script, provided there are no errors. The structure of pbhostent is shown in Table 14-1. Since it's possible for a single host to have multiple names and multiple addresses, the pbhostent structure contains arrays of undefined length.

Figure 14-7: GetHostByName() finds a host's address.

It's a good idea to check the size of these arrays before trying to access their contents. If you assume, as we did in the last example, that one of these arrays has a certain number of elements, your program will crash when that assumption is incorrect. A better way to access the h_addr_list[] array is to first check its size with the PowerScript upperbound() function. The following example is a better version of the last example:

```
pbhostent pbheTmp
string sMessage

pbheTmp = ws.GetHostByName("science.org")
if isnull(pbheTmp) = TRUE then
    // an error occurred, do something about it
else    // no error
    if upperbound(pbheTmp.h_addr_list) > 0 then
        sMessage = string(pbheTmp.h_addr_list[1])
    else
        sMessage = "No Address"
    end if
    messagebox("Address",sMessage)
end if
```

Name	Type	Description
h_name	string	The official name of the host.
h_aliases[]	string array	An array of aliases for the host.
h_addrtype	integer	The type of address in h_addr_list[].
h_length	integer	The length of each address.
h_addr_list[]	unsigned long array	An array of addresses for the host in unsigned long, network byte order format.

Table 14-1: The contents of a pbhostent structure.

If you know the unsigned long, network byte order version of an IP address and would like to convert it to a string in the more friendly "128.64.32.16" *dotted quad notation,* you can use the winsock user object function inet_ntoa(). The inet_ntoa() function accepts a single parameter: the unsigned long, network byte order version of an IP address and returns the string version of the IP address. Here's an example:

```
string sAddr

sAddr = ws.inet_ntoa(209214863)
messagebox("Dotted quad",sAddr)
```

Figure 14-8 shows the result of this script.

Figure 14-8: inet_ntoa() converts an unsigned long address to a string in dotted quad notation.

Getting the Name of the Local Computer

Another useful function in the winsock user object is GetHostName(). This function is used to obtain the name of the local computer. If you don't know the IP address of the local machine, you can use GetHostName() with GetHostByName() to find out what it is. The following example shows you how to do this.

```
ulong ulAddr
pbhostent pbheTmp
string sHostName

sHostName = space(ws.MAXHOSTNAMELENGTH)
ws.GetHostName(sHostName,ws.MAXHOSTNAMELENGTH)

pbheTmp = ws.GetHostByName(sHostName)
if isnull(pbheTmp) = FALSE then
    if upperbound(pbheTmp.h_addr_list) > 0 then
        ulAddr = pbheTmp.h_addr_list[1]
    end if
    messagebox(sHostName,string(ulAddr))
end if
```

Figure 14-9 shows the result of this script.

Figure 14-9: The GetHostName() and GetHostByName() functions work well together.

The GetHostName() function accepts two parameters: a string variable that contains a certain number of characters and the number of characters present in the string variable. The constant value ws.MAXHOSTNAMELENGTH is used to ensure that the string variable will have sufficient space for any possible host name. If the GetHostName() function completes successfully (something serious would have to be wrong for it not to), the string variable contains the name of the local computer. This name is then passed to the GetHostByName() function, and the resulting IP address is displayed on the screen.

Binding the Socket to an Address

After you have the unsigned long version of an IP address, you can use that value to give your socket an address. This is called *binding* the socket to an address and is accomplished using the socket object's bind() function. The bind() function accepts two parameters: the unsigned long IP address of the local computer and the port number to which the socket will be associated. The following example shows how the bind() function is used:

```
ulong ulAddr
socketstream sockSocket

ulAddr = ws.inet_addr("128.64.32.16")

sockSocket = CREATE socketstream
sockSocket.bind(ulAddr,8080)

sockSocket.closesocket()
DESTROY sockSocket
```

This example binds the stream socket sockSocket to the local address 128.64.32.16 and assigns it to port number 8080. This is sometimes known as *assigning a local association* to the socket. Put simply, the socket now has an address. Most client programs don't need to explicitly assign local associations because Winsock does this automatically when the socket needs an address. Server applications, however, must assign addresses to their sockets using bind(). Writing a server application is covered later in this chapter.

To recap, every socket needs an address in order to do anything useful. If you don't give an address to a socket explicitly by using the socket's bind() function, one will be appointed for you when it's needed. Socket addresses have three parts: an unsigned long value representing the IP address of the computer on which the socket exists, a port number and a protocol type. Several functions exist to make it easier to find a particular computer's IP address and work with unsigned long versions of IP addresses.

Sending & Receiving Data Over a Socket

Now that you know how to find a particular computer's IP address, you're ready for socket communications. Five functions in the socket object provide everything you need to send and receive data over a socket:

❏ wsconnect()

❏ recv()

❏ recvfrom()

❏ send()

❏ sendto()

Establishing Connections Between Stream Sockets

The wsconnect() function is used to establish connections between stream sockets. After the connection is established, you can send and receive data using the send() and recv() functions. For datagram sockets, which are connectionless, wsconnect() sets the default destination for subsequent calls to the send() function. The special socket functions sendto() and recvfrom() are meant to be used with datagram sockets, and for stream sockets are no different than the normal send() and recv().

The following example shows the code for using a stream socket to connect to port 7 (the echo port on some UNIX machines). The IP address of the host is 204.94.74.209.

```
socketstream sockTestSocket
ulong ulAddr
blob blobBuffer
integer iLen

ulAddr = ws.inet_addr("204.94.74.209")

sockTestSocket = CREATE socketstream
sockTestSocket.wsconnect(ulAddr,7)

// send data using a blob buffer
blobBuffer = blob("This is a test~r~n")
iLen = len(blobBuffer)
sockTestSocket.send(blobBuffer,iLen,0)

// data was sent, and it should be echoed back
```

```
blobBuffer = blob(space(iLen)) // clear buffer
sockTestSocket.recv(blobBuffer,iLen,0)

messagebox("blobBuffer",string(blobBuffer))

sockTestSocket.closesocket()
DESTROY sockTestSocket
```

First, the IP address 204.94.74.209 is converted to unsigned long, network byte order format using the following code:

```
ulAddr = ws.inet_addr("204.94.74.209")
```

Next, a stream socket is created and is immediately connected to port 7 of the computer with an IP address of 204.94.74.209 using the following code:

The echo port is handy for testing.

```
sockTestSocket = CREATE socketstream
sockTestSocket.wsconnect(ulAddr,7)
```

Port 7 is a special echo port that echoes any data it receives.

Sending & Receiving Data With a Stream Socket

Now that the socket sockTestSocket is connected to another socket, the data can be sent. The next three lines fill a blob buffer with a string to send over the socket. The PowerScript blob() function is used to convert the string value to a blob, then the blob buffer is supplied to the send() function. The string contains the characters ~r~n because PowerBuilder interprets this as a carriage return (~r) and line feed (~n).

```
blobBuffer = blob("This is a test~r~n")
iLen = len(blobBuffer)
sockTestSocket.send(blobBuffer,iLen,0)
```

The send() function accepts three parameters: a blob buffer containing the data to be sent over the socket, the length of the data (number of bytes) in the blob buffer and an integer value representing special flags that change the way send() operates. Zero is the default integer value for send().

Since the data sent to port 7 is echoed immediately, data is now ready to be received over the socket. The following lines receive the data over the socket and display the received data in a message box.

```
blobBuffer = blob(space(iLen)) // clear buffer
sockTestSocket.recv(blobBuffer,iLen,0)

messagebox("blobBuffer",string(blobBuffer))
```

The first line of code clears the blob buffer by storing spaces in it. The number of spaces stored is equal to the number of characters that were sent over the socket because that is also the length of the data to be received. The recv() function then fills the blob buffer with the data that is waiting to be read from the socket. Like the send() function, the recv() function accepts three parameters: the blob buffer in which to store data received over the socket, the length (in bytes) of the blob buffer and a value identifying flags to pass to the recv() function. After displaying the data received, the socket is closed, and the socket user is object destroyed, as shown below:

```
sockTestSocket.closesocket()
DESTROY sockTestSocket
```

Sending Data Using a Datagram Socket

Since datagram sockets don't use connections, sending data using a datagram socket is a bit simpler. To send data using a datagram socket, you create the socket, call the sendto() function, then tell sendto() what to send and where to send it. To receive data using a datagram socket, you can call the recv() or recvfrom() functions. The following example shows how to send and receive data using a datagram socket:

```
socketdgram DGSock
ulong ulAddr
blob blobBuf
```

```
integer iLen

ulAddr = ws.inet_addr("204.94.74.209")

DGSock = CREATE socketdgram

// send data using a blob buffer
blobBuf = blob("This is a test~r~n")
iLen = len(blobBuf)
DGSock.sendto(blobBuf,iLen,0,ulAddr,7)

// data was sent, and it should be echoed back
blobBuf = blob(space(iLen)) // clear buffer
DGSock.recv(blobBuf,iLen,0)

messagebox("blobBuf",string(blobBuf))

DGSock.closesocket()
DESTROY DGSock
```

The first part of this code is similar to that for sending
stream sockets. One major difference is that after you create
the datagram socket, you can use it immediately to send data
using the sendto() function, whereas with stream sockets,
you have to establish the connection before sending the data.
The following lines send the data:

```
blobBuf = blob("This is a test~r~n")
iLen = len(blobBuf)
DGSock.sendto(blobBuf,iLen,0,ulAddr,7)
```

The sendto() function accepts five parameters: the blob
buffer containing data to be sent; the length (in bytes) of the
buffer; a flag value that determines how sendto() operates
(zero for default operation); the unsigned long version of the
IP address; and the port number to which the data in the
blob buffer is to be sent.

The code for receiving data over a datagram socket is the same as that for a stream socket:

```
blobBuf = blob(space(iLen)) // clear buffer
DGSock.recv(blobBuf,iLen,0)

messagebox("blobBuf",string(blobBuf))
```

Datagram sockets have a more specialized purpose than stream sockets. Typically, datagram sockets are used only when it doesn't matter whether the data that is sent actually arrives at its destination. This may seem strange, but at times this makes sense. For example, a real-time data collection device might send data to a collection center using a datagram socket. If the collection center doesn't receive the data, there's nothing that can be done about it anyway because the real-time collection device doesn't have the ability to resend lost information.

Creating Smart Sockets

Creating sockets and using them to send and receive short messages is useful for demonstrating basic concepts, but for most programs, "This is a test" just won't do. Your real Winsock applications need decision-making capabilities. This means that your code needs to watch out for errors, respond to changing conditions that affect sockets and be flexible enough to handle the unexpected. Several PowerSocket functions exist to help you do this:

❑ WSAGetLastError()

❑ wsselect()

❑ ioctlsocket()

❑ getsockopt()

❑ setsockopt()

The following sections describe each function.

Determining the Source of Errors Using WSAGetLastError()

The WSAGetLastError() function is part of the winsock user object. Calling WSAGetLastError() is the only way to determine the cause of an error. When a Winsock function fails, a call to WSAGetLastError() returns an integer value representing the error that occurred. You can determine the reason for the error by comparing the integer value with winsock user object constants. The user object constants are described in the documentation for each PowerSocket Library function.

The following example shows how to use WSAGetLastError() to determine errors:

```
socketstream sockSocket
ulong ulAddr
integer iError

ulAddr = ws.inet_addr("128.64.32.16")

sockSocket = CREATE socketstream

if sockSocket.wsconnect(ulAddr,21) = -1 then
    // an error occurred trying to connect
    iError = ws.WSAGetLastError()
    if iError = ws.WSAETIMEDOUT then
        messagebox("Error","Timed out")
    else
        messagebox("Error #",string(iError))
    end if
end if

sockSocket.closesocket()
DESTROY sockSocket
```

This script creates a new socket and attempts to connect it to port 21 of the host 128.64.32.16. Because 128.64.32.16 is an imaginary IP address, the connect attempt eventually fails due most likely to a timeout, and a message displays indicating this. If the failure isn't due to a timeout, the error code is displayed.

Notice that the script compared the constant value ws.WSAETIMEDOUT to the error code returned by WSAGetLastError(). When coding your error handling routines, it's usually enough just to check for the errors you're interested in and decide upon a default action for the rest.

Checking Socket Activity Using wsselect()

Use the winsock object function wsselect() to check activity on a particular socket, such as checking to see if data is waiting to be read. The wsselect() function accepts four parameters:

❏ A structure containing an array of sockets to check for incoming data.

❏ A structure containing an array of sockets to check for writability.

❏ A structure containing an array of sockets to check for errors.

❏ A timeval structure specifying the length of time to wait for a result.

With the wsselect() function, your program can make intelligent decisions about sending and receiving data on sockets.

You might periodically execute a script similar to the one below to check a socket for waiting data. The significance of this approach is that instead of calling the recv() function once and waiting for data to arrive, you can call recv() only when data is ready to read. In the meantime, other processing can occur.

```
pbfd_set fdRd, fdWr, fdEx
timeval killyourTV
integer iRet

//(0,0) means poll sockets, return immediately
killyourTV.tv_sec = 0
killyourTV.tv_usec = 0

//sockSocket declared, connected elsewhere
fdRd.fd_array[1] = sockSocket
fdRd.fd_count = 1

iRet = ws.wsselect(fdRd,fdWr,fdEx,killyourTV)

if iRet > 0 then
    // sockSocket has data waiting to be read
    // recv( ) it and do something
end if

// continue with other processing, then repeat
```

The following lines from the script set the two elements of a timeval structure equal to zero. Structure element tv_sec specifies the number of seconds to wait, and tv_usec specifies the number of milliseconds to wait. By setting both elements to zero, the wsselect() function is told to return a result immediately, effectively polling the current state of the specified sockets.

```
killyourTV.tv_sec = 0
killyourTV.tv_usec = 0
```

You use three pbfd_set structures to specify which sockets to poll. Each pbfd_set structure contains the following elements:

❏ socket fd_array[128]

❏ integer fd_count

The fd_array element is a 128-item array of socket objects. It is in this array of sockets that you include the sockets to be checked for one of the three conditions: readability, writability or an exception condition. The fd_count element indicates the number of socket objects added to fd_array. In the example script, only one of the three pbfd_set structures is filled with a socket to be checked:

```
fdRd.fd_array[1] = sockSocket
fdRd.fd_count = 1
```

This pbfd_set structure is passed to the wsselect() function to indicate the sockets to check for waiting data. The other two pbfd_set structures are left empty to indicate that no sockets should be checked for writability or exceptions. The sample script assumes that the socket user object sockSocket is created somewhere else before the script is executed.

When all four of the structures are ready, the wsselect() function is called. Remember that the only pbfd_set structure that contains any sockets to be checked is fdRd. The fdWr and fdEx structures are empty to indicate that no sockets should be checked for writability or exceptions. The timeval structure, killyourTV, is set to (0,0) so that a result is returned immediately. The following line performs the actual function call, capturing the return value in iRet:

```
iRet = ws.wsselect(fdRd,fdWr,fdEx,killyourTV)
```

If the socket in the fdRd structure contains data waiting to be read, then the return value will be 1. wsselect() returns the total number of sockets for which the requested condition is true. If none of the sockets specified in any of the pbfd_set structures meet the requested condition, then wsselect() returns zero.

The above example demonstrates how to use the wsselect() function with a single socket object. When wsselect() is used to check the status of several socket objects, a few differences are worth noting. The most obvious difference is that more than one socket is checked by a single call to wsselect(), so there must be a way to find out which sockets meet the condition. The following example shows how to do this.

```
pbfd_set fdRd, fdWr, fdEx
timeval killyourTV
integer iRet, a

//(0,0) means poll sockets, return immediately
killyourTV.tv_sec = 0
killyourTV.tv_usec = 0

//sockets declared, connected elsewhere
fdRd.fd_array[1] = sockOne
fdRd.fd_array[2] = sockTwo
fdRd.fd_array[3] = sockThree
fdRd.fd_count = 3

fdWr.fd_array[1] = sockTwo
fdWr.fd_count = 1

fdEx.fd_array[1] = sockOne
fdEx.fd_array[2] = sockTwo
fdEx.fd_array[3] = sockThree
fdEx.fd_count = 3

iRet = ws.wsselect(fdRd,fdWr,fdEx,killyourTV)
```

```
if iRet > 0 then
    for a = 1 to fdRd.fd_count
        fdRd.fd_array[a].recv( ) // receive data
        // data received, do something with it
    next

    for a = 1 to fdWr.fd_count
        fdWr.fd_array[a].send( ) // send data
        // socket was writeable, so send data
    next

    for a = 1 to fdEx.fd_count
        // an exception occurred, handle it.
    next
end if

// continue, repeat as necessary
```

The first part of this example fills the three pbfd_set structures with sockets. The structure containing sockets to check
for waiting data and the one containing sockets to check for
exceptions are both filled with three socket objects. The
structure containing sockets to check for writability is filled
only with a single socket object.

```
fdRd.fd_array[1] = sockOne
fdRd.fd_array[2] = sockTwo
fdRd.fd_array[3] = sockThree
fdRd.fd_count = 3

fdWr.fd_array[1] = sockTwo
fdWr.fd_count = 1

fdEx.fd_array[1] = sockOne
fdEx.fd_array[2] = sockTwo
fdEx.fd_array[3] = sockThree
fdEx.fd_count = 3
```

The next part of this example calls the wsselect() function, then checks the result. If any sockets meet the requested condition, three *for* loops perform processing for each of the three structures.

wsselect() updates each structure to reflect the sockets that meet the specified condition. The fd_count element is set equal to the number of sockets that meet the specified condition, and the socket object array fd_array is updated so that these socket objects are the first ones in the array. This makes a *for* loop a convenient way to access only the socket objects that meet the specified condition.

```
for a = 1 to fdRd.fd_count
    fdRd.fd_array[a].recv( )
next
```

While this example is only a code snippet, it does illustrate how wsselect() and the resulting arrays are used when working with multiple socket objects.

Commanding Sockets Using ioctlsocket()

The ioctlsocket() function in the socket user object lets you perform three commands on a socket:

❑ winsock.FIONBIO

❑ winsock.FIONREAD

❑ winsock.SIOCATMARK

The winsock.FIONBIO command enables or disables *asynchronous mode* for a socket. Asynchronous mode is also referred to as *non-blocking mode*, while *blocking mode* is a synonym for *synchronous mode*. Synchronous mode is the default socket mode.

Synchronous mode can cause problems when some Winsock function calls won't return control to your program until they're finished processing. A single recv() call, for instance, might block control for a very long time as it waits for data to arrive on a socket. Non-blocking mode solves this problem by using Windows events to notify your program when a particular function call is complete. Detailed instructions on programming with asynchronous mode function calls are provided at the end of this chapter. Use a script like the following one to enable non-blocking mode for a particular socket.

```
socketstream sockA
ulong ulParm

ulParm = 1

sockA.ioctlsocket(ws.FIONBIO,ulParm)
```

The ioctlsocket() function accepts two parameters: the command to perform on the socket and an unsigned long variable. The unsigned long variable contains a parameter for the specified command or serves as a buffer for the command result.

Use the winsock.FIONREAD command to determine the number of bytes of data that are waiting to be read on the socket. The following example shows you how to use winsock.FIONREAD.

```
ulong ulLength, ulAddr
socketstream sockTmp
pbfd_set fdRd, fdWr, fdEx
timeval killyourTV
integer iRet

sockTmp = CREATE socketstream

ulAddr = ws.inet_addr("204.94.74.209")

sockTmp.wsconnect(ulAddr,21)

killyourTV.tv_sec = 5
```

```
killyourTV.tv_usec = 0

fdRd.fd_array[1] = sockTmp
fdRd.fd_count = 1

iRet = ws.wsselect(fdRd,fdWr,fdEx,killyourTV)

if iRet > 0 then
    sockTmp.ioctlsocket(ws.FIONREAD,ulLength)
else
    ulLength = 0
end if

messagebox("Bytes to read",string(ulLength))

sockTmp.closesocket()
DESTROY sockTmp
```

The result of this script is shown in Figure 14-10.

Figure 14-10: Use ws.FIONREAD to find out how many bytes are available to be read.

In the following example from the script, the ioctlsocket() function is called using ws.FIONREAD.

```
sockTmp.ioctlsocket(ws.FIONREAD,ulLength)
```

When the function call is complete, ulLength contains the number of bytes waiting to be read on the socket. The other command accepted by ioctlsocket() is ws.SIOCATMARK. This command is used to determine whether all of the *out-of-band* data has been read.

Controlling Socket Operation

getsockopt() and setsockopt() are used to obtain and set options for a socket. Some of the options available include enabling or disabling debug mode, activating or deactivating inline reception of out-of-band data and setting the send and receive buffer sizes for the socket. Use getsockopt() to read a particular option's value, and use setsockopt() to set a value for an option. The following example shows how to use both functions:

```
linger lingTmp
int iVal, iLevel, iOpt
socket sockA

sockA = CREATE socket
sockA.socket(ws.SOCK_STREAM)

iLevel = ws.SOL_SOCKET
iOpt = ws.SO_BROADCAST
iVal = 1

sockA.setsockopt(iLevel,iOpt,iVal,lingTmp)

iOpt = ws.SO_RCVBUF

sockA.getsockopt(iLevel,iOpt,ival,lingTmp)

messagebox("Receive Buf Size",string(iVal))
DESTROY sockA
```

In this example, the setsockopt() function is called and is passed the following parameters:

❐ ws.SOL_SOCKET as the level of the option (iLevel)

❐ ws.SO_BROADCAST as the name of the option to set (iOpt)

❐ 1 (Boolean TRUE) as the value to set for the SO_BROADCAST option

❐ an empty linger structure

By passing these four parameters, the SO_BROADCAST option is turned on for the socket. This means that the socket can now be used to broadcast information to every computer on the network. The next function call reads the current size of the receive buffer. To do this, the option name stored in the iOpt variable is changed to ws.SO_RCVBUF. The result is stored in iVal, which is then displayed in a message box.

The fourth parameter for both of these functions is a linger structure. This structure is used only for reading or setting the SO_LINGER option. The linger structure has the following form:

❒ integer l_onoff

❒ integer l_linger

When an option other than SO_LINGER is read or set using getsockopt() or setsockopt(), the linger structure is ignored.

Figure 14-11 shows the result of the script.

Figure 14-11: Use getsockopt() to find the current setting for a socket option.

WRITING A TCP/IP SERVER PROGRAM

Writing a TCP/IP server program is very similar to writing a client program. The major difference is that a server program provides a socket to which client programs can connect, while client programs originate a socket conversation with another socket.

Since most server applications that you write will use stream instead of datagram sockets, this section ignores datagram sockets entirely. You use four socket user object functions to create a server application using stream sockets:

- ❏ bind()
- ❏ listen()
- ❏ accept()
- ❏ initsocket()

The following steps summarize how to create a socket connection with a client and begin communicating:

1. Create a socket and bind it to an address using bind().
2. Call the listen() function.
3. When a client program tries to establish a connection to the listening socket, call the accept() function and store the return value produced by accept().
4. Create a new socket object and call the initsocket() function, passing the value returned by accept().
5. The following example incorporates each step.

```
ulong ulAddr
socketstream sockSocket
socket sockAccepted
integer iBufLen, iRet, iPort, iLen
unsignedinteger uiTmp
blob blobBuf
string sTmp
iBufLen = 100

sockSocket = create socketstream
ulAddr = ws.inet_addr("204.94.74.210")
sockSocket.bind(ulAddr,23)
sockSocket.listen(5)
```

```
uiTmp = sockSocket.accept(ulAddr,iPort)
sockAccepted = create socket
sockAccepted.initsocket(uiTmp)

do while "A" = "A"
   blobBuf = blob(space(iBufLen))
   iRet = sockAccepted.recv(blobBuf,iBufLen,0)
   if iRet = ws.SOCKET_ERROR then
      exit
   end if

   blobBuf = blobmid(blobBuf,1,iRet)

   choose case upper(string(blobBuf))
   case "HELP~r~n"
      sTmp = "Available Commands~r~n"
      sTmp = sTmp + "---------~r~n"
      sTmp = sTmp + "HELP - This is the help~r~n"
      sTmp = sTmp + "COMMANDONE - Command one~r~n"
      sTmp = sTmp + "COMMANDTWO - Command two~r~n"
      sTmp = sTmp + "QUIT - Close connection~r~n"
      blobBuf = blob(sTmp)
   case "COMMANDONE~r~n"
      blobBuf = blob("Command one executed.~r~n")
   case "COMMANDTWO~r~n"
      blobBuf = blob("Command two executed.~r~n")
   case "QUIT~r~n"
      exit
   case else
      blobBuf = blob("Invalid command~r~n")
   end choose

   iLen = len(blobBuf)

   iRet = sockAccepted.send(blobBuf,iLen,0)
   if iRet = ws.SOCKET_ERROR then
      exit
   end if

loop
```

```
sockAccepted.closesocket()
sockSocket.closesocket()

destroy sockSocket
destroy sockAccepted
```

The first few lines of this script create a stream socket, bind it to a local address and tell it to listen. The listen() function accepts a single parameter identifying the maximum number of connections that can be placed in the queue of pending connections. A value greater than 5 is treated as 5.

```
sockSocket = create socketstream
ulAddr = ws.inet_addr("204.94.74.210")
sockSocket.bind(ulAddr,23)
sockSocket.listen(5)
```

The stream socket sockSocket is now listening for incoming socket connections. The next step is to call the accept() function to accept an incoming connection. The following lines accept an incoming connection and create a new socket object for the connection.

```
uiTmp = sockSocket.accept(ulAddr,iPort)
sockAccepted = create socket
sockAccepted.initsocket(uiTmp)
```

The accept() function takes two parameters: an unsigned long and an integer variable, both of which are filled with the socket address that originated the connection.

Because this example uses a synchronous (blocking) socket mode, the call to accept() causes the program to wait for an incoming connection before continuing. Once a connection arrives, it is immediately accepted, and a new socket is created. This new socket, identified by the return value of accept(), is connected. The original socket sockSocket continues to listen for incoming connections. A new socket object, sockAccepted, is created and initialized with the number identifying the socket created by accept(). The rest of the script receives a command sent by the client program and sends a response (see Figure 14-12). If one of the socket functions returns ws.SOCKET_ERROR, the script assumes that the connection was broken by the peer and exits.

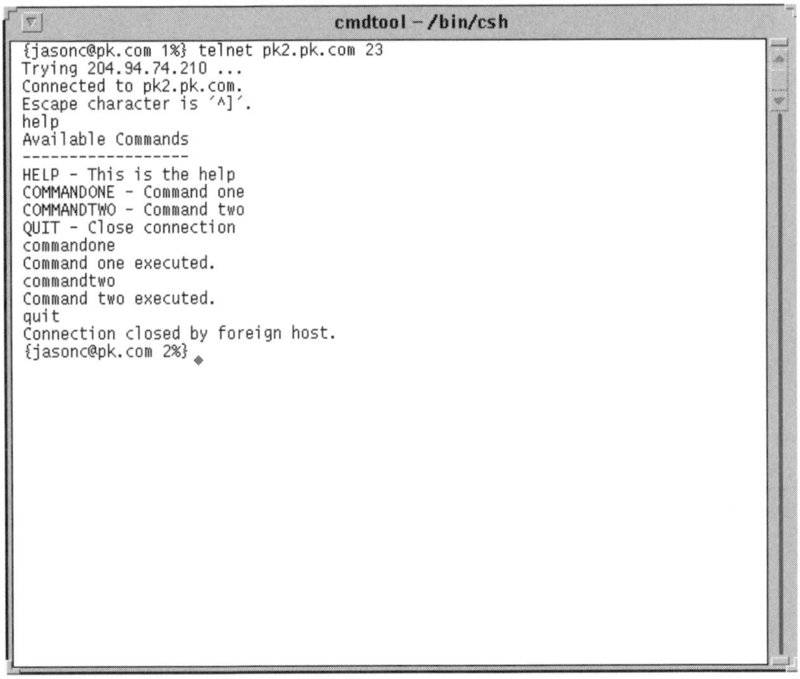

```
┌────────────────────────  cmdtool - /bin/csh  ─────────────────────┐
│ ▽                                                                 │
│ {jasonc@pk.com 1%} telnet pk2.pk.com 23                          │▲
│ Trying 204.94.74.210 ...                                        │
│ Connected to pk2.pk.com.                                         │▽
│ Escape character is '^]'.                                        │
│ help                                                             │
│ Available Commands                                              │
│ ------------------                                              │
│ HELP - This is the help                                         │
│ COMMANDONE - Command one                                        │
│ COMMANDTWO - Command two                                        │
│ QUIT - Close connection                                         │
│ commandone                                                      │
│ Command one executed.                                           │
│ commandtwo                                                      │
│ Command two executed.                                           │
│ quit                                                            │
│ Connection closed by foreign host.                              │
│ {jasonc@pk.com 2%} ◆                                            │
│                                                                 │
└───────────────────────────────────────────────────────────────────┘
```

Figure 14-12: This server program accepts commands from a Telnet client.

This example demonstrates the basics of using any Winsock server program, but overlooks one important aspect: most server programs need to handle multiple, simultaneous connections. Working with multiple socket connections is not practical using synchronous (blocking) mode. For the real power of Winsock programming, you need to switch to asynchronous (nonblocking) mode.

Moving On

Now that you know how to use sockets to communicate across a TCP/IP network, you're ready to learn how to use sockets to interact with the World Wide Web and FTP, or File Transfer Protocol. Chapter 15 takes you into the new and ever-changing world of the Internet.

Programming With Internet Resources

People are arguably the most important resource on the Internet. In many cases, Internet programming means communicating with Internet users—people who access the Internet through client applications such as World Wide Web browsers. Internet programming also involves accessing the vast network of automated information resources. This chapter shows you how to use the PowerSocket Library to write Winsock programs that interact with the two most common Internet resources: the World Wide Web and File Transfer Protocol (FTP).

WORLD WIDE WEB PROGRAMMING

The standard World Wide Web port number is 80. To program using the Web, your applications usually make socket connections on this port. The World Wide Web relies on a standard known as HyperText Transfer Protocol (HTTP) to provide a way for Web browsers to request documents from Web servers. In this section, we'll show you what you need to know about HTTP in order to write useful WWW applications.

At the heart of HTTP is a set of commands that are recognized by an HTTP server. Table 15-1 lists some of the methods defined in version 1.0 of HTTP.

Method	Description
GET	Retrieves the specified document.
HEAD	Retrieves only the HTTP headers for the specified document.
SHOWMETHOD	Returns a description for a given method.
PUT	Stores the specified data in the specified URL.
DELETE	Requests that the server delete the item in the specified URL.
POST	Creates a new object linked to the specified object.
LINK	Links an existing object to the specified object.
UNLINK	Removes link information from an object.

Table 15-1: HTTP 1.0 methods.

GET is the workhorse of the World Wide Web and is most often used to retrieve an item from an HTTP server using a Web browser. The rest of this section shows you how to use GET and other HTTP commands to create a WWW server, retrieve files from a WWW server and submit forms to a WWW server.

Building a Simple WWW Server

Building a complete Web server from scratch is a complex proposition, and PowerBuilder isn't the right tool for the job. However, PowerBuilder is appropriate for building a scaled-down version of a WWW server that supports features required by your application. For example, your

PowerBuilder application can accept the contents of a form written in HyperText Markup Language (HTML) from a Web browser, perform processing or database manipulation based on the form's contents and return an HTML result to the client. Or, your application can accept a simple HTTP file request sent by a Web browser and return the requested document.

The simplest WWW server to build in PowerBuilder is one that recognizes the GET method, searches a database table for the specified document and returns the document to the client. The following summary steps are required to build a simple WWW server in PowerBuilder:

1. Create a database.
2. Create the Web server application.
3. Create the socket, and begin socket communications.

Creating a Database

Create a new database in the Database painter using the following steps:

1. Create a database, and name it WWW. (For steps on creating a database, see Chapter 7.)
2. Create a table named documents, and give the table one char column for the document name and one long varchar column for the document text (see Figure 15-1).

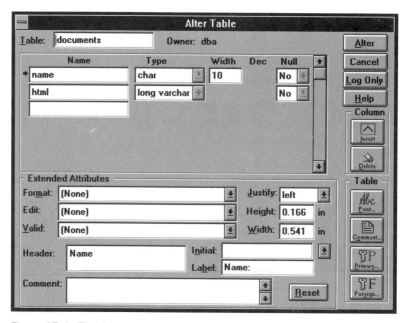

Figure 15-1: The documents table.

Creating the Web Server Application

The next procedure is to create the Web server application that will accept socket communications:

1. Start a new application, and prepare it for Power-Socket programming by declaring a global Winsock variable and adding scripts to the application object's Open and Close events, as described in the previous chapter.

2. Create a new window, and save it as w_main.

3. Add two static text fields to w_main:

   ❐ Type **Number of WWW Accesses**: in st_1.

   ❐ Type **0** in st_2 (see Figure 15-2).

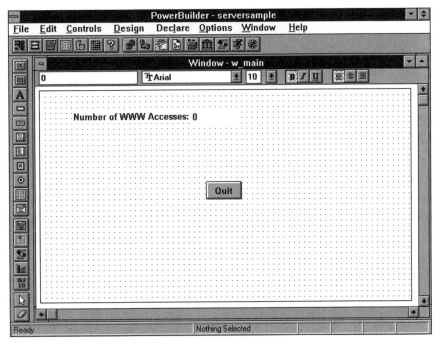

Figure 15-2: Adding two static text fields to w_main.

4. Create a CommandButton, and enter the word **Quit** in the text attribute.

5. Enter **close(parent)** in the Clicked event script so that clicking the button closes w_main.

6. Next, you should create a socketstream variable that will be used to listen on port 80 and accept incoming connections from WWW browsers. Declare a socket-stream instance variable for w_main as well as a long variable.

7. Name the socketstream variable sockSocket, and name the long variable lAccesses (see Figure 15-3). The lAccesses variable will be used to track the number of accesses to this PowerBuilder WWW server.

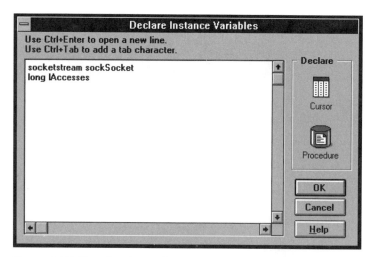

Figure 15-3: Creating the socketstream variable.

8. Open the application object again, and access the Open event script.

9. Add code that connects to the WWW database, followed by an open (w_main) to open the new window. If you're using the Watcom database, your new Open event script will look like Figure 15-4.

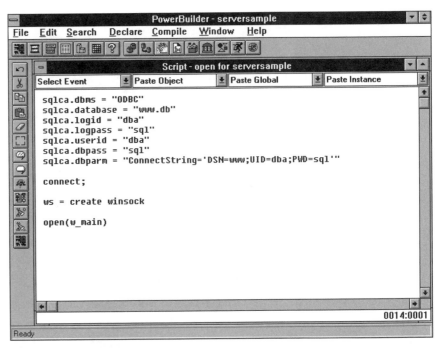

Figure 15-4: The Open event script.

10. Close the application object after saving this new Open event script.

Creating the Socket & Starting Socket Communications

The basic application shell is in place, and you can now add code to handle the socket communications. This section contains many steps and supporting information for establishing socket communications. Please follow it carefully.

1. Type the following in the Open event script for the window w_main, shown in Figure 15-5:

```
ulong ulAddr
integer a

sockSocket = create socketstream

a = ws.FD_ACCEPT
sockSocket.WSAAsyncSelect(handle(this),1024,a)

ulAddr = ws.inet_addr("204.94.74.210")

sockSocket.bind(ulAddr,80)
sockSocket.listen(5)
```

This script does the following:

❏ Creates a new stream socket user object (create socketstream).

❏ Turns on asynchronous event notification for the socket by calling WSAAsyncSelect().

❏ Binds the socket to port 80 of the local computer (bind(ulAddr,80)).

❏ Instructs the socket to listen for incoming connections (listen(5)).

Remember that sockSocket is an instance variable of w_main, so it will continue to exist after this script is executed.

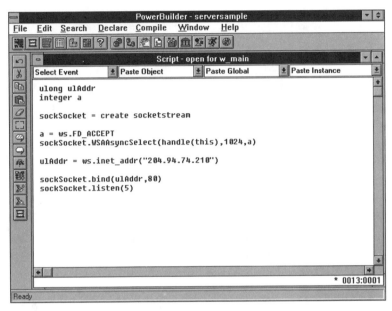

Figure 15-5: Handling the socket communications.

2. Add the following lines to the Close event script in w_main so that sockSocket is destroyed when the window closes:

```
sockSocket.closesocket( )
destroy sockSocket
```

Asynchronous event notification established for sockSocket in the Open event script triggers the specified event in the window w_main when network events occur on the socket. The next step is to create an event script in the specified event that responds appropriately to this network event notification. Event code 1024, the pbm_custom01 event, is used for receiving FD_ACCEPT messages by the call to WSAAsyncSelect().

3. Declare a user event for pbm_custom01 in w_main so an event script can be created for this event (see Figure 15-6).

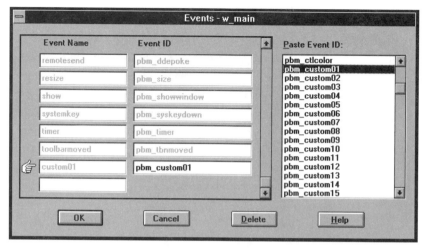

Figure 15-6: Declaring a user event for pbm_custom01.

At this point, the procedure gets a little tricky. The application needs the ability to accept multiple socket connections and to manage sending and receiving data with each one. You can approach this task in these ways:

❏ You could dynamically grow and shrink an array of socket user objects as new socket connections arrive and as existing socket connections are closed.

❏ You could declare a series of user events that contain scripts to manage data communications for a single socket user object.

With the second approach, each time an incoming connection is detected, a new socket user object is created, and asynchronous event messaging is used to trigger the next available user event. While better than loops and arrays, this approach is limiting and inflexible.

A better solution is to think of each socket connection as an object. When a new connection arrives, create an object. Let the object destroy itself when it's no longer needed. The object can encapsulate a socket user object and the processing code associated with it and, by doing so, can handle every aspect of data communications for the socket connection.

4. Create a new visual user object, and save it as a connected_socket.

5. Declare the following variables:

   ❐ A socket instance variable named sSocket.

   ❐ A string instance variable named html.

   ❐ A Boolean instance variable named bWrite.

6. Set bWrite equal to FALSE in the variable declaration window.

   sSocket is the socket user object that is initialized with the number of a new socket connection immediately following a call to accept() for the listening socket. Because sSocket is encapsulated within the visual user object connected_socket, it's better to let the visual user object call initsocket() for sSocket instead of calling initsocket() directly from a script outside of the connected_socket object. Think of it as though connected_socket has assumed all responsibility for sSocket and can only call sSocket's functions.

7. Declare a new user object function for connected_ socket, and name the function initsocket.

8. Define a single unsigned integer argument named uiTmp, and a return value of (None).

9. Type the following code in the Function painter:

```
integer a

a = ws.wsor(ws.FD_READ,ws.FD_WRITE)

sSocket.initsocket(uiTmp)
sSocket.WSAAsyncSelect(handle(this),1024,a)
```

Our function accepts an unsigned integer and passes the value onto the initsocket() function in the socket user object. Remember that the initsocket() function of a socket user object must be called after using accept() to accept an incoming socket connection. After calling initsocket(), the socket user object becomes a valid connected socket user object, and socket communications can begin.

This new socket begins with the same asynchronous message map as the listening socket that created it. This means that Winsock triggers the pbm_custom01 event in the window w_main whenever an incoming socket connection is detected on sSocket. Because sSocket isn't listening for incoming connections, this event notification is pointless.

The important events for this socket are FD_READ and FD_WRITE, so this function's code creates a new asynchronous event notification setting for sSocket. Instead of triggering pbm_custom01 in w_main, Winsock is told to trigger pbm_custom01 in this connected_socket visual user object whenever the FD_READ or FD_WRITE events occur on sSocket.

Now that instance variables are declared and the initsocket function is established for connected_socket, create constructor and destructor event scripts.

10. Type the following in the Constructor event script for connected_socket:

```
socket sSocket
sSocket = create socket
visible = FALSE
```

The first line in this event script is familiar by now. It creates a new socket user object and stores it in sSocket. The next line is new. By setting the visible attribute for this visual user object equal to FALSE, the connected_socket user object is hidden from view even though it's a visual object. Remember that in order to use asynchronous mode for sSocket, the connected_socket user object has to have a Windows handle. Since the connected_socket doesn't have to be displayed on the screen, making it invisible is a reasonable solution.

11. Type the following in the Destructor event script:

```
sSocket.closesocket()
destroy sSocket
```

Calling closesocket() when your program is finished with a particular socket is very important. So is destroying the socket user object that was created in the constructor event script. You're ready to complete the connected_socket user object.

12. Declare a pbm_custom01 user event, and type the following in the event script:

```
blob blobBuf, blobItem
int iLen, iPos, iEvent
string sTmp

iEvent=ws.WSAGetSelectEvent(message.longparm)

if iEvent = ws.FD_READ then
   blobBuf = blob(space(1024))
   iLen = sSocket.recv(blobBuf,len(blobBuf),0)
```

```
sTmp = string(blobmid(blobBuf,1,iLen))
iPos = pos(sTmp,"/")
if iPos > 0 then
    sTmp = mid(sTmp,iPos + 1)
end if
iPos = pos(sTmp," ")
if iPos > 0 then
    sTmp = left(sTmp,iPos - 1)
end if
if sTmp = "" then
    sTmp = "index.html"
end if
iPos = pos(sTmp,"~r~n")
if iPos > 0 then
    sTmp = left(sTmp,iPos - 1)
end if
select html into :html from documents where name = &
:sTmp;
if sqlca.sqlcode <> 0 then
    html = "<html><head><title>Error: Document " + &
    "not found</title>"
    html = html + "</head><body><h1>Error: " + &
    "Document not found</h1>"
    html = html + "Please try again.</body></html>"
end if
iEvent = ws.FD_WRITE
bWrite = TRUE
end if
if iEvent = ws.FD_WRITE and bWrite = TRUE then
    blobBuf = blob(left(html,512))
    do while sSocket.send(blobBuf,len(blobBuf),0) <> &
    ws.SOCKET_ERROR
        html = mid(html,513)
        if len(html) = 0 then
            window parentwindow
            parentwindow = parent
            parentwindow.closeuserobject(this)
            exit
```

```
            else
                blobBuf = blob(left(html,512))
            end if
        loop
    end if
```

This event script is the heart of the PowerBuilder WWW server. It does the two most important tasks in this application: reads the GET request from a WWW browser, and returns an error message or the requested HTML document.

To complete this application, do the following:

13. Close and save the connected_socket user object, and return to the window w_main.

    A user event was declared previously for pbm_custom01, and it needs an event script.

14. Access the pbm_custom01 event script for w_main, and type the following:

```
ulong ulAddr
int iPort
uint uiTmp
connected_socket csTmp

uiTmp = sockSocket.accept(ulAddr,iPort)

if uiTmp > 0 then
    lAccesses = lAccesses + 1
    st_2.text = string(lAccesses)
    openuserobject(csTmp,0,0)

    csTmp.initsocket(uiTmp)
end if
```

This script accepts an incoming socket connection, increments the access counter, creates a new connected_socket user object and calls the initsocket() function for the new connected_socket user object.

467

The last step before running this application is adding records to the documents table.

15. Use the Database painter to type in the HTML to create each document you want to serve through this application.

While this exercise for creating a sample WWW server is interesting, it is very limited. The server can store text documents only, and using a long varchar column type for the document limits the length of each document to the maximum size of a long varchar. However, by using the basic application structure established in this example, you can build a more complete WWW server that can do anything you want.

Getting Files From a WWW Server

Getting a file from a WWW server is easy. Just complete the following steps:

1. Create a new socket user object.
2. Connect to the WWW server on port 80.
3. Send a GET request.
4. Use asynchronous messaging to retrieve the file.

The following script sends the command GET/index.html to the WWW server at the IP address 204.94.74.209. It also establishes asynchronous messaging for the socket using the pbm_custom01 event 1024.

```
ulong ulAddr
string sSend, sFile
int a, b

sSocket = create socketstream

ulAddr = ws.inet_addr("204.94.74.209")
```

```
a = sSocket.wsconnect(ulAddr,80)
if a = ws.SOCKET_ERROR then
    messagebox("Error","No connect")
end if

b = ws.wsor(ws.FD_READ,ws.FD_CLOSE)
sSocket.wsaasyncselect(handle(parent),1024,b)

sSend = "GET /index.html~r~n~r~n"
sSocket.send(blob(sSend),len(sSend),0)

sFile = "c:\temp\file.htm"
iFile = fileopen(sFile,StreamMode!,write!)
```

The next script is placed in the pbm_custom01 event and receives and stores data for the INDEX.HTML file. The variables sSocket, bClosed and iFile are all instance variables of the window or object in which this script is placed.

```
int iLen, iEvent, iBufLen
blob blobtest
ulong ulTmp

iBufLen = 1024
blobtest = blob(space(iBufLen))

iEvent=ws.WSAGetSelectEvent(message.longparm)

if iEvent = ws.FD_READ then
    iLen = sSocket.recv(blobtest,iBufLen,0)
    if iLen > 0 then
        filewrite(ifile,blobmid(blobtest,1,iLen))
        if bClosed = TRUE then
        sSocket.ioctlsocket(ws.FIONREAD,ulTmp)
            if ulTmp = 0 then
                fileclose(iFile)
                sSocket.closesocket()
                destroy sSocket
            end if
        end if
    end if
```

```
            end if
        end if

        if iEvent = ws.FD_CLOSE then
            bClosed = TRUE
        end if
```

Several elements of this script are worth exploring in more detail. You must take extra care when receiving a file over a socket. Unlike sending a file, in which you know when the file transfer is complete, determining that an entire file has been received over a socket is somewhat difficult. You can make the job easier by establishing asynchronous messaging on sSocket for two network events: FD_READ and FD_CLOSE.

The FD_CLOSE event occurs when the socket connection is closed. In the previous example above, the socket connection is closed by the WWW server after the entire INDEX.HTML file is sent. The problem is that the FD_CLOSE event can, and does, occur before your program has received all of the data waiting on the socket. This means that the program must check first for the FD_CLOSE event and then verify that all of the data waiting to be read has been received before it can assume that the entire file has been received.

The bClosed Boolean variable is used to record the occurrence of the FD_CLOSE event. When bClosed is TRUE, the script assumes that the socket connection has closed and begins checking for remaining data after each call to recv(). The following line is used to check for additional data:

```
sSocket.ioctlsocket(ws.FIONREAD,ulTmp)
```

When ulTmp equals zero, all of the data has been read and the file can be closed. With nothing left to do, the socket is ready to be closed, and the socket user object can be destroyed.

Submitting Form Data to a WWW Server

One of the most exciting capabilities that you can get from PowerBuilder and the World Wide Web is writing a program that accepts input from an HTML form. Once it receives input from a Web browser, your application can perform database queries, calculations and even file transfers for constructing the dynamic HTML result. The code required to accomplish this is trivial, but the implications for your PowerBuilder programs are not.

A good first step is to create the HTML form and view it using a Web browser. The sample form used in this section and shown in Figure 15-7 is displayed within Netscape.

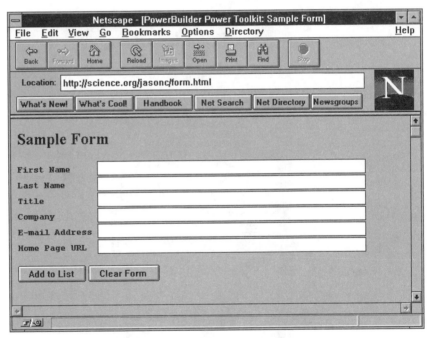

Figure 15-7: A sample HTML form displayed in Netscape.

The HTML source code for this form is shown in Figure 15-9. As you can see, creating an HTML form is very simple once you know the syntax. The important elements to notice in Figure 15-9 are the field names that follow the NAME labels and the ACTION defined for this form. The ACTION is a URL and may seem strange if you've never worked with forms. The ACTION tells the Web browser which URL to access when the form is submitted. In this case, the form is submitted when the user clicks on the Add to List button. This form's ACTION URL refers to port 8090 of the host *pk2.pk.com*. This is the port number that your PowerBuilder application must monitor in order to receive the data entered in the form.

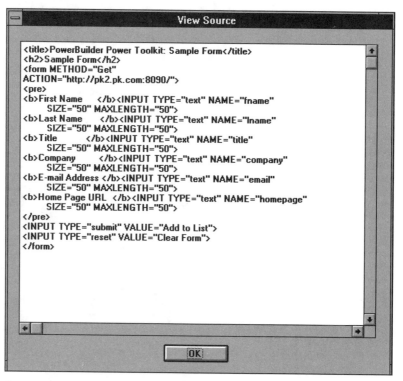

Figure 15-8: The HTML code for a form.

When a WWW user submits this form using a Web browser, the information entered in the form is sent via a GET request to port 8090 of the host pk2.pk.com. Figure 15-9 shows a portion of the GET request. Notice the question mark at the beginning of the data. It represents the beginning of the form data. Each field in the form contains a title followed by the equals sign followed by the data entered in the field. Fields are separated by an ampersand (&).

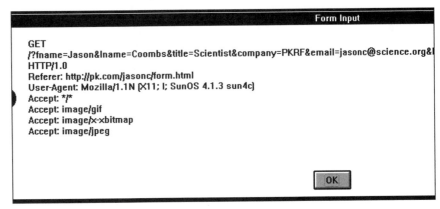

Figure 15-9: Part of a GET request.

Spaces entered in the fields of the form are converted to plus signs. Characters other than letters are converted to hex form and represented as a two-digit hex value following a percent sign. For example, the line *This is a test!* is converted to:

```
&examplefield=This+is+a+test%21&
```

Your PowerBuilder application must parse the fields and field values received from the Web browser. After parsing these fields, the values can be used for just about anything. Store them in a DataWindow, add them to a database table or use them for calculations. After submitting form data, the Web browser waits for a response. Be sure to send at least a confirmation message to the browser after receiving the form data.

PROGRAMMING WITH FTP

File Transfer Protocol, or FTP, is another commonly used method of transferring files across the Internet. FTP is a client-server program. FTP is responsible for file security and for accepting and sending files to and from the part of the file system managed by the FTP server.

FTP security is known more for its public access capability than it is for its security features. Known as an *anonymous FTP site*, a file system that allows the public to log in anonymously through FTP and transfer files has become one of the major sources of distributed files over the Internet. Databases and search utilities such as Archie were developed to provide worldwide locations for files stored in these sites. For this reason, FTP has become a very popular Internet tool.

FTP Commands

The FTP protocol as defined in the Internet RFC documentation is rarely implemented fully. In most cases, the server implements only those commands required for users to log in; add, change and delete files; navigate through the directories and retrieve or store files.

Table 15-2 lists some of the most commonly used FTP commands.

!	cr	macdef	proxy	send
$	delete	mdelete	sendport	status
account	debug	mdir	put	struct
append	dir	mget	pwd	sunique
ascii	disconnect	mkdir	quit	tenex
bell	form	mls	quote	trace
binary	get	mode	recv	type
bye	glob	mput	remotehelp	user
case	hash	nmap	rename	verbose
cd	help	ntrans	reset	?
cdup	lcd	open	rmdir	
close	ls	prompt	runique	

Table 15-2: Commonly used FTP protocol commands.

Using FTP

Chances are that you won't need to implement both client and server portions of the protocol in your PowerBuilder program. Even if you do, you won't need to implement the entire protocol in your server program. As with HTTP, you have to implement only those commands necessary for the task at hand. Besides, many excellent server programs are available for almost any platform. It's easier to install an FTP server and have your PowerBuilder program act as the client for logging in and transferring files.

Building an FTP Client

FTP is not an easy protocol to implement because it uses two communication channels to communicate. One channel is the command interpreter channel, which is the socket connection used to send and receive FTP commands and result codes to and from the server.

The other channel is strictly for file transfer. This channel can be open all the time or only during file transfer. The port number for the second channel is negotiated with the server.

The following steps are for communicating with the server:

1. Connect to the FTP server on port 21.
2. The server informs the client of the port that it has assigned the new connection. (Remember, port 21 is just a listening port.)
3. Log in to the FTP server as an anonymous user or as a user with a user ID.
4. Enter a password. For an anonymous user, it is customary to enter the user's e-mail address as the password.
5. Create a listening socket on the port the server assigned in step 2. This is the data communications socket.

Logging In to the FTP Server

The code in this section shows you how to log in to the FTP server. The first step is creating the sockets for sending and receiving data. In the following code, the socketstream object socks is the socket connection used for sending commands to the server and receiving replies. The other socketstream object created in this code is datasocket, which is used for file transfer.

```
ulong ulAddr, ulAddr2
integer iEvent,iError,iPort,result
socks = create socketstream
datasocket = create socketstream

//Set up the or condition
iEvent = ws.wsor(ws.FD_CONNECT,ws.FD_WRITE)
iEvent = ws.wsor(iEvent,ws.FD_READ)

pbhostent pbstruct
pbstruct = ws.GetHostByName(hostname)
if isnull(pbstruct) then
   ulAddr = ws.inet_addr(hostname)
   pbstruct = ws.GetHostByAddr(ulAddr)
   if isnull(pbstruct) then
      messagebox("Error","Either the host name is " + &
      "invalid or the name server is kaput.")
   end if
end if
ulAddr = pbstruct.h_addr_list[1]
```

The code checks first to see if hostname is a fully qualified domain name. If it is, GetHostByName()returns a pbhostent structure. If not, it tries again assuming that *hostname* is an IP address in dotted quad format (###.###.###.###).

The hostname variable comes from a user interface you create or from some value you have stored in PowerScript code or in a database. Ultimately, you want to have the ulAddr variable set to the host's address as an unsigned login network byte order.

Since the pbhostent structure is set up to handle multiple domains, the address must be extracted from the first element of the h_addr_list array within the pbhostent structure.

```
socks.WSAAsyncSelect(handle(this),1024,iEvent) //notify
whensocket is connected or ready to //read or ready to
write
```

Notice the comment at the beginning of the block of code about setting up the *or* condition. The WSAAsyncSelect() function returns a Windows event when any of the events selected within iEvent occurs. In this case, iEvent is set up to signal an event if a socket receives a connection, is ready to read or is ready to write. The event is sent to the window or visual user object denoted by handle(this).

For this to work, you must first create two custom events in your window or visual user object. You'll need a custom event for your communications socket and a custom event for the data socket.

```
if socks.wsconnect(ulAddr,FTPPORT) = ws.SOCKET_ERROR then
    iError = ws.WSAGetLastError()

    if iError = ws.WSAETIMEDOUT then
        messagebox("Error","Connection timed out.")
    elseif iError = ws.WSAEWOULDBLOCK then
        // just a warning. No error has occurred
    else
        FTPERROR(iError)
    end if

end if

// This creates a listening socket
ulAddr = ws.inet_Addr("204.94.74.211")
linger lingtmp
datasocket.setsockopt(ws.SOL_SOCKET,ws.SO_REUSEADDR,1,lingtmp)
datasocket.WSAAsyncSelect(handle(this),1025,ws.FD_ACCEPT)
socks.getsockname(ulAddr2,iPort)
result = datasocket.bind(ulAddr,iPort)
if result = ws.SOCKET_ERROR then
    messagebox("Error",string(ws.WSAGetLastError()))
else
    datasocket.listen(5)
end if
```

After the sockets are listening and you have contacted the host, you can log in. In this application, all of the FTP commands have been converted to functions. In the following code block, the USER() function sends the user ID to the host. The PASS() function then sends the password.

```
if anonymous then
    USER("anonymous")
    PASS(e-mail)
else
    USER(userid)
    PASS(password)
end if
```

Communicating With the Host

magicsend() is a simple function for communicating with the host that converts the data to blob type and sends it to the host using the FTP send() function.

```
integer result, outbloblen
blob outblob

outblob = blob(sendvalue+CRLF)
outbloblen = len(outblob)

result = socks.send(outblob, outbloblen, 0)
if result = ws.SOCKET_ERROR then
    ftperror(ws.WSAGetLastError())
end if

return result
```

Sending information with FTP is similar to sending information with HTTP in that you need to convert strings to blobs and add a carriage return and line feed. In the following example, the CRLF variable is equal to ~r~n.

The first custom event listening for activity on the communications socket can look like this:

```
blob inblob
integer brecvd
string textbuffer
boolean Failed
Failed = FALSE
// now I'm going to figure out which event has triggered
// this
integer iEvent
integer iError
iEvent = ws.WSAGetSelectEvent(message.LongParm)
iError = ws.WSAGetSelectError(message.LongParm)

if iError > 0 then
    ftperror( iError)
    FAILED = TRUE
else
    FAILED = FALSE
end if

if NOT FAILED then
    // connected
    choose case iEvent
        case ws.FD_CONNECT
    // ready to read
        case ws.FD_READ
    inblob= blob(space(RECVBUFF))
    brecvd = socks.recv(inblob,RECVBUFF,0)

        FTPMessage = left(string(inblob),brecvd)
        mle_1.text = FTPMessage
    // ready to write
        case ws.FD_WRITE
        // This is implemented for writing files to the
        // server and is not implemented in this example
    end choose
else
    FTPMessage = "Error occurred"
end if
```

You can see that the case statement responds depending on which event is received over the communications socket. The multiline edit (mle_1) is updated when data is received from the host.

The other custom event is set up specifically to handle ready to read and ready to write events over the data communications socket. For the example, this was implemented on custom event custom02, which is event number 1025.

Following is some example code for transferring files. You can modify it to suit your needs.

```
ulong ulAddr
int iPort
uint uiTmp
window momnpa

listboxreader lbreader
readtofile rtfreader

//writerobject wobj

uiTmp = DataSocket.Accept(ulAddr, iPort)

if uiTmp > 0 then
    if rwmode = "R" then
        momnpa = parent
        momnpa.openuserobject(rtfreader,0,0)
        rtfreader.initsocket(uiTmp)
        rtfreader.setfilename(getfilename)
    elseif rwmode = "W" then
        momnpa = parent
        // not implemented in this example
    else  //Query response mode
        momnpa = parent
        momnpa.openuserobject(lbreader,0,0)
        lbreader.initsocket(uiTmp)
        //not fully implemented in this example
    end if
end if
```

To simplify data communications, we created more user objects. The lbreader object handles requests for file lists. It sends output to a listbox so it can be displayed in a user interface or referred to from within PowerScript code. The rtfreader object reads to a file. The client then sets the rwmode variable depending on what type of response is expected.

The new user objects are very similar in structure. The custom event for the rtfreader object reads the data using the socket recv() function with a buffer size of 1024 bytes. The buffer size is variable. The PowerScript FileWrite() function is used to write the received data to a file.

```
window w_parent
int iLen, iwhichevent
blob readblob

iWhichEvent = ws.WSAGetSelectEvent(message.longparm)

if iWhichEvent = ws.FD_READ then
    readblob = blob(space(1024))
    iLen = sSocket.recv(readblob,1024,0)
    if iLen > 0 then
        filewrite(iFile,blobmid(readblob,1,iLen))
    elseif iLen = ws.SOCKET_ERROR then
    //oops, an error occurred.
        messagebox("Socket Error", &
        string(ws.wsagetlasterror()))
    end if
    if iLen < 1024 AND closeme then
        w_parent = parent
        w_parent.CloseUserObject(this)
    end if
elseif iWhichEvent = ws.FD_CLOSE then
    closeme = TRUE
end if
```

The example in this section doesn't show you how to create a full FTP client but gives you an idea of how to include FTP client capabilities within your PowerBuilder application.

PROGRAMMING OTHER INTERNET RESOURCES

Other Internet resources are just as easy to work with as FTP and the World Wide Web. For example, you can use Simple Mail Transfer Protocol, or SMTP, to send Internet e-mail, and the Gopher protocol to communicate with Gopher servers and Gopher clients. Better yet, you could invent your own information resources.

MOVING ON

In Chapter 16, we'll look at the sample application developed for this book, the Student Registration System (SRS), which is included on the Companion CD-ROM.

The Student Registration System

This chapter discusses the sample application developed for this book—the Student Registration System (SRS). We'll talk about the application requirements, the database design and the prototype, and we'll give a description of all objects with associated code explanations. The application can be found on the Companion CD-ROM.

This chapter's focus is more on the implementation of the design than on the design itself. We won't discuss the pros and cons of any particular development methodology. We strongly suggest selecting and using a methodology for the design process, however. There are many textbooks that can provide the reader with insight into these methods. Neither will we discuss development tools (CASE, ICASE). Some of these tools, such as S-Designor, ERwin and EasyCase are included as a demonstration version on the Companion CD-ROM. We recommend using these tools to support your chosen methodology, particularly for cross-departmental applications, where explicit, detailed communications are a requisite.

FUNCTIONAL DESCRIPTION

The SRS is a simplified registration application that addresses the primary functions relating to student enrollment that a school might require. These functions are as follows:

- ❏ Class maintenance
- ❏ Instructor maintenance
- ❏ Student maintenance
- ❏ Student/class maintenance
- ❏ Department maintenance
- ❏ Financial transaction maintenance
- ❏ Term maintenance
- ❏ Location maintenance
- ❏ Management overview of revenues

For each of these functions, the following sections provide a description, the associated business rules, and reporting requirements.

Class Maintenance

In most real-world situations, courses are divided into multiple offerings per term, often referred to as sections. We've simplified things by assuming that there will be only one offering of a class per term. Our Class object combines course, class and section attributes into a single object.

Business Rules:

- ❏ The class can be added and updated.
- ❏ The user cannot delete the class, but can change the status to inactive. This is done for audit purposes.

- ❏ A class with students currently enrolled cannot be deactivated.
- ❏ Classes are assigned to departments and can be moved between departments.
- ❏ The class is taught at one of a number of locations. If there is a lab component to a class, the location assigned must be a lab.

Reporting Requirements:

- ❏ Revenue by class.
- ❏ Class list (list of students registered in class).
- ❏ Class list, with grades included (see "Student/Class Object," later).

Instructor Maintenance

The instructor is defined as a person who is currently teaching or has previously taught any class.

Business Rules:

- ❏ The instructor must be approved prior to the first session of his or her initial class.
- ❏ The approval process (not dealt with in our application) involves reviewing credentials, examining letters of reference, reviewing the instructor's published documents, etc.
- ❏ Instructors can be added or updated.
- ❏ The instructor's status will remain active while he or she is teaching a class.
- ❏ An instructor cannot teach more than three classes in a given term.

Reporting Requirements:

- ❒ Class(es) by instructor.
- ❒ Instructor list.

Student Maintenance

The student is a person who has registered for a class. If a student drops the class without registering for an additional class, he or she will remain as a student record with a student identifier (the status will be changed).

Business Rules:

- ❒ The student becomes activated by initially enrolling in a class.
- ❒ The Social Security number is used as the primary key for the student.
- ❒ For those students without Social Security numbers, the system must assign a sequential identifier. The identifier is a nine-character column prefixed with an A and followed by eight numbers.
- ❒ A student can be added and updated.
- ❒ If a student has previously registered but is not registered for the current term, he or she is considered inactive.
- ❒ If a student drops all classes for a term without adding classes, he or she is inactive.
- ❒ The student can request a transcript at any time.

Reporting Requirements:

- ❒ Student transcript.
- ❒ Enrollment history.

Student/Class Maintenance

The key object in any student registration system is the student/class object. This object is the join between a student and the classes he or she has enrolled in or taken. It is initially created when the student enrolls in a class.

Business Rules:

❑ A student can enroll in class up to three weeks after the class has begun.

❑ The student can drop the class for a full refund until the second session.

❑ The refund is pro rata as follows: 75 percent prior to the third session, 50 percent prior to the fourth session, and no refund thereafter.

❑ Full payment is required of students as they enroll in a class.

❑ Payment methods include check, credit card, cash and grants.

❑ The instructor is the only entity that can update grades for a given class.

❑ The grade type (pass/no-pass versus grade lettering) is dependent upon the class type.

❑ Grades must be submitted no later than one week after completion of the class.

❑ The current class enrollment number must be incremented when adding a class for a student, and decrement when a student drops a class

Reporting Requirements:

❑ A class completion notification with the student's grade.

Department Maintenance

The department is an academic department, such as computer science, biology, nursing, general studies, etc.

Business Rules:

- ❏ Each department can have certificate programs for a specific focus.
- ❏ Departments can be renamed after the start of a term. When renamed, all classes assigned to the old department name are moved to the newly named department.

Reporting Requirements:

- ❏ Revenue by department.

Financial Transaction Maintenance

As part of the student enrollment process, a financial transaction is generated. This transaction will eventually update the general ledger. We'll assume that the ledger data is outside of our update authority and will be updated by a specific follow-on process. Our requirement is to create a generalized financial transaction capable of feeding the financial system.

Business Rules:

- ❏ A class add or drop event will trigger the creation of the financial transaction.
- ❏ The add transaction generates a credit transaction, the drop creates a debit.
- ❏ If the student has paid for the class via grant funds, and is dropping the class, and is receiving a refund, the grant amount is credited.
- ❏ The transaction must be generated in a standardized format for eventual financial system update.

❏ The transaction must be date-/time-stamped and carry the operator's ID for audit purposes.

❏ A total of revenues received is kept by class.

Reporting Requirements:

❏ An audit trail of financial transactions.

Term Maintenance

The term is defined as a time period in which classes are conducted. The term length is dependent upon the type of system the school employs—quarter or semester. Our example school uses a quarter-based system.

Business Rules:

❏ The term has a begin and end date that cannot overlap other assigned terms.

❏ It must be assigned a length between a range of minimum and maximum calendar weeks.

Reporting Requirements:

❏ Term calendar.

Location Maintenance

The location is the physical site for the class. It is typically a building of multiple classrooms. The location is uniquely identified by a 4-character code that denotes the general physical location of the classrooms. In our application, the locations are spread throughout the school's region.

Business Rules:

❏ The location must be uniquely identified by a location code.

❐ The location has an effective term range—the *start term* is the term and year classes were initially held at the location, and the *end term* is the term and year classes were last held at this location.

❐ A location is not deleted; instead, its status is marked as inactive and an end term is assigned.

Reporting Requirements:

❐ Location list.

Management Overview of Revenues

We are required to provide management reporting that gives a high-level perspective of revenues. This reporting requirement deals with two reports—the Revenue by Class report and the Revenue by Department report. These reports detail the gross revenues for a specified term, summarized by either class or department.

Business Rules:

❐ Revenues are considered to be gross revenues.

❐ Revenues are reported for a specific term and year.

❐ Revenues are reported at the class and department levels.

❐ These reports are accessible only to those with a management security level.

Reporting Requirements:

❐ Revenue by class.

❐ Revenue by department.

Other Objects

There are several other major objects in a typical registration system that we will not deal with in our sample, including the following:

- ❏ Class schedules.
- ❏ Course catalog.
- ❏ Student mailings.
- ❏ Certificate programs.

The class schedule is a schedule for a term based upon the class length, term calendar (with holiday schedule), special meeting requirements and location availability.

The course catalog is a listing of classes with their descriptions, meeting times, instructor information, locations, prerequisites, etc. The catalog typically contains information about certificate programs, special events, administration and additional marketing information. Our application provides a majority of the information to be able to generate the catalog.

Student mailings are mass mailings sent to current or former students. The mailings can include the course catalog, blanket marketing information and special event notification.

Certificate programs are a set of classes identified as meeting an accepted knowledge base about a particular subject area. They have a certain minimum number of credits associated with them. They typically have a set of required classes and a subset of optional classes to achieve the certification.

DATABASE DESIGN

As we listed the business rules above, we touched on some of the interaction between the data entities in the SRS application. Now let's turn our focus to the database design, where we'll take a closer look at these data entities, their relationships, and data attributes. The basic entities are reflected as individual tables within our application's database, and the attributes are reflected as table columns. These entities are listed below:

- Student
- Class
- Student/Class
- Instructor
- Department
- Location
- Transcript
- Financial Transaction
- Term

The student is uniquely identified by his or her Social Security number. For those without Social Security numbers, the system will generate an identifier. We'll collect basic student contact information, such as address, phone number and e-mail address. We'll also collect demographic data, such as gender and ethnicity.

As mentioned earlier, our Class entity is a combination of course, class and section. The Course entity has generic information such as course title, description, units, fee, and minimum and maximum class length. The Class entity has the specific occurrence of a course, with attributes such as term, year, location, instructor ID and enrollment number.

The Instructor entity contains basic identifying information, demographic information and degree information. The instructor status code denotes if the instructor has an active class assigned for the current term.

The Student/Class entity is a junction entity. It facilitates the many-to-many relationship between students and classes. The primary key is a concatenation of student ID, course ID and class ID.

The Location entity contains individual room locations. It is updated as rooms are added. The status code is changed if a location is no longer in use. The location is related to the class via a foreign key of location ID.

The Financial Transaction is created as part of the add/drop of the Student/Class entity. It carries the student ID, and course and class IDs to tie it to the Student/Class entity.

The Term entity is referenced in the Class and Student/Class entities. It refers to the academic term—such as fall, spring and winter, in a quarter-based system.

TECHNICAL REQUIREMENTS

The primary technical requirements for our SRS application center on the desire to show a business-oriented application incorporating a variety of PowerBuilder capabilities. We want to create an MDI application that demonstrates some common PowerBuilder functionality, including the following:

- ❏ Drag-and-drop functions.
- ❏ A tab user object.
- ❏ Drop-down DataWindows.
- ❏ Modify and Describe functions.
- ❏ Stored procedures.
- ❏ Advanced reporting features.

We'll make no assumptions regarding transaction levels, concurrent update concerns, network traffic issues, DBMS-specific requirements or operating system concerns. All of these issues must of course be considered when creating your "real-world" applications, but here we want to focus on PowerBuilder functionality. We'll assume that you have GUI standards in place or access to GUI design guidelines. Remember the primary goal of any GUI application design—don't place excess restrictions on the user. A good GUI design encourages users to take ownership of the application and utilize the options you've given them. It also assists in the enforcement of the business rules we've discussed.

We've decided to build our own "minimalist" base class. There are a number of excellent base classes on the market as we write this book. The number increases regularly. The decision to purchase a base class or build your own is one you may wrestle with as well. The decision to make or buy requires significant discussion regarding the pros and cons of each base class product. The base class we've developed is named edjebase.

APPLICATION DESCRIPTION

In the following sections we'll look at the objects of the SRS application that demonstrate the areas of PowerBuilder functionality listed above. Let's start by looking at the open script for our application. This will read the SRS.INI file, connect to the database, check for a good return code, open an instance of the login window, verify that the login was successful and open the main MDI frame and splash window.

```
SetPointer( HourGlass! )

//-- Read Application Initialization File

// Declare two local variables
string ini_file, ini_header

ini_file    =  "srs.ini"
ini_header =  "sqlca"

// call a function to read specific entries
// in the INI file.

sqlca.DBMS =  ProfileString( ini_file,&
ini_header, "dbms", "" )
sqlca.database=  ProfileString( ini_file,&
ini_header, "database", "" )
```

```
sqlca.userid  =  ProfileString( ini_file,&
ini_header, "userid", "" )
sqlca.dbpass  =  ProfileString( ini_file,&
ini_header, "databasepassword", "" )
sqlca.logid   =  ProfileString( ini_file,&
ini_header, "logid", "" )
sqlca.logpass =  ProfileString( ini_file,&
ini_header, "logpass", "" )
sqlca.servername =  ProfileString( ini_file,&
ini_header, "servername", "" )
sqlca.dbparm  =  ProfileString( ini_file,&
ini_header, "dbparm", "" )

/* DB connection */
connect;

if sqlca.sqlcode <> 0 then
    MessageBox ("Cannot Connect to Database",&
sqlca.sqlerrtext)
    return
end if

w_login w_login_instance
open( w_login_instance )

//-------- Open Main Window Section

string response
response = message.stringparm

/* Open MDI frame and splash windows*/
if response = "YES" then
    Open (w_main_frame)
    Open (w_srs_splash)
else
    MessageBox( "Login", "Login was cancelled!" )
end if
```

The Splash Window

The splash window (w_srs_splash) is inherited from the base class bw_splash. It will be opened after the main MDI frame opens. It is a generic splash window that has the application name, release number and customer name. It will appear for several seconds while the user initiates the application.

Figure 16-1: The splash window.

The Main Frame

As mentioned earlier, SRS is an MDI application. The main frame used for the application is very simplified. It is named w_main_frame and is inherited from the bw_mdiframe in the base PBL. The window type is an MDI frame with Microhelp. It uses the m_main_frame menu, discussed below.

The Main Menu

The primary menu for SRS is named m_main_frame. As you look at the menu, shown in Figure 16-2, you'll get a better sense of the implemented functionality of the application. The items that are specific to the sample application are Maintenance, Reports and Utilities.

Figure 16-2: The SRS main menu.

The Maintenance menu item allows for adding and updating of the application objects. The selection of any of the application objects will open a search window that prompts the user for search criteria to identify a specific entity. Each of the search windows has a New CommandButton to allow for addition of a new entity.

The Report item offers a list of reports. There's an additional report selection dialog box for some of the reports.

The Utilities menu item allows selection of miscellaneous capabilities with a display of the current key settings (e.g., student ID last selected, instructor ID last selected), as well as user preferences for configuration settings and the ability to export selected data from the database.

The About Window

The About window (w_srs_about) is inherited from the bw_about window. It contains environmental data such as user name, DBMS and software serial number.

Figure 16-3: The About window.

The Search Window

Each Search window is a response window opened by the associated menu item selection from the m_main_frame Maintenance menu. The Search window shown in Figure 16-4 is the student version. All Search windows are inherited from bw_search. The primary function of the Search window is to prompt the user for selection criteria. The user can also select a New CommandButton to go to a data entry window for the object being maintained.

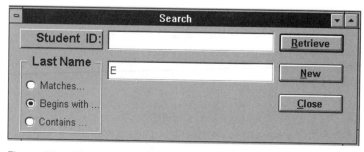

Figure 16-4: The student version of the Search window.

For existing entities (e.g., student, class, faculty, location), the user enters the full selection string, a string to begin the search, or a string contained within the column being searched. The script for the Clicked event of the Retrieve CommandButton follows:

```
// retrieve student data by building
// a search argument that is used as
// a parm in OpenWithParm, used subsequently
// in the match window

SetPointer( HourGlass! )
w_match w_match_instance
string ls_default_sql, ls_mod_rtn
long ll_row

IF sle_student_id.Text = "" and &
    sle_last_name.Text = "" then
```

```
            MessageBox("Entry Error", &
               "Enter either Student ID or Last Name")
        Return
    ELSEIF ib_last_name_changed = TRUE and &
        ib_id_changed = TRUE then
            MessageBox("Retrieval Error", &
               "Choose either retrieve by Student ID or Last Name")
        Return
    END IF


    IF ib_id_changed THEN
        dw_select_list_id.SetTransObject(SQLCA)
        ll_row = dw_select_list_id.Retrieve(sle_student_id.Text)
        if ll_row < 1 THEN
            is_student_arg = sle_student_id.Text
            w_search.TriggerEvent("ue_not_found")
            Return
        ELSE
            MessageBox("ID found", string(ll_row))
            Return
        END IF
    END IF
    //
    IF rb_matches.checked = TRUE THEN
        OpenSheetWithParm( w_match_instance, sle_last_name.text, &
                           w_main_frame, 5 )
    ELSE
        OpenSheetWithParm( w_match_instance, begin_char + &
                           sle_last_name.text + "%", &
                           w_main_frame, 5)

    END IF
```

The Matches Window

The Matches window (see Figure 16-5) displays a selection
list of rows that match the search criteria the user entered in
the Search window. All Matches windows are inherited from
bw_match.

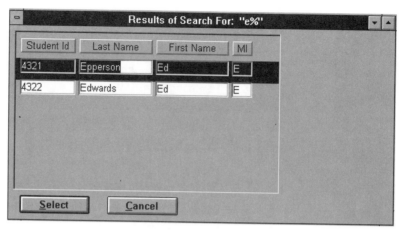

Figure 16-5: The Matches window.

The primary function of this window is to enable the selection of a row and open the maintenance window with the key value as a parm. An instance string variable named is_key_value is used as the parm. It is set in the following Clicked event script for the DataWindow:

```
// this will set the key value
// to the selected student id value
// and trigger the enable or disable
// events
SetPointer( HourGlass! )
long row_number

row_number = this.GetClickedRow()

if row_number > 0 then
    this.SelectRow( 0, FALSE )
    this.SelectRow( row_number, TRUE )
    is_keyvalue = this.getitemstring( row_number,&
"student_id" )
    cb_select.TriggerEvent( "ue_enable" )
else
    cb_select.TriggerEvent( "ue_disable" )
    is_keyvalue = ""
end if
```

The ue_enable and ue_disable events are user-defined events that set the Enabled attribute for the Select CommandButton.

The Student Maintenance Window

The Student Maintenance window (see Figure 16-6) is typical of the data entry windows used throughout the application. It's divided into a series of logical data components exemplified by the tabbed DataWindows. The basic student identification data is contained in the primary DataWindow: dw_student_maint_basic. Data validation is done at the column level.

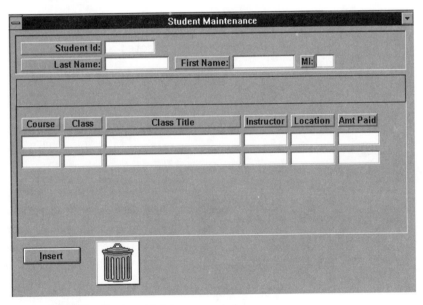

Figure 16-6: The Student Maintenance window.

The window allows the addition and deletion of classes for the student (add/drop). A class is added using the Insert CommandButton. An existing class is selected from a DropDownDataWindow. A class is dropped by dragging and dropping it to a trash can object on the bottom of the window. The first event invoked in the drag process is the Clicked event of the class DataWindow control. The code follows:

```
long ll_row

ll_row = GetClickedRow(This)

If ll_row < 1 then Return // Invalid row clicked.

// Here if ok...
// Toggle the selected status of this row

This.SelectRow(0, FALSE)
This.SelectRow(This.GetClickedRow(), TRUE)
```

The drag is a manual drag and is initiated by invoking a user-defined event named ue_drag. This event is set to the pbm_mousemove Windows event ID.

```
// Script for user-defined event "ue_drag"
// - equated to windows event PBM_MOUSEMOVE
// Determine if the mouse button is depressed from
// the wordparm attribute of the message system object
If Message.WordParm = 1 Then  // Mouse button is down
    If GetSelectedRow(this,0) > 0 Then  // Put this DW into
drag mode
        Drag (This, Begin!)
    End If
End If
```

The DragDrop event of the trash can object invokes a class drop verification message box. If the user responds positively, the class is dropped (the current student_class row status is updated to "d," and a drop class financial transaction is generated.

The financial transaction created as a part of the add or drop class is generated via stored procedures named sp_add_class and sp_drop_class. The stored procedures are passed the current date and time, the student ID, the transaction type, the class fee (transaction amount), the course and class ID, a generated transaction ID and an operator ID.

The Student Transcript Window

The Student Transcript Window allows the printing of a preformatted form that lists the student's classes taken, associated grades, credits, a total of credits received and GPA. The window is inherited from a window in edjebase named bw_report. This base window is a very simple object that contains a DataWindow control and a user-defined event named ue_print.

The DataWindow used is built from the Student, Course, Class, Student/Class and Location tables. The retrieval of the transcript data is done in the Constructor event of the DataWindow control. The transcript must be printed in landscape mode for readability. The printing of the transcript is done by selecting the Print menu item from the File pull-down item on the menu bar, or by selecting the print toolbar item. The Print menu item triggers the user-defined event ue_print. Here is the code for ue_print:

```
// Print the transcript in Landscape mode
dw_transcript.Modify &
("DataWindow.Print.Orientation=1")
dw_transcript.Print()
```

The Tab User Object

The Student Maintenance window (w_student_maint) uses tab files for segregating data components. This widely used metaphor is easily understood and eases the burden of navigating a window with a large amount of data. A number of vendors provide tab user objects, but in the interest of detailing the components of tab objects, we've built our own.

There are two user objects involved in our tab object: uo_top_tab (the tab itself, shown in Figure 16-7) and uo_top_tab_bar (the tab bar, shown in Figure 16-8). The tab is the base object and is inherited into the tab bar. The tab is built as a custom user object. The user object contains two controls: one for static text that will carry the tab name, and the other a picture control that will be used for showing the outline of the tab. The bitmap used for the tab is named TOPTAB.BMP and was created in Paintbrush.

Figure 16-7: Tab user object.

The Clicked event for the tab is sensed in either the static text or the picture control. The Clicked event in the static text triggers the Clicked event in the picture control. This, in turn, triggers a user event named ue_clicked in the parent object (in our case, the tab—uo_top_tab). (The code for this event is shown later in this section.) We also set up an instance variable named ii_tab_idx, which allows us to determine the tab selected.

Figure 16-8: Tab bar user object.

The tab bar is a custom user object that has five (the number is arbitrary) inherited objects of the uo_top_tab. We declare two instance variables to keep track of the tab's getting and losing focus: ii_tab_with_focus and ii_tab_losing_focus. There are two user object functions. The first, uof_get_clicked_tab, obtains a reference to the tab object that has been clicked. The function is passed an integer for the index number of the tab being clicked. It returns a userobject datatype. The code follows:

```
// this function returns
// the user object being
// clicked
uo_top_tab uo_ret_val
CHOOSE case a_tab_bar_idx
CASE 1
    uo_ret_val = uo_1
CASE 2
    uo_ret_val = uo_2
CASE 3
    uo_ret_val = uo_3
CASE 4
    uo_ret_val = uo_4
CASE 5
    uo_ret_val = uo_5
END CHOOSE

RETURN uo_ret_val
```

The second function, uof_set_tabs, sets the number of tabs and their text strings based on a string array argument. This argument is passed from the window inheriting the tab bar. We have an example of the Student Maintenance window passing an array of five tab names. The code for uof_set_tabs follows:

```
// This function sets the text in
// the tabs dependent on values passed
// in the string array argument. It also
// assigns the number of tabs.
//
integer li_idx = 1, li_nbr_of_tabs
uo_top_tab luo_tab
li_nbr_of_tabs = UpperBound( asa_tab_names )
FOR li_idx = 1 TO li_nbr_of_tabs
    luo_tab = uof_get_clicked_tab( li_idx )
    luo_tab.st_1.text = asa_tab_names[li_idx]
NEXT
```

The Constructor event of the uo_top_tab sets the instance variable ii_tab_idx to the appropriate value based on the tab object's number within the bar. It also selects the first tab. The SELTAB.BMP bitmap is a boldface tab outline. Here's the Constructor event script:

```
// this will set the tab index
// values according to the user object
// number and it will highlight
// the first tab
ii_idx = 1
uo_1.ii_tab_idx = 1
uo_2.ii_tab_idx = 2
uo_3.ii_tab_idx = 3
uo_4.ii_tab_idx = 4
uo_5.ii_tab_idx = 5
uo_1.st_1.weight = 700
uo_1.p_1.picturename = "seltab.bmp"
```

Let's look at the code necessary to allow the user to click between tabs. The base uo_top_tab object has a user event named ue_clicked, which is triggered when the user clicks on a top tab object.

```
// instantiate the uo_top_bar,
// set the instance variables and
// trigger the clicked event of the parent
uo_top_tab_bar luo_top_bar
luo_top_bar = parent
luo_top_bar.ii_last_idx = luo_top_bar.ii_idx
luo_top_bar.ii_idx = ii_tab_idx
luo_top_bar.TriggerEvent("ue_bar_clicked")
```

The following code is from a user event named ue_bar_clicked for the tab bar. It is triggered by a Clicked event in the uo_top_tab object. This highlights the current tab chosen and resets the previously used tab.

```
// this will instantiate the top tab
// for the current tab and the previous tab.
// the current tab will be bolded and
// the previous tab will be reset to
// standard weight
uo_top_tab luo_current_tab, luo_last_tab
luo_current_tab = uof_get_clicked_tab( ii_idx )
luo_last_tab = uof_get_clicked_tab( ii_last_idx )

luo_current_tab.p_1.picturename = "seltab.bmp"
luo_current_tab.st_1.weight = 700

luo_last_tab.p_1.picturename = "toptab.bmp"
luo_last_tab.st_1.weight = 400
```

The following is an example of an extension of the ue_bar_clicked event in the user object uo_tab_files for the window w_student_maint. This script will make the appropriate DataWindow visible, based on the user's tab selection.

```
// this sets the datawindow to visible
// dependent on the number of the tab
// selected
parent.setredraw( false )
dw_student_class_list.visible = ( this.ii_idx = 1)
dw_student_maint_addresses.visible = &
```

```
( this.ii_idx = 2)
dw_student_maint_demographics.visible = &
( this.ii_idx = 3)
dw_student_statistics.visible = ( this.ii_idx = 4)
dw_student_maint_misc.visible = ( this.ii_idx = 5)
parent.setredraw( true )
```

The following script is placed in the Open event of the w_student_maint window. It establishes a string array, populates the array with tab names, and calls the user object function to use the tab names in the associated tab objects.

```
string lsa_tab_names[5]

lsa_tab_names[1] = "Class List"
lsa_tab_names[2] = "Contact"
lsa_tab_names[3] = "Demographics"
lsa_tab_names[4] = "Statistics"
lsa_tab_names[5] = "Misc."

uo_tab_files.uof_set_tabs( lsa_tab_names[] )
```

MOVING ON

In this chapter, we described the functional requirements, database design, technical requirements, and highlights of the objects and associated code for a sample Student Registration System application. This application is really a device to assist in the understanding of PowerBuilder capabilities. Additional issues you'll need to consider when designing your own applications include design and development methodologies, use of CASE and ICASE tools, purchase of a third-party base class library, GUI standards, naming standards, and help support software.

In the next chapter, we'll discuss performance issues and offer some tips for improving application performance. We'll also discuss some performance traps to avoid.

A Discussion on Performance

Performance is a primary goal of all developers. The faster an application performs, the happier users will be. The irony of the situation is that we, as developers, tend to have faster, more powerful machines than users have, with more than enough memory to accomplish the job at hand. As a result, if all else fails, we recommend to our users that they throw more hardware at the performance problem so it will go away. Unfortunately, it won't go away. More hardware only disguises the problem until it can resurface later as a larger issue. The solution then, is to understand both our environment and our users' environment, and to remove the problem before it becomes a larger one.

Application performance and user productivity are tied together. The better an application performs, the more productive the user becomes. The converse is also true; if you can make a user more productive, the user perceives that the application performs better. Therefore some of the effort we place on performance revolves around user perception.

DEVELOPMENT STANDARDS

Before you even begin developing an application, take a hard look at your environment for clues about existing development standards. Look at the developers around you. If you've ever worked with other developers, you know each has his or her own style. We each believe our way is the best. In order to work together, however, we must find some common ground.

Imagine for a moment that each person you work with speaks a different language. Imagine how difficult it would be to communicate with one another, let alone work together! There might be one or two people with the same or similar language, but overall, life would be frustrating. The same is true when it comes to working with different developers' styles.

Development standards resolve this communication issue. They put all developers on the same footing. Development standards include more than just naming conventions. They are a set of guidelines that provide direction in application development. The issues that a good set of standards address include the following:

Development standards are guidelines that provide direction in application development.

- ❑ Programming standards
- ❑ Development environment
- ❑ Multideveloper guidelines
- ❑ Database standards
- ❑ Prototyping guidelines
- ❑ GUI standards
- ❑ Extended attributes
- ❑ Application frameworks

Programming Standards

Programming standards do more than define a standard look for the code you write. They also make you more productive. Using well-defined programming standards, you can tell at a glance the scope and datatype of any variable. Control structures, such as FOR...NEXT, CHOOSE CASE...END CHOOSE and IF THEN...END IF can easily be checked for correctness. The intention of your code is easy to determine. You know where to find comments and you know what is and is not acceptable code. Consider, for example, the following code snippet:

```
ll_Row = this.GetRow()
IF ll_Row > 0 THEN
    this.SelectRow(0, FALSE)
    this.SelectRow(ll_Row, TRUE)
END IF
```

You can tell, just by looking, that ll_Row is a local variable of datatype Long. You can tell the IF...END IF is perfectly matched. Because of the indentation, the code is very easy to read. It almost comments itself. If code is well-written, if variables are well named and conventions are followed, you have less work to do as a developer and you are more productive overall.

Are there already programming standards in place? If so, use them as the basis for your development. Otherwise, can you adapt the PowerBuilder development standards to your organization? If not, create your own and stick to them. Regardless, make sure everyone in your organization follows the standards.

One programming standard you might want to adopt is to use CHOOSE CASE instead of the equivalent IF...THEN... END IF. Although the CHOOSE CASE is only milliseconds faster, it's much easier to read and maintain. Once again, ease of use translates into developer productivity.

Programming standards make you more productive.

Development Environment

It doesn't really matter how your development environment is laid out. What matters is that every developer's environment is the same, from directory structure to developer tools. Yes, even the tools you use can affect your performance and the performance of those around you.

Consider all of the documentation, ideas, how-to's, etc., generated within your organization. For each you must take the time to ascertain how this new tidbit of information can be adapted to fit into your environment. If every developer's environment were the same, however, the author can make many assumptions and can be very detailed in his or her description of how to implement a concept in your environment.

What about code you share, tools you pass around and help that is exchanged between developers? Isn't it nice when you can sit down at someone else's computer and "know" where everything is? Doesn't it make you more productive?

When creating objects for an application, where do you store them? Development guidelines should include a definitive way of organizing your PowerBuilder libraries (PBLs). One school of thought is to organize libraries by object type, while another claims organization by function is best. Once again, the choice doesn't matter as long as everyone follows the same guideline.

When organizing your PBLs, never let them contain more than about 60 objects or grow to more than 800k in size. Since PBLs are DOS files, they're subject to the limitations of DOS. One of the most significant limitations is that DOS files become fragmented. The more fragmented a PBL, the longer it takes to access the objects it contains. Keeping your PBLs small and optimized makes them more efficient. Use the Library painter to optimize and organize your libraries. You can move objects from one library to another using the Move item on the Entry menu, and you can optimize a library using the Optimize item on the Library menu.

Never overcompensate for PBL size or content by creating too many PBLs, however—there's more to life than PBLs. For example, examine your environment. Are you using all available extended memory? (Remember, Windows doesn't use expanded memory.) Are you loading as many drivers as possible into high memory? Are you using disk caching? (Disk caching helps improve performance by caching the least used information to your local hard drive.) What about wallpapers? Did you know that wallpaper as a background consumes a lot of memory? Are you using a permanent swap file? If not, examine the reasons why. Permanent swap files help Windows perform faster and more efficiently.

Do you know your configuration? Your CONFIG.SYS file, WIN.INI file and SYSTEM.INI file contain a lot of information that can ultimately affect your machine's performance, and thus your productivity. CONFIG.SYS documentation is provided with your version of DOS. And in your Windows directory there are Write files documenting the WIN.INI and SYSTEM.INI files. Become familiar with these files, especially the 386 enhanced sections. Are you using the appropriate resolution on your monitor? (The higher the resolution, the longer it takes for Windows to paint your screen.)

Take a close look at your hardware. Are you using the fastest possible machine, considering the budget you have to work with? Would a memory upgrade help you? Have you defragmented your hard drive lately? What about using SCANDISK or CHKDSK to look for lost clusters or disk problems? Could you use a newer, faster hard drive? Performance is affected by both hard drive speed and interleaf settings.

Keep PBLs to under 800k in size and containing fewer than 60 objects.

The bottom line is to create a set of standards governing the way your development environment looks and feels. Choose tools that will empower you and last a long time. Create a development directory structure everyone can live with. As a guideline, a typical PowerBuilder directory structure might look like the structure shown in Table 17-1.

Directory	Description
C:\PB4	PowerBuilder development environment (INI, EXE, DLLs, HLP, etc.)
C:\PB4\PROJECTS	Starting directory for projects
C:\PB4\PROJECTS\COMMON	PBLs common to all projects
C:\PB4\PROJECTS\project1	PBLs specific to Project 1

Table 17-1: Sample PowerBuilder development directory structure.

Start with this example directory structure, and then modify it to meet your needs.

Multideveloper Guidelines

Often in client/server application development, there's a need for multiple developers to become involved. Sometimes, each developer has a specific task or subsystem to work on and, thus, can be shielded from the core of the development effort. Other times, developers must jump into the project with both feet and pray they don't land on someone else. In these cases, a clear set of multideveloper guidelines is beneficial. Multideveloper guidelines cover important issues like distribution of code, configuration management and version control. For each of these issues, guidelines need to define who, how, where and what. Who will distribute the code? How is version control handled? Where do libraries reside?

When multiple developers are working on the same project, it's especially imperative that everyone's development directory structure be standardized (see the sample directory structure shown in Table 17-1). Typically, when working in PowerBuilder, you'll want to keep the PBLs you're working with on your local machine. In a multideveloper environment, however, you'll want to keep all of the PBLs on a network where everyone involved in the project can access them. As a guideline, the directory structure layout shown in Table 17-2 might be used on a network.

Directory	Description
N:\PB4	PowerBuilder development environment (INI, EXE, DLLs, HLP, etc.)
N:\PB4\SHARED	Shared resources (ICOs, PBLs, etc.)
N:\PB4\PROJECTS	Starting directory for projects
N:\PB4\PROJECTS\COMMON	PBLs common to all projects
N:\PB4\PROJECTS\project1	Starting point for project
N:\PB4\PROJECTS\project1\VERn	Version of project
N:\PB4\PROJECTS\project1\VERn\DEV	PBLs under development (to be checked in and out)
N:\PB4\PROJECTS\project1\VERn\TEST	Test version of the project application (PBL, PBD, PBR, EXE, ICO, BMP)
N:\PB4\PROJECTS\project1\VERn\PROD	Production version of the application (PBL, PBD, PBR, EXE, ICO, BMP)

Table 17-2: Sample network directory structure.

Unfortunately, network traffic and PBL contention can bog you down at development time. PowerBuilder provides the check-in/check-out features to help with this problem. With a check-in/check-out system, you keep all the PBLs associated with the application on your local machine, along with an empty PBL called a work PBL. When you want to work on an object, you check it out from its home PBL and into your work PBL using the Library painter. PowerBuilder marks the object as being checked out and will not let anyone else check it out until you've checked it back in. Furthermore, when you check an object back in, PowerBuilder alerts your version control package so that each version of the modified object can be saved.

Part of your multideveloper guidelines must describe when objects are to be checked in, where they are to reside when they are checked out and what the steps are to update the developers' local libraries, as well as how to build a test or production version of the application. In addition, your guidelines will also define developer roles and responsibilities.

The first key role you might want to define is that of the version manager, who is responsible for maintaining the various versions of each object and, ultimately, for creating the executable versions. The version manager might use a product like PVCS, ENDEAVOR or LBMS to assist in version control.

The version manager works under the project leader, who is responsible for delegating the work to each developer and overseeing the entire project. As time-consuming as it is, the project leader will want to bring all of the developers together on a weekly basis to share ideas. The primary purpose of this interaction is to determine if there are any common objects that can be shared. The project leader will use a predefined set of standards to distribute code among the developers on the team. Usually, these standards follow very closely the PBL layout, assigning the development of objects by function or type.

If the project is very large or involves a large number of developers, the project leader might want to break the project up into subsystems and assign a lead to each subsystem. Each subsystem lead has basically the same responsibilities as the project lead, but on a much smaller scale.

A project team should also include others who will never write a line of PowerScript. These individuals are responsible for developing the documentation and help files as well as creating and implementing a test plan.

Database Standards

In any development effort, a solid understanding of the database is essential, primarily because of the effect the database has on the performance of the application. Stored procedures, triggers and referential integrity, when properly defined, can have a positive influence on your application.

A stored procedure is compiled, optimized SQL code stored on the database. The primary benefit of stored procedures is twofold. First, the code for the stored procedure does not need to traverse the network, making the calling process quick and efficient. Second, stored procedures are executed independently of your application, making them fast.

Triggers are also compiled, optimized SQL code stored on the database. Triggers, however, are tied to a table. The code is executed when an insert, delete or update to a row occurs or is triggered. The primary benefit of triggers is they can be very complex, containing a great deal of business logic that is not application-specific.

Referential integrity is the relationship between two tables. It defines what activities can take place when the parent or child table is updated. Referential integrity is usually implemented through stored procedures and triggers.

Both stored procedures and triggers can execute without interacting with your application. The stored procedures and triggers can be fired in your database and then your application can continue processing. This being the case, you don't have to write PowerScript to accomplish these tasks.

Consider a parent-child relationship between an Order Header table and an Order Item table. When a parent (Order Header) row is deleted, *all* the associated child (Order Item) rows must also be deleted. In order to make this happen in PowerBuilder, you might load the header and child information into separate DataWindows, delete the parent row, delete all the child DataWindow rows and update. On the other hand, using CASCADE DELETE stored procedures and/or triggers, you need only delete the parent row and reset the child DataWindow. The database does the rest.

If you weren't aware that a DELETE CASCADE trigger or stored procedure existed, however, you might write code to delete the child rows. If your code attempts to delete child rows after the parent, errors will be generated by the database, because the trigger will have deleted the child rows automatically when the parent row was deleted. Or if your code causes the child rows to be deleted first, followed by the parent row, you'd be duplicating the functionality of the database trigger without getting any additional benefit.

Consider using a data-modeling tool.

Since a strong knowledge of the database is required, it's a good idea to have a data model on hand. If you have the time, you might consider purchasing and learning a data-modeling tool such as ERwin, S-Designor or System Architect. Determine how tables will be named and how to name columns. Include in your standards when you will define DELETE CASCADE referential integrity and what additions you'll make to any triggers you use. Make sure your standards include what your data models will look like and what they must include. Once again, a good set of standards and a clear understanding of them will lead to increased performance on the development side as well as the end user side.

Prototyping Guidelines

In developing applications, we tend to interface with the end users as little as possible, probably because we find it difficult to interact with users. This is especially true during the prototyping phase of application development. For this reason, the prototyping phase is often avoided, much to our detriment. Prototyping is one of the most, if not the most, important phase of development.

Prototyping helps us to find the weak spots in our design and gauge the users' needs and desires. It helps us understand the way the users work and how we can write an application that works with them. It demonstrates to the users the way the application will eventually look and shows them that it will work. Pay particular attention to the way users interact with your prototype. This interaction will help you determine if users will be productive on the interface you've designed.

Remember that you're building a *prototype*. Don't write code except to connect the components together. Developers have a tendency to write all the code for each of the components so that when the prototype is finished, so is the application. The problem is that if a change needs to be made, we're hesitant to make it for fear of destroying the code we've spent so much time writing. Changes *will* need to be made, and prototypes *will* need to be trashed.

Before beginning to prototype, you need to make some decisions. First, determine how many iterations you'll allow.

Next, determine how long each iteration will be and how long you'll allow between each iteration. Remember, each iteration builds upon the last one and includes the fixes the users requested in the previous prototyping session. Probably the most important point in prototyping is to save each iteration after showing it to the user. Undoubtedly, they'll want to see a previous version.

Keep Users Involved

When you develop an application, you usually start by interviewing your users. Sometimes this interview is done for you by management or other staff. Unfortunately, user involvement usually stops there, and that's where the problems start. Involving the users from the beginning, and keeping them involved, can help you develop well-thought-out, efficient applications. Users can tell you where you've gone astray and where you've done well. Your users know what they want—they just might not be able to express their needs well.

GUI Standards

When developing an application, the area where we spend the least amount of time yet which yields the greatest user productivity gain is the interface. A good graphical user interface (GUI) can mean the difference between an understandable, productive application and an ineffective, unused application. As you might have guessed, the key to good interface design is standards.

GUI design guidelines are available from a variety of sources. To begin with, they can be found on the Windows SDK CD-ROM. In addition, the *Application Design Guide* from Microsoft Press is available at most bookstores. Christine Comaford's company, Corporate Computing, has a great deal of information and software on GUI design guidelines.

Powersoft also offers a course in GUI design. Most importantly, GUI design guidelines can be found just by looking around your own environment.

Is there a framework in place, or are there de facto GUI design standards? If your end users are used to working with Microsoft applications and your standards are already in place, they merely need to be documented. The same is true if your company has standardized on WordPerfect or Lotus products. If standards do not exist, now is your opportunity to read the user interface design guides and create your own set of standards.

Familiarize yourself with the available GUI guidelines, both internal and external. Although GUI guidelines can be quite extensive, there are some general rules of thumb you can follow:

- A user interface should be intuitively obvious to the most casual of observers.
- Always leave 25 percent blank area on every window.
- Use window controls as designed.
- Place command buttons either horizontally along the bottom right or vertically along the top right of a window.
- Learn and use the Common User Access (CUA) guidelines.
- Light backgrounds indicate an editable field, dark backgrounds the opposite.
- Command buttons on a window indicate a response window to users.
- Consider using drag and drop, but remember that this functionality isn't obvious to your users.

Take the time to set and use GUI standards. For the most part, examine your *current* environment. The applications currently in use, especially the ones your users interact with most often, are your guides. If your development environment is new, you can design your own guidelines, or, more correctly, implement the proper guidelines. Remember, your standards can be different than everyone else's as long as yours make sense.

APPLICATION PERFORMANCE

Rarely when building an application do we focus on performance. Usually performance is a secondary consideration, after getting the application to actually work. There are, however, certain actions you can take right from the beginning that will have a tremendous impact on performance. In PowerBuilder application development, there are three major factors that can affect an application's performance:

- ❐ Script execution
- ❐ Object creation
- ❐ Data retrieval

When initially creating your application, knowledge of these factors and the related performance tips can yield significant benefits. Later, when your application is near completion, you can review your work looking for specific places to improve the performance.

Script Execution

Optimizing PowerScript comes, in part, from understanding the language. Understanding the language comes from understanding the environment. This understanding will help you write effective code in your applications.

PowerBuilder is an event-driven environment, and the scripts you write are attached to events to define their behavior. PowerScript is pseudo-code, meaning that it is partially interpreted at run-time. As you already know, Windows notifies you each time something occurs through events. Your code or PowerScript always answers the question, "What do I want to do next?"

Your performance comes from correctly answering the question. In part it comes from correctly identifying where scripts should be placed and what they should be doing. For example, it seems natural to write code to access the current window and perform all of the save functionality in the Clicked event of the Save menu item. If you did, however, not only would you be violating object orientation, but you'd also be doing more work than necessary. The most efficient, reusable script you can write is on one line:

```
ParentWindow.TriggerEvent("we_update")
```

This single line of code in the menu item doesn't free you from having to write code elsewhere, but it does free you from the alternatives. The problem with this line of code is that it takes time to look up a user event in the window's event queue. The major benefit to the code is that it is portable and reusable. It also allows true polymorphism in that if the ParentWindow does not have a we_update event, the TriggerEvent is ignored. An alternative would be to call a function on the active window:

```
w_base_sheet   lw_sheet
window      lw_activesheet

lw_activesheet = ParentWindow.GetActiveSheet()

IF IsValid(lw_activesheet) THEN
    lw_sheet = lw_activesheet
    lw_sheet.wf_update()
END IF
```

Although these few lines of code perform faster than triggering an event, there are a couple of challenges. First, we're assuming that w_base_sheet has the wf_update() function on it. Second, the code must find out what the active sheet is and check to make sure it's a valid one. Finally, we can assign the active sheet to the lw_sheet variable and call the wf_update function. The optimal solution is a variation of the above code:

```
w_base_sheet   lw_sheet

lw_sheet = ParentWindow
lw_sheet.wf_update()
```

While this solution provides the best performance, there are still a couple of challenges. First, we're assuming the w_base_sheet class contains the wf_update() function. Second, the menu that contains this code, or one of its descendants, will always be associated with a sheet. In other words, that ParentWindow will always refer to a descendant of w_base_sheet. This means that the menu is not very portable. All things considered, then, the optimal solution is the single line of code that triggers an event on the ParentWindow.

Unfortunately, as we mentioned, there's a performance penalty in that single line of code as well; the time it takes for PowerBuilder to search through the event queue in the specified window for the specified user event. It takes more time, in fact, than it takes to find a PowerBuilder defined event. The question you have to answer is whether the penalty is worth it.

Throughout the development effort, you'll have to ask that question. If the penalty isn't worth the gain, why bother? If you're only going to gain a millisecond of performance, what difference does it make? Is this millisecond going to add up? Is it going to make a difference? If it takes your user 10 seconds less to enter an order because of the work you've done, so what? Unless, of course, the user enters 1,000 orders per day. Then, that 10 seconds turns into 2¾ hours. That's a benefit!

As you write your PowerScript, there are a number of areas you can concentrate on that will provide performance benefit. Again, you must understand object orientation and event-driven development to be able to quickly identify potential problem areas. Some of the basic guidelines can be found throughout this book, but the following points provide a refresher:

❏ An object knows everything about itself and nothing about anything else. Therefore, one object should never know the intimate details of another. Thus, a DataWindow should never interact with another DataWindow, but it *can* interact with the Parent-Window that knows all about both DataWindows. This is the fundamental concept of encapsulation.

❏ Always make your scripts short—about 30 lines, excluding comments. Long scripts tend to cause other events not to be "heard" and can have a detrimental effect on your application.

❏ Never compensate for long scripts by creating functions. Only create a function when the code needs to be used more than once. Functions occupy memory and take longer to load and run than the existing code in the current script.

❏ Never scope variables higher than necessary. In other words, never create a global variable where an instance variable will do. Never create an instance variable where a local variable will do.

❐ Never use global functions and structures where object functions and structures will do. Globals are loaded and unloaded for each use and thus take time away from your application. They also consume resources, which can degrade your application.

When working with script, resource usage is a very important consideration. Rarely in application development do we consider resources. Unfortunately, resource usage can have a tremendous effect on the performance of your application.

Resources come in two forms: resources can refer to icons, bitmaps and other auxiliary files, or resources can refer to available memory, in all its forms. For our purposes, resources refer to memory. The concern we have is anything that can degrade or reduce the amount of available memory.

Memory is a volatile thing. It is created and destroyed with virtually every script run in PowerBuilder. The trick, then, is to control the manner in which memory is used. One of the ways to control memory has already been mentioned: by limiting the use of global variables, functions and structures. Another is the use of variables as a whole. Consider the following code for the RowFocusChanged event:

```
SelectRow(0, FALSE)
SelectRow(GetRow(), TRUE)

IF GetItemStatus(GetRow(), 0, Primary!) = &
    DataModified! THEN
    is_names[UpperBound(ls_names)+1] = &
                GetItemString(&
                GetRow(), "emp_name")
END IF
```

Assuming that the array is_names is an instance variable designed for dynamic allocation, there are a number of ways this script can be improved. Focusing on the memory usage issue, there are two ways to improve performance. Each time an embedded function is called, a temporary variable must be created to hold the return value. (An embedded function is one embedded within or used as an argument to another function, as in the case of the GetItemString() above.) Variable creation takes time to allocate the memory and to subsequently destroy it. The same is true of the array used in the example code above. Each time the array counter is incremented, memory must be allocated to hold the new value being added. Again, this allocation takes time and, more importantly, it may not be contiguous, which can take time during retrieval. If you know in advance how big the array will be, you can initialize the array to the proper size during declaration:

```
String is_names[100]
```

If, on the other hand, you have no idea, you might initialize the array to a large size for starters:

```
IF UpperBound(is_names) = 0 THEN
    is_names[100] = ""
END IF
```

The use of the UpperBound() function to determine the size of the array should also be avoided. The reason for this is that PowerBuilder determines the upper and lower bounds of an array the same way that we might—by counting. Counting takes time and should be avoided at all costs. Another approach is to create an instance variable to hold the number of elements in the array:

```
Long il_name = 0
```

Next, notice that the function GetRow() was used in the script a number of times. Since the value returned by GetRow() never changes throughout the life of the script, it should be stored in a local variable. Anytime you find a function called more than once in the same script, make sure it returns a different value each time. This is especially true when the function is used to determine the upper or lower bound of a loop.

Finally, notice that none of the object functions reference the object that owns them. The problem here is that PowerBuilder must go "look" for the function to determine what kind of function it is, what type of object and which specific object owns it. The moral is to always preface object functions with either a pronoun or the name of the owning object. Pronouns are always faster because PowerBuilder "knows" to which object the pronoun refers.

> Use pronouns whenever possible. They're faster and more portable than using object names directly.

When coding, watch out for bad object references. In PowerBuilder help and in some of the authorized Powersoft training materials, you'll see a function passing the object as the first argument:

```
object-function(object, arg1, ..., argn)
```

This is wrong and, in some cases, can cause the function not to work. No errors, no return codes, no results—the function just won't work. The correct syntax is as follows:

```
object.object-function(arg1,...,argn)
```

Even if the function does work, it generally performs much more slowly than with the correct naming convention.

Now, back to our example. With all of this knowledge, we can rewrite the script. First, start with our instance variables:

```
String is_names[]
Long   il_name = 0
```

Next, the script itself. Notice how it has changed:

```
Long    ll_Row

ll_Row = this.GetRow()

IF il_name = 0 THEN
    // Allocate Memory for the Array
    is_names[100] = ""
END IF
// De-Highlight the Old Row, Highlight the new one
this.SelectRow(0, FALSE)
this.SelectRow(ll_Row, TRUE)

// Add modified names to the array
IF this.GetItemStatus(ll_Row, 0, Primary!) = &
    DataModified! THEN
    il_name = il_name + 1
    is_names[il_name] = &
                GetItemString(&
                ll_Row, "emp_name")
END IF
```

There's a bit more code here, but in terms of performance, it's a significant improvement. It's faster and more efficient. The only problem with the tuned script occurs when the array needs to be deallocated or reallocated. In actual fact, deallocating an array has very little effect on performance except to reduce the amount of memory your application uses. Setting all of the elements to an empty string is not the way to deallocate an array. Actually, it's much easier and faster:

```
String ls_dummy[]
is_names = ls_dummy
```

In our example, this script is in the RowFocusChanged event of a DataWindow and as a result, we have a tremendous performance improvement. Long-running scripts in any event that can potentially occur a large number of times are seldom a good idea. These events include the RowFocusChanged, ItemFocusChanged, ItemChanged and RetrieveRow events of a DataWindow. Anything you can do to enhance the performance of scripts in these events will provide immediate performance improvements.

Perception vs. Reality?

Long-running scripts in some events will cause a user to *perceive* that an application is slow. These events include the Open, Activate, Clicked, DoubleClicked, Close and CloseQuery events. In the case of the Open and Activate events, consider Posting a user-defined event to allow the Open or Activate to complete immediately before processing continues. You might also want to Post a user-defined event to perform some data retrieval. This is especially true if the data retrieval currently occurs in the Open or Activate event. You might also consider using the Retrieve Only As Needed attribute of a DataWindow to speed up retrieval.

Keep in mind that sometimes "performance" can be a function of user perception. When users have to wait for something to happen, it feels like an eternity to them. Sometimes, to improve performance, you just need to let your user know that something is happening—for instance, by changing the mouse cursor shape or displaying the record count. As long as there's some kind of activity, the user tends to be satisfied.

Some events can degrade the performance of your application just by having script in them. One of these is the SQLPreview event of a DataWindow. Another is the RetrieveRow event. In fact, any code (even comments) placed in the RetrieveRow event will slow down retrieval by

25 to 50 percent and should be avoided. Another event of this nature is the Other Event of a window, which traps virtually every other activity not specified in the predefined window events.

Script in PowerBuilder, or code in any language, must be evaluated and executed. Just as in any language, some PowerBuilder functions, such as Modify() and Describe(), take longer than others. It's never a good idea, however, to replace one of PowerBuilder's functions with one of your own. PowerBuilder's functions are highly optimized and can perform much faster than any PowerScript function you might write.

With Modify() and Describe(), you can reduce the number of times the function is called by using compound commands. During debugging, we have a tendency to call Modify() and Describe() a number of times. By using the tab character (~t) to create compound commands, the number of calls might be reduced to one:

```
dw_1.Modify("emp_id.color =255~temp_id.protected=1")
```

When optimizing user-defined and external functions, consider passing arguments by reference. Normally, when passing arguments to user-defined functions, it's far faster if the arguments are passed by reference. This is because PowerBuilder will not need to make a copy of the argument. This is not true of objects or arrays of objects. Objects are automatically passed by reference, and specifying that an object or array of objects is to be passed by reference is passing a reference to a reference. This can create performance degradation at best and system failure at worst.

Object Creation

One of the most common ways to degrade memory and reduce resources is in object creation. The most common mistake developers make is to create an object that is never destroyed. For example, if you need a second transaction object in your application, it's very easy to create one:

```
transaction ltr_sybase
```

```
ltr_sybase = CREATE TRANSACTION
```

The problem is that we tend to use this object and then exit the script. Once the object has been created, memory is allocated. When the script is completed, the variable is destroyed, but the memory is never recovered. As memory degrades, the application slows down, and this can eventually be the cause of a general protection fault. Remember, you must DESTROY any object you CREATE.

Remember to DESTROY any object you CREATE.

Create objects sparingly. Creating an object, whether a window, menu, application or user object, takes time. If your application relies on a custom class (non-visual) object, consider making the object global, shared or an instance variable, so that it doesn't need to be rebuilt each time it's needed.

Additionally, when creating windows, consider using inheritance. Inheritance does not just apply when developing your application. It applies at run-time as well. Remember, when a window is loaded into memory, all of the ancestors are loaded as well. If the ancestors are already in memory, it will take less time to load than the equivalent single window, because there's less to load. The more same-level descendants that are loaded, the more your application's performance will improve compared to an application with the same number of open windows with no ancestors.

There is, however, a limit to the number of levels of inheritance. There's no *physical* limit; PowerBuilder doesn't discriminate. But experience shows that seven descendants in the inheritance chain is the maximum before performance begins to be affected. This degradation occurs because the area of memory containing the object classes (called the *class pool*) begins to fill up, and Windows must start swapping to disk.

With Windows, object creation extends beyond the window itself to the controls on the window. Each control is constructed or built before the window is displayed. If the window consists of several user objects, remember that each user object counts as several objects. This means that PowerBuilder must load the ancestor object(s) into memory before the descendants can be created.

When the controls are created and the window is displayed, the order of the objects is very important. Windows are painted from top left to bottom right. If an object is not listed in the proper order, it may take several passes to paint the window completely. To remedy this situation, you might consider consecutively selecting the window controls and selecting Send to Back from the popup menu.

Good GUI design tells you to leave 25 percent blank space on each window you create. This means limiting the number of controls you place on a window. This affects more than just GUI design—it also affects the length of time required to create and display a window. As mentioned earlier, when a window is opened, all the objects on that window are constructed. The fewer controls on a window, the faster it opens.

Data Retrieval

Quite frequently we, as well as our users, expect the data to be displayed when a window opens. Unfortunately, this isn't always practical. Sometimes, there's an enormous amount of data to be retrieved. Other times, it just takes a long time to even get the data. There are a few things we can do to enhance the performance of our application.

Consider the data that you're retrieving. Do you need to retrieve all of it? If not, can you limit the user to a specific query? In other words, can you retrieve the data based on a retrieval argument? Perhaps you can place a DataWindow into Query mode to directly modify the WHERE clause of a DataWindow's SELECT statement.

If, on the other hand, there's no way to reduce the number of rows retrieved by query, can you limit the number of rows using some other method? For example, you might use the RetrieveRow event to count the number of rows being loaded into the DataWindow, then cancel retrieval if the number of rows exceeds some predefined number. Or you might create a cursor to load data into the DataWindow:

```
Integer li_emp_id
String ls_emp_fname, ls_emp_lname
Long    ll_Row = 0

DECLARE data CURSOR FOR
 SELECT emp_id, emp_lname, emp_fname
   FROM employee
  USING SQLCA ;

OPEN data ;

DO WHILE SQLCA.SQLCode = 0
   FETCH data
    INTO :li_emp_id, :ls_emp_lname, ls_emp_fname ;
   IF SQLCA.SQLCode = 0 THEN
      ll_Row = ll_Row + 1
      IF ll_Row > 500 THEN
         MessageBox("Limit Reached!", &
               "The Maximum number of " + &
               "rows has been retrieved!")
         EXIT
```

```
            END IF
            dw_1.SetItem(ll_Row, "emp_id", li_emp_id)
            dw_1.SetItem(ll_Row, "emp_fname", ls_emp_fname)
            dw_1.SetItem(ll_Row, "emp_lname", ls_emp_lname)
         END IF
      LOOP
      CLOSE data ;
```

Embedded SQL is not as efficient as a DataWindow.

Beware of using cursors, or any embedded SQL. Embedded SQL is not as efficient as a DataWindow, and because the embedded SQL is executed as part of a script, it's often very slow. Unfortunately, there isn't a lot you can do to enhance the performance of embedded SQL except not to use it.

If you choose not to use a cursor or the RetrieveRow event, your remaining option is to use the Retrieve As Needed attribute of a DataWindow. The challenge you'll face using this attribute is that you may not use any aggregate functions within the DataWindow—no Sums, Averages, Mins, Maxes, etc. You may not sort or group the DataWindow either. Anything that requires all rows to be present overrides the Retrieve As Needed attribute. If you decide to use Retrieve As Needed, you might consider turning the option off after the initial retrieval has taken place. That is, in some event of your window, perform the Retrieve, then Post an event to get the rest of the data:

```
dw_1.Modify("datawindow.Retrieve.AsNeeded = no")
```

There are still other options you might consider. For example, you might cache infrequently-used data on the user's machine, using the SaveAs() function to export the data and the ImportFile() function to get it back. Perhaps you could save the data with the DataWindow using the Data item on the Rows menu in the DataWindow painter.

Instead of retrieving all the data, perhaps you can have the server do some of the work for you. This is especially true of aggregation where the server performs SUMs, GROUPs, ORDERing, etc. The server is much faster and more efficient than the client machine. If your application doesn't need the complete result set, but just the summarized version, let the server do the work. Save the display and data entry for the client application.

Here's one last performance tip to consider. If you need to move data from one table to another, there are two ways to accomplish the task. First, you can write a stored procedure to accomplish the task behind the scenes. The drawback to a stored procedure is flexibility. All options must be considered and planned for in advance.

On the other hand, you can use a data pipeline. Once again, there are benefits and drawbacks. The benefits are that the pipeline handles virtually every possible situation from table creation to data replication. The data source is a SQL statement, and thus is incredibly flexible. The destination can be any table in any DBMS. The extended attributes can be moved with the data. The drawback is that the pipeline is an object and is slightly slower than a stored procedure, but its flexibility makes up for its sluggishness.

MOVING ON

Performance is an all-encompassing issue. It involves virtually every aspect of application development, starting with your development environment and finishing with the resulting application. Be aware of the size and number of objects in your PBLs, and consider the user-perception concepts versus performance concepts. Sometimes the things you do during development can affect performance; other times you'll review your application just before you go to final beta or production. Whichever the case, take the time to understand your application and the options you have in the development environment to enhance the performance. You won't be disappointed.

About the Online Companion

The *PowerBuilder Online Companion* is your one-stop location for PowerBuilder resources on the Internet. It serves as an informative tool as well as an annotated software library aiding in your exploration of PowerBuilder's powerful development environment.

The Online Companion links you to available Power-Builder newsgroups, Web pages and e-mail discussion groups. So you can just click on the reference name and jump directly to the resource you're interested in.

Perhaps one of the most valuable features of the *PowerBuilder Online Companion* is its Software Archive. Here, you'll find and be able to download the latest demos, utilities and other software that is freely available on the Internet. Also, with Ventana Online's helpful description of the software, you'll know exactly what you're getting and why. So you won't download the software just to find that you have no use for it.

The Online Companion also links you to the Ventana Library, where you will find useful press and jacket information on a variety of Ventana offerings. Plus, you have access to a wide selection of exciting new releases and coming attractions. In addition, Ventana's Online Library allows you to order the books you want.

The *PowerBuilder Online Companion* represents Ventana Online's ongoing commitment to offering the most dynamic and exciting products possible. And soon Ventana Online will be adding more services, including more multimedia supplements, searchable indexes and sections of the book reproduced and hyperlinked to the Internet resources they reference.

To access, connect via the World Wide Web to
http://www.vmedia.com/powerbuilder.html

About the Companion CD-ROM

The Companion CD-ROM included with your copy of *PowerBuilder 4.0 for Windows Power Toolkit* contains a wealth of valuable software. Most of the tools on the Companion CD-ROM are third-party products that enhance the performance or usability of PowerBuilder. Also contained on the CD are examples created by the authors of this book that provide instructions for building the applications reviewed within the chapters. Remember to visit the PowerBuilder Online Companion to obtain updates to these tools and applications.

To install the *PowerBuilder 4.0 for Windows Power Toolkit Companion CD-ROM*, load the CD and double-click on the CD icon. Then double-click on the Viewer icon. The onscreen help will explain how to navigate, run and install the programs. The Companion CD-ROM interface is very user-friendly. You will have the choice of viewing the README files, running a sample of the program or installing the program onto your hard drive.

The *PowerBuilder 4.0 for Windows Power Toolkit Companion CD-ROM* contains the following limited version programs:

- ❐ PowerFrame
- ❐ PowerClass
- ❐ PowerTOOL 4.0
- ❐ Component Toolbox for PowerBuilder
- ❐ ObjectStart
- ❐ ERwin
- ❐ Visual Voice
- ❐ Enterprise Builder for PowerBuilder
- ❐ BACHMAN Generator
- ❐ Graffman
- ❐ EasyCASE

The Companion CD also contains the PowerBuilder Winsock Library developed by Ted Coombs. Other examples and mini applications created for the book by the authoring team are also available on the Companion CD.

LICENSE, DISCLAIMER & LIMITATION OF LIABILITY

The *PowerBuilder 4.0 for Windows Power Toolkit Companion CD-ROM* is offered without support other than the README file on the disk and the information in the *PowerBuilder 4.0 for Windows Power Toolkit* book. The publisher and authors assume no responsibility for the suitability of the files and programs contained on the disk. Programs on the Companion CD-ROM are intended only for your personal use and may not be duplicated or used for resale.

The Companion CD-ROM compilation and its design are ©1995 Ventana Communications Group, Inc. Individual programs and files are copyrighted by the manufacturer. All copyright and disclaimers that apply to the *PowerBuilder 4.0 for Windows Power Toolkit* book also apply to the *PowerBuilder 4.0 for Windows Power Toolkit* CD-ROM.

HOW DO I GET IN TOUCH WITH VENTANA?

Ventana Communications Group, Inc., welcomes your comments and questions about the *PowerBuilder 4.0 for Windows Power Toolkit* (or any of our other books). If you'd like to contact Ventana, use your pen or pencil, phone or fax to reach us at:

Managing Editor
Ventana Communications Group, Inc.
PO Box 13964
Research Triangle Park, NC 27709-3964
Fax: (919) 544-9472

Technical Support is available for installation-related problems only. Phone (919) 544-9404, extension 81, or via the Internet at help@vmedia.com. Fax back service is also available by dialing (919) 544-9404, extension 2000.

PowerBuilder & Windows 95

The following is a paper presented to the 1995 Mid-Atlantic PowerBuilder Users Conference by Dave Rensin, Gregory McIntyre, and Timothy Jarrett of American Management Systems, Inc. Although it is certainly not *the* definitive work on how PowerBuilder programming will change with Windows 95, it attempts to address some of the major structural changes to the operating system and how they are likely to affect PowerBuilder programmers.

Windows 95: The New Paradigm & PowerBuilder

by Dave Rensin, Greg McIntyre, and Tim Jarrett
American Management Systems, Incorporated
1777 N. Kent Street
Arlington, Virginia 22209
703-841-6000

Respectfully submitted to the
1995 Mid-Atlantic PowerBuilder Users Conference,
April 13, 1995.

ABSTRACT

Windows 95 presents a new paradigm for the desktop operating system. Its enhanced technical features and user interface will impact existing PowerBuilder applications, as well as influence the design of future software development efforts. This paper discusses the effects of Windows 95 on PowerBuilder applications and presents strategies for capitalizing on the changes in the operating system.

Biography of Authors

Dave Rensin is a developer at American Management Systems, Inc. (AMS) on the CARDSS project, a large scale migration effort from DOS based applications to PowerBuilder environments. He has worked in the field of database design and systems engineering for the last six years. Mr. Rensin holds a BS in Management Science and Statistics from The University of Maryland.

Greg McIntyre is a developer at AMS on the Procurement Desktop project, a PowerBuilder application. He has also served as a Business Process Reengineering analyst on numerous procurement and logistics projects. Mr. McIntyre holds an M.S. in Operations Research from The George Washington University and a B.S. in Engineering Management from The United States Military Academy.

Tim Jarrett is also a developer on the Procurement Desktop project at AMS. Previously, he was a developer of a business process reengineering application in PowerBuilder for AMS. Mr. Jarrett holds a B.S. in Physics from The University of Virginia.

The forthcoming Windows 95 operating system from Microsoft attempts to redefine the basic premise of a personal computer (PC) desktop operating system. The flow of many PowerBuilder applications will also need to change to accommodate the new paradigm. This paper provides a first look at Windows 95 and discusses how this new operating system and interface will affect PowerBuilder applications in the following areas:

- 32-Bit Architecture
- Interface Paradigm Shift
- Interconnectivity

SHIFTING FOUNDATIONS: 32-BIT ARCHITECTURE

One of the most significant changes in Windows 95 is "under the hood"; it's the first mainstream version of Windows to have a 32-bit architecture. Changing the bit depth of an addressing scheme from sixteen to thirty-two adds several layers of convenience, ability, and stability to an operating system. The improved memory access of Windows 95 is related to the 32-bit architecture. Unfortunately, changing an architecture also occasionally creates problems with programs developed for the previous, 16-bit incarnations of Windows. The memory-protection scheme that Windows 95 uses to keep Windows from crashing when an application crashes is only effective when all the applications involved are 32-bit clean. It is less effective when dealing with 16-bit applications. Windows 95 can protect memory against a single 16-bit application, but (as in previous versions of Windows) cannot protect 16-bit applications against each other. This means that most existing PowerBuilder applications will not be more stable under Windows 95 than they currently are under Windows 3.1x.

For programmers who have watched with dismay as PowerBuilder or PowerBuilder applications deplete the Windows 3.1x resource heap, Windows 95 provides a much-enlarged resource space. However, it's still finitely large—this means that, while it may no longer be possible to exhaust Windows' resources by building a window with forty-five controls on it, opening three of those Windows could still deplete the resources.

A NEW LOOK: INTERFACE PARADIGM SHIFT

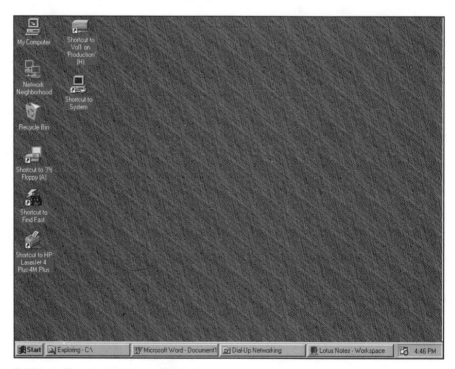

Exhibit 1: The new Windows 95 desktop

Besides the power of 32-bit computing, Windows 95 presents a new interface (Exhibit 1) which PowerBuilder developers must consider during GUI design. This section addresses two differences between Windows 95 and Windows 3.1x—the more objected-oriented desktop and the softer feel of windows—and discusses their impact on PowerBuilder applications in the new environment of Windows 95.

The Object-Oriented Desktop

Another big change to Windows is the greater emphasis on object-oriented (OO) workspaces and principles. Where there were once command buttons, there is now drag and drop. For example, let's say that we have created an inventory system in PowerBuilder where the user enters some information about an inventory item in a datawindow control and clicks a print button to print a stock form.

The same system developed in Windows 95 would probably have a printer window in the corner of the desktop. When the user wants to print the inventory form, he would minimize the entry window and drag it to the printer. This example can be expanded even further. Let us also say that each piece of inventory is associated with a particular warehouse. In our new system each warehouse could be an open sheet on the desktop with a bitmap in each sheet representing various inventory components. To print the information about a specific inventory item, the user might drag the bitmap from the warehouse sheet to the printer.

In systems where individual components are distinct but related (i.e., a database system), this use of an object-oriented desktop will be most important. Because PowerBuilder is a database application tool, the use of the OO desktop design will be a necessary interface choice since the operating system interface so strongly promotes it.

While Windows 95's Program Manager may promote drag and drop, Windows 95 eliminates one common method used by PowerBuilder developers to achieve this OO design goal. This is because of a Windows 95 innovation: the omnipresent task bar along the bottom of the interface which encourages multi-tasking. The task bar is composed of applications which have been minimized. Likewise, applications also have task bars composed of windows that have been minimized. An icon is not created when you minimize a window; instead a rectangular piece is added to the application task bar on the bottom of the application frame. This has implications for PowerBuilder Windows 3.1x applications with drag and drop features implemented via minimized Multiple Document Interface (MDI) sheets.

For example, a PowerBuilder application in Windows 3.1x may have allowed the user to print a document by dragging it onto a printer icon. Surprise! In Windows 95, that printer icon has become a rectangular block on the application task bar and it may no longer be intuitive for a user to drag and drop as previously with the printer icon. This same problem will arise for any application icons such as file cabinets, outboxes, etc. If the developer wants to preserve the drag and drop metaphor, a bitmap will have to be created to provide the icon and significant code will need to be added. Perhaps with time, it may become accepted practice for users to drag and drop over a task bar item. Until then developers need to be aware of how the new task bar will affect their applications, especially since the drag and drop metaphor is familiar to users and is prevalent throughout Windows 95.

Softer Look & Feel

Windows 95 has a distinctly different feel than Windows 3.1x, characterized by softer lines and a less obtrusive program manager which more closely resembles an actual desktop. In this spirit, PowerBuilder applications running in Windows 95 should place their emphasis on the content of windows rather than border information. This concept, along with Windows 95's softer, rounder windows, may lead the designer to consider an unorthodox, yet effective method of creating popup windows. Using this method, the designer creates a round-looking popup window by laying a datawindow with rounded corners over the expanse of a child type window. So that the window performs like a popup, create the window without any border or title bar. Since the window lacks a border or title bar, the Windows operating system will not allow any other window to gain focus on top of the popup window. To enhance the rounded look of the popup, choose a neutral transparent color for the window so the user will not see its corners. To make the window look three-dimensional, the designer may also lay an additional rounded datawindow between the datawindow and window. Exhibit 2 summarizes the steps involved in creating this window.

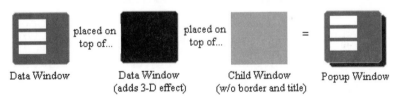

| Data Window | Data Window (adds 3-D effect) | Child Window (w/o border and title) | Popup Window |

Exhibit 2: Construction of rounded window popup.

Exhibit 3 shows an example popup window.

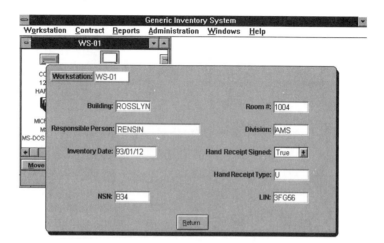

Exhibit 3: Completed rounded window popup.

"PLUGGED IN": INTERCONNECTIVITY

This section discusses the connectivity mechanisms which Windows 95 provides PowerBuilder developers: the ability to communicate effectively between applications and between machines.

Between Applications: OLE

Although PowerBuilder allows developers to create powerful applications, often system requirements mandate the integration of the PowerBuilder application and another Windows application. A common case occurs when a database application needs to do financial calculations or document generation. Instead of writing a word processor or spreadsheet, a clever system developer might use Dynamic Data Exchange (DDE) to talk to Word or Excel. This will no longer occur in Windows 95 where DDE has been replaced by the Object Linking and Embedding (OLE) 2.0 standard.

The applications that come with Windows 95 use OLE extensively to communicate with each other. New PowerBuilder applications will have to use OLE to do some of the things formerly accomplished with DDE, as well as fully integrate into a client's specific work environment as OLE servers.

The new shift to an object-oriented interface scheme as well as stronger application interconnectivity means that application developers can expect the complexity of their system requirements to rise enormously. Where it was once sufficient to develop an inventory system that simply captured data, it will now be vital to capture processes as well. With the increase in average computing power and drive space, it will be necessary to integrate many PowerBuilder applications with a wide range of input systems such as imaging and mail, as well as a variety of output mediums more diverse than the standard monitor and printer. The reason that developers of PowerBuilder applications can expect to see these changes is simple: database systems often require an extended capability to capture new data (i.e., via electronic mail and imaging systems). Since PowerBuilder is a database application development tool that allows the developer to access large volumes of data from varying data sources, it seems likely that PowerBuilder developers will be among the first to feel these changes.

Between Machines: Networking

Another feature of Windows 95, extensive built-in networking capabilities, will increase the available capabilities for any PowerBuilder application. With built-in peer-to-peer networking, Novell, and TCP/IP support, a PC running Windows 95 has a huge array of options for sharing information. As such, whole new horizons for developing distributed applications may become possible within PowerBuilder. The distinction between Windows 95 and previous Windows-plus-networking-software solutions is not necessarily the technology (although there are improvements in that arena as well)—it is the availability and integration of that technology. In integrating all possible networking options into the operating system and providing APIs for each, Microsoft has created *de facto* standards for coding TCP/IP and Novell functionality in Windows, eliminating a PowerBuilder programmer's uncertainty about which WINSOCK.DLL and TCP/IP stack will be used with his application.

With every machine running Windows 95 potentially its own Novell server, visible from any machine on a Novell network (a capability provided at the OS level), PC networking may finally be edging close to universality and even ease of use. As such, it should theoretically become possible, using OLE and DDE, to distribute a PowerBuilder application's operations across one's local Local Area Network (LAN) or even over a TCP/IP connection—that is to say, the Internet.

These networking features enable PowerBuilder applications to become fully "client-server," not just in the atrophied sense of data servers alone, but in the expanded and far more powerful sense of application servers. The combination of greater interoperability and the enhanced user interface, together with PowerBuilder's powerful development environment, expand the potential feature set of new client-server applications.

PBORCA Reference

Powersoft's Open Repository CASE API (ORCA) provides advanced developers and CASE vendors with a simple way to access PowerBuilder's library functions. Although this information is free from Powersoft, it is not officially supported, and you will be unable to obtain technical support for it from any Powersoft technical representative. Chapter 9, "Advanced Programming Topics," discussed in some depth the basics of using this interface. The following document is a reprint of the available documentation on this subject from Powersoft. The authors of this book extend their thanks to Powersoft for allowing its use.

POWERSOFT™ OPEN LIBRARY API

As part of the Powersoft CODE (Client/Server Open Development Environment) initiative, Powersoft has developed an Application Programming Interface (API) to the Powersoft library facilities, the Powersoft Open Library API. This Open Library API (ORCA), provides comprehensive access to all PowerBuilder, PowerMaker, and PowerViewer library entities.

This API, which is part of the PowerBuilder Version 3.0 Enterprise Edition, is delivered as a DLL (PBORC030.DLL). The files PBORCA.H and PBORCA.LIB required for development of C programs that use the Open Library API are supplied on PowerBuilder Enterprise Edition disks.

ORCA Functions

This paper describes the ORCA functions you use to access PowerBuilder, PowerMaker, and PowerViewer libraries and objects. The functions are divided into the functional groups described below and are discussed alphabetically within each group. Prototypes of the callback functions and their structures are described at the end of the paper and are also in PBORCA.H.

Session Management

All functions within ORCA operate within the context of a *session*. This is analogous to opening a file, performing some set of operations on it, and then closing the file. The session management functions allow sessions to be established and terminated. This group also includes session service functions that are used to set the current library search path, set the current application, and perform error handling.

Note: The library search path must be set before the current application is set.

The system management functions are:

- ❐ PBORCA_SessionClose
- ❐ PBORCA_SessionGetError
- ❐ PBORCA_SessionOpen
- ❐ PBORCA_SessionSetCurrentAppl
- ❐ PBORCA_SessionSetLibraryList

Library Management

The library management functions allow libraries and library entities to be manipulated outside the context of a current application or library list. Libraries can be created and deleted, and library comments can be modified. In addition, library entities (objects) can be copied, deleted, exported, and moved. A library directory facility is also provided.

The library management functions are:

- ❏ PBORCA_LibraryCommentModify
- ❏ PBORCA_LibraryCreate
- ❏ PBORCA_LibraryDelete
- ❏ PBORCA_LibraryDirectory
- ❏ PBORCA_LibraryEntryCopy
- ❏ PBORCA_LibraryEntryDelete
- ❏ PBORCA_LibraryEntryExport
- ❏ PBORCA_LibraryEntryInformation
- ❏ PBORCA_LibraryEntryMove

Compilation

The compilation functions allow for importing and regeneration of library entities. *All* compilation must occur within the context of a current application and library list.

The compilation functions are:

- ❏ PBORCA_CompileEntryImport
- ❏ PBORCA_CompileEntryImportList
- ❏ PBORCA_CompileEntryRegenerate

Object Query

The object query functions allow for querying of objects for object reference explosion and object hierarchy traversal. Object querying must occur within the context of a current application and library list.

The object query functions are:

❏ PBORCA_ObjectQueryHierarchy

❏ PBORCA_ObjectQueryReference

Function: PBORCA_SessionClose

Prototype

```
void    PBORCA_SessionClose( HPBORCA hORCASession );
```

Description

Terminate an ORCA session. This function will free any currently allocated resources related to the ORCA session. Since an ORCA session has no connection to anything, failure to execute this function will not result in any loss of data.

Parameter Description

HPBORCA hORCASession

Handle to previously established ORCA session.

Return

Function: PBORCA_SessionGetError

Prototype

```
void    PBORCA_SessionGetError( HPBORCA hORCASession,
        LPSTR   lpszErrroBuffer,
        INT iErrorBufferSize );
```

Description

Get the current error for an ORCA session. This function should be called any time that another ORCA function call results in an error. Functions always provide some useful error code (along with a set of #defines detailing the errors), but if you choose to utilize ORCA's own text representation for the error, you can just call PBORCA_SessionGetError. If there is no current error, "" will be placed into the error buffer.

Parameter Description

HPBORCA hORCASession

Handle to previously established ORCA session.

LPSTR lpszErrorBuffer

Pointer to buffer for current error string to be returned into.

int iErrorBufferSize

Size of error buffer. #Define PBORCA_MSGBUFFER in the header file sets the message buffer size to 256.

Return

Function: PBORCA_SessionOpen

Prototype

```
HPBORCAPBORCA_SessionOpen( void );
```

Description

Establish an ORCA session. This call must be made before any other ORCA function calls. There is no overhead or resource issues related to keeping an ORCA session open, therefore once established it should be left open as long as it might be needed.

Parameters

Return

HPBORCA - Handle to ORCA session. This handle will be used on all subsequent ORCA calls. Since there is no need to actually connect to anything, this call will fail *only* if all storage has been allocated.

Function: **PBORCA_SessionSetCurrentAppl**

Prototype

```
int PBORCA_SessionSetCurrentAppl( HPBORCA
hORCASession,
    LPSTR   lpszApplLibName,
    LPSTR   lpszApplName );
```

Description

Establish the current application for an ORCA session. This function must be called after PBORCA_SetLibraryList and before execution of any ORCA function that compiles objects or queries objects. The application library name should be fully qualified wherever possible.

Parameter Description

HPBORCA hORCASession

Handle to previously established ORCA session.

LPSTR lpszApplLibName

Pointer to name of application library.

LPSTR lpszApplName

Pointer to name of application.

Return

int - Return code. An error will occur if:

❏ Bad parameter list is passed

❏ Referenced library name does not exist

❏ Referenced application does not exist in referenced library

❏ Referenced library is not part of current library list

The typical return codes are:

PBORCA_OK - Operation successful.

PBORCA_INVALIDPARMS - Invalid parameter list.

PBORCA_BADLIBRARY - Bad library name.

PBORCA_LIBLISTNOTSET - Library list not set.

PBORCA_LIBNOTINLIST - Library not in library list.

Function: **PBORCA_SessionSetLibraryList**

Prototype

```
int PBORCA_SessionSetLibraryList( HPBORCA
hORCASession,
        LPSTR far *pLibNames,
        int iNumberOfLibs );
```

Description

Establish the library search path for an ORCA session. This function must be called before execution of any ORCA function that compiles objects or queries objects. The library management functions and query functions listed below can be called without setting the library list. Library names should be fully qualified wherever possible.

- ❒ PBORCA_LibraryCommentModify
- ❒ PBORCA_LibraryCreate
- ❒ PBORCA_LibraryDelete
- ❒ PBORCA_LibraryDirectory
- ❒ PBORCA_LibraryEntryCopy
- ❒ PBORCA_LibraryEntryDelete
- ❒ PBORCA_LibraryEntryExport
- ❒ PBORCA_LibraryEntryInformation
- ❒ PBORCA_LibraryEntryMove

Parameter Description

HPBORCA hORCASession
Handle to previously established ORCA session.
LPSTR far *pLibNames
Pointer to array of pointers to library names.
int iNumberOfLibs
Number of library name pointers in array pointed to by pLibNames.

Return

int - Return code. An error will occur if:

❑ A bad parameter list is passed

❑ Any libraries in the passed library names list does not exist

The typical return codes are:

PBORCA_OK - Operation successful.

PBORCA_INVALIDPARMS - Invalid parameter list.

PBORCA_BADLIBRARY - Bad library name.

PBORCA_LIBLISTNOTSET - Library list not set.

PBORCA_LIBNOTINLIST - Library not in library list.

Function: PBORCA_LibraryCommentModify

Prototype

```
int PBORCA_LibraryCommentModify( HPBORCA
hORCASession,
        LPSTR   lpszLibName,
        LPSTR   lpszLibComments );
```

Description

Modify the comment for a PowerBuilder library.

Parameter Description

HPBORCA hORCASession

Handle to previously established ORCA session.

LPSTR lpszLibName

Pointer to library name.

LPSTR lpszLibComments

Pointer to new library comments.

Return

int - Return code. An error will occur if:

❑ Bad parameter list is passed

❑ Library name could not be found

❑ I/O error

The typical return codes are:

PBORCA_OK - Operation successful.

PBORCA_INVALIDPARMS - Invalid parameter list.

PBORCA_OBJNOTFOUND - Object not found.

PBORCA_BADLIBRARY - Bad library name.

PBORCA_LIBLISTNOTSET - Library list not set.

PBORCA_LIBNOTINLIST - Library not in library list.

PBORCA_LIBIOERROR - Library I/O error.

Function: PBORCA_LibraryCreate

Prototype

```
int PBORCA_LibraryCreate( HPBORCA        hORCASession,
        LPSTR  lpszLibraryName,
        LPSTR  lpszLibraryComments );
```

Description

Create a new PowerBuilder library.

Parameter Description

HPBORCA hORCASession

Handle to previously established ORCA session.

LPSTR lpszLibraryName

Pointer to library name to create.

LPSTR lpszLibraryComments

Pointer to library comments.

Return

int - Return code. An error will occur if:

❐ Bad parameter list is passed

❐ Library name is invalid

❐ Library already exists

❐ I/O Error

The typical return codes are:

PBORCA_OK - Operation successful.

PBORCA_INVALIDPARMS - Invalid parameter list.

PBORCA_BADLIBRARY - Bad library name.

PBORCA_LIBLISTNOTSET - Library list not set.

PBORCA_LIBNOTINLIST - Library not in library list.

PBORCA_LIBIOERROR - Library I/O error.

PBORCA_OBJEXISTS - Object already exists.

Function: **PBORCA_LibraryDelete**

Prototype

```
int PBORCA_LibraryDelete( HPBORCA        hORCASession,
        LPSTR  lpszLibraryName );
```

Description

Delete a PowerBuilder library.

Parameter Description

HPBORCA hORCASession

Handle to previously established ORCA session.

LPSTR lpszLibraryName

Pointer to library name to delete.

Return

int - Return code. An error will occur if:

❐ Bad parameter list is passed

❐ Library name could not be found

❐ I/O error

The typical return codes are:

PBORCA_OK - Operation successful.

PBORCA_INVALIDPARMS - Invalid parameter list.

PBORCA_BADLIBRARY - Bad library name.

PBORCA_LIBIOERROR - Library I/O error.

Function: **PBORCA_LibraryDirectory**

Prototype

```
int PBORCA_LibraryDirectory( HPBORCA    hORCASession,
        LPSTR   lpszLibName,
        LPSTR   lpszLibComments,
        INT iCmntsBuffSize,
        PBORCA_LISTPROC    pListProc,
        LPVOID pUserData );
```

Description

Explode the directory for a PowerBuilder library.

Parameter Description

HPBORCA hORCASession

Handle to previously established ORCA session.

LPSTR lpszLibName

Pointer to library name.

LPSTR lpszLibComments

Pointer to library comments buffer.

int iCmntsBuffSize

Size of buffer pointed to by lpszLibComments.

FARPROC pListProc

Pointer to the PBORCA_LibraryDirectory callback function. Entry information will include entry name, comments, size of entry, and modification time.

LPVOID pUserData

Pointer to user data to be passed to the PBORCA_LibraryDirectory callback function with each entry.

Return

int - Return code. An error will occur if:

❑ Bad parameter list is passed

❑ Library name could not be found

❑ I/O error

The typical return codes are:

PBORCA_OK - Operation successful.

PBORCA_INVALIDPARMS - Invalid parameter list.

PBORCA_BADLIBRARY - Bad library name.

PBORCA_LIBLISTNOTSET - Library list not set.

PBORCA_LIBNOTINLIST - Library not in library list.

PBORCA_LIBIOERROR - Library I/O error.

Function: **PBORCA_LibraryEntryCopy**

Prototype

```
int PBORCA_LibraryEntryCopy( HPBORCA     hORCASession,
        LPSTR   lpszSourceLibName,
        LPSTR   lpszDestLibName,
        LPSTR   lpszEntryName,
        PBORCA_TYPE    otEntryType );
```

Description

Copy a PowerBuilder library entry from one library to another.

Parameter Description

HPBORCA hORCASession

Handle to previously established ORCA session.

LPSTR lpszSourceLibName

Pointer to source library name.

LPSTR lpszDestLibName

Pointer to destination library name.

LPSTR lpszEntryName

Pointer to entry name.

PBORCA_TYPE otEntryType

Enum for entry type (PBORCA_APPLICATION, PBORCA_DATAWINDOW, PBORCA_FUNCTION, PBORCA_MENU, PBORCA_QUERY, PBORCA_STRUCTURE, PBORCA_USEROBJECT, or PBORCA_WINDOW).

Return

int - Return code. An error will occur if:

❏ Bad parameter list is passed

❏ Source and/or destination library name could not be found

❏ Entry name could not be found

❏ I/O error

The typical return codes are:

PBORCA_OK - Operation successful.

PBORCA_INVALIDPARMS - Invalid parameter list.

PBORCA_OBJNOTFOUND - Object not found.

PBORCA_BADLIBRARY - Bad library name.

PBORCA_LIBLISTNOTSET - Library list not set.

PBORCA_LIBNOTINLIST - Library not in library list.

PBORCA_LIBIOERROR - Library I/O error.

Function: **PBORCA_LibraryEntryDelete**

Prototype

```
int PBORCA_LibraryEntryDelete( PBORCA   hORCASession,
        LPSTR   lpszLibName,
        LPSTR   lpszEntryName,
        PBORCA_TYPE   otEntryType );
```

Description

Delete a PowerBuilder library entry.

Parameter Description

HPBORCA hORCASession

Handle to previously established ORCA session.

LPSTR lpszLibName

Pointer to library name.

LPSTR lpszEntryName

Pointer to entry name.

PBORCA_TYPE otEntryType

Enum for entry type (PBORCA_APPLICATION, PBORCA_DATAWINDOW, PBORCA_FUNCTION, PBORCA_MENU, PBORCA_QUERY, PBORCA_STRUCTURE, PBORCA_USEROBJECT, or PBORCA_WINDOW).

Return

int - Return code. An error will occur if:

- ❏ Bad parameter list is passed
- ❏ Library name could not be found
- ❏ Entry name could not be found
- ❏ I/O error

The typical return codes are:

PBORCA_OK - Operation successful.

PBORCA_INVALIDPARMS - Invalid parameter list.

PBORCA_OBJNOTFOUND - Object not found.

PBORCA_BADLIBRARY - Bad library name.

PBORCA_LIBLISTNOTSET - Library list not set.

PBORCA_LIBNOTINLIST - Library not in library list.

PBORCA_LIBIOERROR - Library I/O error.

Function: **PBORCA_LibraryEntryExport**

Prototype

```
int PBORCA_LibraryEntryExport( PBORCA   hORCASession,
        LPSTR   lpszLibraryName,
        LPSTR   lpszEntryName,
        PBORCA_TYPE   otEntryType,
        LPSTR   lpszExportBuffer,
        LONG   lExportBufferSize );
```

Description

Export the source for a PowerBuilder library entry.

Parameter Description

HPBORCA hORCASession

Handle to previously established ORCA session.

LPSTR lpszLibraryName

Pointer to library name.

LPSTR lpszEntryName

Pointer to entry name.

PBORCA_TYPE otEntryType

Enum for entry type (PBORCA_APPLICATION, PBORCA_DATAWINDOW, PBORCA_FUNCTION, PBORCA_MENU, PBORCA_QUERY, PBORCA_STRUCTURE, PBORCA_USEROBJECT, or PBORCA_WINDOW).

LPSTR lpszExportBuffer

Pointer to export buffer.

LONG lExportBufferSize

Size of storage pointed to by lpszExportBuffer.

Return

int - Return code. An error will occur if:

- ❏ Bad parameter list is passed
- ❏ Library name could not be found
- ❏ Entry name could not be found
- ❏ Buffer size was insufficient
- ❏ I/O error

The typical return values are:

PBORCA_OK - Operation successful.

PBORCA_INVALIDPARMS - Invalid parameter list.

PBORCA_OBJNOTFOUND - Object not found.

PBORCA_BADLIBRARY - Bad library name.

PBORCA_LIBLISTNOTSET - Library list not set.

PBORCA_LIBNOTINLIST - Library not in library list.

PBORCA_LIBIOERROR - Library I/O error.

PBORCA_BUFFERTOOSMALL - Buffer size is too small.

Function: **PBORCA_LibraryEntryInformation**

Prototype

```
int PBORCA_LibraryEntryInformation( HPBORCA
hORCASession,
        LPSTR   lpszLibraryName,
        LPSTR   lpszEntryName,
        PBORCA_TYPE   otEntryType,
        PPBORCA_ENTRYINFO  pEntryInformationBlock );
```

Description

Return information for PowerBuilder library entry.

Parameter Description

HPBORCA hORCASession

Handle to previously established ORCA session.

LPSTR lpszLibraryName

Pointer to library name.

LPSTR lpszEntryName

Pointer to entry name.

PBORCA_TYPE otEntryType

Enum for entry type (PBORCA_APPLICATION, PBORCA_DATAWINDOW, PBORCA_FUNCTION, PBORCA_MENU, PBORCA_QUERY, PBORCA_STRUCTURE, PBORCA_USEROBJECT, or PBORCA_WINDOW).

PPBORCA_ENTRYINFO pEntryInformationBlock
Pointer to PBORCA_ENTRYINFO block (See below). Entry information includes comments, size of source, size of object, and modification time.

Return

int - Return code. An error will occur if:

❏ Bad parameter list is passed

❏ Library name could not be found

❏ Entry name could not be found

❏ I/O error

The typical return values are:
PBORCA_OK - Operation successful.
PBORCA_INVALIDPARMS - Invalid parameter list.
PBORCA_OBJNOTFOUND - Object not found.
PBORCA_BADLIBRARY - Bad library name.
PBORCA_LIBLISTNOTSET - Library list not set.
PBORCA_LIBNOTINLIST - Library not in library list.
PBORCA_LIBIOERROR - Library I/O error.

Structure for PBORCA_LibraryEntryInformation

```
typedef struct pborca_entryinfo
{
    /* Comments */
  CHAR      szComments[PBORCA_MAXCOMMENT + 1];
  LONG      lCreateTime;  /* Time of entry create/mod */
  LONG      lObjectSize;   /* Size of object */
  LONG      lSourceSize;   /* Size of source */
} PBORCA_ENTRYINFO, FAR *PPBORCA_ENTRYINFO;
```

Function: **PBORCA_LibraryEntryMove**

Prototype

```
int PBORCA_LibraryEntryMove( PBORCA     hORCASession,
        LPSTR  lpszSourceLibName,
        LPSTR  lpszDestLibName,
        LPSTR  lpszEntryName,
        PBORCA_TYPE   otEntryType );
```

Description

Move a PowerBuilder library entry from one library to another.

Parameter Description

HPBORCA hORCASession

Handle to previously established ORCA session.

LPSTR lpszSourceLibName

Pointer to source library name.

LPSTR lpszDestLibName

Pointer to destination library name.

LPSTR lpszEntryName

Pointer to entry name.

PBORCA_TYPE otEntryType

Enum for entry type (PBORCA_APPLICATION, PBORCA_DATAWINDOW, PBORCA_FUNCTION, PBORCA_MENU, PBORCA_QUERY, PBORCA_STRUCTURE, PBORCA_USEROBJECT, or PBORCA_WINDOW).

Return

int - Return code. An error will occur if:

- ❏ Bad parameter list is passed
- ❏ Source and/or destination library name could not be found
- ❏ Entry name could not be found
- ❏ I/O error

The typical return values are:

PBORCA_OK - Operation successful.

PBORCA_INVALIDPARMS - Invalid parameter list.

PBORCA_OBJNOTFOUND - Object not found.

PBORCA_BADLIBRARY - Bad library name.

PBORCA_LIBLISTNOTSET - Library list not set.

PBORCA_LIBNOTINLIST - Library not in library list.

PBORCA_LIBIOERROR - Library I/O error.

Function: **PBORCA_CompileEntryImport**

Prototype

```
int PBORCA_CompileEntryImport( PBORCA   hORCASession,
        LPSTR   lpszLibraryName,
        LPSTR   lpszEntryName,
        PBORCA_TYPE   otEntryType,
        LPSTR   lpszComments,
        LPSTR   lpszEntrySyntax,
        LONG    lEntrySyntaxBuffSize,
        PBORCA_ERRPROC pCompErrorProc,
        LPVOID pUserData ) ;
```

Description

Import the source for a PowerBuilder library entry and compile it.

Parameter Description

HPBORCA hORCASession

Handle to previously established ORCA session.

LPSTR lpszLibraryName

Pointer to library name.

LPSTR lpszEntryName

Pointer to entry name.

PBORCA_TYPE otEntryType

Enum for entry type (PBORCA_APPLICATION, PBORCA_DATAWINDOW, PBORCA_FUNCTION, PBORCA_MENU, PBORCA_QUERY,

PBORCA_STRUCTURE, PBORCA_USEROBJECT, or PBORCA_WINDOW).

LPSTR lpszComments

Pointer to entry comments.

LPSTR lpszEntrySyntax

Pointer to entry syntax.

LONG lEntrySyntaxBuffSize

Length of storage pointed to by lpszEntrySyntax.

PBORCA_ERRPROC pCompErrorProc

Pointer to compile error PBORCA_EntryImport callback function. Error information will include error text and line number.

LPVOID pUserData

Pointer to user data to be passed to callback function with each compile error.

Return

int - Return code. An error will occur if:

- ❏ Bad parameter list is passed

- ❏ Library name could not be found

- ❏ I/O error

- ❏ Compile error

The typical return values are:

PBORCA_OK - Operation successful.

PBORCA_INVALIDPARMS - Invalid parameter list.

PBORCA_OBJNOTFOUND - Object not found.

PBORCA_BADLIBRARY - Bad library name.

PBORCA_LIBLISTNOTSET - Library list not set.

PBORCA_LIBNOTINLIST - Library not in library list.

PBORCA_LIBIOERROR - Library I/O error.

PBORCA_COMPERROR - Compile error.

Function: **PBORCA_CompileEntryImportList**

Prototype

```
int PBORCA_CompileEntryImportList( PBORCA
hORCASession,
        LPSTR   far *pLibraryNames,
        LPSTR   far *pEntryNames,
        PBORCA_TYPE   far *otEntryTypes,
        LPSTR   far *pComments,
        LPSTR   far *pEntrySyntaxBuffers,
        LONG    far *pEntrySyntaxBuffSizes,
        INT iNumberOfEntries,
        PBORCA_ERRPROC pCompErrorProc,
        LPVOID pUserData  );
```

Description

Import the source for a list of PowerBuilder library entries and compile them. Each member of the list is identified by a set of corresponding entries in the arrays passed as input parameters. All entries will be imported first and only their type definitions will be compiled, and then assuming everything works, the entire entry list will be fully compiled. This call can be used to import several interrelated objects. For example: a window, its menu, and perhaps a user object that it uses.

Note: Ancestor objects and user objects must be imported (that is, in the list) before any objects that are descended from them.

Parameter Description

HPBORCA hORCASession

Handle to previously established ORCA session.

LPSTR far *pLibraryNames

Pointer to array of library names.

LPSTR far *pEntryNames

Pointer to array of entry names.

PBORCA_TYPE far *otEntryTypes

Pointer to array of enums for entry type

(PBORCA_APPLICATION, PBORCA_DATAWINDOW, PBORCA_FUNCTION, PBORCA_MENU, PBORCA_QUERY, PBORCA_STRUCTURE, PBORCA_USEROBJECT, or PBORCA_WINDOW).

LPSTR far *pComments

Pointer to array of entry comments.

LPSTR far *pEntrySyntaxBuffers

Pointer to array of entry syntax buffers.

LONG far * pEntrySyntaxBuffSizes

Pointer to an array of lengths of storage buffers pointed to by *pEntrySyntaxBuffers.

int iNumberOfEntries

Number of entries in each list.

PBORCA_ERRPROC pCompErrorProc

Pointer to compile error callback function. Error information will include error text, line number, and entry that error occurred in.

LPVOID pUserData

Pointer to user data to be passed to callback function with each compile error.

Return

int - Return code. An error will occur if:

- ❏ Bad parameter list is passed
- ❏ Library name could not be found
- ❏ I/O error
- ❏ Compile error

The typical return values are:

PBORCA_OK - Operation successful.

PBORCA_INVALIDPARMS - Invalid parameter list.

PBORCA_OBJNOTFOUND - Object not found.

PBORCA_BADLIBRARY - Bad library name.

PBORCA_LIBLISTNOTSET - Library list not set.
PBORCA_LIBNOTINLIST - Library not in library list.
PBORCA_LIBIOERROR - Library I/O error.
PBORCA_COMPERROR - Compile error.

Function: PBORCA_CompileEntryRegenerate

Prototype

```
int PBORCA_CompileEntryRegenerate( PBORCA
hORCASession,
        LPSTR   lpszLibraryName,
        LPSTR   lpszEntryName,
        PBORCA_TYPE   otEntryType,
        PBORCA_ERRPROC pCompErrorProc,
        LPVOID pUserData );
```

Description

Compile a PowerBuilder library entry.

Parameter Description

HPBORCA hORCASession

Handle to previously established ORCA session.

LPSTR lpszLibraryName

Pointer to library name.

LPSTR lpszEntryName

Pointer to entry name.

PBORCA_TYPE otEntryType

Enum for entry type (PBORCA_APPLICATION, PBORCA_DATAWINDOW, PBORCA_FUNCTION, PBORCA_MENU, PBORCA_QUERY, PBORCA_STRUCTURE, PBORCA_USEROBJECT, or PBORCA_WINDOW).

PBORCA_ERRPROC pCompErrorProc

Pointer to compile error callback function. Error information will include error text and line number.

LPVOID pUserData

Pointer to user data to be passed to callback function with each compile error.

Return

int - Return code. An error will occur if:

❏ Bad parameter list is passed

❏ Library name could not be found

❏ Entry name could not be found

❏ I/O error

❏ Compile error

The typical return values are:

PBORCA_OK - Operation successful.

PBORCA_INVALIDPARMS - Invalid parameter list.

PBORCA_OBJNOTFOUND - Object not found.

PBORCA_BADLIBRARY - Bad library name.

PBORCA_LIBLISTNOTSET - Library list not set.

PBORCA_LIBNOTINLIST - Library not in library list.

PBORCA_LIBIOERROR - Library I/O error.

PBORCA_COMPERROR - Compile error.

Function: PBORCA_ObjectQueryHierarchy

Prototype

```
int PBORCA_ObjectQueryHierarchy( HPBORCA
hORCASession,
      LPSTR   lpszLibraryName,
      LPSTR   lpszEntryName,
      PBORCA_TYPE   otEntryType,
      PBORCA_HIERPROC   pHierarchyProc,
      LPVOID pUserData  );
```

Description

Query a PowerBuilder object for other objects in its ancestor hierarchy.

Parameter Description

HPBORCA hORCASession

Handle to previously established ORCA session.

LPSTR lpszLibraryName

Pointer to library name.

LPSTR lpszEntryName

Pointer to entry name.

PBORCA_TYPE otEntryType

Enum for entry type (*only* PBORCA_WINDOW, PBORCA_MENU, or PBORCA_USEROBJECT).

PBORCA_HIERPROC pHierarchyProc

Pointer to hierarchy callback function. Hierarchy information will include ancestor object names.

LPVOID pUserData

Pointer to user data to be passed to the callback function with each hierarchy object found.

Return

int - Return code. An error will occur if:

- ❐ Bad parameter list is passed
- ❐ Library name could not be found
- ❐ Entry name could not be found
- ❐ I/O error

The return values are:

PBORCA_OK - Operation successful.

PBORCA_INVALIDPARMS - Invalid parameter list.

PBORCA_OBJNOTFOUND - Object not found.

PBORCA_BADLIBRARY - Bad library name.

PBORCA_LIBLISTNOTSET - Library list not set.

PBORCA_LIBNOTINLIST - Library not in library list.

PBORCA_LIBIOERROR - Library I/O error.

PBORCA_INVALIDNAME - Invalid name.

Function: **PBORCA_ObjectQueryReference**

Prototype

```
int PBORCA_ObjectQueryReference( HPBORCA
hORCASession,
        LPSTR   lpszLibraryName
        LPSTR   lpszEntryName,
        PBORCA_TYPE   otEntryType,
        PBORCA_REFPROC pRefProc,
        LPVOID pUserData  );
```

Description

Query a PowerBuilder object for references to other objects.

Parameter Description

HPBORCA hORCASession

Handle to previously established ORCA session.

LPSTR lpszLibraryName

Pointer to library name.

LPSTR lpszEntryName

Pointer to entry name.

PBORCA_TYPE otEntryType

Enum for entry type (PBORCA_APPLICATION, PBORCA_DATAWINDOW, PBORCA_FUNCTION, PBORCA_MENU, PBORCA_QUERY, PBORCA_STRUCTURE, PBORCA_USEROBJECT, or PBORCA_WINDOW).

PBORCA_REFPROC pRefProc

Pointer to reference callback function. Reference information will include object referenced, library it was found in, and object type.

LPVOID pUserData

Pointer to user data to be passed to callback function with each reference.

Return

int - Return code. An error will occur if:

❒ Bad parameter list is passed

❒ Library name could not be found

❒ Entry name could not be found

❒ I/O error

The return values are:

PBORCA_OK - Operation successful.

PBORCA_INVALIDPARMS - Invalid parameter list.

PBORCA_OBJNOTFOUND - Object not found.

PBORCA_BADLIBRARY - Bad library name.

PBORCA_LIBLISTNOTSET - Library list not set.

PBORCA_LIBNOTINLIST - Library not in library list.

PBORCA_INVALIDNAME - Invalid name.

Callback Function: PBORCA_CompileEntryImport

Prototype
```
typedef void (FAR PASCAL *PBORCA_ERRPROC) (
PPBORCA_COMPERR, LPVOID );
```
Parameter Description

PBORCA_ERRPROC

Far pointer to a type PBORCA_ERRPROC.

PPBORCA_COMPERR

Pointer to the structure PBORCA_COMPERR.

LPVOID

Long pointer to user data.

Return

Structure for PBORCA_CompileEntryImport callback function

Prototype

```
typedef struct pborca_comperr
{
int iLevel;/* Error level */
  LPSTRlpszMessageNumber;    /* Pointer to message number
*/
  LPSTRlpszMessageText;  /* Pointer to message text */
  UINT iColumnNumber;/* Column number */
  UINT iLineNumber;  /* Line number */
} PBORCA_COMPERR, FAR *PPBORCA_COMPERR;
```

Callback Function: PBORCA_LibraryDirectory

Prototype

```
typedef void (FAR PASCAL *PBORCA_LISTPROC) (
PPBORCA_DIRENTRY, LPVOID );
```

Parameter Description

PBORCA_LISTPROC

Far pointer to a type PBORCA_LISTPROC.

PPBORCA_DIRENTRY

Pointer to the structure PBORCA_DIRENTRY.

LPVOID

Long pointer to user data.

Return

Structure for **PBORCA_LibraryDirectory** callback function

```
typedef struct pborca_direntry
{
    /* Comments */
  CHAR szComments[PBORCA_MAXCOMMENT + 1];
  LONG lCreateTime;   /* Time of entry create/mod */
  LONG lEntrySize;    /* Size of entry */
  LPSTRlpszEntryName; /* Pointer to entry name */
  PBORCA_TYPE otEntryType;  /* Entry type */
} PBORCA_DIRENTRY, FAR *PPBORCA_DIRENTRY;
```

Callback Function:
PBORCA_ObjectQueryHierarchy

Prototype
```
typedef void (FAR PASCAL *PBORCA_HIERPROC) (
PPBORCA_HIERARCHY, LPVOID );
```

Parameter

Description

PBORCA_HIERPROC

Far pointer to a type PBORCA_HIERPROC.

PPBORCA_HIERARCHY

Pointer to the structure PBORCA_HIERARCHY.

LPVOID

Long pointer to user data.

Return

Structure for **PBORCA_ObjectQueryHierarchy** callback function

```
typedef struct pborca_hierarchy
{
  LPSTRlpszAncestorName; /* Pointer to ancestor name */
} PBORCA_HIERARCHY, FAR *PPBORCA_HIERARCHY;
```

Calback Function: **PBORCA_ObjectQueryReference**

Prototype

```
typedef void (FAR PASCAL *PBORCA_REFPROC) (
PPBORCA_REFERENCE, LPVOID );
```

Parameter Description

PBORCA_REFPROC

Far pointer to a type PBORCA_REFPROC.

PPBORCA_REFERENCE

Pointer to the structure PBORCA_REFERENCE.

LPVOID

Long pointer to user data.

Return

Structure for **PBORCA_ObjectQueryReference** callback function

```
typedef struct pborca_reference
{
  LPSTRlpszLibraryName;  /* Pointer to library name */
  LPSTRlpszEntryName;/* Pointer to entry name */
  PBORCA_TYPE otEntryType;  /* Entry type */
} PBORCA_REFERENCE, FAR *PPBORCA_REFERENCE;
```

Index

Power Toolkits & Visual Guides

CUTTING-EDGE TOOLS & TECHNIQUES

Paradox 5.0 Power Toolkit for Windows

$49.95, 560 pages, illustrated

Boost database application development with this insider's look at the true power of Paradox. Complete with advanced techniques, tips for creating user-friendly applications and an overview of third-party tools. The companion CD-ROM features sample routines from the book and selected third-party tools and controls.

Visual C++ Power Toolkit

$49.95, 832 pages, illustrated

Add impact to your apps using these 10 never-before-published class libraries. Complete documentation plus professional design tips and technical hints. The companion CD-ROM contains 10 original class libraries, dozens of graphics, sound and toolbar utilities, standard files and demo programs.

Visual Basic Power Toolkit

$39.95, 960 pages, illustrated

Discover the real force behind Visual Basic's pretty face with this unique collection of innovative techniques. Hundreds of examples, images and helpful hints on data security, color manipulation, special effects and OLE automation. Demystify fractals and master multimedia as you push the power of VB! The companion CD-ROM contains all the routines from the book, sample Custom Controls, animated clips, MIDI music files and more.

The Visual Guide to Visual Basic for Windows, Second Edition

$29.95, 1282 pages, illustrated

The definitive reference for Visual Basic is completely
revised for Visual Basic 3.0—packed with useful, easy-to-
understand examples, more than 600 illustrations and
thorough explanations of every Visual Basic command
and feature.

The Visual Guide to Visual C++

$29.95, 888 pages, illustrated

A uniquely visual reference for Microsoft's next-generation
programming language. Written for both new and
experienced programmers, it features a complete
overview of tools and features in each class of the
"Visual C++ Foundation Class Library"—including names
and prototypes, descriptions, parameters, return values,
notes and examples. Ideal for day-to-day reference! The
companion disk contains code examples, including programs and subroutines from the book.

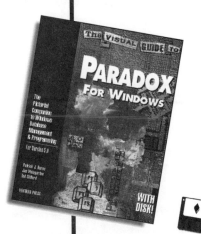

The Visual Guide to Paradox for Windows

$29.95, 692 pages, illustrated

A pictorial approach to Paradox! Hundreds of examples
and illustrations show how to achieve complex database
development with simple drag-and-drop techniques. Users
learn how to access and modify database files, use Form
and Report Designers and Experts, program with
ObjectPAL and more—all with icons, buttons, graphics
and OLE. The companion disk contains sample macros,
forms, reports, tables, queries and a ready-to-use database.

Books marked with this logo include a free Internet *Online
Companion*™, featuring archives of free utilities plus a
software archive and links to other Internet resources.

Internet Resources

Mosaic Quick Tour for Windows, Special Edition

$24.95, 224 pages, illustrated

This book was a national bestseller straight out of the gate in its first edition, thanks to its down-to-earth approach to Mosaic™—the "killer app" that changed the face of the Internet. The Web, with its audio, video and graphic capabilities and hyperlinks between sites, comes to life in this important update that focuses on Ventana Mosaic™, the newly standardized commercial version of the most famous free software in the world. Includes information on audio and video components of Ventana Mosaic, along with a guide to top Web attractions. Two companion disks feature Ventana Mosaic and Win32s, which is required to run the program.

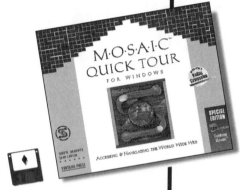

Internet Roadside Attractions

$29.95, 376 pages, illustrated

Why take the word of one when you can get a quorum? Seven experienced Internauts—teachers and bestselling authors—share their favorite Web sites, Gophers, FTP sites, chats, games, newsgroups and mailing lists. In-depth descriptions are organized alphabetically by category for easy browsing. The companion CD-ROM contains the entire text of the book, hyperlinked for off-line browsing and Web hopping.

Acrobat Quick Tour

$14.95, 272 pages, illustrated

In the three-ring circus of electronic publishing, Adobe® Acrobat® is turning cartwheels around the competition. Learn the key tools and features of Acrobat's base components in this hands-on guide that includes a look at the emerging world of document exchange.

TO ORDER ANY VENTANA PRESS TITLE, COMPLETE THIS ORDER FORM AND MAIL OR FAX IT TO US, WITH PAYMENT, FOR QUICK SHIPMENT.

TITLE	ISBN	QUANTITY	PRICE	TOTAL
Acrobat Quick Tour	1-56604-255-0	_____ x	$14.95 =	$ _____
HTML Publishing on the Internet for Windows	1-56604-229-1	_____ x	$49.95 =	$ _____
Internet Publishing Kit for Macintosh	1-56604-232-1	_____ x	$149.00 =	$ _____
Internet Publishing Kit for Windows	1-56604-231-3	_____ x	$149.00 =	$ _____
Internet Roadside Attractions	1-56604-193-7	_____ x	$29.95 =	$ _____
Mosaic Quick Tour for Windows, Special Edition	1-56604-214-3	_____ x	$24.95 =	$ _____
Paradox 5.0 for Windows Power Toolkit	1-56604-236-4	_____ x	$49.95 =	$ _____
PGP Companion for Windows	1-56604-304-2	_____ x	$29.95 =	$ _____
PowerBuilder 4.0 Power Toolkit	1-56604-224-0	_____ x	$49.95 =	$ _____
Visual Basic Power Toolkit	1-56604-190-2	_____ x	$39.95 =	$ _____
Visual C++ Power Toolkit	1-56604-191-0	_____ x	$49.95 =	$ _____
The Visual Guide to Paradox for Windows	1-56604-150-3	_____ x	$29.95 =	$ _____
The Visual Guide to Visual Basic for Windows	1-56604-063-9	_____ x	$29.95 =	$ _____
The Visual Guide to Visual C++	1-56604-079-5	_____ x	$29.95 =	$ _____
The Visual Guide to Visual FoxPro 3.0	1-56604-227-5	_____ x	$34.95 =	$ _____
The Windows Internet Tour Guide, 2nd Edition	1-56604-174-0	_____ x	$29.95 =	$ _____

SUBTOTAL = $ _____

SHIPPING

For all standard orders, please ADD $4.50/first book, $1.35/each additional.
For *Internet Publishing Kit* orders, ADD $6.50/first kit, $2.00/each additional.
For "two-day air," ADD $8.25/first book/$2.25/each additional.
For "two-day air" on the kits, ADD $10.50/first book, $4.00/each additional.
For orders to Canada, ADD $6.50/book.
For orders sent C.O.D., ADD $4.50 to your shipping rate.
North Carolina residents must ADD 6% sales tax.
International orders require additional shipping charges.

SHIPPING = $ _____

TOTAL = $ _____

Name _____ Daytime telephone _____

Company _____

Address (No PO Box) _____

City_____ State_____ Zip_____

Payment enclosed ____VISA ____MC ____ Acc't # _____ Exp. date_____

Signature _____ Exact name on card _____

Mail to: Ventana Press • PO Box 13964 • Research Triangle Park, NC 27709-3964 ☎ 800/743-5369 • Fax 919/544-9472

Check your local bookstore or software retailer for these and other bestselling titles, or call toll free: **800/743-5369**